SOCIOLOGISTS ON SOCIOLOGY

For Norman Dennis

Sociologists on Sociology

Second Edition

BOB MULLAN

Avebury

Aldershot • Brookfield USA • Hong Kong • Singapore • Sydney

Published by
Avebury
Ashgate Publishing Limited
Gower House
Croft Road
Aldershot
Hants GU11 3HR
England

Ashgate Publishing Company
Old Post Road
Brookfield
Vermont 05036
USA

British Library Cataloguing in Publication Data

Sociologists on sociology
    1. Sociology
    I. Mullan, Bob
    301

    ISBN 1 85972 316 0

Library of Congress Catalog Card Number: 96-84695

Printed in Great Britain by the Ipswich Book Company, Suffolk

Contents

Preface to second edition   vii

Preface and acknowledgements   x
Key to transcripts   xiii

Part I

Introduction   1

Part II

1   John Rex   9
2   Ralf Dahrendorf   39
3   Peter Worsley   65
4   Anthony Giddens   101
5   Howard S. Becker   127
6   Laurie Taylor   157
7   Michael Mann   183
8   Ann Oakley   207
9   Peter Townsend   229
10 Stuart Hall   255
11 Robert K. Merton   295

Part III

12 Personal postscript: The relevance of C. Wright Mills   321

Bibliography   329

Preface to second edition

I think it's important to make connections with the people that
sociology is supposed to be about.   That is I do think it is
important to write little introductory books and to do the sort
of work ... that people would dismiss as 'pop sociology'. I'm
very much against the protection of social science as a kind
of restricted discourse.

Anthony Giddens (1987, p. 114)

Almost ten years after Giddens' remarks about the relative inaccessibility of
sociology it is evident that such potential 'connections with the people' have
failed to materialise. Quite simply sociology tends not to be taken seriously.
Witness *The Guardian's* announcement of Stuart Hall's 64th birthday
(February 2 1996) which concludes with the remark - 'he's OU Professor of
Sociology - now there's a period piece of a phrase'.

Some sociologists continue to talk and write in a 'restricted discourse' and
in so doing enable on-lookers to view the discipline as an unimportant means
of understanding society and indeed ourselves. There is the issue of jargon.
For instance in his rejection of conventional family studies, which use the
distinction between the public and private spheres, Tony Fahey prefers to
talk of the 'multiple, cross-cutting, context-specific zones of privacy found
in social life' (1995, p.687). Meaning what precisely? Similarly Trevor
Purvis and Alan Hunt in their attempt to retrieve the concepts of 'discourse
and ideology' state that their conceptual strategy involves the following steps
(1993, p. 473):

We first engage with the debate over ideology within modern western Marxism and explore the suggestive distinction proposed by Larrain between a negative and a positive conception of ideology. Next we explore Foucault's version of discourse theory. Our third investigation focuses on the work of Ernesto Laclau and Chantal Mouffe who opt for a rupture between discourse and ideology; their solution will be contrasted with the Gramscian position espoused by Stuart Hall - the approach closest to the solution we will propose - that retains the concept ideology whilst benefiting from the advances secured by discourse theory.

The reader is exhausted before the authors actually begin their substantive investigations. Sociological *naivete* also ensures that the discipline is not embraced by a wider public - 'sociology is common sense camouflaged by jargon'. For example in their plea for women workers to be included in social mobility studies Bernadette Hayes and Robert Miller rightly castigate such traditional studies for only including *male* experiences, but when they conclude that employed females exert an important 'independent influence on the social class or prestige position of their families as a whole', and that female children benefit from having working mothers as positive role models, they are surely - in the 1990s - stating the obvious (1993, pp. 667-68).

But this is not to suggest that *all* sociological enquiry - whether strictly theoretical or essentially substantive - is of the same somewhat banal sensibility. Bjorn Eriksson, for example, in his imaginative and thoughtful discussion of the 'first formulation of sociology' argues convincingly that sociology *proper* began with the model propounded by the *Bureau of Applied Research* in the 1940s, but that the sociological sensibility had its origins much earlier and not with Comte, but rather with the so-called Scottish Historical School of the 1760s - Adam Smith, John Millar, William Robertson, *et al* (1993, p. 252). More substantively W.G.Runciman has recently posed the question 'has British capitalism changed since the First World War?'. In his confident analysis of the question he asserts that his essay 'is written from the standpoint of sociology, not of economic or social history'. For Runciman this means, therefore, that his concern 'is solely with the question whether there has or has not been a qualitative change from one to another distinguishable sub-type of the capitalist mode of production in Britain'. Despite such clear-mindedness and confidence in his project even he feels it necessary to conclude his essay with a cautionary note. 'Sociology is not and cannot be a predictive science - which is why sociologists can, and do, make just as big fools of themselves in trying to forecast the future as do the politicians, journalists and other non-academic fellow-members of their society whose behaviour and attitudes they study' (1993, p. 66).

When *Sociologists on Sociology* was first published in 1987 many of the contributors, sociologists themselves, said they were not especially interested in the various disputes and issues *within* sociology, but rather were more concerned about how *social science* - a more generic term than *sociology* - could answer questions about *societal issues*. Almost a decade later the importance of sociologists addressing societal problems rather than sociological ones is even of greater urgency, especially if sociology is to genuinely enter public debate. In his 1992 Presidential Address to the American Sociological Association, James Coleman talked of the 'crumbling of the primordial social organisations' that contemporary American society consisted of. He argued that it was the 'task of sociologists to aid the process of the rational reconstruction of society'. This involved 'training sociologists, both undergraduates and graduates, to be the architects and architectural aides in the design of social institutions' (1993, p. 14). As we approach the next millennium it is hard to imagine that sociologists will play *any* important role in public decision making, unless they collectively begin to imaginatively examine societal processes rather than sociological conundrums, describe their findings and ideas in a precise but jargon-free manner and until they begin to learn how to use institutions of the mass media more profitably and persuasively.

Preface and acknowledgements

Robert Merton is surely right when he notes that 'ours has become an age pervaded by sociology', and that we habitually think in sociological terms partly because a great variety of sociological terms have 'drifted into our everyday language' (1981, p. 42). Perhaps more importantly sociology is relevant because our age is one of great social dislocation, conflict, and transformation, and sociology is best placed to examine and understand this modern world.

This preamble serves, I hope, to emphasise that this book is in no way intended to be defensive of sociology's possibilities or potential, nor is it another sociology of sociology (see Friedrichs, 1970). Rather, it elicits the views of some of the leading contemporary sociologists concerning the state of the discipline in order to demonstrate both its plurality and current good health.

The book consists of interviews with eleven leading sociologists. It was a personal choice exercised under the constraints of who were in fact willing or able to be interviewed, and no doubt I could have chosen differently. I do hope however that I have chosen imaginatively and, more importantly, that I have consequently discussed the majority of vital issues in contemporary academic sociology. *Sociologists on Sociology* concludes with a personal postscript in which I outline C. Wright Mills' substantive and methodological programme. I do this in agreement with Irving Horowitz who while discussing *The Sociological Imagination*, argues that the ideas contained in the book are 'probably more relevant in Britain in the 1980s than they were twenty years earlier' (1983, p. 100).

Many people assisted me with the project in quite different ways not least Michele Allen and Christine Jope who helped with the arduous task of transcribing the taped interviews; Diane Flegg at the University of Wales Swansea; Bryan Heading of the University of East Anglia who offered helpful advice, as did John Cockburn; and most importantly, of course, Howard Becker, Ralf Dahrendorf, Anthony Giddens, Stuart Hall, Michael Mann, Robert Merton, Ann Oakley, John Rex, Laurie Taylor, Peter Townsend, and Peter Worsley who gave their time and hospitality in allowing me to interview them.

Finally, it is Norman Dennis to whom I dedicate this book. He, as a most committed teacher, first kindled my interest in sociology and then made me understand that sociology should always include *both* theory and empirical research.

'There would be no social science if there were not perplexities in living in culture that call for solution. And it is precisely the role of the social sciences to be troublesome, to disconcert the habitual arrangements by which we manage to live along, and to demonstrate the possibility of change in more adequate directions.'

Robert S. Lynd (orig. 1939, 1970, p. 181)

Key to transcripts

[ ]   information added by editor

...   pause

(...)   material edited out

Part I

Introduction

British sociology today stands in the shadows of academic life after a quarter of a century of rank, rancorous and resisted growth, its proponents weary from internal schism and dispirited by both establishment rejection and popular misunderstanding. Yet these tribulations are largely the consequences of its own success - enthusiasm for an intellectual apparatus promising enlightenment on public issues of immense importance, the over-rapid university expansion of a single decade after nearly a century of official neglect. It is a time for defence and consolidation and at such moments of uncertain direction any group is wont to appraise its own history. Appraisals appear and can bear fruit provided that they are harnessed not to recrimination about the past but to defining work for the future.

A.H. Halsey (1984), p. 15.

Sociology can only be a society's understanding of itself and this, of course, is contested and constantly in flux; in other words no orthodoxy exists (Mann, 1983, p.v.). However despite this plurality advances are made and which are in a sense forms of cumulative knowledge. For example following the conceptual clarifications made by Bachrach and Baratz in their study of power, who would dare not to include non-decisions in their analyses of power (Barach and Baratz, 1963). More specifically because social life is complex and beyond the grasp of most, sociology is about demystification, and some would add that it is therefore also subversive.

1

In the late Raymond Aron's opinion, the trouble with British sociology is that it is 'essentially an attempt to make intellectual sense of the political problems of the Labour Party' (in Halsey, 1982, p. 150). And certainly the investigation of social inequality and a commitment to social reform have been prominent in the development of British sociology. However, although the development of British sociology - and, the year 1834, the date of the *Report* of the Commission on the Poor Law and the founding of the Statistical Society of London, is 'about as rational a date', argues Abrams, 'for beginning a history of British sociology, as one could hope to find' (1968, p.vi) - has been a history of a struggle to become institutionalised and a solid reliance on both the 'founding fathers' on the one hand and survey-dominated empirical research on the other, 1968 changed the discipline out of all proportions. Rex may well be overstating the case, but he certainly has a point that following the 1960s a new generation of sociology of students 'emerged in Europe as well as in Britain, who had little knowledge of Weber but considerable acquaintance with the applications of Marxist theories in the pages of the *New Left Review*' (1983, p. 1003). Rex concluded that (1983, p. 1005);

> What most young sociologists were receiving by the early seventies was a sociology based on a political critique of capitalism on the one hand and an understanding of deviance on the other ... there was little place in this for the study of Weber and Durkheim. If they were prepared to make some obeisance to theory they did so by quoting half understood themes from Giddens, Althusser, Garfinkel, or Habermas.

The 1970s produced all sorts of developments some of which seemed to threaten the status of sociology as a coherent discipline. For instance the emergence of micro-sociology and in particular ethnomethodology, a development which John Goldthorpe talked of as having an 'increasingly divisive effect within the sociological community at large' (1973, p. 449). But the most sustained pressure came from Marxism, feminism, and the renewed interest in epistemology derived from the work of such strange bedfellows as Althusser, Kuhn, and Feyerabend, and which resulted for a time in a new 'subjectivism'.

2

Anthony Giddens

'If western sociology is to be saved from its continuing crisis, Anthony Giddens may be the author to achieve it', says John Urry (1977, p. 911), and certainly without doubt Giddens has been the most oft-quoted *British* sociologist in the past decade of sociology. Indeed, in his publications his own name is printed larger than his titles. Rex, in a quite succinct account, notes the Giddens' work represents 'in a very striking form the philosophization of sociology', indeed an attempt to 'rewrite sociology' (1983, p. 1005).

The initial reaction of philosophers to sociology had been hostile and their view of the essential impossibility of a science of sociology had been summed up by Peter Winch in *The Idea of a Social Science* (1958). Increasingly, however, the idea gained ground that if a 'simplistically conceived *science* of sociology was impossible, there was a space to be occupied by a philosophic discipline' (Rex, 1983, p. 1005). In a series of books Giddens has reviewed the schools of critical theory, hermeneutics, positivism, ethnomethodology and structuralism, and has now begun to develop his own theory of 'structuration'. Rex is surely not too cynical when he concludes that (1983, p. 1005);

> There are many who would argue that Giddens represents the major significant development in English sociology. This claim, however, is difficult to assess, since it is extremely unlikely that there are many practising sociologists who even begin to understand the issues with which he is concerned.

Perhaps, in extreme summary form, what can be noted is that Giddens' work emphasises more than many the role of human agency, and that Giddens' claim that his work has major significance for the understanding of late capitalism and communism is somewhat difficult to evaluate.

The State Of Sociology

Of course at any given moment, sociology or social science consists of 'what duly recognized social scientists are doing - but all of them are by no means doing the same thing, in fact not even the same sort of thing', and of course social science is also 'what social scientists of the past have done - but different students choose to construct and to recall different traditions in their discipline' (Mills, 1970, p. 26). Mills' comments point to a difficulty in discerning trends or drifts in sociology over the past few decades, namely different sociologists are doing all sorts of different things for all sorts of different reasons. However I suspect a great number of sociologists are carrying out their craft in what they see as a quite traditional manner; namely small-scale empirical research using survey techniques and interviews, policy oriented, and *possibly* linking the research to middle-range theories.

Also we must remember that sociology, quite simply, is not merely the work of sociologists. Non-professional sociologists can make, as well as use, sociological knowledge and insights. Just think of the likes of Raymond Williams and Richard Hoggart, and furthermore George Orwell who, in *The Road to Wigan Pier* (1937) for example, brilliantly captured aspects of traditional working class family life. Indeed Worsley talks of the 'mystique of professionalism' which assumes that the 'only significant thinking about society which sociologists need take account of seriously is that done by sociologists, i.e. that which is "occupationally real"' (1974, pp. 4-5).

Sociology (and social science) has suffered over the past few decades from the deaths of some of the more free-thinking members of the discipline, who were also original and powerful thinkers; for example, Raymond Aron, Philip Abrams, Michel Foucault, Erving Goffman, Alvin Gouldner, T.H. Marshall, and, of course, C. Wright Mills. In addition, influential 'sociology' books over the decades have been few: Vance Packard's *The Status Seekers* (1961) demonstrated the investigative nature of sociology; politically connected works like Anthony Crosland's *The Future of Socialism* (1956) and Galbraith's *New Industrial State* (1967); the sophisticated accounts of J.W.B. Douglas in *The Home and the School* (1964) and David Glass's *Social Mobility in Britain* (1954); Rex and Mooore's forceful *Race, Community and Conflict* (1967) which also made *The Times* editorial; Hoggart's quite classic, and still neglected, *The Uses of Literacy* (1957); Runciman's imaginative *Relative Deprivation and Social Justice* (1966); Abel-Smith and Townsend's reformist *Poor and the Poorest* (1965); Winch's *The Idea of a Social Science* (1958); Goldthorpe and Lockwood *et al.* and *The Affluent Worker* series (1969); Stanley Cohen's edited *Images of Deviance* (1971); all of Parsons, Goffman, and also Garfinkel's *Studies in*

Ethnomethodology (1967); Reisman's *The Lonely Crowd* (1950) was not as influential as in its home, but Robert K. Merton's *Social Theory and Social Structure* (1957) and Mills' *The Sociological Imagination* (1959) were; Giddens' *Capitalism and Modern Social Theory* (1971).

If we can discern drifts over the past few decades of British sociology, notwithstanding the features already noted, they would probably be the following. Firstly, there is more plurality than ever in terms of methods, theories, and indeed over the purpose of the discipline. Secondly there is the *claim* which is hard to substantiate, that the contemporary climate is essentially anti-positivistic. Thirdly - and this is not so surprising following the dissatisfaction with functionalism - there is increasing stress on the side of human agency as opposed to structure (although of course the two are not *in fact* separable). Structuralism was short-lived. Finally, following a period of 'epistemological anomie' and a partial decline in research output, there is a counter-attack with an emphasis on theoretically-informed empirical research.

Part II

1 John Rex

John Rex is currently Emeritus Professor at the Centre for Research in Ethnic Relations, at the University of Warwick, is probably most well known for two important books published in the 1960s and constantly re-printed. *Key Problems of Sociological Theory* (1961) was both one of the first attempts to take 'theory' seriously in British sociology and also provided a cogent critique of functionalism. In 1967, and with Robert Moore, Rex published *Race, Community and Conflict* which was an imaginative fusion of the ideas of Weber and the Chicago School (of urban sociology), together with a detailed empirical investigation of a region of Birmingham.

In *Race, Community and Conflict* Rex and Moore coined the term 'housing classes', in describing a class struggle over the use of houses which in fact they saw as the central process of the city as a social unit. The housing market they saw as distinct from the labour market since men in the same situations in the latter may have differential degrees of access in the former. Despite criticisms (see Saunders, 1980, pp. 67-76) the concept has remained extraordinarily useful. Over a decade later, Rex carried out another empirical study in Birmingham, this time with Sally Tomlinson, and in 1979 published *Colonial Immigrants in a British City*. In this Rex continued his theme that 'race relations was utterly dependent upon some form of class analysis' (1983, p. 162), yet this could not please a new generation of 'radical' and often black, theorists in the area of race relations. Prescod, for example, in a review of the book talks of Rex and Tomlinson as 'policy researchers par excellence in the period of black militancy ... [and] ... He is still making contributions to the sociology of race relations but he is now a liberal pessimist' (1979, p. 200). While Lawrence in *The Empire Strikes Back*, a kind of anti-white-sociologists-in-race-relations-research book, talks of Rex's 'closer contacts with the Home Office' and of his embracing 'their rationalisations' (1982, p. 131).

Two prevailing themes in British sociology have continued to preoccupy Rex, namely empiricism and functionalism. His own position is often termed 'structural phenomenology', which refers to his methodological commitment to a neo-Weberian conception of the phenomenology of social action, and in part upon a theoretical commitment to the ubiquity of conflict in social relations. It is Rex's status as an 'all-rounder', his ability to carry out empirical research and his commitment to theorising, that has given depth to his analysis and endowed it with credibility as serious social criticism. On the role of sociology he is unequivocal (Rex, 1974, p. ix).

> sociology is a subject whose insights should be available to the great mass of the people in order that they should be able to use it to liberate themselves from the mystification of social reality which is continuously provided for them by those in our society who exercise power and influence.

Firstly, can you tell me something about your background in South Africa?

Yes. I went to university in South Africa in the immediate post-war period, having grown up in a poor white South African family which therefore had various natural inclinations towards racism. But as a result of my experience in the war I came back very critical of the South African social system, and was also able because of the grants available to ex-servicemen to go up to university [Rhodes University College, University of South Africa] which I wouldn't normally have been able to do (...)

What did you go to read - sociology?

No, I went up actually to read for a BA with a view to going on to a BD to go into the Presbyterian Church and become a minister ...

Was there a Chair in the Department of Sociology there?

There was an excellent teacher called James Irving, who'd been, was a man of working class origins from Scotland who had been trained as an anthropologist, had taught in Nanking, then been an extra-mural teacher in England, and he was made Reader in Sociology, and when I met him he was just beginning to read McIver and Page's textbook [1950].

Just before I forget, can you tell me what date and where you were born?

I was born on the 5th March 1925, in Port Elizabeth.

You've said that you moved to England by accident and found English sociology very disappointing and that it was engaged in 'the book-keeping of social reform' [1975, p. 1]. That's the first thing - and the second thing, that you accept Mannheim's perspective that displaced persons are in a better position to do sociology, and people who are most aware of sociological problems are the people who by accident go outside of society. Can you tell me then why you were disappointed in English sociology, and was there anything good about South African sociology?

Well, yes.   I mean we used sociology in order to achieve political understanding as people who were radically against the system, we recognised then that there were lots of things to do politically, but that in order to do effective things politically one had to understand the world and particularly one had to try to understand what made one's enemies tick. And, I mean, it's always seemed to me absolutely essential to reverse Marx's eleventh thesis and to say that hitherto sociologists have tried to change the world or politicians have tried to change the world; the important thing if anyone wants to change it effectively is to understand it.   And actually the kind of analysis which one made of the South African situation was some sort of a class analysis because very few of us believed that Afrikaaners were wicked because they were Afrikaaners, rather we looked

11

at the interests of white workers in that particular situation so that we thought of our sociology as being based on a kind of class analysis, as being Marxist. When I came to England ...

Can I just ask you what you were working as in South Africa?

I wasn't working, well ... when I left university I went briefly to teach in a mission school in what was then Rhodesia and I was deemed undesirable as an inhabitant or visitor, largely because somebody who had a personal axe to grind against me used his influence in the Department of the Interior. But they had a dossier on me, and so I had to leave my job, went back to South Africa, worked for a very brief period, as the Superintendent of an African village, or location, and I'd hardly got there when I was also successful in getting a job at Leeds University, where my own professor had previously taught; and coming to England, and looking at the sociological tradition which existed there, first of all it didn't seem to me to be *sociology* as I understood it.

Let me just come back ... tell me about 'displaced persons' doing sociology. Are you just saying they tend to be able to understand and be aware of sociological problems more?

I don't know that I would take a very strong view on this - it's a psychological question rather than anything else (...). Well I think that the sociologists who were growing up in England at that stage shared a lot of assumptions that they never turned their back on and looked at critically. I mean if you look for instance at the shared assumptions in the work of people like Halsey, Goldthorpe and Glass, they belonged to a certain political culture, they haven't turned round and criticised the assumptions of their culture, and somebody coming in from the outside is going to look more critically at it.

We'll come to Weber later, but who were other early influences?

Well, I think before I turned to Weber I dismissed Weber as rubbish. The very first influence on my thinking was George Lundberg's *Foundations of Sociology* [1939]. Sometimes I say I was a teenage positivist. Er ... I think the other person who influenced me a lot at university was Karl Mannheim whose sociology led me to have grave doubts about the nature of social science, and also I had read *The American Dilemma* [1944] and I was very impressed by Myrdal's appendix on facts and valuations in sociology. I left university in 1948-49 and by that time Parson's *The Structure of Social Action* [orig 1937, 1968] was just getting quoted and I remember laying my hands on a copy just after I'd graduated, and then when I was working in Middlesbrough found a copy of *The Social System* [1952] in the municipal library, and I began to try to understand Parsons. But in a way I was reading Parsons because I saw that as the high intellectual culture of my subject, not because at that stage it seemed to me to speak to my condition in any way.

Just going back to Mannheim, you said that he threw grave doubts about the possibility of there being a social science project. Could you just talk a little bit about that?

Yes, I thought that the ... I always felt that there is a great deal of naivete about people who said that their views were scientific and objective, and that Mannheim was saying what I always felt, that much of what people, especially the people who call themselves *the* most scientific people, were saying, was actually said unconsciously to promote their interests. But I was particularly struck by Mannheim because he not merely made an indictment of ideology but had the courage, as it were, to turn on his own side and say let's look at our position. One thing I never actually saw as a particularly important part of his work was suggesting that in some way intellectuals had a privileged status - in fact I don't think he really ever said that. What he did suggest that we should do if the accidents of history and personal biography knocked us out of a social position was ... that we should analyze everything in relation to a specific point of view, but having done that to complement it with analyses from opposite points of view.

Quite recently, well I think it was in fact 1980 but it's been printed recently, you were talking about early British sociology [1983]. One thing was that you saw two themes, one that as an imperial nation the British have remained concerned with social evolution and moral progress in the tradition of Spencer, and the other is the concern for inequality. Could you expand?

Well, I think that the importance of the Spencer, Hobhouse, Ginsberg tradition was not so much *what* they said but the fact that because they were looking at social evolution and looking at sociology of societies comparatively that they were bound to transcend the insularity of the Fabian tradition of the LSE, although that's not to say that they didn't discuss those kinds of problems because I think one of the profoundest moments in the work of Hobhouse is when in *Morals in Evolution* [1951] he has a chapter on property and poverty which ends with a discussion of the Minority Commission of the Poor Law, which relates him really to the LSE tradition, puts it into perspective.

(...) So you applauded their lack of insularity, and also presumably because it was theory, and there was a lack of that?

Yes, it ... the word theory is a funny one - I'm never quite sure what it means. I think that they had a conception of societies as structures of social relations which occurred in the course of meaningful action. And incidentally, in that context of the evolutionary/anthropological tradition, I think I should say something about Malinowski. In some sense I didn't like him because as a functionalist he turned his back on evolution, but one of the books which seemed to me to be extraordinarily useful when I was a student, and when I was taught anthropology by Monica Wilson who was one of Malinowski's students herself, was *A Scientific Theory of Culture* [1944] where he defined the social institution as the legitimate isolate of sociological analysis, talks about it, and he has there a concept of meaningful social relations, as indeed does Radcliffe-Brown, and that sort of tradition was what seemed to me to be a more theoretical view than just counting up the number of people and saying how many of them were women, how many were poor, and so on.

(...) Obviously you see limits to [Fabian sociology]. What interests me is, do you think it's true to say that after a while there's nothing that that kind of sociology can do, because if you've looked at educational inequality, social mobility and a couple of other areas it's exhausted?

14

Well, first of all I think I reacted against Glass's work from what I thought of then as a Marxist stance, because he seemed to have no conception of class conflict. The assumption behind those statistical tables seemed to be that you collected the statistics of inequality, and that having collected them you would then make them available and that 'we' the government would then do something about it. Strangely enough, Glass always thought of himself as a Marxist as does his pupil John Westergaard, and there seems to me to be a very large gap between that sort of empiricism and the concept of social class and class struggle, which one finds in Marx and which seems very important to me.

What about contemporary sociologists such as Goldthorpe, Halsey, Townsend, et al. Is their work still in the LSE tradition of the 1950s, albeit more sophisticated?

Well, I think all the people you mention actually seem to assume that they are part of the government, even Peter Townsend who I know to the most radical and courageous person amongst all of them. He and Donnison, in talking about policy problems, often use the word 'we', and it's a word which I don't understand because when I'm talking about these problems and what government might do about them I do resoundingly say 'they', and 'they' are people whom one has to do something in terms of power to ...

...Why do you think they see it that way then? I mean, why, is it just a slip, or ...

I think they come out of a more aristocratic tradition than I do, I think they've all been to Oxford or Cambridge ...

Okay, I'll come back to that.

But ... there are other things involved. I think that there are really mandarin assumptions in the work of Goldthorpe and Halsey, and the thing which I've often quoted, and I know that John Goldthorpe doesn't like me quoting it in this way, is John Goldthorpe's address to the British Association for the Advancement of Science in Exeter, something which Halsey quoted later ...

15

And, the assumption is that we are talking amongst policy makers, the working class don't enter into the scene at all, we're talking about what 'we' should do to them. This is just very alien to me.

(...) Something Perry Anderson said, which I'm sure you know, from 'Components of the National Culture', about the 'absent centre'; 'why did Britain never produce either a Weber, a Durkheim, a Pareto, or a Lenin, Lukacs or Gramsci?' [1969, p.219]. He gives his own interpretations - are your interpretations the same?

No, I mean my interpretation is that there were too many people like Perry Anderson which stopped the emergence of this - I mean, this is said by a man who went to Eton and Balliol and who never studied sociology (...) I have the utmost admiration for Perry Anderson's learning and his intellect let me say, but his attitudes towards sociology always seemed to be compounded by sheer class snobbery. There's one of his post-1968 pieces in which he refers to the 'dreary provincialism' of British sociology, by which he means that it was taught in the provincial universities and therefore not worthy of his thought ... I remember meeting him in Soho Square once on the way to the Left Club, and he was like a man who like Paul having newly seen the light on the road to Damascus and the thing which he had in his hand, was Leach's *Rethinking Social Anthropology* [1961] and he was saying 'at last - British sociology has an intellectual basis', and he really never had read any sociology, he thought it was beneath his notice, it wasn't something in the PPE syllabus.

(...) I won't comment on Key Problems of Sociological Theory [1961] *itself until a bit later, but obviously one of the things about the book and its historic importance within sociology, is the importance of theory. Simey, who reviewed it, talked about the fact that it didn't help us with the 'worrying problems of modern societies', it wouldn't come in useful, 'it's speculation which may sometimes be magnificent' but it is 'not sociology' [1962, p.118]. Can you tell me a bit about the experience you felt of the 'disinterest' in theory in Britain in 1960 ... Was it hard to get theory done?*

It's very funny that Simey should have said that, and I was very surprised when you quoted it because I remember not long after that giving a very

16

favourable review myself to a book by Simey, where Simey was talking most interestingly about Weber and he clearly knew a great deal about Weber, and he could recognise that somebody with Weber's theoretical positions would have a very strong position on a whole lot of policy questions, and yet when he responded to my book he responded to it as though he were a foolish enough man to believe that sociology was concerned with solving a lot of social work problems, and indeed I think that he got into that sort of position in Liverpool. We're not talking about Simey in particular but it seemed to me when he produced his later book which involved this stuff about Max Weber that he wasn't doing himself justice when he said things like that. There's a close relationship between theoretical understanding in terms which I use the notion of theoretical understanding and a concern for political problems if not policy problems.

How else would you characterise sociology departments that you knew of in British universities around that time?

Well we had all those social studies departments around the country which were run by failed economists and social workers. There were very few centres where anything else was happening (...) Anthropology was preventing the development of sociology. The figures of Gluckmann on the one hand and I think Little on the other at Edinburgh were preventing the development of sociology in those places.

In what sense? Their personalities or ...

No, because they saw to it that their universities provided money for anthropology rather than sociology. A break began to come in the late sixties, and it began partly because intelligent men like Grebenik, who was my professor at Leeds, who didn't like to admit to being intelligent, who was a demographer, saw that he had the need for sociological thinking in his department, and a number of the younger people at the LSE amongst whom at that stage one must count David Lockwood and Asher Tropp were dissatisfied themselves with the empiricism of the LSE ... and Lockwood's book *The Blackcoated Worker* [1958] we saw as a big breakthrough because it started to ask the Marx/Weber kind of class questions which on the whole Glass didn't ask.

17

(...) Let me get on to something else you've said in your Lancaster talk (I imagine in Social Forces *[1983]), one of the things you said was that a new generation of sociology students emerged in Europe, and in Britain, with 'little knowledge of Weber, but considerable acquaintance with the application of Marxist theory in the pages of the* New Left Review' *[1983, p. 1003]. Before we go on to that, could you talk a bit about* New Left Review *and Stuart Hall, and the early days of that?*

Just before I mention that, just let me correct you, that was not a talk which I gave at Lancaster. Interestingly that was a talk which I gave to the American Sociological Association; when I tried to give something similar in Lancaster at the British Sociological Association, my remarks, because they referred to such things as the Marxist incursion into British sociology produced almost a kind of witch-hunting hysteria in things like *Network* [1980], where Alan Waton wrote a piece calling *me* a Macarthyite for having raised intellectual questions about the relation between the Marxist tradition and sociology ...

The New Left Review ...?

The NLR emerged from the merger of two things, the *New Reasoner* and the *Universities and Left Review*. The *New Reasoner* was a body largely of ex-communists around Edward Thompson, who was a colleague of mine in the extra-mural department at Leeds. The *Universities and Left Review* was run entirely by young men from Oxford. I was attached to the *New Reasoner* group as a very marginal member. I was involved in various campaigns with Edward Thompson, and I ran my own campaigns on Africa, and because he didn't understand anything about Africa he asked me to write on Africa. Well, when the merger occurred, there were a number of people added to the board, and for the first time actually you had people - it's interesting that those who were added to the board were people who had in some sense a little bit of knowledge about sociology. They included apart from myself Ralph Miliband who had never been in the previous journals, Norman Birnbaum, who was actually a sociologist like myself, Alisdair MacIntyre, Raymond Williams - these were all new people - but I think we really hung together because we respected each other individually rather than having a common position. Various people I suppose gave direction to the movement because they were more intellectually impressive than others, and perhaps *the* most striking figure was E.P. Thompson, but Thompson never liked the situation in which he wasn't editor, even though he'd given up editing and asked Stuart [Hall] to be editor of the new journal. Stuart was a much more modern character from the world of both young Marxism and Mary Quant and that sort of thing. This was a phenomenon of the sixties. We had Left Club meetings in a ball-room in Oxford Street rather than in the sort of dreary church halls where the left used to meet. And for a long time - well for a while - the thing ran as an eclectic movement finding its day-to-day basis for reflection in the history of the nuclear disarmament movement. And then the point arose at which we couldn't ask Stuart Hall any longer to work for a pittance for us, because I think we paid him five hundred pounds a year and at the same time abused him continually for the inadequacy of things, and with perfect goodwill the organisation decided that we would find an editor to replace Stuart after a year. We accepted that we would have to have someone whose views were roughly within our area who could write and could live on next to nothing, and so we found Perry Anderson, who fulfilled all of those criteria. We had a splendid meeting at Keele at which Perry said that Britain lacked a political sociology, it lacked a tradition of Marxism, and it would be our job to give Britain this tradition of political sociology akin to what he thought Marx had given to the world in the 1880s. And we all thought that was fine. Laurence Daly of the NUM, I remember, who was on the board said 'will your journal sell at the pithead?', and Perry Anderson said 'oh yes, of course', and then he brought out his first number with an article by R.D. Laing called 'Series and Nexus in the Family' [1962] which didn't actually seem to have sales potential. But the new ... the thing was that then Perry introduced a new intellectual rigour *and* dogmatism into the journal, and I think the first flirtation was with Frankfurt and Gramsci.

In your Social Forces *piece you say that 'many philosophers now felt they had the right to intervene in most sociological debates' [1983, p. 1008] ... Why is it they felt that they had the right?*

I'm sorry to be dreary about this but it turned upon the class distinction in British education - at Oxford and Cambridge there were hundreds of philosophers and they had no sociology there, and I suppose with that kind of training they felt that their discipline was the one which was best, and a lot of them were going, because they, having run out of empire - which used to entitle them to go and rule British Somaliland, they were beginning to look for jobs in provincial universities. I'm being nasty now, but ...

You add that Giddens began to 'rewrite sociology', and that Giddens claims that his work has 'major significance to the understanding of late capitalism and communism' [1983, p. 1008]. Do you think he genuinely believes that his work has significance for the understanding of capitalism and communism?

I think you'd have to ask him that ... I mean the first thing I want to say about him is that clearly the man has a command of difficult philosophical texts in foreign languages which I can only envy. But also I think, following from that, he addresses himself to a set of debates which are common amongst the highest intellectuals of the European tradition, which I find sometimes quite, very difficult to understand. And which I probably at heart have a kind of earthy disrespect for, I mean, if - I actually find myself more in sympathy with Habermas than with Giddens, but when so much of what was being written in Germany was how the economic crisis was now over and the crisis was being displaced to other parts of the system, at all the times that I read that I was seeing around me people for whom the old economic crisis was still the main point.

Could you briefly characterise for me what you think the 'philosophisation of sociology' represents?

(...) It seemed to me that what I was trying to do as a sociologist was to describe social structures of greater or less extensiveness and the way in which they affected human behaviour, in order thereby to understand the way in which human beings could control their own destiny a little more satisfactorily, and by comparison with that it seemed to me that the European philosophers of society, or whatever is the appropriate term, were speaking about very intellectual issues which were very far removed from that rather direct and simple empirical goal of being able to describe and understand society. And actually I suppose if I understood Giddens on the question of structure, I would say that's where he seems to me to philosophise away the very subject matter of sociology.

You say that what most sociologists were getting in the early seventies was a sociology based on a political critique of capitalism on the one hand and an understanding of deviance on the other, and that there was 'little place in this for the study of Weber and Durkheim, and if they were prepared to make some relation to theory they did so by quoting themes from Giddens, Althusser, Garfinkel and Habermas' [1983, p. 1008]. Could you talk a little ...

I'm sorry. I must say something else between the last question and this one which turns on Giddens' concept of 'structuration', and that is that it seems to me that one of the things that the philosophical kind of sociologists want to do is to describe the world as it really is. Now that seems to me as a neo-Kantian myself an impossible goal ... that we cannot know the world as it really is, all that we can do is make more or less satisfactory models of the world, and it seems to me that Weber has a very adequate and satisfactory concept of structure, and that the concept of structuration doesn't improve on that - nor does the Levi-Strauss concept of structure. That's the thing that I want to hold onto; the concept of structures of social relations as compared with the abstract study of the structure of social systems which you get in what is called 'structuralism', and also the ethnomethodologisation of structure which you get in Giddens' concept of structuration. But now coming then to the things that occurred in England ...

I'm particularly interested in what you say about the Marxist incursion of Althusser and also the National Deviancy Symposium ...

I want to say something about the deviancy symposium. I had great hopes for that, and I thought that there would be some communication between sociological theory and deviance theory. In fact in my book *Discovering Sociology* [1973], there is a chapter which has been less commented on than any other thing I've ever written about sociological theory and deviance theory, in which I try to discuss the place of deviance theory in sociological theory. Now, in my own department at Durham, when I appointed Stan Cohen who was one of the founder of that [NDS], and he was, is and will always remain a very very close and much loved friend ... that I was always very disappointed that instead of the development of deviance teaching providing something which was a specific exemplification of and enrichment of the general sociological theory which we were doing, it became a little slick - not because of Stan but because of the way it was institutionalised -

it became a little slick paradigm of its own, where each person went off and did his own study of this and that form of deviance. I mean, a book called *The Tearoom Trade* [Humphreys, 1970] was typical of the sort of thing that captured people's imagination.

And your particular objection was because they were looking at actions of deviance rather than looking at a kind of deviance structure, that was the ...

Well, I think I was interested in the action of deviance, but I would have wanted to connect the limited action sequences in which the deviants were involved on particular occasions with larger social structures. I mean, one of the things which disappointed me enormously was a favourite essay of theirs, Becker's essay on becoming a marijuana user [1963], because Becker leads one to expect at the beginning of the essay that hitherto what one had in this field were sort of correlation studies - and as a Weberian I want to go from correlation studies which are in Weber's sense causally adequate to explanations which are adequate on the level of meaning - and I would have expected Becker to have been writing about the meaning of marijuana smoking in the context of quite far-reaching structures of social relations, instead of which the essay seems to me to be about how you inhale, and things of this kind.

Right. What about the Marxist incursion? Do you mean that the period came when sociology was not just sociology but politics and ideology, and that they all became mixed up. Is this through Louis Althusser?

Well first of all, before discussing Althusser it has always seemed to me to be possible to be politically engaged, yet at the same time to try to speak objectively - one does this particularly by being critical of one's own position (...) Now what began to happen at the time of 1968 was first of all a rejection of the idea of academic objectivity and I think also the refection of the liberal university as an institution. And I think that was disastrous for civilisation. I think that it actually opened the way to - I know I'll be criticised for using the term - opened the way to left-wing fascism in the sense of the systematic acceptance of unreason and force in debate. Now none of that in any sense depends upon Althusser, and in fact it is not merely an expression of Marxism, but seems to me to be at odds with very

22

important traditions in Marxism. Now as to Marxism itself (...) Marxism itself has always claimed to be *an alternative to sociology*, but it has been possible nonetheless for some people to read out of Marx a Marxist sociology. But whether one's speaking about social science or whether one's speaking about political life, there are many different kinds of Marxism. Let me say one of the great books that I ever read, probably the greatest book I ever read, was Ernst Troeltsch's, *The Social Teachings of the Christian Churches* [orig. 1931, 1956], and in that Troeltsch shows that in fact Christianity has been used to support every political position that there ever was, and so also has Marxism, and there are many facets of Marxism. I have always found it quite extraordinary that young English social scientists and students should take as the standard of what Marxism was, something which emanates from a man at the Sorbonne who like many other French academics was a communist and a Marxist, but whose special interest was Spinoza, and who in the light of that set about reflecting on, not on sociology as such of which he knew nothing, but upon the sort of crude sociology of Plekhanov and Bukharin, and revising that in terms of Spinoza and Freud and a few other things - how this very impoverished form of Marxism could come to ...

Yes, why? Some critics say that it's 'radicalizing Parsons', it's another form of functionalism ...

Well Althusser's influence has not been universal around the world, I mean it has in fact flourished in those places like Britain which have a very poor sociological tradition, and amongst people who knew very little about sociology who took this up as an alternative. One of the most ludicrous things in the Althusser tradition, is a remark by Poulantzas - who unlike Althusser does seem to have read some sociology - where he dismisses what he calls the historicist problematic of 'class in itself and class for itself' which he sees as characteristic of the social thought of Lukacs and Weber. Now, I mean there's several things about that. First of all, I cannot feel that you can treat Weber adequately as a kind of appendage to Lukacs; the actual historical reality was the opposite, but also if I have a Marxism myself it centres around that particular problematic, and although in practice I'm sure Poulantzas does himself implicitly use that problematic, its dismissal from the scene there in favour of a systems theory in which one talks about the independence of the ideological and the political, and never gets down to the

23

question of individual and collective actors as historical agents ... it seems to me quite extraordinary and quite unacceptable as Marxism.

At the other end of the scale, 'subjectivism' and ethnomethodology. Have you much to say on ethnomethodology?

Well I wish that I understood it. I find it very difficult to understand because its main writers don't actually write in English and I find it very difficult to understand sentences that don't have a verb in them, and I have pointed this out to some of my colleagues, my ethnomethodological colleagues, with regard to Garfinkel's work, and when I point to paragraphs which I don't think have a verb - although it's always in doubt - they say 'God he's good! Look how he fractures language!'. There's a kind of methodological irrationalism about that. I think that there are certain things which ethnomethodology brings forward which are of value. Incidentally I can claim to be one of its founding fathers. Aaron Cicourel's book *Method and Measurement in Sociology* [1964] quotes me and Max Weber as the two chaps who write about what sociology is!

Was it both, as you I think might have hinted, a reflection of the time, which was, if you like, a rejection of politics, and again was there something in sociology it was reacting against?

Yes. I mean that it turned away from what we can crudely call positivist empiricism ... It also of course in its Californian forms took a stand against more political action; it was connected with the cultural revolution rather than hard political change. But I mean, I think it is true that the world 'out there' is made by the people who participate in it and they are in their own way skilled sociologists, and actually a sociologist trying to describe social reality has to be aware both of the constructs about the social world which have been produced by observers and the implicit rules of action and so on which people are using, and I did try to write about this once in another essay of mine which has the dogmatic title 'Thirty theses on epistemology and method in sociology' [in Rex, 1973]. And I mean in there is a definition of my position as against ethnomethodology. But they have produced their own mystery, and it is very much a mystery (...) I think that there is something to be salvaged from the ethnomethodological position, that

24

along with the concepts of structural description which one gets in Max Weber, there's another notion which is to be found in Simmel's essay 'How is Society possible?' where he speaks about the possibility of a sociological *a priori* as compared with that of natural science, and then he goes on to say that we have this problem in sociology that it's not simply sociologists having concepts but the people 'out there' making their own *a priori* ...

(...) What would be a quick definition of the sociological enterprise?

I don't think there is a quick definition of it an attempt to understand the structures of social relations which influence and limit the goal fulfilment of individuals, and this is something which one might tackle on a micro-level, or one might be more ambitious and tackle it on a macro-level. I think that if one does tackle it on the highest macro-level that necessarily there's going to be a much greater degree of uncertainty about what one says. Although very often it is also very true that one can't really adequately understand the micro unless one knows how its implanted in the macro.

Your work has been described as 'structural phenomenology', in that there's a methodological emphasis on a neo-Weberian conception of phenomenology of social action, and a theoretical commitment to what some people call neo-Marxist - although we don't really know what that means - about the inevitability of conflict in social relations. Those two things, are they the central ...

Yes, I was told after I'd written *Key Problems of Sociological Theory* [1961] by a number of Germans that I was a phenomenologist ... I would certainly deny that the kind of sociology that I was talking about had very much in common with Husserl's enterprise. I was always interested in Schutz as a sort of footnote to Weber, but I didn't see Schutzianism as replacing Weber. I did want a concept of structure which was related to the concept of action, and that was something which I was prepared to do without calling myself a phenomenologist. But when I started to say about Glass's statistical tables, please let's look at the meaning of those categories in terms of which he's classified the population and that might lead us to some concept of classes as historical actors, that's the particular thing I had in mind. If that was phenomenology I was a phenomenologist. But it soon became apparent to

25

me that ... if we were to go back to those tables, what I was saying is let's look at this, not in order that we should abolish tables altogether, but perhaps we should have better tables. Cicourel wanted to concentrate the whole effort on looking at the people who made the tables rather than the data to which they referred. He said about Goldthorpe, 'I've just been to have lunch with John Goldthorpe. They're going to do another study of social mobility.' Cicourel said 'I said "Why don't we instead of doing that do a study of people studying mobility"', and that was the sort of thing that was happening. And, so very soon phenomenological sociology and ethnomethodology had gone way beyond my ken, just as on the other front my emphasis upon conflict theory had been submerged in Marxism, which claimed to be about conflict theory but took a form which didn't have any place for conflict in it at all.

Could you talk very briefly about 'conflict theory' which although a vague term is associated with you, Dahrendorf, and Randall Collins, for example?

I find that encapsulation of conflict theorists are always rather surprising - I accept it because sometimes people who would not be interested in what I have to say otherwise are prepared to listen to me if I'm encapsulated in that group ...

Why - does it seem to be more radical?

I don't know. I mean, actually conflict theory is a bit old-fashioned nowadays, but occasionally people who want to cover the full range of things have a place for conflict theorists, and all I can say is that my sociology is basically Weberian, and if one has the notion that structures of social relations arise in the course of human action, whose nature is determined by the meaningful action of individuals, then it is always possible that that social structure one individual is trying to sustain will be different from the structure which somebody else is - so the notion of conflict arises from that. I wouldn't want to say that I'm a conflict theorist.

(...) Right. I'll move on. The value debate, it's an area hardly talked about today. You once said that 'one problem has been quite central to me, the

relationship between detached sociological work and political engagement' *[1975, p. 8]. Could you talk a little about this?*

Well, I mean one of the most really ultimately stupid pieces of writing I've ever seen was Gouldner's 'Anti-Minotaur' essay [1963] where he discussed Weber as though Weber had invented positivism. I find it very hard to know how a man of Gouldner's culture and learning could have written such a trivial and misleading essay. My guide on the question of values and actions is Gunner Myrdal, who says in his 'Facts and Valuations' piece [1944] which I think is a piece of central sociological importance which should be taught to every student, is that first of all in making any kind of sociological analysis of something serious one should begin by making it clear what sort of state of affairs one is concerned with either promoting or stopping. Myrdal asks us to ask, given such a set of desired social states what institutions and patterns of social action are conducive to the attainment of that state of affairs, and what are not? He also goes on, I think, to go beyond that sort of approach, which is the basis of a serious kind of critical sociology, to the possibility of prediction, where he says you can look at a society from a number of different points of view and by and large you concentrate on those 'goal states' or values which actual groups are seeking and then you try to make some sort of prediction in terms of the result of the interplay of the power which those groups of people use to achieve those objectives (...) I certainly don't want to commit myself to a situation in which the people I know as brother or sister sociologists have responsibility for our affairs. That's the task of politics.

(...) Two things you said in Discovering Sociology *on C. Wright Mills interested me: 'Despite the systematic attempt to denigrate and devalue the work of the late C. Wright Mills' [1973, p. 178], that was one thing you say, I want you to tell me what was the systematic attempt; and secondly, that 'Mills would not have settled for a quiet, professional definition of his role. Like Comte and Marx and Weber before him ... he saw it as his task to make sense of his time ... British sociology has never yet been challenged by such a man' [p. 184]. Just tell me briefly why he's important to you?*

I think when I wrote that bit about the systematic attempt to denigrate his work I'd just read a review of one of his books written immediately after his death by Shils, and it just seemed to me to ... I mean he was criticised for things like faking his samples when he was a coder for a project in New York and things like this, as though that made a great difference to the man. I thought that he was a political intellectual, who dealt with the things which were really important and had agonized over the problems of how a little individual in American society has any influence over it at all, and I said somewhere, sometime that Mills said - it's in *The Sociological Imagination* [1959], I think, or was it in *The Causes of World War Three* [1958] - he said sociologists face two alternatives: one is to go into the administration as an advisor, thinking one can do something but having to accept all its assumptions, or to stand outside and not have any influence. And Mills' answer to that was absolutely to choose the second, in the hope that somehow, some way by preaching, his ideas would have some kind of impact. It may actually be an irrational and emotional thing, but I feel much happier - that's why I said that I don't like the way some of our social administration people say 'we' when talking about the government.

Alright. We'll come now to research and race relations. Donald Macrae in 1970 stated: 'Empirical research is easy, as well as quite often being generally useful. Most of it, like most natural science, could be done by well-designed mechanical mice' [in Halsey, 1982, p. 166]. Does it surprise you that somebody like Donald Macrae can say that?

Well, I think that I would ... It depends what you mean by research. I think that the concept of research which is continually wished upon people like myself by those in government and my own employers in the SSRC [ESRC], that we do research to make up for some sort of simple deficiency of fact, and that things may be going wrong because people haven't got the facts. Myrdal's 'Facts and Valuations' piece that I keep coming back to, was precisely an attempt to make a statement about what he should do in race relations research in the United States, when he was called in by people who said 'you're a distinguished objective outsider - give us the facts'. Now his answer to that was that sociologists do not just talk about the facts, they say that certain facts are necessary facts, and as soon as that notion of necessity is introduced, Myrdal says we have to say 'necessary from what point of view'?

(...) Alright. 16 February 1967, headline in the Times *was 'The danger of*

Sparkbrook' which referred to Race, Community and Conflict *[Rex and Moore, 1967]. That was quite important in the discussion leading up to the election. How influential do you think that sociological research is, even if it's on sensitive issues and written incisively, like say* Race, Community and Conflict - *how influential can it be? Think of your own work, cast your mind back ...*

When I look back on *Race, Community and Conflict* as compared with *Colonial Immigrants in a British City* I'm astonished at the moderation of the book. I was ... one is influenced by these sorts of political circumstances, and I was addressing people in Birmingham who were in a state of panic about the arrival of black people there, and I was trying to suggest there a model of race relations in the urban system which involved looking at mechanisms whereby the coming of such people did not lead to the disruption of the social structure, and the people themselves became, either as separate groups or as individuals, part of British society, and it's a very moderate book in that way. It is in fact almost seeking to advise Birmingham how it can avoid racial conflict. Now, unfortunately that book got the most extraordinary publicity apparatus working for it because of Jim Rose's relationship with the press. And we launched it at various public dinners and so on, and of course it was *my* intention all the time while writing to draw the attention of people in Britain to the dangers of the forms of racial discrimination which were going on, in terms of the kinds of conflict to which they'd ultimately lead, and obviously implicitly asking them - as indeed I did as a citizen, I ran a campaign against discrimination in the allocation of housing particularly. Now, I'm afraid that some of the reviews of that piece, in saying it was an important book, said that it was an important book for almost the opposite reason. I mean the *Times* first leader actually said that what this book shows is that we need a better immigration control act which would enable us to keep out the Pakistanis and so on and still let in the Australians. And Enoch Powell reviewed the book in the *Telegraph*, and used it as a taking-off point for talking about the dangers to Britain of the presence of these blacks. There's nothing in my book that justifies that, but that's one of the difficulties that one finds oneself in.

Do you think now though that the period is such, take the case of Peter Townsend, that the media is not particularly interested in the outpourings of sociology any more, or that the political climate is such that it is of no consequence?

(...) Actually I have tried, I may not have succeeded, to write books which help those who are in oppressed groups, subordinate, oppressed groups, to understand their situation in order to be able to act politically against it, and to give an answer to those questions one must give a quite complex answer. The question of immigration in British politics and as presented by the media, has no place for complex issues. It allows itself to be dominated by questions posed by Enoch Powell, and the most that one can expect is to be allowed to appear as the other side. In the various requests which I've had, which have been very small in numbers since I've been here, to appear in the media have always been in relation to some question posed by Enoch Powell, so that there is a kind of blackout of serious discussion.

(...) I won't rehearse all of the arguments about housing classes. In Colonial Immigrants *you and Sally Tomlinson argue that 'In particular we were still inclined to the view that, however much immigrants might be integrated in the workplace (an integration which we saw in any case as only partial), this did not mean that they were accorded the same rights as their native peers in matters of residence and education' [1979, pp. 192-93]. To me, that's a good summary of housing classes ...*

I must say that statement which you read of mine seems to me as you read it to be the most irrefutable statement I've ever made; it seems to me to be so true of British circumstances. Whether one uses the term *class* here does depend a little upon one's theoretical background. You see there's a Marxist objection to suggesting that class arises anywhere else than at the point of production, and it is a Marxist view that other things belong to something which is the sphere of consumption. I would say rather that people are seeking various ends and that there are a number of important means and resources to those ends, and that one way of using the word class is to refer to the extent to which people control those important resources necessary for life, and that along with the relations to the means of production the relation to having a house or having access to schooling is a very central thing in modern life, and that it is possible in Weber's terms to refer to the groups of people who have the same relationship to those other resources as classes.

... I'll just read you a piece from a review of Colonial Immigrants *by Colin Prescod: 'Rex and Tomlinson, [are] policy researchers par excellence in the period of black militancy', and that you are still 'making contributions to the sociology of race relations', but are 'now a liberal pessimist'. On the book itself he says 'how are we to apprehend the intention of a book which starts with a scientific race relations project, and finishes with an emotional Third Worldist programme? There is something almost racist about the implication that it is necessary to inform social change in the metropole with some kind of science whereas mere revolutionary rhetoric will do for the Third World periphery' [1979, p. 201]. Now, I've read quite clearly your views on this, and it's quite clear to me that you do not belong to the race relations industry of liberal sociology ...*

The first remark that I would make, and I would hope that when you edit that you would keep this in, is that one shouldn't really feel bound to reply to every observation that individuals make, even when it is based upon irrationalism and defies all kinds of logic. And it doesn't seem to me from the things that Prescod has written and said that he merits reply. However, treating him rather more generously than he deserves, one of his major objections to me - three objections to me which he has made at various times - one is that although he doesn't know my ancestry which is mixed, he objects to the colour of my skin, he takes a racist view of that; secondly he believes that the fact that I talk about Max Weber is dangerous; and thirdly he feels that what I write is threatening to his own claim to political power. Those three objections are important to understand what he's saying. But I think the thing which I found most strange about his piece was that when he looked at the back part of my book in which - because I believe in the interpretative understanding of social action and social relations - I tried to give as sympathetic account as I could of the world view of Rastafarianism and the way certain practices followed from that. I was very surprised when Prescod reviewed the book to find him saying that for black people I accepted irrational rhetoric, because I have a great respect for Rastafarianism, which I would have expected a man who himself wears a Rasta hairstyle might have shared. Why he should wish in the course of a review of mine to attack Rastafarianism I don't know, to represent it as irrationalism. I can only think that although, so far as I understand Prescod's position, it attempts to balance a relationship between black consciousness and Marxism - when it comes to it the ultimate commitment is to a certain kind of political Marxism (...) I think it would be very

31

important for someone in Britain to produce a piece of work, which would be set upon and attacked, but which would look at the groups of people presently claiming leadership of the black community, groups of political intellectuals, and asking things about their interests. I think that these are early days in the development of race relations in Britain and that one is likely to find all sorts of opportunists claiming that leadership. Now I want to say this - I don't feel that doing research is the most important thing from the point of view of achieving a just society in terms of race relations, it just so happens that doing social research is my job, and I try to do it in ways that are helpful to and not hurtful to oppressed black groups in this country. I will go on trying to do that work, because I justify it in terms of my reversal of Marx's eleventh thesis again, and I think it can be of value. But because the channels for the dissemination of research findings are in fact manipulated in Britain [the result is] that those who have power can see to it that the sorts of information that people like myself produce never get anywhere. I'm not sure that I really feel that I want to go on for the rest of my life doing research on race relations. I would be happier and considerably liberated if I could go back to the politics of race relations. Only one can't just go as an individual, politics involves a relationship with movements, and the difficulty I would find at the present time is finding a political audience to talk to. I would like to live in a situation where we had something like a civil rights movement in this country which was interested in research results, and which was interested in careful, rational interpretations of political situations as a guide to action. We don't have that at the moment, and it does make it therefore very difficult, either to see how research can be used, or how to see ways in which black politics can be effective.

(...) On Marx you once said that 'in the contemporary world we have again a number of doctrines claiming a Marxian heritage, which probably have as little relation to Marx as Calvinism has to Christianity' [1975, p. 8], and you talk particularly about the Frankfurt School and about Althusser. Could you expand and talk about Marxism and social change?

A number of points ... The first is that until fairly recently I gave a very old-fashioned answer; I did believe in the role of the working class and indeed of the oppressed peoples of the earth, of whom the British working class were one in a sense ... and I really believed that in England the agent of change would be the working class, and that there wasn't really any alternative to the Labour Party ... I mean I'm worried about that now, I mean I think that the decline of the class base of the Labour Party makes it difficult to feel sure that it's going to re-assert itself - that a labour movement can change or even check and balance capitalism. When you talk about revolutionary change, [or change towards the 'good society'] I must I think record that I have some deeply pessimistic views here, as a result of my visits to Eastern Europe.

Meaning?

(...) if one visits Poland or Bulgaria or East Germany, the places which I've been to, what one sees there is something which does so little actually to advance the happiness, the standard of life and so on of the most numerous class, that one asks oneself whether one can any longer seriously say that there is a model in which a centrally planned and bureaucratic system can produce better results for the people than a market economy. In fact, it seems to me very clear that the most revolutionary thing which could happen in Poland is to open branches of Marks and Spencers and Sainsbury's there, and to allow the market mechanism to operate. And so, if one takes that point of view, surely one has to say, horrible and morally and aesthetically displeasing though the market mechanism is, it's the best way that we know at the moment of providing the basic necessities of life for people. The important thing is to *control it*, so that in fact social goals are nonetheless achieved. Now that's a very moderate sounding thing to say, some people might even suggest that compared with my earlier positions it's a sort of 'social democratic' thing to say. Now I don't mind if there is a political group which advocates an acceptance of the market economy but with an attempt to control it for very definite social goals and for equality. I would support such a group. The thing is that I don't see such a group as existing in Britain in any of the political parties. I think it's far more likely to emerge in the Labour Party than it is to occur amongst the various right-wing refugees from Labour who've joined the thing called the Social Democratic Party.

(...) I think that demystification has been a central element to sociology for you both in terms of unmasking the social world and sociology. Could you

33

talk about your own style of sociology and influence within it, and sociology's future as you see it?

I think I was trying to say in the 'demystification' book [*Sociology and the Demystification of the Modern World,* 1974] that most sociologists whose work I look at, whether it's Giddens or Goldthorpe or anybody else in Britain, write in ways which are extraordinarily inaccessible to people 'out there'. They are accessible to intellectuals, and intellectuals who are engaged in politics and that may be important. Practically everything that I do in sociology consists of unpacking words, if I've made any contribution to conflict theory or the study of functionalism it's usually been by rewriting what clever people have said in simple and straightforward language about action, which suggests that it isn't a thing out there that we have to deal with by science. And, people may say Weber had an awkward and Teutonic style, but I think to some extent he did that sort of rewriting too ... now as to influence. First of all I don't think that at the present time I will have much influence in British sociology. In fact the people who are interested in the kind of sociology which I do tend to be scattered around the world rather than in England. The kind of ideas which I put forward, in very simple language, seem naive and child-like to the really clever people who exclude them from discourse; and I'm also now older than other people, and I don't belong to any group which would lead to my ideas being taken up for non-academic reasons.

(...) Do you think there are any baselines at all that exist or should exist between sociologists of different 'species', or is sociology simply, as you quoted in another article, just a 'Micky Mouse' subject [1975, p. 10], something that anyone could do?

Well all sorts of people have moved into sociology and colonised it and used it for their purposes, and it's actually very difficult nowadays for anybody who's a sociologist to get a job in a sociology department, because on the whole there are all sorts of deviants and criminals and gangsters - to exaggerate somewhat - who have moved in, and I suppose it's a case of the lunatics have taken over the asylum, which is very sad. I don't know whether we'll ever get back to a stage where there will be a position in which sociologists can occupy, where they demystify the world and give people a clearer view of it so that they can act. Every time I listen to something like the BBC news, which compared with others which one sees around the world like the Polish news and so on, is actually relatively honest, but even so it is still loaded with distortions of reality, and I want sociology teachers at least speaking to their students, to create people who have an understanding of the world, which makes them proof against that sort of propaganda.

Thinking of what you said earlier about the 'philosophisation of sociology', do you think a lot of contemporary 'sociologists' are in fact philosophers? Or doesn't it matter?

One can't really say any more what is a sociologist and not a sociologist, because the gatekeeper's opened the gates to everybody, and now those who've got in make the declarations. I would say that, I hesitate to be dogmatic, but I really feel that sociology is what Max Weber did, and that if one starts from Max Weber one can get a great deal from Marx, even occasionally from Durkheim, and Simmel was also I think a very significant figure. But of course sociology should be cumulative, there should be other figures one could point to - I think one could point to Parsons - I can think of precious few people after that, because Habermas in fact is engaged in a larger enterprise than sociology. But I can't see in what developed in the 70s in the United States and in Europe a development of a sociological tradition ... if the subject is to exist in the future as what I regard as sociology, it would have to go back to something like Weber.

(...) What about the priorities? Should there be priorities?

Well one thing that Weber wrote about was bureaucracy and people becoming cogs in machines and so on. He regarded bureaucracy with people in jobs with job descriptions as a threat. We now live in the world of computerised administration, and a totally new and much more disturbing world has come into being. That seems to me to be an extra problem. Things which arise out of Weber's conception of the rationalisation of the world - with all of the inverted commas and ironies which he attaches to that term - I think we need them to deal with that kind of problem. I mean we live in a world of right-wing political extremism. I think we need to understand the forces which have created that right-wing political extremism and the possibility of checking it. And because the world has moved on from the nineteenth century, the groups of people who are brought into conflict with one another are no longer simply the metropolitan bourgeoisie and proletariat, but all of the people of the rest of the world. Those are the sorts of problems that sociologists should go to.

(...) What is the real value of the sociological enterprise, and secondly what for you is the 'good society'?

Well I think that amongst the other ways of helping human beings to control their environment is an understanding of social structures and the ways in which they can be changed. I mean that is what is contained in [that] sentence about the paradox of sociology, that these things have been made by men and can be changed by men. And that statement was made at a very high level of generality, but there are all sorts of levels at which one can apply it. As to the 'good society' ... (...) First of all let us consider the 'Green alternative'. When I was entertained to forest mushrooms and vodka by a peasant family in Poland who had nothing, I was conscious of being in touch with people who were very close to the good life, and that makes me sound very romantic. It's necessary to say that because one oughtn't automatically to accept that the world which has arisen as a result of capitalism and bureaucratization is a step on the way to the 'better life', but if we've got there and we're going to do something about it clearly the question becomes how you impose on formal rationality - the rationality which produces efficient car plants and so on - some sort of goals, you can call it substantive rationality or anything else, how do you impose it on that ...?

A morality?

Well, I mean ... the welfare of the most numerous class or something, can one create a system which does that - that's still a legitimate question. What's much more in question today is whether the bureaucratically run societies of Eastern Europe, which are our models, go anywhere near providing an answer to that, and if not is there any sort of social democrat or mixed alternative, which involves using the mechanism of the free market but developing the political institutions to control it. But maybe, and one of the things that I said in the 'demystification' book, is that if one lives in the First world it's pretty nasty, if one lives in the Second world it's pretty nasty, of one lives in the Third world it's pretty nasty. We're *never* going to have a system of social institutions which guarantees happiness to everybody; all of them have their structural problems and defects, and if I was teaching students drawn at random from the First, Second and Third world I would be trying to equip them to cope with the forms of oppression and alienation which arise from the free market, from the Party, and from whatever it is we have in the Third world. So the recommendation of that 'demystification' book which appalled Peter Worsley, who really does believe that somehow or other we can gather the troops and morale should still be high and the fight is on; I used the word stoicism - he didn't like that.

2 Ralf Dahrendorf

Lord Dahrendorf, Warden of St. Antony's College, Oxford, is one of the few sociologists to have been prominent in public life having served as a Commissioner for the EEC, as a Junior Foreign Minister in Germany for the Free Democratic Party (FDP), and more recently as Director of the London School of Economics and Political Science.

Often viewed as *the* sociologist of liberty, and certainly as Hall points out he was profoundly influenced by Popper and his notion of 'open-ness' (Hall, 1981, p. 120), Dahrendorf is best know for his critique of Marx in *Class and Class Conflict in Industrial Society* (1959), and for his belief in the ubiquity of social conflict as characterised in his brilliant essay 'Out of Utopia: Toward a Reorientation of Sociological Analysis' (in Dahrendorf, 1968, pp. 107-28). Interestingly enough, another of his works *Homo Sociologicus* (1973), in which he develops what he considers to be the central concept of sociology, *role*, has not received as much attention. However, in Germany the book led to a fully-fledged public controversy, while conversely his works on class and the theory of conflict failed to stimulate discussion.

The question of values also figures strongly in his thinking and indeed as Bryant notes, Dahrendorf has attempted to restore a discussion of values in sociology (1976, p. 295). Dahrendorf states his position against Weber, in that he wishes to advance the thesis that 'whereas sociology as a value-free science in Weber's sense may be desirable, the sociologist as such must always be morally committed if he is to protect himself and others from unintended consequences of his actions'. In fact, for Dahrendorf 'our responsibility as sociologists does not end when we complete the process of scientific inquiry; indeed, it may begin at that very point' (1968, p. 17 and p. 18). This stress on the public significance of sociology is another of Dahrendorf's claims, as is his insistence on bridging the Weberian divide between science and politics.

On conflict, Dahrendorf argues that the notion wherever there is social life there is conflict 'may be unpleasant and disturbing', yet not the presence but the absence of conflict is surprising and abnormal, and 'we have good reason to be suspicious if we find a society or social organization that displays no evidence of conflict' (1968, p. 127). In his model of social conflict, Dahrendorf points out that societies are held together by constraint not consensus, by the 'coercion of some by others', and that 'quite apart from its merits as a tool of scientific analysis, the conflict model is essentially non-utopian; it is the model of an open society' (1968, p. 128).

In *Class and Class Conflict in Industrial Society*, Dahrendorf criticises Marx for believing that power or domination 'is derived from the possession of property when in fact the possession of property is only a special case of the capacity to dominate' (Bryant, 1976, p. 269). Dahrendorf extends Weber on power, and defines class in relation to *authority*; the ability to exercise or be excluded from authority. Bryant, in a thorough review of Dahrendorf's work, sees his vision as one of a (1976, p. 295)

> humane meritocracy in which competition is tempered only by the existence of a floor through which no one shall be allowed to fall lest the resultant demoralisation preclude any realistic chance of participation in social, economic and political processes and by restrictions designed to prevent the elite from so changing the rules of participation as to perpetuate itself indefinitely.

Despite Dahrendorf's own public career, and his concern to discuss the public significance of sociology, he is hardly optimistic (1968, p. 274)

> Rich as the country of sociology with its open frontiers may be in potential, however ... its glories do not extend to practice. Sociology is theory, and no amount of 'decided reason' will set it to dealing actively with the social and political problems of our time.

Could you tell me a little about your background?

I was born in 1929, and I was born into a political family, that is, my father was a Social Democratic member of the Weimar Reichstag towards the end - he was himself quite young at that time of course. So he was first arrested when virtually all Social Democratic MP's were arrested after they had voted against the 'enabling law' in the late Spring of 1933. We moved house in order to be less visible than we were in Hamburg where he was well known, and moved to Berlin. He was arrested on and off, and for the final time after the 20 July 1944. At that time we had been evacuated from Berlin to a small place about thirty miles outside, and at the school there we had, well, a sort of an organisation, which in itself was not to be taken terribly seriously ... it has a beautiful high-sounding name, 'Freedom Association of Secondary Schoolboys of Germany', and consisted essentially in producing flysheets which we typed ourselves and distributed to a small number of people (...). A friend of mine was living about ten miles away and we were exchanging letters and they of course - our letters at least - were opened by censors, and that was how they found out what had been going on, and after two slightly disagreeable interviews we were arrested early in December 1944 ... both taken to be imprisoned in Frankfurt-on-the-Oder which is [now] the boundary of Poland, and then to a camp to the east of that where we spent the following eight weeks. Basically, my friend and I were lucky because when the Russians came at the end of January we were just kicked out ... we were given a marvellous mixture of total confusion and bureaucratic cruelty. We were each given a piece of paper saying that we were both hereby forbidden ever to attend secondary school in Germany again, which we took along with us and found our way home with the last refugee groups, went to Berlin and awaited the end of the war ... my father survived. But I think perhaps the main point about this is that I had grown up in an environment where outside political events were one of the main influences - even on personal life in a certain sense, and that, of course, is something one does not forget.

Yes. I don't know if you know the John Hall book where he says that the concentration camp experience particularly leads you, or rather reinforces the desire for freedom [1981, p. 120] ...

Yes, and yes I suppose it does. I tend to have a fairly detached view of what I did and all the more so since I have children who have themselves been fifteen at some stage, and therefore I have seen how young one is when one is fifteen. While we were imprisoned in Frankfurt, we were in cells by ourselves and that's quite an experience for a young person and one does learn a bit about what one wants ... it's a desire for freedom almost in a claustrophobic sense. I wouldn't make too much of it but I've certainly been impressed by what happened to my father then and again in late 1945 early 1946 when he was Deputy Chairman of the East German Social Democrats and refused to go along with the merger with the Communists *under pressure*. So we went through an almost similar experience at that time or would have done, had it not been for the British occupation ... people in Berlin flying us out, and so it's more precarious than direct.

Okay. So you joined the SPD?

I joined the SPD on my eighteenth birthday which was in 1947, and I don't think I ever attended a ward meeting, but I did attend quite regularly the student group meetings at the University of Hamburg. The fact is that when I came to England my membership lapsed.

In my notes here I've got '1952; no longer a socialist?' ...

I don't know whether I was a socialist or not, but certainly between 1952 and 1954 I didn't pay any dues and at that time the SPD was still quite a strict party in that respect ... nowadays they're delighted if they have any members at all, and so they just took me off the register which I discovered six years later when I wasn't sure myself.

I've read that you studied classics at the University of Hamburg but got interested in social science through Marx. Is that true?

What happened was that ... its really a story of how university teachers *should be* in an ideal world. I did classics and philosophy, and I had a teacher in classics who wanted me to write a dissertation in Greek, but I had become much more interested in philosophy and so I went to my philosophy

42

professor and said that I wanted to write a dissertation on Hellenistic philosophy and the concept of society, and he said 'what are you really interested in', and I said 'what do you mean' and then we talked about politics and I explained to him what I've said to you, and so he said - surprisingly rather, in Germany in 1950 - 'do you know Karl Marx's dissertation?'. I said 'no' and he said 'why don't you go and read it', and so I did, well what's left of it, and lo and behold his dissertation was on Hellenistic philosophy and was the beginning of a much wider - although he was essentially interested in natural philosophy - study of whatever, and so gradually we got on to a very different subject, namely Marx. The reason was that he wanted me to write about a subject which had some personal meaning for me, not in the sense in which one talks about Marxism today but in the sense that I was obviously interested in the history of political thought and so on, and then somehow or other we decided that one needed a vantage point to write about this, and that's how I got to the rather fascinating subject of the concept of justice, fascinating because it doesn't exist in Marx because of course he believes in the inexorable necessity of the historical process, the inevitability of historical processes and therefore doesn't need a moral category in order to motivate people to do certain things ... anyway that's how it happened.

You came to the LSE?

Yes, I went to the LSE not knowing where I was going.

The influence of Popper is obvious, it's also just that T.H. Marshall ...

Tom Marshall was my supervisor.

(...) Could you just tell me what to you is the crucial importance of Popper, and the importance of Marshall as well?

No, not of Marshall as well, that's quite different and not as easily answered. I think the *crucial* importance of Popper, certainly for me and I think for us, is the assumption of *fundamental uncertainty* and everything that follows from it. It's such a simple and obvious one, that once you assume that we cannot really know what is true - let alone what is right - you get pretty quickly to the trial and error notions and falsification is an extreme way of putting it ... that I think is the fundamental influence and of course it's a very important one. I recently had an American PhD student here who was writing a very interesting dissertation on what he calls 'Liberal thought in the mid-20th Century'. He argues that Popper as well as Raymond Aron and Hayek [1945] in *The Road to Serfdom* and also Talmon were all really primarily influenced by the experience of totalitarianism and this whole uncertainty, openness, trial and error approach was directed to the experience of totalitarianism. Now this had an obvious appeal to me I'm bound to say, because both the Nazi and the Soviet encounter in my early years had left quite considerable thoughts in my mind at any rate and of course my own father's role in it all. I might add that this PhD student's main thesis is an approach which is spent because the danger of totalitarianism does not exist, because there are no longer any respectable intellectual groups in the world who explicitly or implicitly advocate this sort of approach, so nowadays a congress for cultural freedom is totally out of place and makes no sense at all. There is an interesting fact which Aron mentions in his memoirs. He says that he accepted the world presidency of whatever it's called - some new organisation of this kind founded three years ago - and he regretted it, but he discovered too late that they were the ones now in charge and they weren't the opponents of 1945 or 1950. So I would say this uncertainty idea, the trial and error notion which follows from it applied to thought as a notion that we cannot know whether something is true, we can only know if it is wrong and therefore we have to proceed by refuting or ideally falsifying earlier theories ... applied to political theory as *The Open Society* [1945] does, as the rejection of all closed systems is perhaps the most important intellectual result of the age of totalitarianism.

Marshall, was he ...

Tom Marshall's influence on me wasn't very great. He was my supervisor and we had numerous conversations; what impressed me about Marshall, and that's why I quote him so frequently, is the *style* of *Citizenship and Social Class* [1950] because my dream has always been social analysis, that is to say, the really thoughtful penetration of social processes by a mind which could have written abstract theory but has decided instead to bring real processes to life. Now Durkheim has done this in a fairly mechanical way

44

but nevertheless I believe his *Suicide* belongs to this tradition, and I think that the long essay on citizenship and social class is a masterpiece in this history of social analysis in which there are not many masterpieces. *The Protestant Ethic* is a masterpiece in this history and there are other books, but *Citizenship and Social Class* has certainly had an influence on me in style as well as substance. I would today regard the style as the more important aspect.

(...) You became Professor of Sociology at Hamburg 1958, then in 1967 Free Democratic Party Junior Foreign Minister, then the EEC in 1970 as a commissioner. Did being a sociologist make you do the job differently or did that in fact matter?

It didn't matter at all. I've recently thought about this quite a lot and of course people have often said to me even in Brussels, but also in Bonn after a cabinet meeting, they would say this must have been fascinating for you as a sociologist, and I then noticed that I hadn't been there as a sociologist at all, I'd been there either to get something through or prevent something, in other words just like anybody else. I think it's an illusion to believe that if a sociologist goes into politics he applies sociology to it. Similarly the effect of these experiences on one's thinking is much more indirect than most people seem to think and certainly not immediate, because when you're fighting a particular corner, the last thing you think about is how this is translated into sociological analysis.

Okay. Your contribution to the Adorno-Popper dispute edited by David Frisby; one thing you say that's interested me, you say, quote 'thus Popoer and Adorno were in complete agreement that the attempt at a sharp demarcation between sociology and philosophy would have detrimental effects for both' [in Adorno et al., 1976, p. 124]. (...) Can you say why there shouldn't be any demarcation because of, say Giddens's approach - or is this simply the difference between German and English sociology?

At the time I was professor in Tubingen. I was intrigued by the apparent incompatibility of the two approaches which were both meta-sociological approaches - they were not in themselves sociological nor would their authors have claimed that - and so I organised this meeting in Tubingen. It

45

was really a disaster because they didn't talk to or about each other but passed each other, and at best an observer could watch two minds at work, and at worst even that wasn't particularly impressive. I had to write a kind of summary and pointed out tongue-in-cheek really that this was one of the similarities if not much of a similarity. Having said that I suppose ... let me say that I do think that there are boundaries, the question is to what extent does one have to respect them (...) Having said that, I don't believe that not separating sharply has made a particularly negative difference. I think I'm now bored by the methodological debate, and I think contributions can come from all sorts of corners and one of the corners is one in which philosophy is regarded as very close to sociology. Habermas, Luhmann, the German tradition if you want to put it that way, I don't mind it, but I'm really bored by these methodological disputes. I note that in this country sociology has become highly empirical in the best sense of the word, and that all the good sociologists I know have areas in which they do quite important research and want to move up to the kind of analysis, which I hinted about earlier - whether it's in industrial relations, or race - but I still believe that there is this other approach ...

At the symposium, you say that too much time and too much of the subject matter is dominated by neither Popper nor Adorno but by a 'third man', variously called 'empiricism', 'empirical research', 'positive method' and so on [1976, p. 125]. Do you think this is merely a straw man or is there something really substantial that these authors are obsessed about?

It's a straw man if you want to regard it as an enemy, but there is now a very real tradition of, I believe, highly significant empirical research which is carried on by people who probably have a sneaking sympathy for Popper *but* don't like the prescriptions implicit in his rigour. That is to say, in a sense Popper could lead you to do nothing because there aren't any theories to falsify and too many sociologists have therefore taken to building up some phoney hypothesis and then writing the rest of their dissertation in an attempt to do something about this hypothesis. I quite like especially macro-empirical research as it's been done by some of my own disciples (...). It is a straw man in methodological terms, but it is quite real and should be.

In Halsey's article on LSE's sociologists, Raymond Aron was quoted as saying that British sociology 'was essentially an attempt to make intellectual sense of the political problems of the Labour Party' [1982, p. 156]. Do you think that tradition is still quite strong? I'm thinking of John Goldthorpe, Peter Townsend, and so on.

My own impression is that there's been quite a significant change in the last few years from prescriptive social policy research, which either by obvious implication or by deliberate intent, was supposed to resolve problems to the analysis of the effects of social policy, and I see much more of that than one did in the past. I think there's been a change; it is a strong element in the history of British social analysis - and where we are talking we're talking in an institution started by the Webbs - and that's precisely what they had in mind, although they also had it in mind - well Sidney did - that unbiased and unfettered research would have its own effects even if you didn't add any prescriptive element. So they are both there, and more recently I detect more analysis than prescription.

Two more questions and then I come on to your own work. Robert Merton was saying that he still believes with Parsons that albeit through the mechanisms of middle-range theories, we should go for general theories, general laws; is that your position?

Yes, I'm not sure about the word 'we' in this ... I'm not sure I would say if I was in charge of a department of sociology, that I'd say I'm only going to appoint people who want to do that, but if you ask me what I believe is our most worthy task, then I would say yes, Merton is right.

Because sociology is a scientific discipline if done properly?

You can't get me with that, because I couldn't care less whether it's called a scholarly discipline, an intellectual discipline or a scientific discipline. No it's not because we're natural scientists, it's because understanding presupposes explaining and explaining means having a general notion of the structures and processes which we are concerned with.

We talked earlier about sociology and philosophy and its boundaries; how do you then locate Marxism?

Well I view it first of all sociologically, that is to say, in a discipline in which there's a great deal of uncertainty about it and about the individual in it, people have done what people do in the real world, they've given themselves labels, and by labelling themselves, made discussion unnecessary ... in a sense you don't need these discussions, all you need is somebody who carries a poster around his neck which says symbolic interactionist and everything else ... Any intelligent sociologist can then deduce from that on virtually any subject. So I've always been terribly bored by all that, and that's not what I mean by philosophy. (...) I'm now thinking a lot about the social contract, not Jack Jones but Hobbes and Locke and Rousseau; now there we're very close to, it's an interesting subject, we're very close to two things, on the one hand this quite fundamental problem of law and order and on the other hand, the equally fundamental problem of how as I would put it, is society necessary, not how is it possible, but why is society necessary and there you are in a sort of borderline area and I don't mind being in this borderline area, that's all I'm saying. Incidentally, I would increasingly tend to describe myself not as a sociologist but as a social scientist, and that is another comment on your question. I think I like the implicit generality of the term social science, without once again wishing to say that it's got to be precise like physics or whatever.

But your own knowledge of Marxism say, is it simply a tool for social analysis?

In my view, it is simply a tool for social analysis in so far as it is useful.

Okay, in your Essays in The Theory of Society *[1968], in the preface, you say in Germany* Homo Sociologicus *led to a fully-fledged public controversy, while the works on class theory and conflict failed to stimulate discussion. The opposite trend is true for Britain. Could you expand?*

There's a whole load of literature on the subject, and it's partly technical which we can perhaps leave on one side, it's partly about whether role theory is precisely this or precisely something else, and it's partly been taken

48

for actually what it was, as a contribution to social theory or even political theory and a slightly anarchist one which I think it is, because of this odd separation of the individual and his roles which I tried there or human beings and *Homo Sociologicus* - that is the real and the construct - one sort of implicitly assumed that society and its normative arrangements, sanctions, and all, are imposed on something else that can be regarded as real underneath it all (...). So the full-fledged debate was really a debate on the social theory-political theory implications rather than the strictly sociological implications, and I detected something in my thinking which I would probably put differently today, but which is there.

Turning to the actual book you say that the central concept of sociology is role (...). What I'm interested in is how different is your idea of role, which actually is very new to me, to, say, Goffman's work on role?

I tell you I think there's quite a fundamental difference which is a bit unfortunate because I don't want to have any term patented. I'd much rather have the ability to communicate with others in the same language. I have almost been obsessed throughout my thinking about society with the identification, and I'm going to use a word loosely which you shouldn't use loosely, of the almost objective reality of structures, and so I have tried to detect things which are quite independent of the individuals who act in certain situations. Indeed I have made statements which imply that once individuals slot into these places there will be variations and so on and so forth, but nevertheless these are underlying structures. I have a notion of structure in my mind, quite a strong one.

Durkheimian?

Which is probably Durkheimian in the sense that he talks about social facts ... and Goffman I think starts at the other end, I think he starts at the things that human beings actually create and quite often create as individuals. Indeed the fact that he likes to talk about 'eccentric' individuals and what they create is indicative of this. Now I would see the creation of roles as it were as falling out of a sky of norms and sanctions and so on, and crystallising somewhere on the way; that's not the way he sees it at all, and I think this is actually the real confusion about the concept of role - is it a

49

regularity which comes about by individuals creating it, ir is it a regularity which individuals find, can mould, and change and so on, but which can be looked at independently. I strongly belong or I strongly believe in the latter approach, and the person who's closest to me, and is almost totally unknown and that's [Heinrich] Popitz who's written in my view one of the most important theoretical criticisms in recent years, which only has 96 pages, but it is beautiful and is called *The Normative Construction of Society*. In it he tries to explore what ... he takes off from Theodor Geiger's philosophy of law and some of the ideas in there about norm senders and norm receivers and asks how do these relationships harden into something which we can then call 'norm' and why are 'norms' constitutive of society. Now that's again thinking at a level of structure which almost ignores the individual for quite a long time, and that's always concerned me - incidentally, both in *Homo Sociologicus* and in the class book deep down what I want to talk about is the structure of processes apart from history, apart from specific cultural conditions, apart from individual input.

(...) 'Values and social science'; you argue that 'our responsibility as sociologists does not end when we complete the process of scientific inquiry; indeed, it may begin at that very point' [1968, p. 18]. I'm very impressed with your writings on the social role of sociologists and the value debate in Weber. Could you briefly summarise your views on this?

I think Max Weber's own position has been much misunderstood, although I too would believe not as a theoretical position, but as a practical position it is virtually untenable. The centre of Max Weber's position is the very simple statement that a statement of fact and a statement of value have a different logical status, they are not just the same statements. Now he wasn't at that time directly involved in the kind of discussion of the so-called unity of theory and practice which we have had thanks to critical theory, but he was involved in the phoney politics of a whole generation of German social scientists, who thought that they should pronounce from university what he called the *Katheder*, from the rostrum, about political issues, and he just pointed out that there are these two different kinds of statements. Now he then went very far in arguing that it is not the business of the scholar ever as a scholar to pronounce or to make statements of value; he should confine himself entirely to statements of fact and that's where one of the fundamental conflicts in Max Weber's personality comes up, because he felt quite passionately about value questions, but he tried to separate the two things to such an extent that - if this amateur psychology is permitted - then I am convinced that this is at least a contributing cause to the explosiveness of the personality of Max Weber to the fact that he just couldn't bear it at certain points, because he was equally passionate about the cleanliness of scholarship and about the need to do certain things in practice. Of course there are famous occasions like his opposition to the unlimited submarine warfare in the First World War where his political passions became perfectly evident but *he never confused the two*. Now I share, first of all the conviction that it is right to draw the distinction and I think we are thinking in a muddled way if we don't draw the distinction, and to me the statement that theory and practice are one and the same or that theory emerges from practice or that practice emerges from theory are, I'm sorry to say meaningless statements, and quite often they are the statements of those who have no actual practical experience and want to substitute statements of this kind of the absence of that practical experience. Incidentally, one must be a bit careful - theory and practice, fact and value, are not entirely the same but one does readily get into similar territory with this terminology. Where I differ from Max Weber is that I'm as interested in the ethics of scholarship as I am in the logic of scholarship and so I would feel it is perhaps one of my main concerns to cross boundaries in every sense of the word, so accept boundaries but cross them, and just as I wouldn't for one moment argue that Britain and Germany are the same or are identical societies or one flows from the other ... but would feel quite happy crossing from one society to the other, so I feel we should in a conscious sense and not as sociology but as sociologists in our definition of our own role, find it possible to cross the boundary and say so and that's what I've been trying to argue for quite a long time ... I think that possibly there are other boundaries for which this is true, but never forget the existence of the boundaries because otherwise, you get terribly muddled.

One thing I feel in your work, possibly I'm just reading something into it, but it seems that you want to say that the whole notion of elites *is underplayed in sociology - is that a thing you feel strongly about?*

I know exactly what you mean and I've published quite a bit in this area but what I really feel ... in my thinking when I start with norms and sanctions, I immediately get on to power; that is, I think that the contract of society and the contract of association one would have said in the eighteenth century and the contract of domination are very close to each other, in fact they are probably one and the same and the terminological distinction doesn't get you very far. That is, you cannot think in my view about sanctions without thinking instances which are capable of applying sanctions and once you do that, you are in the field of power; you cannot think about norms without sanctions, nor sanctions without power, and so since these are connected I would regard this as the core of my analysis and then the next step would be to talk about legitimacy (...). And incidentally, I've just been invited to give the Hamlyn lectures here in 1985 which are really in law, and I've just decided to give them on the social contract so you will find some of these ideas in 1985 in these lectures. What I think must be argued if one wants to understand what is going on, is that legitimacy must be seen as an essentially negative phenomenon, it is the absence of protest, it is the contribution of the many to the process of legitimation or delegitimation as essentially a negative contribution; and then I'm left with the quite important question from my understanding of social processes, where does initiative come from? That is, who actually formulates the next trial after the errors of yesterday and it is in this connection and in no other that *the few* play a very great part in my thinking, that's perfectly true, but I would like to put it in this context in other words, I'm not talking about a static system in which there is a nice elite. I'm talking about the role of the few and the same is true in some other respects. I personally, although it's gone almost totally unnoticed, regard my contribution to the Merton *festschrift* on representative activities [also in Dahrendorf, 1979] as quite important, and so does Merton ... but that's again about the contribution of the few, the position of the few, it's not elite in the static sense in which they are talked about, it's the relation between the contribution of the many and the contribution of the few in the process of legitimacy and change.

(...) I've heard you speak disapprovingly of much of contemporary sociology - have you just seen this as the sociological equivalent of 1968, the disillusionment with the possibilities of 1968, or is that too simple?

I have never engaged in an ideological analysis - which is a perfectly legitimate thing to do - and I would have to invent an answer now, which I don't want to do. I'm not surprised that there's a whole variety of approaches to social thought under the name of sociology both in this

52

country and on the continent, although not in the United States really, it's all terribly second rate there ... and I don't think that it's second rate here in view of what I've said earlier, namely people want to feel at home somehow, they can't stand Popper's world, just as many human beings can't stand the world of liberty, so I'm not surprised about that, but I haven't seen it in connection with 1968 (...).   I no longer think about sociology as a subject at all, I'm just interested in particular contributions to our understanding of society and the subject as such, I don't think you will find another statement from me in the foreseeable future about the subject as such.   It's a subject of no interest, that is, I'm interested in what Albert Hirschman does, who doesn't call himself a sociologist, because in my view, he has more to say about development than almost anybody else, now he's a political economist.   (...)   I wouldn't wish to comment on sociology. However, I think in the last decade there's actually been quite a lot of ... I am most impressed by macro-empiricism which I think is immensely courageous to look at total societies over 150 years back and see how much material one can get about it, and how much we can therefore learn. Incidentally, some developments in demography go even further back, and are marvellous and really immensely telling and Tony Wrigley has made magnificent contributions.   On the other hand, in sociology, I notice some quite interesting theoretical attempts, I wouldn't dismiss Habermas for one minute, much as I find myself amazed at the revival of Rousseau towards the end of the twentieth century.

(...) *Your work, despite your stress on conflict has been linked with Daniel Bell and the 'end of ideology' theorists.   How have you seen the relationship between your work and the investigators of 'post-capitalism'?*

Well, there's bound to be some confusion in the perception of my work, because on the one hand, I am interested in and odd though this may sound to you, most passionately interested in, these structures which we have talked about; and on the other hand, I have occasionally tried my hand at social analysis.   I personally don't think as highly of what I've tried to do in this field as I do of the attempts of structural analysis and I have a lot of unpublished stuff ... I don't know about Merton, he probably has as much as I do if not more, but I have two 600 page books at home, which I won't publish - one is *Elements of Sociology* and the other is called *The Eclipse of Modernity* - and they are two quite different ones and they still lead me to say my most passionate interest is in the understanding of the structure of social processes. Daniel Bell, I think has a primary interest in social analysis and would probably regard this as his main and dominant theme and I think that is quite an important difference, I don't regard it as bad company at all.

Okay, it's all labels. In 'Out of Utopia' you talk about the 'ubiquity of social conflict', and the notion that wherever there is social life there is conflict may be 'unpleasant and disturbing', but not the presence 'but the absence of conflict is surprising and abnormal' and there is 'good reason to be suspicious if we find a society ... that displays no evidence of conflict' [1968, p. 127], and you talk about the continuum of conflict. Is this from sociologists like Simmel, or simply further back in human history?

Kant ... well I think the most explicit philosophical statement, if it is indeed philosophical, is Kant's essay 'The Idea of a General History with a Cosmopolitan Intent', I think that's the title [*'idea of a universal history from a cosmopolitan point of view'*] in which he talks about antagonism, as he calls it; and incidentally, I've often looked for a more generic term for what I've called conflict. Let me just say this in passing, I've since come to the conclusion that expressions of conflict are manifold, and some of them are individual and the word conflict conveys quite rightly group conflict; where it *is* possible to translate group conflict into individual action, or the energy that goes into group conflict into individual action, I should say, he calls it antagonism, and has a very important passage in which he roughly says man wants harmony, but nature knows better what's good for him, it is the antagonism and so on and so forth, and unless this is there men would sleep like the sheep on their meadows, live a useless and forever purposeless life or whatever. I feel very very strongly in a tradition of thinking which is entirely contrary to the Plato, Hegel and in a certain sense Marx line of thought, because I've always regarded synthesis as the crucial category in Hegel's dialectics. I know that negative dialectics are trying to do away with this, but I have regarded synthesis as the crucial one and not position and opposition or thesis and antithesis, and I think this is true for Marx as well ... it's the dream of synthesis which motivates it. Not in my case though I feel in the Aristotellian or above all Kantian tradition, and that's been more influential than Simmel whom I discovered *after* I had formalised some of these things; although of course, Lewis Coser's book - I found out about

Simmel through Lewis Coser!

Next you talk about the continuum of conflict which ranges ...

It ranges from individual competition to the 'crowd in the French Revolution', that is, to the actual role of visible ... we've seen a lot in our age, Iran ... continuum of expressions of the same fundamental energy. I've since as you know, from occasional remarks I've made about Britain, thought quite a bit about Marx's distinction between individual competition and collective solidarity. That is to say, Marx was upset by what he saw as workers being far too engaged in individual competition and not being ready. Well, that's his philosophy of history underlying it, the distinction itself is a very useful one, because I do believe that individual competition has in the United States, over long periods, taken the place of the great collective conflicts carried on by the Labour Movement in the more rigid societies of Europe. So it's not that sooner or later this must happen everywhere, there are different expressions of similar fundamental relationships, so that's why this notion of a continuum is really quite important.

And the final thing I want to talk about, is that you speak of the suppression, channelling, and regulation which are all kinds of temporary *modifications of conflict. To me that seems a crucial element in political sociology.*

I don't know whether it's *temporary*. I would regard as important an essay I've written from my own point of view about 'Uncertainty, Science and Democracy' [in 1968] in which I'm trying to apply the uncertainty idea and what follows from it, to what may be called the regulation of political conflict. Now while I don't believe that the same set of political institutions will do the job at all times, I think on the whole institutions which allow change without revolution can reign for very long periods of time especially if there is a built-in adjustment mechanism; in other words if constitutions can be changed and are changed, if there are amendments as there are in the United States; so there are forms of conflict regulation, certainly in the political field which endure, or at any rate for a long time, whether the same is true in the industrial field may be regarded as an open question. Even so, I think what's called the Constitution of the Enterprise in Germany - indeed it's called that in legislation, has at any rate, served the country quite well

and all involved as a system of conflict regulation for about thirty years -
which is not temporary in quite the sense in which one normally uses the
word.

*I know you hate labels, but you've been associated with 'the conflict model
of society'. In the ' Out of Utopia' essay you talk about the conflict model's
three elements: change - all units of social organisation are in constant
change; ubiquity of social conflict; and constraint, that societies are held
together not by consensus but by constraint, by the coercion of some by
others. That to you then is the conflict model of, say sociology?*

Well, here I have to say that I've since thought further about it, and I think
that for a very long time and perhaps in all the available publications, I have
underestimated, or perhaps failed to understand fully, the other dimension
of Marx's analysis of change (...), that is to say one does detect in Marx's
use of the word 'production' an obsession with something that was of
primary importance in his time so I don't like the notion of forces of
production and relations of production. I do think that the concepts which
you have quite rightly mentioned as central for me make sense only once
they are related to a sub-strata of forces and conditions - leave production
out and then the very important question is what is this sub-strata about, and
probably what one is talking about, and I think one is probably talking about
the social construction of human lives ... and I've recently been quite
interested in work and the future of work. You see in some ways, those
who've accused me of being overly formal have been right, because I have
in a sense talked only about the formal aspects of conflicts and not related
them to institutions and forces working on these institutions whereas in fact
they are related. That is to say, it undoubtedly makes sense to say that if
there is a group which demands something new it is likely to be successful
to the extent to which it represents a potential which is present in the society
and can be pointed to, and which is somehow prevented from expression or
implementation or realisation by existing institutions and those who defend
them, so there is this sub-strata of analysis as well as the formal analysis,
and what I want to do is write three short treatises, one on the social
contract, one on revolution and one on liberty. The second one would make
a lot of the missing dimension in my own analysis of conflict, so I would
add a whole dimension to the concepts you've mentioned.

56

Something you said in the essay I found very important and wondered if you would expand on; you say 'quite apart from its merits as a tool of scientific analysis, the conflict model is essentially non-utopian; it is the model of an open society' [1968, p. 128] ...

If one works on the assumption that none of us can know whether the answers we think we have to the issues of our time to great problems are actually right, and will continue to be right, if we work on the assumption that none of us can know this, then I think the most important single thing is to keep open the possibility of giving different answers and keeping open the possibility of giving different answers. It is just another way of saying, create institutions in which a clash of views, differences of views and their clashes are possible and are indeed real, and so I think that actually this process is itself the 'open society' and that's why I continue to believe that conflict and its existence and its open existence is indicative of a free society.

Class and Class Conflict in Industrial Society; *Marx's basic mistake according to you is to assume that power and domination is derived from the 'possession of property', when the possession of property is 'only a special case of the capacity to dominate' [1959]. Presumably it's not just Weber, it's more than that, yes?*

No, it's more than Weber. I suppose why it's important for me is that I've had the good or bad fortune of living over 100 years later than Marx, and so I've seen conditions much more clearly in which power has been exercised without any actual relationship to property and whatever people say about big industry financing the Nazis, the property in Nazi Germany existed almost side by side with the power structure, or underneath it or tucked away, and of course the same is true of many of the communist societies and yet I would wish to apply an analysis of conflict to them as well because it's quite clearly there ... so in some ways power can look for a whole variety of vehicles or instruments and property can indeed be one of them and indeed, may have been a very important one in long periods of history. But a party like the state parties of totalitarian regimes are not property and yet nevertheless an instrument by which power is exercised. So power seeks its appropriate vehicle and should not be linked totally to one particular vehicle if one wants to produce an analysis which helps us in

57

understanding social processes under different conditions.

On Marx, you talk about the rise of the new middle class, the service class, increasing social mobility, no polarisation and so on, and one conclusion you make is not only that Marx is inaccurate and not particularly helpful, but also that notions like false consciousness are illegitimate. Can you then just say firstly, something about false consciousness and, secondly, if all these things are true, which they are empirically, why is it that Marxism in England is such an important intellectual force?

Well there I can give you a straight answer - a label, it's utterly bourgeois, I believe that the importance of Marxism is simply for people simply to be able to say I'm against this, that and the other, it isn't in any sense a strict interpretation of Marx or an application of Marx to new conditions or anything of that kind ... and if you look at critical theory which is the most interesting, if you want to analyse it in terms of intellectual history what they've done is gone back from Marx to the left Hegelians, really to *The Holy Family* which Marx attacked fiercely, they've turned Marx downside up again and I don't mind that. I'm always amused when Habermas calls himself a Marxist which he doesn't do very often but occasionally does, essentially because he doesn't want to be confused with anything else, which could easily happen if one just looked at his writings, and I'm firmly convinced this is the case for many others as well. They don't actually believe in the kind of historical inevitability which is associated with Marx, let alone in the process which Marx claimed would happen in all advanced societies of (linear) intensification of conflict and then the revolution. They don't even believe in the economic determination of politics and ideology, occasionally they do if it's a particular analysis, but quite often they do the opposite, quote Adorno, perhaps a prime example of somebody who at least from what he has said seemed to believe in the spiritual or mental intellectual determination of things real. So I'm unimpressed by this, it's more an identification of a position *vis-a-vis* the system in which we live, than a strict description of an intellectual tradition in which people find themselves. False consciousness has merely become just a polemical instrument, and everybody accuses everybody else of it ... Of course if you can identify social forces, supposing you can in a particular situation, and if you then look at how people argue it does make sense at times to state an absence of congruence between argument and reality. To give you two examples; one is the fight against inflation... now the rhetoric of the fight against inflation is quite general in our societies, and yet I wonder whether in a society of debtors, the actual interest isn't the other way, and whether there isn't an interesting incongruity between the manifest interest in reducing one's debt by inflation, and the apparent interest in fighting inflation by whatever means, control of money supply or what have you. The other area is work or labour, for example, if the German Minister of Economic Affairs says 'what is necessary is for people to work harder', surely he must know if people work harder, unemployment will rise quite rapidly and the only hope to keep it at present levels if for people not to work too hard, so there are incongruities. I'm not saying it's a meaningless concept, I'm saying that it is used quite often for purely subjective polemical reasons rather than for a strict analysis of the relationship between interest and what people say.

(...) Is there much in Marxism to be saved in order to assist social analysis?

Yes, lots; because I think the concepts are all there. I think he is the greatest analyst of social change, and all you have to do is free these concepts of the deterministic or dogmatic context in which he has put them. I think if you generalise forces and relations of production into something which forgets about production, or rather makes production a special case, if you generalise some of the things he said about individual competition and collective action, if you generalise the property relationship in class to one of power, you do have many, many of the tools which one would need and I'll do just that when I write my treatise on revolution.

Okay. The second point of the book is the extension of Weber and power, and class being defined in relation to authority; 'classes are social conflict groups in which the determinants for which can be found in the participation or exclusion of exercising authority'. A lot of people argue that you didn't theorise enough on authority, how do you see it?

That's entirely correct and is related to what I said a moment ago. You see it's not just the people who exercise authority, it's really the people who have an interest in the exercise of authority at a given time in the way in which it is being exercised, and that's how you relate what I called the substratum a moment ago. I think that's the major shortcoming of what I've done and unless I manage to bridge the formal analysis of the exercise of authority or exclusion from it to interests and underlying forces, I don't think I'll succeed in producing anything even faintly resembling a theory of change, so I would accept that.

And how many classes can there be? I mean some people say that there can only be two ...

In my view, it is essentially always two. Yes. Which is not to say that you don't get in a given situation remnants of historical classes which have a very strange place because yesterday they were protagonists of a class struggle - yesterday being one or two hundred years ago - today they are semi-irrelevances. But semi-irrelevances with a very interesting function, it isn't directly a comment on class, but nevertheless not irrelevant to say that for instance in Britain, members of the real aristocracy like the working class much better than they do the bourgeoisie which they regard as distasteful and awful ... now this is not totally irrelevant, this is a class which had function and now doesn't have a function, filling a very funny place in contemporary conflicts, indeed, they are described correctly by these rather simple labels.

Is there an over-emphasis on conflict in your work?

First of all, I'm here talking about analysis and not about the evaluation of things. Once conditions are such that conflicts are allowed to take on revolutionary dimensions, I would say that many people are likely to suffer not only before the explosion but afterwards too. There's no revolution in history that has had immediate effects for the large number, which made the large number much better off, happier or whatever ... the immediate after effects of revolution are often very similar to the situation immediately preceding it, after the short explosion of hope which then dies down, and the pattern of revolution is one which leads one to think that it takes a generation before improvements for the many can happen. So there certainly are conditions under which the effects of conflict may well be regarded as undesirable, if that's what you want to say, I also didn't ever - and this is where we get back to values and social science - wish to say that stimulating conflict is the great task of teachers or whoever, so when 'conflict theory' entered into the curriculum debate in the part of Germany in Hesse and the so-called *Konflikt pedagogik* was invented, I found myself with a certain amount of embarrassment because that hadn't been what I'd said.

In Society and Democracy in Germany *[1968a, p. 123] you say that 'conflict should be regulated* rationally.' *What do you mean?*

I don't use terms like rationality and rational very often. What I had in mind is that there is the kind of regulation which we talked about earlier, that is to say, institutions which enable conflicts to take place and have an effect on the course which a society takes.

Also that 'elites should reflect the colour and diversity of social interests ...' [p. 267] ...

This is not very high level theory, this was rather for purposes of classification ...

... How does one get elites to reflect those interests?

By not having one impermeable and unified class at the top, but by having competing groups ... by having within *the few* checks and balances through their differences. I think this is a very important feature of a healthy free society and often absent. The British establishment if anything is too unified, which is one of the reasons for the fairly high intensity of conflict throughout British democratic history, it's a mistaken belief ... actually Britain's been a very violent country really (...). When I saw this film on 1911, and then went further back and looked at newspapers in the 1850s, 60s and 70s, where every single day, workers were shot dead by the army ... It's been extremely violent because of a tradition of a fairly unified and permeable elite.

Finally the importance of 'public virtue ... ' [p. 304]. How do we instill it?

I don't know how we instill it because I've never believed that education can be regarded as an instrument of change. I think probably educational institutions essentially follow suit and I've often argued that both the right and the left are wrong. The right is wrong in believing that once the left takes over the educational institutions the revolution is near, and the left is wrong in thinking that if only they can take over they can bring about fundamental change. I really don't know where certain public virtues come from, I mean values which facilitate a process of reasonable discourse ... something like fairness of queuing. Now queuing, where does it come from and what happens once it goes which it may well do in this country - to some extent? But one of the first things people notice when they go on the continent is that queuing doesn't exist, and you somehow try to move in sidewards, you use your elbows, and if there's a child in the butcher's shop you will say 'oh, you're just a child you can wait', whereas here it's the other way. Now what makes this? I haven't speculated on this, this is a very descriptive set of categories.

In what ways do you think you have been influential in social science?

I suppose ultimately in political theory, but in a political theory which I would hope is based on an understanding of social processes which one can only have if one's thought about these processes themselves ... You see Popper once said to me 'if I had been engaged in political theory, I would have written precisely what you now write, I think you're the only one who fully understands, but of course, I have so much more important things to do, so I have to concentrate on these important things'. In other words, he doesn't think very highly of political theory, he thinks that, for instance, quantum theory is infinitely more important than any amount of political theory and in a sense, he'd prefer not to have written *The Open Society* [1945], although I have a hunch that he'll be remembered for *The Open Society* much longer than for some of his contributions to natural science ... that's different from his hierarchy. Now my interest is in a sense in writing the political theory part of Popper's approach.

If you had a say in what sociologists would be doing over the next couple of decades, would you ... would it be about values?

Not at all. What I implied earlier, is that a strict methodological position is always at risk, always runs the risk of discouraging people who are actually working in the field, this is one of the greatest weaknesses of Popper and in a sense one of the great disasters of the reception of Popper in the social sciences. He should have been received in the natural sciences perhaps, but even there people beaver away at endless experiments which are not related to theories, you know serendipity is more important than systematic attempts to identify the experimental cruces, and refute a particular theory. No, my recommendation would always be to engage in courageous empirical research, and I emphasise the courageous. On several occasions in our conversation, I've talked about this macro-research which I regard as courageous because you have to do things which aren't fully justifiable if you compare figures about crime in the early nineteenth century in six different countries because you know perfectly well that your statistical base is thin and so on. Courageous macro-social research is what, it's an idiosyncratic view, but I wouldn't recommend the general approach to everybody at all.

And you would want a more multi-disciplinary approach?

I would wish there to be a much greater concentration on *problems*, and if you deal with a problem there cannot conceivable be an argument for saying 'I only deal with the sociological aspect and leave the others to others'.

A question on the 'classless society'; what is your idea of the 'good society', or is this it?

Pretty close to it, in a certain sense, because the good society is an imperfect society in which certain imperfections have been dealt with reasonably well. Can I say that's why I am quite worried about the fact that we now seem to have reached a point of development in some advanced societies in which the imperfections we thought we had dealt with, reappear. That is, the reappearance of an underclass, using the class term loosely, which actually doesn't have citizenship rights, which may even be illiterate, and illiteracy in advanced societies is growing at a frightening rate. In that sense, it is quite a disastrous testimony to our ability even to maintain a level which we had more or less reached. But I think once one's reached a level of potential participation as we have and have the institutions which make change possible, one's gone a very long way and from that point of view I'm quite pleased with the arrangements under which we operate, and can concentrate on the contents of what has to be done.

Your future?

The trouble is the bug of politics which is one of the threads that runs through my life ... I think it's at least conceivable that I will find it possible to return to a more academic existence in which occasional forays into the margins of politics are part and parcel of my life, but the centre is one of producing these three treatises which I have talked about on the social contract, on revolution, and on liberty, and I would very much like to do that.

How long will all of this take?

Well I can write the social contract book in two years. I think I'll find the revolution will take longer, and I don't even know - despite the fact that I've published a lot about it - how to begin the third and final one, which is clearly the most important.

3 Peter Worsley

Born in Cheshire, 1924, Peter Worsley a social anthropologist trained at Cambridge, was Professor of Sociology at the University of Manchester from 1964 until his retirement in early 1984. He has written widely in social anthropology, for example his highly successful *The Trumpet Shall Sound* (1957) which has both been reprinted and translated into many languages, but he has also written on Marxism, introductory sociology, Third World studies and on China.

Peter Worsley would concur with the view that the distinction between sociology and social anthropology is a social rather than a logical one, and that the distinction can 'best be understood not by looking at some neat dividing line in the subject matter of the disciplines or in their method, but in the concrete, and hence untidy, factors which operated in various times and places to cause people to class themselves as "sociologists" and as "social anthropologists"' (Gellner, 1973, p. 107). Worsley himself has developed his skills and interests non-dogmatically over the years.

Worsley observes that people are interested in China because, amongst other things, there is the 'revival of hope in the possibility of change, including very radical and revolutionary change' (1975, p. 12). One feature of China that he noted was the 'virtual absence of social science as we know it': 'theory and research are no longer left to specialists, but have become mass practices' (1975, p. 198 and p. 200). However actual attempts to 'restore' sociology have partially succeeded since 1979 (see Cheng and So, 1983). Nonetheless Worsley's views are quite clear on the matter, views he forcibly made clear in 1974: 'Little wonder that the country which has made the most spectacular and world-historic developmental break-through of the post-war period, People's China, has done so without the benefit of Western sociological theory or indeed of institutionalized sociology' (1974, p. 16).

On the Third World, his conclusions concerning the relationship between the 'major powers' and the Third World are sobering. He argues that if the major powers 'act in less than rational ways, as they are doing, the prospects of containing a world full of revolutionary peasants are nil, as the resistance of such a petty country as Vietnam to the might of the USA shows' (1975, p. 327).

Marxism, both intellectually and politically, has attracted Worsley and one of his contributions has been to continually stress the plurality of Marxism; that is that there are many versions of Marx, with the majority of them being challenging. In *Marx and Marxism* Worsley neatly contextualises the nature of the growth of Marxist ideas (1982, p. 10).

> in his own lifetime, Marx's ideas had little impact. Only after his death did the first explicitly 'Marxist' mass party come into existence, in Germany. Since then, in the advanced capitalist countries, Italy and France apart, Marxism has still not 'gripped the masses' much. Where it has taken root has been in impoverished agrarian countries dominated by the industrialized powers. The Chinese Communist Party, for instance, was established in 1921, only a year after the *Communist Manifesto* was translated into Chinese and had 57 members. Within five years, it was leading a general strike in Canton, and less than 30 years later was in power in the country with a quarter of the world's population. The British Communist Party, on the other hand, founded in 1921, numbers around 25,000 members and the Communist Party in the USA, according to one black joke, probably had a majority of FBI members in the McCarthy era.

In keeping with his interests in global affairs, Worsley has recently chided British sociology for having 'contributed virtually nothing to the nuclear debate' (1984, p. 14). He points to a rare exception, Emmanuel de Kadt's *British Defence Policy and Nuclear War* published in 1964, in which he uses the literature on disaster studies to discuss what life would be like after the

66

nuclear war (Worsley, 1984, p. 14). Worsley argues that if sociologists are to contribute anything to the debate it calls for a high degree of 'criticality towards our own value-assumptions', and concludes by saying that what we do know is that 'anything recognizable as human civilisation, anywhere, would disappear after a nuclear war, and that frantic preparations are being made for precisely that war. If ever there was a self-fulfilling prophesy, this is it' (1984, p. 14).

Could you tell me a little about your early life?

Okay, swept into the army in World War II - I was at Cambridge ...

Born where?

Born Birkenhead, lower-middle class father who had his own estate agent's business, we lived in a very respectable part of Cheshire, Wallasey, and his business was in Birkenhead. I was always struck from the beginning by the terrible contrast of what I thought was the despicable comfort of Wallasey and the poverty of Birkenhead. I remember guys in the street literally selling matches who had been blinded at the Somme, who has their medals on and that sort of thing. Then war interrupted my nice comfortable career. Nevertheless I ended up at Cambridge to read English Literature. I only got interested in it because I was taught it very well by a Leavis protege (which has affected my recent work), so I went up to Cambridge, and after a year I was called up to the army and went off in East Africa. In East Africa I served with African troops and then went with them to India and South-East Asia. In 1946 I went back to Cambridge, and said 'I want to switch from English Literature to Anthropology', and my senior tutor said 'Well ninety-five per cent of you people who've come back from the war want to change, how inconvenient' ... so I switched to Anthropology. Anthropology was terrible at Cambridge, I mean absolutely abysmal, it was before the epoch of modern anthropology; however the best work written in the field, by people like Gluckman, was locked up literally in a special private

67

cupboard in the professor's private study and you could get it only if you asked his permission. Then I went back to Africa, being fascinated by Africa (...) on the Groundnut Scheme, teaching mass education, and came back and managed to get a job as a research assistant with Max Gluckman - which was the the the thing in life I wanted - at Manchester. Marvellous, Max was at the height of his powers, it was a privilege to be in his company.

Was it his teaching, his research, or was it something else?

It was his ideas. He was as it ultimately turned out - I mean the same kind of thing works positively and negatively - he was an authoritarian personality, but he had good ideas (...) also although he was an orthodox kind of anthropologist ... Central Africa, we did every bloody tribe in Central Africa inside and outside. But then Max turned his own attentions to British society and he put Tom Lupton to work wielding a broom in a factory in Manchester (...) and Max's ideas that he'd developed in the context of the Zulu were shown to be relevant and interesting, so relevant and interesting that when he went on Third Programme broadcasts (I've tried to find the documentation for this and failed) at the time there was an extremely popular comedy show called *Take It From Here*, and Max's programmes were only second or third in the ratings behind *Take It From Here*. I mean he was so good, he could fascinate people, they could see the relevance of discussing the mother's brother in South Africa - or some ridiculous topic like that - to the situation in Britain, it was marvellous; we could feel it, and the British public could feel it when they listened to him on the radio. He built up a tremendous department here. Then I went off, I was a communist and a Marxist at the time; I got into a lot of political trouble in Australia, I was banned from New Guinea, and was virtually told by some senior anthropologist that I would never get a job (...) I was in Australia between 1951 and 1953, I had a big public scandal, so I came back and I wrote *The Trumpet Shall Sound* [orig. 1957]. I did fieldwork with Australian Aborigines. I wrote the book because I was interested in the cults and the world was being transformed - it was the Third World coming alive, and here were these people reacting to the advent of this incredible civilisation. So I wrote that book and at the end of it thought, there's not going to be a future for me in anthropology, so Max said 'Look, you'd better get a job in sociology'. By that time we were heading towards the Robbins era, and I went over to Hull and applied for a job in sociology (...)

somehow or other, I don't know why, I got the job. I went up to Hull and I built up a department there in eight years. (...) Then I went off to Canada for a year, and then Robbins started and then like a bolt out of the blue Manchester said 'Would you like to come and discuss whether you might like to become Professor'. So I said 'Alright', and the way things were done in those days I never heard a word for literally a year, and I'd forgotten about it, and I was very happy for reasons I won't discuss, when I got a letter saying 'You have been appointed' a year later. So I went to Manchester and it was great, marvellous - you could get money for anything, you could pick your staff. We literally rang around universities, I remember ringing Chelly [Halsey] and saying 'Have you got any human body capable of teaching sociology?', and he said 'There's this fellow who's just come back from Chicago who's very good' and he turned out to be; it was as good or as bad as that. We were looking for staff ... I mean there was nobody. I was an anthropologist and lots of people came from other disciplines, and I must say, now - what's wrong with that?

(...) You argued something in The Trumpet Shall Sound *which I imagine in 1957 was something quite radical, it might not be now but I imagine it was then, and that is about anthropology a social control assisting the colonial administrators. What could we learn from that or what could we add to that?*

It was an incredibly daring, not to say outrageous, provocative, and wildly communist thing to say in those days. I cooled it down as much as I dared do, consonant with my conscience.

So what you are saying is if anthropologists, say, learnt something about forms of social control within a group themselves, that information could be passed on to administrators and assist them?

Indeed a lot of anthropologists advocated precisely that, it was called 'applied anthropology'. Lucy Mair wrote a whole book about it. We should be at the service of the colonial government, that is virtually it. I resisted that of course, and believed that we should be at the service of those trying to liberate themselves. As you say that was a dangerous, radical thing to say, it meant virtually you would not be able to do anthropology, you would be banned. I was banned firstly from Central Africa, I was appointed to the Rhodes-Livingstone Institute, around 1948 by Max Gluckman, but the British MI5 turned me down. So then I was an Africanist, I had spent several years by then turning myself into an Africanist, and I was really fascinated by Africa; but I had to switch overnight. Max said 'Try Australia, it has just opened up'. So I went out there and I was banned from New Guinea, the night before we were due to go out to the Central Highlands to do a perfectly orthodox study of the culture of the Central Highlands. So I decided that I would not get persecuted like that. I'd fight; we caused a hell of a row, it was in the Australian Parliament and in the *Sydney Morning Herald*, in the end I thought 'Christ they cannot stop me going to the Australian mainland, to one of the Aborigine reserves', although they could have done. Eventually I got into a reserve and I did my PhD at four months' notice, I switched from having worked on Melanesia, and from having been an Africanist, to working with the Australian Aborigines, and as a result of that I think my eleven months field work and my six months PhD thesis is not very good - what do you expect?

Does anything linger on from that in anthropology as a discipline? Is it still tainted by that kind of mentality and history?

No, because I think there has been a fundamental change - that is the end of direct colonialism, and therefore it [Marxism] is now perfectly possible or respectable (...). But we are talking about the McCarthy period. Max Gluckman once came into my office and saw two or three copies of the theoretical journal of the Communist Party *The Marxist Quarterly*, and he said 'For Christ's sake get those bloody things out of here', he was terrified. *Now* Marxism is an integral part of university courses in anthropology, sociology and economics - you name it. It is respectable, there are journals about it, it is perfectly alright, there are seventeen different varieties, many of them are quite unconnected with any particular political action and so forth, but it was not like that then ... this was the epoch of the Rosenbergs. So as colonialism has gone, Marxism has become perfectly acceptable and tolerable (...). I would like to say that the common image I found among my radical students, for example those at City University in New York a couple of years ago, is that they think *all* anthropology done in the colonial epoch was pro-colonial - I think that is balls. Most of the anthropologists I lived with, and worked with and respected, were at the least liberals, many of them were socialists, and I would say that even those who were rather conservative were highly critical of colonial governments, their regimes and relationships, and strongly defensive of their people, 'my tribe' ... I reject entirely this notion that Kathleen Gough has expressed - much as I love Kathleen - that anthropology is a child of imperialism, which of course in one sense is true - chronologically it is - but the idea that anthropologists were uncritically, totally and universally slaves of imperialism is not true at all (...) Basically most colonial governments took no notice of anthropologists or they hated their guts. They regarded them as liberals or even worse as dangerous Reds; and the Director of the Rhodes-Livingstone Institute in Rhodesia, who was a pacifist not a left, Dr Godfrey Wilson, committed suicide under the impact of the beginning of World War II. He could not stand the harrassment he was getting. Max Gluckman was treated as a dangerous agent of Moscow. Now Max to me was a middle-of-the-road Fabian, so I do not buy for one minute this notion of anthropology as the tool of imperialism.

(...) One of the things you say is there can be no absolute division of spheres of influence between anthropology and sociology, because the subject matter that they divide between them has not always been the same and is still changing. Would you say that there can be no point making any distinction?

There can be no *absolute* division of spheres, but there is a division of spheres. I mean basically they were dealing with people who lived in colonial societies, some of whom were tribes by any kind of definition - that is a very vague term, for many of them were not, for example the Ashanti, Zulus, great empires, centralised state systems and God knows what - but the one thing they had in common was that they were all subject to colonial control. Secondly there was a different *method* of investigation; that was in-depth, intensive fieldwork, which was not typically the method of sociology at that time, although it became as much. So there has always been an ambivalence about how you define anthropology: in terms of the type of society it focuses upon, of the set of methods it uses to study: and you could go on arguing for ever. It is quite clear that Nardel was studying one or two villages and Gluckman was studying one or two villages, in extremely numerous state societies, with sophisticated technology and all that, and they were not hunting-and-collecting societies of a few individuals armed with blow-guns. But of course these methods can be applied in Brixton and they

71

are. Off the top of my head I think the breakthrough was [Michael] Young, and I remember talking to Young at an anthropology do at the LSE and he had just written this article in *Man* comparing his mother-centred families in East London (Bethnal Green) with the Ashanti or someone, and we were arguing about whether these were strictly comparable or not, but basically Young was influenced by anthropology through Firth who had also done kinship studies in London. So the methods of anthropology involve intensive casework and close fieldwork, which was not of course characteristic of much of sociology perhaps. If you go up and ask any Englishman on the street 'What do sociologists do?' he will say 'Surveys', and that it is what they always have done ... Booth, Rowntree, the Mersyside studies of unemployment ... and in the minds of most people in Britain sociology means surveys. Well sociology now includes what we would call anthropology; so the borderlines have changed, also, of course, sociologists are studying the Third World.

Fine. One thing you say is that 'much remains to be done before social anthropology can resume its rightful place as a branch of historical science' [1970, p. 274]. Is your argument against functionalism because of its bias against history?

There are two reasons; one the bias against history, and two the absence of any dialectic - a sense of contradiction, conflict and so forth. Everything fitted together beautifully in what was ultimately a harmonious, functioning model of society. I think actually, as we speak - this year - I have just done a review of Eric Wolf's book *Europe and the People Without History* [1982] and I think it is changing: for the first time he shows how the expansion of Europe, the French, the Dutch, the British etc., all over the colonial world (and firstly actually in Eastern Europe), has profoundly transformed all those societies - the Indians of North America, the peoples of Africa, new states arose, societies collapsed, gigantic movements of population took place, all this Eric show in 500 pages ... tremendous, and in those pages somewhere are all the peoples famous in anthropology (...) whom we always studied as self-enclosed tribal societies. Now I never believed that they were self-enclosed tribal societies, but functionalist theory made them self-enclosed tribal and timeless societies. Now I think therefore by the time we have reached 1984, with Eric, we have reached a watershed in which that kind of anthropology had been dominant. You see anthropology has basically gone through three phases - nineteenth century evolutionism and the influence of Darwinism ... fantastic, up to Malinowski, the revolution when functionalism took over and that I think has lasted to the present day (in theoretical terms). Now a lot of anthropologists have been very unhappy for the last ten to fifteen years with what to put in its place and the only thing they could find which was ready-made intellectually as a system was Levi-Strauss. It never took on in Britain very much, I wrote a small critique ... I would like to have been more critical than was possible at the time, because it was in vogue you know, and you might have been considered a stupid old fuddy-duddy resisting this innovatory wonder. But I thought that it was wrong, and what I tried to show in a very characteristic, if you like British empiricist way, was that it did not work with the empirical data on my people.

How would you characterise ... I mean a lot of people are very interested in Levi-Strauss and if one wanted to be a Levi-Straussian anthropologist, what does it tell you about the world and what do you do?

It tells you that the way we and anybody else perceives the world is structured by the culture that they were born into, and that this culture has an extraordinary coherence and persistence, that there are different cultures and that therefore there are different ways of perceiving the world. It also of course has the classic relativist argument that all anthropologists have, that there is no reason to assume arrogantly that our way of perceiving the world is any better than their's it is just that they are different.

But is that any different an approach to that which an anthropologist would use anyway, if he was thinking about what he was doing?

Yes well, there is a terrible tension between that relativism and the nineteenth century evolutionism which still persists in certain vulgar, popular thought - that these people were savages. The idea that we might learn something from them or that these societies might be as good, better or just different had been unimaginable.

So why did you criticise Levi-Strauss?

73

Well it is a primitive old system in itself. It is all based on the notion of binary opposition, okay - all intellectual thought must be based upon similarity and difference but there are many different modes and permutations in which this can take place (...) In the nineteenth century they were bugged about the dialectic, the thesis, the antithesis and the synthesis and now Levi-Strauss reduces it to two. Now is one any more valid than the other? - I do not think so. What I tried to do, in that simple paper of mine [1970a], was simply to say that the Aborigines have in fact multiple different ways of perceiving reality, according to the context of the situation - whether it is religious, secular or whether it is 'social' in the popular sense, that is whether they are considering the structure of their society, whether they are considering their environment or, whether they are considering their cosmological conceptions of the world. They use *different* conceptions and you cannot reduce this to a simple opposition between plus and minus.

So you say three phases. Darwin because he started anthropology, because of the notion of evolutionism: functionalism because of its neatness and the importance of looking for functions, and thirdly Levi-Strauss ... the lack of ethnocentrism if you like. Presumably you've replaced all of those with Marxism, or do you see them all as conceptual and methodological tools?

Marxism had literally a revolutionary effect in the 1930s, intellectually speaking. (Then it was economism.).

Are we talking about anthropology now? I mean if you talk about Eric Wolf bringing back history, how would you characterise your position?

Well I think the thing I've tried to put at the centre is the concept of *culture*. I think Marxism did a great job - and basically that job was political economy - in the late 1930s it was economism, and then we developed the notion of *political* economy, and I think perhaps the supreme tribute to that is Perry Anderson's work - absolutely magnificent - *The Absolutist State* [1974], the perception that political forms of society were an important factor in the whole of the centralisation and transformation of social relationships. Now Perry is brilliant at that, but in that book he mentions two institutions of crucial importance - and he says that himself - that don't actually fit that theory. One is the Roman Catholic Church, which persisted

74

from Christ to the present day (including Socialist Poland) and the second is Roman Law; now why the hell does the law and the Church persist? And the fact that they *do* persist tells us that values - intellectual orientations, cognitive maps, whatever you like to call it, *culture* I call it - persist and are tremendously important. The fact that people in Poland consider themselves to be Catholic is of great, great, practical importance. For example Marxism itself is a theory - it's a body of ideas, it's spread all over the world - it has tremendous impact, once people have got it, they see the world in a different way and they behave in a different way. This is a transformation of reality by theory, and therefore, any economistic theory as I call it, any theory like Althusser ('history has no subject', economy is where you've got to look, and people's aspirations or struggles are really rather irrelevant, it's some gigantic system working itself) personally I don't accept that.

(...) So if an anthropologist was about to carry out some research, you'd say 'focus on culture, you'll learn a lot' ...

I'll give you an instance. What's one of the classic studies of Britain since sociology started in the 1950s - Rex and Moore on Sparkbrook [1967] - right? I happen to think that it's a very limited if not bad book ... because at the same time there was a Pakistani called Dahya - whom I've never met or heard of subsequently - who wrote an article, [see for example, 1974] and he said to understand why Pakistanis come to Britain, and why when they've arrived in Britain they behave in the characteristic way they do even down to such mundane matters as the kind of housing they find for themselves, (that is multi-occupancy: those that have a bit of capital buy a house, a poor bad run-down house and they split it up and they get those with whom they already have some social relations) - to understand all that, you have to go back to Pakistan, you have to understand the kind of values, ambitions, orientations, aims, ends, values in life which they come to Britain with, and ultimately they aim to go back to Pakistan having made a killing. And of course they never do; most of them will stay here forever and become British. Now Badr Dahya takes into account the meaning of the action to the actor, it is very Weberian. Now Rex and Moore who think they are Weberian do not understand the meaning of the action to the actor, in fact they do not even ask themselves that question. They call these people 'proletarians'. Proletarians! They are buying houses, they are renting them out to kinsmen, members of fellow-castes, in other words non-economic relationships are intrinsic to the nexus between them, non-economic or extra-economic. You cannot call these people proletarians, proletarian implies the whole business of a cash nexus, a person who has nothing in life other than in the relations of the means of production, these people are not interested in the means of production, they are interested in the means of consumption and of property (...).

Do you think that it is just a formalistic type of worry or do you think that there actually is something meaningful called comparative sociology?

You have hit your finger on it. I mean what is comparative sociology? I have just been looking at this splendid prospectus of the next British Sociological Association Conference [1984], there must be seventy papers on unemployment and employment, work and leisure - obviously very exciting, tremendous diversity, a lot of work being done *is* tremendous, and at the end of the day it will tell you something about Britain. But you are never sure whether this is peculiar to Britain, you can't be sure unless you look at France or Germany. I would say that is the most sociologists ever do. Comparative sociology means comparing Britain with France and Britain with Germany, and if you are really wild and 'way out' you will compare Britain with the USSR - sorry the first thing you do is compare Britain with the USA. I think that anthropology is the *really* comparative dimension of sociology (...). Well what about looking at ethnicity in South Africa - in Johannesburg - or Sao Paulo, Brazil or ethnicity in Mexico City; I mean *there* is some wonderful material which I can guarantee you that 99 out of 100 sociologists would never dream of looking at, partly because some of it is written in foreign languages.

Do you think that in contemporary anthropology there are too many individual case studies, which interesting as they are in themselves, simply miss the point?

Yes absolutely, most of the individual cases do. Anthropologists have always been absorbed in their own people ... I think that it was Ernest Gellner who said that there is nobody more tribal than anthropologists, it is always 'my tribe', and it is very hard to get them out of that even to compare one tribe with the tribe next door, or with a tribe in their region, or a *type* of society. For example, if they are studying hunting and collecting societies in Africa, they might also look at hunting and collecting societies in Australia ... but the idea of comparing them with, say gigantic state systems or with the Soviet Union would not cross their minds. They are frightened, they are very timorous creatures ... but I think that that is what they have got to do.

So although they are interesting in their own right they are denuded because of this lack of historical and comparative perspective?

So are we, how many sociologists ... for example, they are writing about men and women, like some of the best sociologists, Ann Oakley, and do they ever look at the anthropological data, which is the truly comparative dimension? And when they do look at this data, I am afraid, because they do not know their stuff, they get it wrong, and there are incredible myths about men and women in primitive societies. The myth of matriarchy for example, which Engels believed in as did a lot of the nineteenth century people, is still believed in by a lot of feminists, and it is an absolute nonsensical myth without any empirical foundation (...)

Okay. The Third World. Could you start by talking about Wallerstein and Frank, because they are two of the most important figures ...

Absolutely, tremendous influences and rightly so, they have transformed our whole perception of modern history, and the emergence of what has become the dominant form of social organisation since the fifteenth and sixteenth centuries through to the present day and that is capitalism. America is still the number one power, and the Western world is far more powerful by any criterion than the whole of the communist world. They are right, it is a world society which has existed since about 1885, since the triumph of imperialism over the colonial world. I think that what is wrong about that is - and I have said it in this book [1984a] - is that you have got to look at the impact of this incredibly powerful Western world or Western power on the people who have been conquered in terms of a dialectic, and I would have thought that this would be a very Marxist thing to do. That is, there are existing societies, cultures, which interact and actively respond to the

77

colonising powers; for example, I wrote about those Melanesian people, and their response to the colonising powers was cargo cults, but the response of the *Chinese* people to the Western world was communism, not 'cargo cults'. Now why do the Chinese people respond in this way and the Melanesians in another way? To understand and answer that question you have got to understand Melanesian society and culture and Chinese society and culture, and therefore, if you like, that's an anthropological enterprise. You cannot answer it in terms of colonialism. Now I think that Frank and Wallerstein see the world as a kind of two-sided interaction between the West and the 'rest'. I do not even accept the notion of the 'rest', I think that there are Bushmen in the Kalahari, tribal societies; there are all kinds of intermediary societies, there are world religions like Buddhism, Hinduism, Islam; and to call all these the 'rest' is simply an ethnocentric residual kind of classification that the West adopts towards the people it conquers. It is not valid. Now it's not valid because there are structural differences between all those cultures (...). So to talk about the world having been capitalist since the sixteenth century as Frank does, it is perfectly inadequate.

So the important contribution was simply seeing the world as a whole in the first place?

Yes and that is a marvellous contribution.

In other words we do not see anything without looking at its relationship to something else. Is your argument though, that this is a mere beginning?

It's a fundamental beginning, I think Lenin summed it up in 1918 with *Imperialism*. The world became, as I put it in *The Third World*, a 'social system for the first time' and that is very fundamental. The other very important thing that Frank and Wallerstein don't, I think, really come to terms with, is that no sooner had that world been created it was dissolved or at least broken up - 1885, the triumph of imperialism; 1917, the Russian Revolution. Now after the Russian Revolution there was a Second World, composed of one member. It didn't get any followers until 1945, but today the Soviet Union is the number two power in the world (...) the communist world is one-third of the human population. We have also something called the Third World, which is extremely variegated: some of it (most of it) takes its models and lessons and aspirations from the First World - some from the Second - but the notion of an 'integrated world system' I think misses all that diversification that began in 1917 (...). I don't want to leave out for one minute or forget about the economy, power, political economy, relationships of domination, hegemony - not one iota, but that model omits the cultural diversity of the world; the fact that today India is still a caste-ridden society. What does caste mean? Is that a category of capitalism? No, it is something that existed before capitalism, persisted into the epoch of capitalism, and I wouldn't at all be surprised, if India went that way, persisted into the epoch of socialism. Like Roman Catholicism existed before capitalism, it persisted and was made compatible with capitalism and it still exists today very healthily in capitalist Poland; therefore to talk about, to ignore ... the relative autonomy of cultural traditions or values and talk of the world as being capitalist, as if capitalist were the only ...

You mention the Third World growing by '60,000,000 every year', and of the chances that it will fast get 'beyond the control of anybody, even the greatest of Powers acting in the most rational of ways, is a sober probability on the basis of present trends'. And you add that if the major powers act in 'less than rational ways, as they are doing, the prospects of containing a world full of revolutionary peasants are nil, as the resistance of such a petty country as Vietnam to the might of the USA shows' [1975, p. 327]. Could you add anything to that?

I would have thought that the major problem isn't what is implied here - the demographic problem - it does imply that the poorer of the world are growing at a hell of a rate. I think the major problem is indeed the problem between the two Superpowers - it's a problem of power rather than of demography. There is no problem of demography actually; we could solve the problems of world poverty and world hunger and world underproduction tomorrow morning (...). In the First World I go round talking to people - I'm worried myself - about the ultimate World War III. In the Third World, and I've been round a lot of it, people aren't terribly concerned about it, and I keep saying to people in the Third World 'Shouldn't you be a bit more worried about what's going to happen with nuclear weapons?' - 'Nuclear what?' Meantime back at the ranch we've got no food, we've got the Americans screwing us like hell, and they're preoccupied with mainly the problems of their relationship with the First World, not with the Second

World. They're not worried about communism, so when you try and interest them in what we see in the West, in what ... the Chinese call the 'principle contradiction', for us the nuclear contradiction - what they, in the Third World, see as the principal contradiction is poverty. Now I think unhappily the two problems will come together, because there will be a lot of Third World countries that will soon have nuclear weapons, like Argentina, Brazil, Iraq and so forth - and that's what [that] Israeli attack on that Iraqi nuclear reactor was about - India and maybe up to fourteen countries. Conversely, of course, the terrible desperate problems of poverty which manifest themselves in international conflicts between Third World countries, or sometimes between Third World countries and First World countries, like the Falklands War, will sooner or later - just statistically - provoke the Third World War: that is, it is a matter of probability. You cannot go on having so many sources of conflagration, intimately linked with the alignments of the Superpowers who want to interfere in Afghanistan, in Vietnam, in Nicaragua - and one of these days it will blow up. If you think the opposite I think you're being sweet and naive.

In your book on China, Inside China, *you say that people are interested in China for, amongst other reasons, it gives rise to the 'revival of hope in the possibility of change, including very radical and revolutionary change', but you add that cynics do not believe that China has the 'human capacity to create new structural societal arrangements - even less to change "human nature"' [1975a, p. 15]. How do your remarks strike you today?*

Well since then I'm sorry to report that the cynics feel that they have been proved right. My view is that China is going through at the present moment what the Russians went through in 1921, called the 'New Economic Policy', in which they obviously couldn't push through the kind of socialism they wanted - highly centralised and so on - so the mass of the ordinary people, who are individualists and entrepreneurs, saw the best chances they could to make of life - making more money by producing things and buying things, and that's what they're doing in China - at an enormous rate, it's quite staggering the difference since 1972, when I was there. My daughter's just come back, and it's quite unbelievable.

Nevertheless ... positively speaking what has always struck you about China?

Equality ... it is striking and it still is probably today even with television sets. Okay it's enforced equality, I know that (...)

You've commented that China has made the most 'spectacular and world-historical developmental break-through of the post-war period' and has done so 'without the benefit of Western sociological theory or indeed of institutionalised sociology' [1974, p. 16]. Could you expand on that?

Well the world has existed I think ... well for ninety-nine per cent of human history without sociology. Conversely, you might say, if you look at the great struggles and the things that people thought they were fighting for ... I was thinking particularly of the Reformation, Protestants versus Catholics, well what was that all about? You can say it was about individualism, you could say it was about nationalism, you could say it was about a lot of other things, it was an idiom or a language or a mode of expressing relationships which were actually more of a kind of phenomenal ...

China and sociology ...?

Well ... I think they've made a lot of mistakes. Let me give you an extremely mundane but terribly historically important one, the creation of the communes. I said in that book [*Inside China*] that I think that the creation of the communes was a historical watershed, like very few things or institutions which are created in society. Trade unions are new, co-ops are new, in the nineteenth century; communes are new, soviets are new, this is something ... a fantastic break with the past, an innovation. I think that the Chinese communes were of that quality, like that. But they're always working within the framework of a Marxist theory basically taken from the Russians, Leninism; for example, the whole structure of their society is still democratic-socialist in Leninist sense, the *Party* dominates society; the economy is more important than anything else; ideology is subsidiary to what they call the basis , or infrastructure ... In more concrete terms, in the field of agriculture, which is eighty-five per cent of the Chinese population, they borrow their model of the communes from the Soviet Union, that is the centralisation of the means of production, and the system of renumeration according to work-points. Classically Leninist.

Social science?

Social science could help ... they made such balls ups in the early days when they were creating the communes. They created out of the innumerable, many hundred thousands of villages of China, they formed them together to create twenty-four thousand communes. Nutty! I mean elaborate intellectual work has been done by brilliant sinologists like [George William] Skinner to show that these corresponded to no historical entity in Chinese society, economy or polity; it was crazy, it was like imposing a grid on Chinese society, like as if we were to reform the whole local government structure of Britain and divide England up into four regions and nothing else, it would be nutty, it wouldn't correspond ... If they'd [China] had social science they wouldn't have done that, and in fact because they've got a lot of Chinese empiricists they found that out a year or two later, and they divided up China into seventy-four thousand communes which corresponded with what Skinner called the lowest level of marketing zones. These were historically established areas within which people traded and exchanged goods and so on. Now if you had good social science you would have found that out maybe. On the other hand, if you had not got the Chinese Communist Party with its drive towards the future and its ideological commitment towards equality, towards socialist society, we would not have communes anyhow (...)

Okay, Marxism and Sociology. I will read you a quote from C. Wright Mills who asserts that there is 'no Marxist social science of any intellectual consequence. There is - just social science: without the work of Marx and other Marxists, it would not be what it is today; with their work alone, it would not be nearly as good as it happens to be. No-one who does not come to grips with the ideas of Marxism can be an inadequate social scientist; no-one who believes that Marxism contains the last word can be one either. Is there any doubt about this after Max Weber, Veblen, Karl Mannheim - to mention only three? We do now have ways - better than Marx's alone - of studying and understanding man, society, and history, but the work of these three is quite unimaginable without his work' [in Horowitz, 1983, p. 198]. Do you think that is fair?

I think that that is dead right.

I will tell you why I ask, it is because some people regard sociology and Marxism as incompatible ...

That is nonsense, Marxism versus sociology. I am emphatically against that (...). You cannot understand the twentieth century without using the intellectual tools of Marxism, which have added a great deal. And also Marxism itself *is a fact*, it is institutionalised in the form of world communism and if you want to understand the twentieth century you have got to understand that: it is a third of the world. But as a social science ... it is either one-dimensional Marxism, economism, reductionism. Then, somewhat better than that, is political economy - which is what most of it is, 'mode of productionism', if you like. It misses crucial dimensions of social life which are the 'ideal': that is values, norms, cognitive sets, intellectual orientations and the forms in which these are institutionalised and handed on over the centuries ... Take the persistence of Islam or Christianity, you cannot explain that in the categories of feudalism and capitalism. Then there are a lot of other big gaps - it is a very good societal theory; it has tremendous explanatory power at the level of *the* society or the state, in modern terms, but it has no explicit theoretical apparatus for coping with the dynamics of personal interaction - which the symbolic interactionists beautifully elaborated and worked out. Now it is interesting that when Marxists do field studies and they have to get down to the nitty-gritty - it is no use talking about the role of the state if you are studying the internal dynamics of a factory in Manchester, it does not help you very much to explain the logic of the social system, the relationships that are happening there - they fall back onto symbolic interactionism. So you have a funny book, which is macro-Marxist theory at the beginning and the end, a kind of sandwich with most of the middle being symbolic interactionism or some other kind of unrecognised, implicitly-borrowed theories.

In Marx and Marxism *you talk about inadequacies in Marxism and how they've borrowed from, say, Freud, but you add that 'most of these hybrids have not been very impressive' [1982, p. 11]. Were you particularly thinking of critical theory?*

Frankfurt, yes. Because I don't find it very rewarding, Frankfurt sociology. I haven't honestly spent much of my life immersing myself in it. I've read enough to know that I don't find it immensely profitable. Why? Because

I think it comes out of the tradition of German (Hegelian) idealism. *It's not Marxism*, a dialectical sociology which implies a relationship between the object and the subject. Those people typically seem to me never to do any contemplation of the object, and what empirical research of any use is there that came out of that entire school, except *The Authoritarian Personality* [Adorno, *et al.*, 1969] - that was a major thing, and the follow-up *The American Soldier* [Stouffer, *et al.*, 1949] studies - but that's about the end of it. The lucubrations of Adorno, Horkheimer and all those people about jazz and everything they wrote about seem to me of no great illumination.

Is Habermas included?

I don't know a lot about Habermas, I'll be perfectly frank ...

But you obviously don't want to, do you?

I don't want to no, I keep picking up bits of it and reading what he has to say about the State, and I find it's based on nothing, except some abstract categories. Where is the research? And I'm afraid I can't tolerate that kind of stuff, I don't regard that as social science, as a matter of fact. I think scientific research means doing some work. The categories we use when we think about the State must be based on knowledge of the actual State as it is out there in the world, and if Habermas just sits in his study and thinks about it, or looks on the financial pages of the *Frankfurt Allgemeine Zeitung*, that isn't research! And I'm not really terribly interested - he might be a brilliant chap, and he might be *right*, but I don't think it's social science.

You constantly talk about Marxisms, the varieties of Marxisms. But obviously you prefer some versions over others ...?

Any complex body of theory - take Christianity - in principle, intrinsically - is based on a set of complex propositions, always more than one, about the nature of the world, the place of man, society, *et cetera*, the relationship of human society to nature and so on. Now any one of these major propositions is a very general statement isn't it? A huge proposition about the world, and it requires specification, applying to particular times and

84

circumstances. If we talk about *the* State, for example, do we mean the Zulu State, the liberal 'nightwatchman' State of the nineteenth century - you know minimum government interference - or the macro-state today, which runs everything? Or the Soviet State? So there are different states. So a theory of the state, or any other aspect of society is necessarily a very general statement, and obviously you soon start saying there are different *kinds* of states (...) I've just been reading the history of Christianity; movement after movement, the Dominicans, the Franciscans, the monastic movement, the movements of poverty and of the abandonment of the world and so forth ... the way in which Christianity became '*the* religion', the official state religion of the Roman Empire (and later you were hung if you didn't accept it). So that there's Christianity of rebellion, of retreat from the world, there's the Christianity of the State. Are they all Christianity? Yes. In other words Christianity, like Marxism, is a plural phenomenon, which has to be situated sociologically and explained how it came to be hooked up to the State by the Emperor Constantine, how there came to be a new reading of Christianity, that suddenly emerges, that we call 'Protestantism' (...)

What has been your experience of Althusser's work?

I think it was one of the most stultifying disasters that swept over this country in the last decade and thank God it's over. I think Edward Thompson did a wonderful (and definitive) job in dismantling it. I had contemplated doing the same myself, as did other people I've talked to. I remember talking to Jon Halliday, and he said well he'd always rather hoped that it would go away, if he waited long enough. But it doesn't go away, you know; these things do have to be confronted intellectually, and you have to do what Edward did.

Did Althusserianism catch on because of a surfeit of 'humanistic Marxism'?

Well I don't think we do have too much humanistic Marxism. No, I think it's part of a wider sea-change going on in social science and perhaps the end of a long epoch. I think it was part of the whole revolt against British empiricism, which, now you know and I know, that British sociology was largely Fabian - surveys and empiricism - much remains so. Then with the

85

explosion of the universities, which meant the explosion of sociology, too, we had an explosion of research, which was very empirical research and much needed. We knew nothing about the family. Until Young and co., [and Willmott, 1957], there was nothing known. Actually the first article I ever wrote in sociology was called 'Britain - Unknown Country?', which appeared in the *New Reasoner*, which was the predecessor of the *New Left Review*, because Britain was pretty well an unknown country then ... We had a minimal corpus of studies of our own society and culture (...) A revolution happened in sheer volume, let's say ... So we do know a bit about Britain that we did not know in 1957. However the great bulk of that work was very empirical, even empiricist in the sense that it was either eclectic or within a broadly Fabian-socialising tradition, and when the right-wing attack us - that sociology is a kind of leftism - there's a certain amount of truth in it. So I think that the next generation, people who then occupy the lecturing positions in the universities, their social positions have changed; they are not researchers, they are not going out there. In fact, their job prevents them from researching; they are professional teachers, in other words they are synthesizers and communicators of ideas and that generation I think wanted theory and that is what they damn well did. That applied to Marxism of course - a highly theorised form of Marxism, highly systematic, integrated, coherent, I would say scholastic, indeed mandarin. *NLR* was the epitome of it, that is what the *NLR became*, we founded it as part of a social movement and it went through a fundamental transformation. That is why Anderson and Thompson ended up at each other's throats so often - because they represented two utterly distinct attitudes towards Marxism; one which was trying to produce an austere, self-contained internally coherent philosophy of the world, and the other was concerned with changing the world, and I think that Edward's subsequent career in CND has shown that he kept on doing that, and I think that that is more important. But it was not only that. Then there was the vogue of ethnomethodology; there was a minority of people who took up Frankfurt. When I wrote those first Penguin textbooks the dominant theoretical mode - which, again, was borrowed and not indigenous - was symbolic interactionism. We were all bowled over by Becker and Goffman and co., not just because they had been out in the world, but because they had produced some theoretical tools - primary and secondary socialisation, the internalisation of values, the concept of the primary group. All this was a body of theory, which symbolic interactionism developed. It was very fine theory, very useful theory, and researchers used it but of course it was a theory with tremendous limitations

... so Althusser was part of a search for theory.

(...) On page 16 of Marx and Marxism *[1982] you say that Marx was able to 'discern the outlines of what a socialist society might look like'. Really?*

Well, yes it was a few simple, indeed you might say ingenious and naive principles, and he was a very young man when he wrote it - [the 'hunting and fishing' phrase]. He was a Hegelian idealist, and it was sweet, but I do think it was correct: it was the dream of equality and fraternity and there's nothing terrible about that. Of course Marx never spelt it out ... I think Lenin said that they were very annoyed with Marx when they got power because they looked through all the books and there was nothing to tell them how to run the country, there's very little in Marxism (...). There are a few hints on the actual organisational structures that would be consistent with socialism, what socialism would look like, what would we have to do in the countryside, you see. So his outline is really a few general principles, 'from each according to his ...', *et cetera*, so how do you interpret that? What does that mean with regard to the real differences between mental and manual labour, between a peasant and an industrial worker, what does 'according to their ability' mean?, and this is an issue we talked about before - those general principles have to be *interpreted* (...)

In Marx and Marxism *you observe that there was a 'further scenario that Marx never envisaged', namely that one of the Superpowers could 'pull down the whole temple, by provoking nuclear war, rather than allow the frustration of their private interests'. Mao of course called this the 'principle contradiction', and as you add he was optimistic and believed that 'evolution would start all over again after such an Armageddon' [1982, p. 110]. It doesn't sound too convincing does it?*

Yes I think I quote it in my new book, but not in the *Marx and Marxism* book, that Mao says ... well, human life could get wiped out on the planet and he said something like 'But of course evolution would start up again, monkeys would turn into men and then the whole thing would start up again'. That is the ultimate optimism. Even if the whole of human society as we know it was wiped out, or human physical stock was wiped out evolution would begin again. Now I think that that is lunatic optimism -

lunatic and also very frightening, because it does imply that preparedness to contemplate the ultimate, and I think to start dealing in those terms leads to a totalitarian mode of thought and practice (...).

You talk about the contradictions and difficulties in Marxism which have to be overcome. The first one, and I think that this is a very interesting quote: 'it is my contention that the model of base and superstructure that most Marxists including Marx took as the key image through which to express the essence of their theoretical system is in fact quite incompatible with the idea of a dialectical science of society, since it implies not only conceptually isolating economy in an unacceptable way but also assumes that the latter is somehow necessarily more decisive than anything else' [1982, p. 130]. One thing that interests me is that you seem to be the only person these days who uses the word dialectical, now can you explain that again?

Well I mean the relation between the knowing subject and the objective world outside the knowing subject. I think that most sociology ... there is a classical Marxist statement about 'bourgeois' thought which divides it into either materialism or idealism. I think this is actually true of most Marxism, as well. I think a social science would have to be *dialectical*, in that the categories through which we think about the world and therefore act are of course subjective categories: norms, ideals, values, ends, purposes. These are not by-products of the economy; indeed the opposite ... What they have in the Soviet Union is a model, a set of theoretical postulates: values about equality and fraternity, about the socialisation of the means of production and the fair distribution of the product to the producer. These are ethical values, and the entire economy is structured in accordance with those ethical values. That is not a materialist strategy; it is a dialectical strategy, because the subjective norms and values of socialism structure and condition, and interact dialectically with the formal organisation of society.

This is the thing that gives people problems, namely that if you get rid of the famous Marxist statement 'that it is not the consciousness of man ... et cetera', how can you still claim that your account is Marxist? Would you say that it is because of its method? (...)

I do not even know that I would say that my account is Marxist. I am not really concerned about what label one puts on it. Obviously I come out of an intellectual formation of Marxism, but 'out of' is a significant little phrase, because I have very little sympathy, indeed antipathy, towards many *forms* of Marxism. For example, I regard myself as an undying enemy of Althusserianism, I would also regard myself as an undying enemy of subjective idealism such as ethnomethodology. But many of the conceptual notions in Marxism and key ideas I do accept. I think that they need an awful lot of change, refinement, criticism, but there are many other fundamental propositions of Marxism I do not accept.

Fine. The second crucial contradiction in most varieties of Marxism is a temptation 'shared with other systematic sociologies and indeed scientific frameworks in general', and that is the holistic temptation to 'over-connect everything', for instance to treat the family as an ideological state apparatus. Such Marxisms are 'over-systematic, over-deterministic, and over-economistic', and that to you it seems to be a temptation with Marxism [1982, p. 114] ...

I am thinking of Wally Secombe's article in the *New Left Review* on 'housework and the family' [1973] in which he tries to reduce the domestic relations between husband and wife and families to the requirements of the capitalist market - capitalism requires a workforce and it requires cheap labour, different kinds of labour - and so women fulfil this role and so forth, and this has direct repercussions inside the home - and indeed it does. But I have become very conscious lately, having lived a peripatetic life all over the world, out of touch sometimes for years and years with my kin, that I am becoming less and less out of touch with my kin as I grow older, because they are getting older as well and becoming more dependent on me. For example, my mother, why do I feel such a tremendous moral imperative to support and associate with my mother? Because she is imprinted on me at an early age and I feel a sense of obligation - kinship is a deep commitment in our culture and in any culture and it cannot be explained in terms of the logical requirements of the capitalist system.

You say that it is 'perfectly understandable why these distortions have come about ... for Marxists have taken materialism as the essence of their world-view', and this can lead to a 'one-sided materialism in response to a one-

sided idealism', and that neither alternative begins to 'resemble what Marx said he was engaged in: producing a dialectical science of society' [1982, pp. 114-15]. Can you elaborate?

Well Marx you know has given the whole world a bad steer because he spent his whole life producing *Capital*, which was a fine piece of work, but it was about the economy. It was not really even about the political economy, and, as Marx said, it was only a part ... it was going to be, what, one of six major segments as mentioned in the *Grundrisse*. It was not a sociology. It did not even begin ... But it has been taken as the model. Indeed in the Althusserian period, *Lire le capital* and I have seen them in the university reading *Capital*, pouring through the pages ... trying to find the magical strategy, you know you got this magical strategy from *Capital*. But you know you don't, because *Capital* does not provide one. It does not provide a model of society, it is not a sociology, and unfortunately it is his greatest work and it has steered people into economism. And the effects are of course practical as well. The whole model of base and super-structure was elaborated actually by Stalin - as a matter of fact Marx is very much more flexible about that. It is only an image that occurs in one or two little places. It is not a central concept, although he did eventually in fact use it ... Marx is full of contradictions.

So you would look at the whole corpus of Marx's work, and not stress (say) the 'younger Marx' or emphasise the 'epistemological breaks' ...

Well there are different phases of Marx. I do not agree with this tremendous epistemological *coupure*, I reckon Marx went on retaining and thinking in terms of those categories he formulated in his youth about alienation - Hegelian categories. Now I think that he went on believing all that and thinking in those terms, but at the same time he was writing a different kind of thing in *Capital*. It is a contradiction in Marx. Really you cannot square the materialist-reductionism of a base and super-structure model with the socialist ideals that he derived from Hegel. They are two different kinds of Marx. Now they are both locked up in the same brain; unfortunately the dominant one tended to be the economistic one.

You say that Marx 'clearly emphasised the necessity of producing' and that at the 'heart of his sociology' as no other sociology does, he puts the 'theme of exploitation' [1982, p. 115]. What do you mean by the 'necessity of producing'?

Oh what I meant was ... You see as Marx said his object in life was, when he was a young man, to turn the Hegelian dialectic on its head. You know that he was talking about Feuerbach, that is, to put a materialism in place of idealism. Now I think that that is really a bad formulation because it lays itself open to precisely what Weber said, to substitute a one-sided materialism for a one-sided idealism. They are both one-sided. That is why I say that a sociology must be dialectical, including a Marxist sociology. Here I am taking on the dominant Marxism, which is still economistic or political economy. For example, that journal *Review of African Political Economy*, a Marxist journal ... Political economy is what they say they are doing and indeed it is what they are doing. They are not doing sociology; they are doing political economy. They are leaving out of their conceptual apparatus a whole field. Now that field I would loosely call 'culture'. What I mean by that is that it provides you with cognitive orientations, evaluative standards, it provides you with a conative model, it tells you, classically, 'what is to be done'. Now that is what culture provides you with, rules to live by (...). Now in countering economistic or reductionist, or defective one-dimensional or two-dimensional forms of Marxism, I inevitably - like Marx (with all modesty) struggling with Hegel - tend to overemphasise or pay a lot of attention to those cultural aspects because people have not thought of them. I want to draw attention to them. But a man has to live and produce, that is what I meant by that; we have got to have factories, we have to grow food, we have to have industrial relations, we have to have trade unions ... as Marshall Sahlins puts it very well in *Stone Age Economics [1972]* 'society has to be provisioned'. So Marx was quite right to tell idealistic Hegelians in his day (...) get your feet on the ground where people produce things; exchange, where there is a market, etc. He was saying that sociology without any economics is nutty and will inevitably be idealistic. Now Marx was right (...)

In terms of the theme of exploitation does this mean that unlike sociology, Marxism is about prescriptions?

I think implicitly in any analysis, at the end of the day, the analysis must lead somewhere, intrinsically *does* lead somewhere ...

... like functionalism leads to stability?

Right. It is built-in to the categories (...) or at best symbolic interactionism leads you to the identification with the insulted and the injured of the world, and to a preoccupation with primary groups (...) the whole thing is in fact diffused with what Gouldner called a 'metaphysical pathos'. There are values, concepts, prejudices you call them if you do not like them, in the way in which everything is presented ...

(...) In Marx and Marxism *you argue that if 'material interest' is central to Marxism so are the concepts of 'immaterial* mystification *and of* false consciousness' *[1982, p. 118]. Could you elaborate?*

False consciousness is a mode of talking about a dissonance between people's objective interests and their perception of those interests, their subjective understanding, and what it says is that these people are mystified, they're making mistakes, or they're being induced to make mistakes by people who are making them mis-think. Now I think that occurs in life; it's analogous if you like to conspiracy theory (...) I think people *do* conspire to fool, deceive, delude, trick other people in their own interests and against the interests of other people. Now I'd defend the concept of false consciousness because I do think people have interests that they sometimes don't appreciate. I don't think the interests of the working class are the same as those of guys who were getting paid five hundred thousand a year for doing their terribly burdensome jobs.

It does have this ring though, doesn't it, of us *telling working class people what is in* their *interests?*

You mean we have the truth and they don't? Well if you have any conception of truth ... some forms of knowledge are better than others, the whole of science is based on the assumption that there is truth and falsity, or error, these are elemental categories. Now you have got to be aware of that terrible arrogance of thinking, that you have some kind of monopoly and that you're always right, and that's why I think it's the inspection and critical attitude towards one's own values which is absolutely crucial. It's easy to be critical about other people's ... demystification of the self and the groups and categories with which one belongs. But I think, re false consciousness ... if you do away with the conception of false consciousness you've got to do away with the conception of truth.

You also note that Marxism has failed to develop a social psychology [1982, p. 118]. I can personally think of the attempts to fuse Marx and Freud, and work like that of Lucien Seve [1975], but it is all inadequate, so why do you think that such a social psychology has not been developed?

It's neglected the subjective, really, and because they've also neglected the sub-societal, the level of interaction between real persons, their theory is about society with a capital S, and about structures, and systems and sub-systems, as much as Parsons [did], that's why it's functionalist-Marxism. So I think once you begin to operate with that kind of model you have no place really, you don't feel any urgency to construct appropriate categories for the level at which life is lived (...).

In a recent article you talk about people's, including sociologists', 'ignorance of Soviet society' [1984, p. 14] ...

Phenomenal. Well most people's knowledge of the Soviet Union is gained from *Animal Farm* and *1984*. They were very interesting fables and very accurate presentations of Stalinist Russia in the 1930s, I think ... but that is half a century ago, the world has changed including the Soviet Union. It is no longer under mass terror; there are no longer tens of millions of people being bumped off in prison camps ... we know all the nasty forms of social control and cancer wards and psychiatric hospitals and so forth, but the Soviet Union isn't the regime of mass terror it was in the 1930s. It's also a lot more prosperous, and in my book [1984a] I give some evidence of this; vastly more prosperous than it was even in the 1950s; the standard of living of the average Soviet citizen has gone up immensely. The controls on the peasantry have been taken off, they don't need an internal passport, they are getting welfare services for the first time in human history. So I think the Soviet Union has changed a great deal ... what was your question?

... people's ignorance ...

Well people never read about the Soviet Union, all they ever read about of course is bad doings, which are quite a lot, especially in foreign policy.

You were saying that sociologists share this ignorance ...

Sociologists know nothing. I'd like us to go to a meeting, and we'd ask the first ten sociologists what they have read of serious literature about Soviet society. I bet none of them, none of them would have read a work like David Lane's. David Lane has written quite a lot of work now [for example, 1978], and I'd like to bet that nine out of ten sociologists haven't read them and therefore they are quite ignorant about the nature of Soviet society.

Okay, on to Giddens. In his Sociology: a Brief but Critical Introduction *he says that it's important for a 'critical social theory' to 'outflank Marx from the left' [1982a, p. 169]. Does that mean anything to you?*

I think it's very funny, the idea of Tony Giddens outflanking Marxism from the left. I wouldn't have thought that there's that [many] differences between him and me, and as a consequence of that I wouldn't want to put us to the left of Marxists, God forbid. I believe in a sort of humanistic socialism and so does Tony I should think, and that's not outflanking Marxism from the left. What he's saying is that Marxism in its institutionalised - and I would say ossified forms, has failed to grapple with race and gender in particular, and is now desperately trying to catch up - how does it catch up? Usually by firstly picking up and developing ideas generated outside it, by the women's movement for example ... It is almost pathetic to see men in general, not just Marxists, trying to hook themselves onto ... desperately trying to show they are now cognisant of and sensitive to the women's issue when they haven't been for the whole of their lives, and I apply that criticism to myself as well. So they borrow ideas which have been generated in the Women's Movement about gender, not necessarily good ideas - I think that there is a lot of mythology, tremendous mythology in some feminist writing - but I think that it is very diversified

94

and ideas are being batted about. Marxism and ethnicity: as a theory of ethnicity and race, it is almost laughable. I have a whole chapter in [this book] on class and ethnicity ... Frank Parkin refers to the Rand Rebellion, when the white miners, in 1920-odd it was, rose in rebellion. Working class? They had to be put down by guns, artillery and aeroplanes, and the slogan was 'Workers of the world unite for a White South Africa' - how do you explain the ethnic division of the working class of that cosmic nature between Black and White in South Africa, and talk about the 'unity' of the working class? (...) Let me give you another illustration. Frank Parkin's marvellous little book *Class inequality and Political Order [1971]* in which he talks about the working class. People talk about *the* characteristic outlook of the working class; Marxists do, non-Marxists do; they talk about working class values, working class ideals, working class consciousness, and Frank says 'There isn't; the working class is a kind of field, in which people absorb and generate ideas which reflect their interests in life, their needs, wants and aspirations and so forth'. Some of them come, 'hegemonically', from the ruling class - a third of British Trade Unionists have always voted Conservative since the war - that is part of the working class, a working class tradition ... In other words, if you like, it has been injected into the working class from the outside, but it *is* rooted in it. There is the counter socialist, radical, liberal tradition which is very alive - but, Frank says, 'and in the middle there is a whole range of people who are neither, a sort of grey area, probably the majority, who accommodate, who get by in social life'. Now which of these are the working class? They are *all* the working class.

So a 'critical' social theory will not outflank Marxism from the Left?

Well I don't think that Tony has provided us with one!

Okay relatedly, do you see Giddens' work as the 'philosophisation of sociology'? As obscurantist?

Well that grandiose claim about outflanking Marxism from the Left ... despite what I said earlier about over-systematisation, I think that anything that would help cope with Marxism would have to be a lot more systematic than what Tony has produced, which I think is basically a kind of eclectic

95

bits of this, that and the other put together, not into any kind of very coherent ... lacking the qualities of a system. I think that is just pretentious. What the political implications might be we are not told.

(...) In your BSA address you were quite critical of ethnomethodology, as opposed to symbolic interactionism [1974, p. 10] ...

I think the ethnomethodologists are right when they themselves rigidly and fiercely distance themselves from orthodox and earlier symbolic interactionism (...). Ethnomethodologists are concerned with, as the term implies, the logic of the situation as perceived by the actor, with the interpretation ... and they say we can only perceive the world using the categories that they use. But the way that they use it, ends up as a kind of solipsism, that each individual perceives the world - is constantly constructing reality as they put it - each *person*, not each category, group or major social entity, but each person. In [this] conversation I am modifying your world because I am putting views, perceptions and trying to change your thinking ... it [ethnomethodology] is *a-social*. Because where do we get these concepts and ideas from - from our education and the world around us. They are institutionalised: the ideas of socialism, Christianity, individualism (...)

So what is to be gained from ethnomethodology?

Well I think that the only thing to be gained is a refinement of the techniques of analysis of interpersonal situations like the famous telephone studies. So what? I do not think it is worth the intellectual effort that has gone into it (...) At the end of the day you are really given a few formal procedures, because really if you do not have a theory of societies, composed of sub-systems, of entities, of sub-categories, then you have a world composed of atoms, which are persons, interacting. All you can do, therefore, is produce propositions which will be true for the properties of *any* kind of social situation. I think you end up back with a formal sociology (...) which says, telephone conversations have beginnings, closing motions, and ends. Well, marvellous. *I* mean, I could have figured that out.

(...) Do you think that the question of the relationship between Oxbridge and sociology is an interesting one?

Oh, I think Oxbridge is the bastion of social orthodoxy ... I was very surprised to see the Cambridge class lists recently and a huge page full of people graduating in natural science. Oxbridge is not stuffy, out of touch with reality, it is highly oriented into the needs of industry and science and so on. It *is* a centre of social orthodoxy, it is the top apex of the pyramid (...) So you wouldn't expect would you, to find a very vibrant critical thinking about society and questioning of society at a place like that. And I've sat around tables with some very famous conservative professors of other disciplines listening to them discuss the horrendous prospect that they might actually have to have some sociology eventually, though they really had nothing but contempt for it - and fear, I think - because it contained a lot more criticality (...) They saw sociology as both an intellectual and a social threat. In Cambridge, you can see ... well Meyer Fortes is now dead, so we can speak well of him, I think deliberately he fought as hard as he could to keep sociology - not to resist it totally, I think he was on the committee that brought it in - but to make sure it didn't threaten too much the position of anthropology. It's significant, I think, that John Barnes (for whom I have the greatest personal respect as a friend and a liberal human being), is (like I was) an anthropologist by training. And he became the professor of sociology there. I think that suited Cambridge, they didn't want a sociologists' sociologist as professor of sociology, and in fact the two best I would have thought at the time - the most productive and stimulating, when was it the late 50s early 60s - were Lockwood and Goldthorpe. Both were at Cambridge and both were, I would say, squeezed out. How they were squeezed out I don't honestly know, but they obviously felt it would be good to leave, and I think it was a tragedy for Cambridge and a tragedy for sociology, only partly rectified now because we have one or two good people like Tony [Giddens] and Runciman around in Cambridge. But you have *not* got a major centre of sociology in either Oxford of Cambridge.

How would you like to be influential in your work?

One's influential as an intellectual if you've affected the ideas of other people. You do that through your teaching and also through one's books. Now the average readership, I read recently, of an article in a learned journal is four, so you're not influencing too many people. But some articles and books do get read by more people (...)

Without being quite so coy, if you'd really liked to have influenced people in what way would it have been?

Oh I wouldn't have been in academia at all, I would have liked to influence people towards changing the whole structure of our society to a socialist one ...

Don't you think your work kind of works towards that?

Yes I do, it's pretty limited ...

So the aim is to change the world?

Yes changing the world; that's exactly it.

What would the 'good society' look like? Or perhaps, as Ralf Dahrendorf would say, is this more or less it?

Lipset said the same thing about America in *Political Man [1960]*. What Dahrendorf means is that it is a society in which you can speak your mind, and be critical of other people, and be critical of your own ideas, and so forth. Now that is excellent; I don't buy this denigration of 'bourgeois' values and thought from ultra-Marxists. I think the freedoms were won by struggle, I may say, in the bourgeois epoch - the *habeas corpus*, the secret ballot and all those things - they are marvellous, are always under threat, and must be maintained, they're always trying to take them off us (...) and not only that, they must be extended. I think what we've got is very limited, and at the moment socialism (if you talked to any ordinary people - we could do this experimentally) - means two things. It means the Soviet Union, that means *Gulag archipelago*, and they're not going to have that over their dead bodies, because that's what it would mean - *their dead bodies*, they think. Secondly, it means bureaucratic nationalisation, and I

98

think Mrs Thatcher still has a lead over the parties combined, she's very popular, and she's popular because socialism has a very negative *indigenous* history (...). Now until people begin to see socialism as meaning *more* freedom, more economic freedom and more economic justice, instead of massive unemployment or living on welfare, until they see more political freedoms, they won't want it. In the Soviet Union, they've been *reduced* compared to the 'bourgeois' world.

Is there a model?

An existential model, a country in the real world, no. There are aspects, in places, about the criterion of equality between say mental and manual labour. Some other aspects are not so good (...)

Regarding your current work, The Three Worlds *[1984a], what essentially is its message?*

The message is firstly don't blow the world up. It's not nuclear weapons that are the problem. What we need is to eliminate the social problems of the world. We produce nuclear weapons like we produce any other weapons because we have enemies, or perceive them as enemies, I think therefore it's very important to start ... We have to move beyond 'co-existence', which means living in armed mutual terror, to actually interacting with persons in the Soviet Union; now how the hell do you do that? It means maximising contacts. They're all monitored and controlled by government, but nevertheless I think it's possible for trade unionists, for astronomers, for businessmen, for academics. I think more material interdependence is a good thing - I'm delighted at the prospect of this new natural gas pipeline from Siberia coming to Western Europe. The more our economics become interdependent, the more possibilities of living together, of co-operating. Now we're a long way from that, but that's what we've got to aim towards, and that is the only way in which we'll avoid dropping the weapons. The second message is that until those weapons are dropped between the two Superpowers, vast sums of the world's resources are being wasted on military hardware, and of course innumerable wars, any one of which might spark off World War III. Look at [how a] little island like Grenada threatens the peace of the whole Caribbean and possibly the whole world, as it might have done. It could happen at any minute. And of course there's the fundamental thing: that most of the people in the world are living lousy lives still, and it's not necessary. Tomorrow morning we could wipe out world poverty; you see this is why I think we need a flash of the old utopian vision (...) It was as long ago as 1957 when a good solid old Stalinist like J.D.Bernal, but a brilliant scientist, wrote a book called *World Without War*, and what he did was make a few simple calculations: how much money was being spent globally on war and missiles. Now if that were re-allocated (...) ten cities the size of Moscow, and another thirty cities the size of Paris could be built within the next two years out of the world armament budget (...) It *can* be different. We've never had that kind of vision updated in recent times. We've become very pessimistic. We've lived through a century that's seen concentration camps, hydrogen bombs, torture on a scale perhaps unique in history. We've got very gloomy and pessimistic about the human condition. And I think people like Bernal and C.Wright Mills were trying to say it needn't be like this, and it can be different. That's utopianism.

4 Anthony Giddens

Anthony Giddens, Professor of Sociology at the University of Cambridge, has recently been described as 'un-English' (Inglis, 1982, p. 215) which is not surprising given his determined attempts to introduce European theorists to British sociology. Born in 1938, he is best known - apart from his sheer output of books - for taking the 'founding fathers' seriously, and of developing and extending their insights. As Giddens notes, the overwhelming interest of Marx, Durkheim and Weber was in the 'delineation of the characteristic structure of modern capitalism as contrasted with prior forms of society', and he himself has attempted to develop and extend such analyses for contemporary capitalism (1971, p. xvi).

Relatedly, of course, is Giddens' interest in the relationship of positivism and sociology. Interestingly, and quite correctly, Giddens notes that the word 'positivism' like the word 'bourgeois' has become 'more of a derogatory epithet than a useful descriptive concept, and consequently has been largely stripped of whatever agreed meaning it may once have had' (1974a, p. ix). He sees three principal sets of issues specific to the importation of positivism into sociology: whether the methodological procedures of natural science may be directly adapted to sociology; whether the goal of sociological analysis can and must be to formulate law-like generalisations; whether sociology has a 'technical character' and like natural science is neutral in respect of values. He is negative in reply to each of the issues (1974a, pp. 3-4). Much of the debate about positivism is misguided anyway. Indeed as Gouldner notes in his most under-rated work *Enter Plato*

(1965) there has always (since Plato) been a dualism in terms of *knowing*, namely *episteme*, the understanding by 'theorists' and *techne*, the technical manipulation of facts. As Gouldner adds (1965, p. 268)

> Far from being archaic, the distinction between these two different forms of knowing is at the root of many major controversies in the social sciences today, and, particularly, in sociology. Indeed, it has been implicated in these since the nineteenth century, when a distinction was formulated between the natural and the cultural (or human) sciences, each presumably having its own different object and appropriate method, corresponding to the two forms of knowing. This nineteenth-century distinction between the natural and the cultural sciences generated a polemic, echoing to this day in the social sciences, concerning whether sociology was a natural science, like biology or physics, and was to be pursued with the same methods as these disciplines employed, or whether sociology required a special and distinctive method and training, for example, *verstehen*, clinical intuition, or some kind of awareness.

Giddens' own approach to social theory is essentially in terms of his theory of *structuration*, in which he argues that neither subject (human agent) nor object ('society' or social institutions) should be regarded as having primacy. Rather, *'each is constituted in and through recurrent practices'*; that is, for Giddens the notion of human 'action' presupposes that of 'institution', and vice versa. As he himself puts it, 'explication of this relation thus comprises the core of an account of how it is that the structuration (production and reproduction across time and space) of social practices takes place' (1982, p. 8).

In a recent textbook, *Sociology: a brief but critical introduction* (1982a), Giddens argues that 'good sociology' uses 'several related forms of sensibility', indeed his own version of the 'sociological imagination': 'these forms of the sociological imagination involve an *historical,* an *anthropological,* and a *critical* sensitivity' (1982a, p. 16). Indeed, he goes further to say that sociology *'necessarily* has a subversive quality' (1982a, p. 2, italics added). Briefly Giddens argues that (1982a, p. 26)

> As human beings, we are not condemned to be swept along by forces that have the inevitability of laws of nature. But this means we must

be conscious of the *alternative futures* that are potentially open to us. In its third sense, the sociological imagination fuses with the task of sociology in contributing to *the critique of existing forms of society*.

———————————

I just want to know a little about your background.

Well I was born in North London in Edmonton, and I went to the local grammar school and then I went to Hull University ... and that was actually a good thing at the time because Peter Worsley was there then - that was in the late 50s. He was always a very energetic and lively character and he was the main influence I suppose on anyone who was doing sociology. He was probably the main person responsible for the department being a very lively one ... and so I suppose I just struck lucky actually. When I went to Hull I was originally going to real philosophy. I think there was only one philosophy lecturer there and he was away for a year so you couldn't do philosophy. I looked around for something else to do. I didn't know what sociology was but it was one of the things that I could do, not having very good academic qualification! Then after that I did an MA at the LSE in sociology. I was supervised by David Lockwood for a year and subsequently by Asher Tropp for a year ... but I'd only been there for a year and a half and then I got a job in Leicester; in those days everybody used to get jobs when they were fairly youthful. I was at Leicester for about seven years or so, but also worked in the USA for about two years then. I've been here since about 1970, that's about it, the whole sketch.

So apart from Peter Worsley who else or what else, in terms of books, were influential?

(...) I'm afraid this isn't very helpful but there weren't any main books which influenced me particularly, and there weren't many main authors who influenced me. At Hull there was a very strong Socialist Society. Peter Worsley was very active in that and most people belonged, but I suppose I always had more mixed feelings about it than most of the other

103

students did, so although I was quite involved and interested in politics I wasn't as straightforwardly a member of the Socialist Society as everybody else was, and so I was never at any point straightforward Marxist, for example, as a student or subsequently ... and I just can't think of any single author or book at that stage that had a profound influence on me at all ...

Was Capitalism and Modern Social Theory *[1971] the result of your postgraduate work?*

Not really, no. Originally I was not planning an academic career, I was going to be a civil servant and like you I was always interested in football and so I wrote an MA basically about football - the development of football in the nineteenth-century. It discussed other sports as well, and I suppose at the time I didn't take it all that seriously. I didn't have any broad-ranging interests in the social sciences and I wasn't thinking about an academic career at all, so *Capitalism and Modern Social Theory* derives from other interests that I established in Leicester basically.

(...) In the book you say that Marx's writing shares a good deal more in common with those of Durkheim and Weber than was apparent to either of the latter two authors, but that that having been said 'there are irreconcilable differences' between Marx and the other two authors [1971, p. 244]. What do you mean share a good deal more in common?

Looking at *Capitalism and Modern Social Theory* you have to put it in its context. When I wrote it about fourteen to fifteen years ago - and it's hard to believe that now - it was very common in sociology departments not to teach much about Marx at all. The usual view, or at least a prominent view, of the development of social theory in the nineteenth-century was essentially a Parsonian one, that is that Marx belonged to a prior tradition to Durkheim and Weber and basically that they improved upon most of the key ideas in Marx's writings ... What I tried to do in that book simply and bluntly was to provide a comparison between the three thinkers of equal status, the idea being that certainly Durkheim and Max Weber couldn't be regarded as just having somehow filled in all the empty spaces in Marx. I tried to set them up as each worthy of comparison with each other. I suppose I reacted against both the Parsonian version of what social theory was like, and what

104

at that time was mainly a fairly crude alternative Marxist version, that Durkheim and Weber were essentially just bourgeois apologists in the face of the superior claims of Marxist thought. I've never really believed that either. It's actually only more recently that everybody has come to accept Marx, Weber and Durkheim as the key nineteenth-century figures. I don't think that they did then, and it's become much more common place (...)

You say that the 'overwhelming interest of each of these authors was in the delineation of the characteristic structure of modern "capitalism" as contrasted with prior forms of society' [1971, p. xvi]. That seems to be obviously true, and if true what is left then and what can we learn from them?

Well actually you say it's *obviously true* but again I'm not sure if everybody thought so or thinks so. A good deal of discussion of those authors at the time was mainly about methodological issues. One of the things that I tried to show in the book was that they were all concerned with fundamental problems of social development and that their ideas are still the basic parameters within twentieth-century social thought ... I was concerned to try to establish that they'd all been very much bound up in their writings with phenomena specific to a particular phase in the development of western capitalism, and although they'd all written in a very generalised way I tried to give a lot of attention to the political context in which they wrote and particularly given the backdrop of the more methodological discussion in Parson's book [*Structure of Social Action*, 1937].

If they're 'founding fathers' what do they tell us that we should take heed of? What is it that they've founded, that we should hold on to?

In my opinion 'the' problem in sociology, 'the' thing that gives sociology some distinctiveness is a concern with social changes initiated over the last couple of hundred years. In my opinion these are much, much more wide-ranging than any other social changes that have occurred in anything like such a time period in any previous era. The modern world, I think, is substantially so different from any pre-existing forms of society. These writers ... lived at the time of the main period of transition, and established some of the main parameters in terms of which that issue has been handled.

But I would not be prepared to defend more than certain segments of their views as being relevant now, because changes they identify have just expanded so ...

As you say what remains is the focus on the 200 years and the changes that have come on ...

Yes I think the focus on *radical* social transformation with an open-ended result. As far as I can see the modern world is just a stupendously disquieting and difficult world to understand. It's a really fearsome world, twentieth-century world, given all the things that have happened ... I think the twentieth-century is very different from the nineteenth-century, therefore, although to understand the origins of modern social thought you must come to terms with authors like those three. It's no good supposing you can just use any of them as a basis any longer for our overall perspective on what's happened. Many of the things that have come about either they couldn't have predicted or certainly they didn't, I think, adequately grasp (...) In *Capitalism and Modern Social Theory* one of the things I tried to stress and still would stress is that those three writers also held very different views not just in the content of their ideas but in the nature of their careers and what they were doing. Weber and Weber's writings don't fall into any single easily identifiable category in my opinion. If I was going to look for some sort of simple characterisation it wouldn't be that [BM; determinism] one, that is I wouldn't try and link Weber to some kind of deterministic view of history - whatever deterministic means - I'd be inclined I suppose to think the opposite, that Weber was very alive to contingent changes that have affected the courses of world history ... very much concerned with unintended consequences of events that nobody really foresaw, and concerned with the results of struggle and military power that don't really fall into any easy framework of history. I'm not favourable I suppose to the new interpretations of Weber which try to put Weber into an evolutionary framework. I'm much more inclined to emphasise the historical aspects of Weber's writings. That is to see Weber as an historical writer, as someone who was always very alive to the switchways of history as it were, switchways which have pushed different societies on different paths. But Weber was such a complicated person I think, that one should resist any simple characterisation of his writings. I don't think that's true of Durkheim. One can set out a very coherent and a fairly consistent appraisal

106

of what Durkheim was doing ... Durkheim had a definite sociological programme and he very self-consciously advocated that programme, trying to show how it would work out in particular forms of study. He changed his views certainly in some respects, but I didn't think he abandoned the essentials of that stance, within which he produced a very sophisticated style of sociological reasoning. The boundaries of his work were fairly clearly defined, he had a definite school of followers and in some part was consciously interested in building up a group of followers who would follow Durkheimian methods ... Weber was always much more ambivalent and difficult about such things.

Can you talk a little about the 'great divide' which you discuss in your article on the 'four myths in social theory' [1977, pp. 208-34]?

What I was attacking, in relation to that, was the idea that there's a major watershed at some point between a time in which the social sciences were philosophical and speculative and where they became scientific and therefore took on the mantle of something similar to the natural sciences ... It seemed to me that kind of view has been repeated across the generations at least from Montesquieu onwards, maybe even from Vico onwards, and the fact that it's been repeated is some reason to be a bit cautious about it. But I've tried to show that in fact it is a myth in the sense of being a false version of what social sciences can be like, that is, it's not just historically an invalid account. I think ... it's a logically suspect claim that there is that kind of divide. In my opinion philosophical issues are necessarily relevant to the social sciences - without at the same time at all implying that they're not empirical. I just don't believe that there is such a period at which there was this transformation, and the reason I don't believe it is that I don't believe analytically it's valid that such transformation is possible. So therefore you're quite right to pick it up. I think it's quite important because it connects some of the stuff I wrote on the history of social thought with other material that I've been writing on the logical status of the social sciences.

(...) What about the myth of the 'problem of order'?

The 'problem of order', as defined by Parsons anyway, is a specific way of formulating what sociology and the social sciences should be about, and depends upon a very specific version of how the concepts of social science should be organised. According to Parsons this is in terms of coping with the fundamental issue of how it is that a society coheres in the face of potentially conflicting interests. Now I think that Parsons is quite right to show that in the eighteenth-century certain ways of formulating such a problem were misconceived, but then wrong to suppose that it remains as *the* fundamental problem for the social sciences. What I try to do in the article you have in mind and also in subsequent books is actually to dismember it and to reformulate the problem of order. I see it as primarily a problem not of how a society coheres but how it comes about that societies stretch across time-space, that is how they are constituted and reconstituted temporally and spatially, and I don't see that as having any intrinsic connection with contractual theory, with Hobbes, or therefore with the counter version of that - Parsons' theory of consensus. I think that the problem of what a society *is* is much more difficult to formulate than anyone who belongs to that tradition does, and therefore I think it's awfully important actually to get away from the idea that that formulation of the problem of order is somehow *the* basic problem for sociology. That's again I think somewhat part of an American-European divide, because it's primarily in American sociology I'd say that 'the problem of order is the problem of sociology'. There is less inclination to see things this way in Europe. But that's where that 'schism' thing came from, because it was in reaction to Parsons's view that writers like Dahrendorf, Lockwood and Rex invented 'conflict theory' and 'coercion theory'. In my view that's an extension of that idea of the problem of order. It seems to me that if the original notion isn't viable then the idea of complementing it with another one simply complicates the situation, and compounds the difficulty in the original formulation. So I've never been at all happy with that sort of division, which I think is the kind of disguised version of Marxism versus an orthodox sociology, conflict versus consensus theory. In the United States it still has quite a strong hold ... lots of sociologists there still believe in something called 'conflict theory' and see it as a sort of adventurous form of social science, and I suppose Randall Collins' book [1975] is probably the main organising focus for that. It's interesting to remark that it's quite a famous book in American sociology but I would say virtually unknown in Europe (...)

Okay, the New Rules. *In the conclusions where you're summarising the 'new rules' you say that 'the production and reproduction of society ... has to be treated as a skilled performance on the part of its members' [1976, p. 160]. Do I gather that ethnomethodology is quite important for you?*

Well for me ethnomethodology is much more important than probably most writers working outside the specifically designated ethnomethodological tradition. *Much more important* in my opinion. That having been said, it wouldn't be true to say that I just draw uncritically upon ethnomethodology. I regard some of the insights of ethnomethodology as comparable to those which you can draw from other sources, and I've tried to draw from those as well. These include continental hermeneutics, especially hermeneutic phenomenology and the later Wittgenstein. Some of the philosophical implications of those traditions are much more profound than those of ethnomethodology. But I think ethnomethodology is important for at least two reasons. One is that it's in the forefront of those schools of social theory which have recovered to importance of mundane actors as knowledgeable about what they do and why they do it. In that sense ethnomethodology is a sort of empirical programme of the later Wittgenstein's philosophical method - I regard it as that -although that's a crude formulation - an attempt to put into practice an empirical study of the idea that all of us know a great deal about why we act, about the condition of our actions, and even about the consequences of our actions. A lot of this knowledge is tacit, it's not knowledge which you can discursively formulate. This view of the social actor I think is simply repressed in most orthodox schools of social thought and ethnomethodology is extremely significant from that angle. But second I think ethnomethodology is important for the specific contributions that it's made to the constitution of meaning, the nature of what meaning is. Meaning is related to the situated nature of human activities, and the modes in which contextuality is implied in making talk and making things happen. What I try to do - especially in my most recent book, *The Constitution of Society* - is to try to show how we might develop a view of social analysis which recognises the knowledgeability of social actors, but at the same time acknowledges the bounds of that knowledgeability, and thereby allows you to use some of these insights in a context which doesn't sacrifice institutional study. It's a fundamental error to suppose ethnomethodology is about trivial things, and it's an equally fundamental error to think it's not historical. To me what it does is expose to view some of the main foundations of social institutions. So for example Garfinkel's notorious experiments with *trust* I think are really brilliant, because they show that apparently very trivial features of talk and conversation have extraordinary moral binding force, and that they are integral to the institutional components of what society is like. And I think Goffman's work is similar in this respect. It's quite wrong to suppose that Goffman is a sort of portrayer of a cynical society of role-players. What Goffman does is to illuminate some of the most fixed and constraining aspects of social institutions. Again he's fundamentally a historical thinker - not 'historical' in the sense of charting out a sort of sequence of development of a particular society, but 'historical' in showing how temporality is involved in the way in which human institutions work.

(...) Another thing you say from New Rules *is that 'the realm of human agency is bounded. Men produce society, but they do so as historically located actors, and not under conditions of their own choosing' [1976, p. 160]. How different is that from Marx and 'men make history ...'?*

Well in *The Constitution of Society* I use that celebrated phrase 'human beings make history but not under conditions of their own choosing', arguing that that's an unobjectionable statement, but when you try to tease out its implications it becomes extraordinarily complicated. What each of the terms involved mean has to be thought through in detail. What 'human beings' are, that is, how you theorise them as agents; what the 'making' involves in making history is; and also what 'history' is because that's not at all easy to puzzle through. I've built the whole book really around trying to work through those three elements of Marx's statement. It doesn't in any way mean it's a Marxist book, but yes I regard that statement as a sort of pithy statement of what social life is like, although terribly difficult to amplify.

(...) If we turn to Profiles and Critiques *you say that 'in the theory of structuration, I argue that neither subject (human agent) nor object ("society", or social institutions) should be regarded as having primacy. Each is constituted in and through recurrent practices' [1982, p. 8]. So in other words 'action versus structure' is a non-debate, yes?*

Well it's a non-debate, I think it's just been miscast as a discussion of the relationship between either 'society' and the 'individual' or 'subject' and 'object' or whatever kind of terminology is used. I don't think it's a mistaken focus for analysis because I can't see how you could ever do social

110

science without having some kind of grasp of the relationship between the two, what I've tried to show is that the one presupposes the other (...) My view is that the social sciences certainly have been divided between two traditions. One accords some kind of primacy to institutions, and talks in terms of structure and constraint. It has been quite good at analyzing institutions but rather bad at analyzing human action because human beings appear as basically 'socially caused' in some way, socially constrained. On the other side there are those traditions which tend to accord primacy to the agent - which do treat the agent in some sense as knowledgeable about what that agent does and which are quite often quite good at analyzing human beings as actors. But these traditions are not very good at analyzing institutions and don't talk much about constraint, structure, conflict, power, and so on ... What I've tried to argue is that the two traditions have been in opposition, but that it's a mistake to treat them as mutually exclusive. We have to theorise the main concepts involved differently from the traditional usages on both sides. We must rethink what agency is, what it is to know why you act as you do, and what it is you know when you know why you act as you do, on the one hand; and on the other to reconceptualise what structure is, what structural properties of social systems are and how they exist. And I've tried, I suppose, to break away from various sorts of pre-existing imagery in relation to structure and action, to break away from the idea that social structure is like the walls of a room, which you may collide with, and which constrain you in a quasi-physical sense. That doesn't seem to me to be of much use in relation to a theory of action ... I've also tried to break away from theories of action which failed to situate action in some kind of time-space context. Most philosophical theories of action just talk about intentions and reasons as though they were discrete elements of activity, whereas it seems to me perfectly obvious that social life unfolds across time and space, it's a continuous thing. Day-to-day life is a duration.

(...) *What are the empirical implications of 'structuration' theory?*

I'm fairly clear about what the empirical implications are. Of course it doesn't follow that any kind of social analysis which is primarily theoretical *does* have immediate empirical implications, and one can't judge it wholly in those terms. Therefore I think it is wrong to suppose that that's the only criterion in terms of which to judge a theoretical interpretation of the social sciences. We must assess it also in terms of its coherency, in terms of what

111

kind of problems it generates, in terms of what kind of insights it might offer. However I do think the theory of 'structuration' does have quite powerful empirical implications, which can quite easily be pointed out by critical reference to existing forms of social science ... and it's best if I just list them. One main respect I think in which a great deal of empirical science is misconceived is that it simply fails to recognise large areas of human knowledgeability. For example a researcher will go along to someone say working on a production line and ask 'what do you think of your work?', 'are you happy in your work?', and the worker says 'well it's okay, you get used to it after a few hundred years'. The sociologist marks down 'well adjusted to labour' or whatever. To me that ignores this tremendously important arena of human knowledgeability which is carried in types of discourse which sociologists often ignore - humour, irony, wit, and so on [Willis, 1977]. Secondly much existing empirical work ignores the vast areas of tacit knowledgeability which agents have about the nature of their activities. Such things have to be studied empirically, otherwise the result is that as soon as you find that someone is not very good at talking about why they act as they do, you immediately start looking for structural forces that somehow constrain them. That's one reason why many people are rightly suspicious of the claims of sociologists, who suggest they are being moved by forces which they don't understand or control. They *may* be being moved by such forces but they often know far more about what they're up to than sociologists give them credit for, although they cannot explain what they know discursively.

All social research, as it were, has 'an ethnographic moment' which is the correlative of the 'hermeneutic moment' looked at in terms of analytical social theory. That is, all social research - even if it's questionnaire research or highly statistical research - presupposes an ethnography. When studying one's own culture this may be largely an implicit ethnography - some kind of unwritten understanding of the reasons and intentions people have for acting the way they do. Uncovering that ethnography is absolutely crucial to empirical research. I don't believe that this in any way comprises the use of statistical methods or hard-nosed empirical research, to recover the whole area of human knowledgeability, its discursive expressions and its tacit expressions. Second, I think that it's essential to do empirical research which picks up the unintended consequences of human activities without treating them in a functionalist mode - either defining problems functionally or attempting to explain their outcomes functionally. I'd regard Willis's book as a very good example of this. One of the attractions of Willis's book [*Learning to Labour*, 1977] is that it conforms to these two criteria. It does take the agents seriously in terms of giving a range of expressions of their discourse, it does take them seriously as knowledgeable agents. But also it recognises that they do things that have consequences in contexts which range beyond what those agents actually know about, and that these consequences influence the overall institutional structure of capitalist society. They don't do so because of any functional need, they do so because of an interestingly paradoxical consequence. Because these kids are particularly knowledgeable about school - because they're contesting its authority all the time - they take up jobs which are relatively unrewarding. Since they in some part 'understand' their fate, they actively bring it about. The result is something which is 'functional for capitalism'. But it would be hopeless and quite wrong to suppose that there is any necessarily functionalist element in it. I would want to promote empirical research which is sensitive in those respects - which investigates unintended consequences while discarding any kind of functionalist framing of empirical research. Third, I think that structuration theory stands in opposition to any kind of research which supposes that you can have universal laws of social life. In my opinion knowledge of social life is part of what social life is, and that breaks any kind of *universal* connection you could establish between say what happens in a car factory in one country and what happens in a car factory in another. You *can* generalise in the social sciences, but all generalisations operate through certain mixes of intended and unintended consequences of activities. They are malleable in terms of what people think and know about what they are up to. Therefore the programme of formulating a set of analytical laws of some kind in social science is simply a futile programme ... and a potentially alienating one because it again suggests an analysis of social milieux which is inaccurate, and makes them appear as more fixed and solid than they really are. This has relevance, for example, to the 'Luton' [*Affluent Worker*] experience. Important aspects of the workers' attitudes and behaviour somehow hadn't been picked up in that research - suddenly these workers were on strike.

(...) *Frank Parkin's 'Reply to Giddens': 'social analysis requires an examination of the range of potential choices, and the kinds of constraint brought into play, as these occur in specific social contexts. Although both are important, they are nevertheless different things; the language we use*

113

must therefore signify this difference. An "integrated terminology", whatever that might be, seems like a recipe for doing just the opposite' [1980, p. 893]. Has he misunderstood you?

Yes. Well I'm prepared to agree this platitude thus stated, of course. But once you start to examine it, and pursue what's involved, then you are at the heart of some of the most important, difficult and complex issues in social science. Once you start to seriously examine these problems, it no longer becomes a platitude, but on the contrary it can be extremely demanding. Generations of social scientists have wrestled with such matters precisely because they are at the core of what defines the character of the social sciences (...)

Why was Peter Winch's The Idea of a Social Science *[1958] so important in the 60s and the 70s? Or was it?*

Winch's book *was* important and *is* important because at the time it was a very unusual book. When it was first published [1958], the dominant view was one I have often described as the 'orthodox-consensus'. Most writers in the social sciences believed that social sciences were something like natural sciences, give or take a few differences. It was a long while since anyone had set out a sophisticated version of a radically different view - as Winch did. In doing so he helped fuel the modern debate which has been swelled by the recovery of hermeneutics, by ethnomethodology and other schools of thought that we've talked about. Personally I think that some of the claims that Winch makes are valid and have to be defended. I don't consider that the programme - as far as there is one - for the social sciences which his book contains is coherent. The book has major shortcomings, but some of the ideas in it are essential. The book was very important in its context, because it provided a partially valid characterisation of a viewpoint which was at that time very unfashionable. Why it's been so much the centre of the debate I think is partly accidental ... If you look at the writings of the later Wittgenstein, Wittgenstein made, as it were, a move in his writings towards a quite strongly sociological position. If it's true that language is primarily a phenomenon of social practice - that is, it's in the forms of life and social activities that language is enmeshed and is intelligible - then it's surely true that there's a strong sociological component to what philosophy is. Now Wittgenstein himself focused most of the comments he made about the social sciences upon psychology and quite a few of his earlier followers, Melden, Peters - and Charles Taylor a bit later - chose to focus those ideas primarily on psychology. Winch was the only writer, I think, who focused directly on the social sciences, and for that reason his book achieved a peculiar pre-eminence in the literature.

Rex, in a recent review of contemporary British sociology, argues that 'Giddens' work represents in a very striking form the philosophization of sociology, even though Giddens claims that his work has major significance for the understanding of late capitalism and communism' [1983, p. 1008]. Could you talk a little about the 'boundaries' of philosophy and sociology?

Well how I'd answer that sort of question is to say that it seems to me to be essential for people who work in the social sciences to be alive to philosophical problems. That is, I don't think you can do social science effectively without being clued into philosophical debates, because at the heart of the social sciences are major difficulties in characterising what human beings are like and what human agency is. Such questions are in some part philosophical, and to be alert to what philosophers are writing about those issues seems to me important. This isn't at all the same as arguing that the social sciences are essentially philosophical in some sort of unique fashion. That's the sort of claim Winch made and I don't think it's at all valid. So when I say that social sciences have to be alert to philosophical questions I don't at all mean to collapse them into philosophy. What I write is not a surrogate philosophy of some sort. Nearly all my work is centred upon a fairly coherent range of empirical issues in fact. These issues certainly have much to do with what Rex calls late capitalism - how you characterise modern societies, indeed how you characterise the tremendous break with the past which has been initiated from the late eighteenth-century. What are the implications of such analyses for practical political programmes? ... these things I see as basic to what I do (...) I try to skirt epistemological issues especially. What I'm trying to produce is, as it were, an ontology of human society as a theory of action and structure. There's probably been too much philosophising about epistemological questions of truth, validity, falsification and so on. I am not so interested in those as in developing a coherent account of agency and structure for problems of concrete sociological analysis. So I resist very strongly the idea actually that what I do is some kind of misconceived philosophy. That's one of the reasons that in *The Constitution of Society* I've got a long section trying to detail out the implications of structuration theory for empirical research. I actually think it's a very odd accusation because it depends upon the idea that there is some way of or some sense in keeping empirical work untainted by philosophical considerations. I think the opposite really; most of the best empirical research is done by people who have quite acute theoretical sensitivity. Willis's work is a very good example of that (...) In *The Constitution of Society* I try to rescue Goffman as a theorist. I think Goffman is a very systematic theorist, not just a brilliant ethnographic observer, so I do see these things as tied up with each other pretty closely.

Right, I'll move you on to Positivism and Sociology *the book you edited in 1974. In the introduction you make the point that there are three sets of issues specifically pertinent to positivism in sociology; one I think we have already gone through - can the procedures of natural science be directly adapted to sociology, and are the subject matters the same? Well clearly they weren't, but we've gone through that ...*

Well have we gone through it enough to make it clear to people reading this?

Well okay, we'll go through the three; are the subject matters the same?; is the goal of sociological analysis to formulate law-like generalisations?; has 'sociology' a technical character, and is sociology like natural science neutral? The one I'm particularly interested in is the final one, but if you want to go through the first and second you can.

Well I just wanted to make sure that if you do write this stuff up that ...

... it comes out verbatim.

Well it's quite common for commentators on my work to suppose that I'm arguing that the natural and social sciences are completely discrepant, and that I'm arguing for a form of humanism. Actually I'm not.

116

I think that you've already said what the subject matter of sociology is, and how it cannot be examined in natural scientific terms. I think you've said that clearly.

Yes. Okay with the proviso ...

(...) Well on the issue of 'law-like generalisations' Merton himself thought that perhaps law-like general theories can come about through a collection of middle-range theories put together. Presumably your argument would be that that is not a fruitful goal of sociology?

Well my argument would be that it's logically wrong. Merton apparently used to believe - I don't know if he now does not - that there probably could be law-like generalisations in the social sciences. However, in his view it's very hard to get the material to prove them and they tend to be very abstract. Therefore it's better to go for these 'middle-range generalisations', which can be tested. I don't attach any such particular importance to 'middle-range generalisations'. My opinion is that there are generalisations of many kinds in the social sciences which are perfectly valid. Such generalisations have a logical form substantially discrepant from laws in the natural sciences, whether these be universal laws or whether they be statistical-type laws. The difference is in the nature of connections which they presuppose, something which comes back to what I was talking about before ... In social science to generalise about something means generalising also about people's knowledge of the circumstances of the action involved. All generalisations are generalisations that link what people know about what they are doing with the boundaries of that knowledge, and the things that influence them beyond those boundaries. Those things are not fixed, they can't be fixed because they depend in some part upon what people precisely do know about the conditions and outcomes of their action. Therefore generalisations in the social sciences are certainly more limited, more contextual than most sociologists are prepared to acknowledge.

The third issue is whether sociology has a technical character. Could you discuss this in relation to Habermas's views?

You mean how Habermas's view relates to it?

117

Yes.

Because I think my view is different from Habermas and Habermas's own views change, the answer might be a bit confusing. Habermas's earlier writings in *Knowledge and Human Interests* [1972] involve a definite view of the association of scientific-type knowledge with attempts at technical control and prediction. He argues that where those kinds of interests become the only ones accepted as justifiable - as in positivistic philosophy, in modern politics and modern culture - claims to knowledge become ideological. Other perfectly legitimate questions which concern the moral role of science and a range of other issues about the uses to which science is put, are excluded. That was his position in his earlier writings. In his later writings he has modified that position. Perhaps he even no longer believes that there are 'knowledge constitutive interests'. It seems as though he's abandoned the attempt to handle the issues in that kind of way. He now sees them against the background of an ideal speech situation as being embodied in language, and treats this as a sort of conceptual yardstick in terms of which ideological implications of social practice can be as it were measured out. My view? I don't think one is likely to reach a systematic treatment of such issues which is going to be satisfying to everybody. I don't accept the notion of an ideal speech situation. Moreover, I don't really hold it either necessary or possible to build the kind of epistemological position from which you can sally out confidently in the world and say what is a valid judgement and what isn't ... So my view about the practical implications of the social sciences comes back to the idea that social science is itself a form of knowledge about agents who are themselves already knowledgeable. I think it's necessarily 'political' because anything you claim to say about the origins of human conduct is a claim which can affect the nature of that conduct. That means that there is no way of severing off, as it were, the practical implications of social science from what it is that social scientists do when they describe or attempt to explain things ... and to me a whole nest of interesting issues centring around the so-called value-freedom debate and so on have to do with that. The issues involved there are very complicated. The social sciences are a constituent part of the society they claim to analyze. Social science isn't just a way of studying modern society, it's become constitutive of what modern societies are like. For example economics only exists because of certain forms of behaviour influenced by the taking over of some of the concepts that the economists themselves invented. That kind of double-hermeneutical relation is a really basic thing in what social science is about. Complicated to pursue, but exceedingly important. From it you can argue that the traditional view - that natural science has influenced the world a lot; while the social sciences haven't, and that the social sciences have few practical implications - might be totally wrong, if you see that social science and the concepts of social science help to constitute the reality they describe. An example I use in *The Constitution of Society* is Machiavelli and others on sovereignty. The discourse of sovereignty is a new kind of discourse that comes into being at a certain particular period, but it's not just a description of what's going on, it helps to actually constitute and inform new types of state. It becomes part and parcel of what a modern state is. That 'citizens' have some kind of concept of sovereignty seems to me to be essential to the modern state but not to traditional states. If that's true - and it is only one example among many others which could be afforded - social science has fundamentally influenced its subject matter, in a way which doesn't have a parallel in the natural sciences. The 'practical' character of social science is fundamental to its character.

In Central Problems *you say 'we cannot treat the natural and the social sciences as* two independently constituted forms of intellectual endeavour' *[1979, p. 259]. What do you mean by that?*

That's exactly what I wanted to talk about before, because it bears upon how I would situate my views in the debate about whether the social sciences and the natural sciences are similar. My argument is that modern philosophy and social theory lead one to reformulate the nature of *both* social and natural science *simultaneously*. It wouldn't be true to argue that I'm claiming that social science is radically unlike natural science. What I'm claiming is that the traditional model of social science was formulated against a background of a particular model of natural science, both of which are now compromised. So that you are, as it were, changing two parameters at the same time, redefining natural science as involving far more to do with intelligibility, meaning frames, even ordinary conversation (...) The social sciences are being redefined at the same time through developments we talked about earlier. That means that it's not just a question of saying social science is a much more humanistic discipline than many social scientists used to think it was. It means saying that in some respects social sciences and natural sciences do share a similar logic, do share some interests while in other respects they don't, and each of these things is the case in rather different respects from those traditionally discussed. I regard that as a sort of logical parallel to changing the axis(es) of the action-structure dualism and making it a duality.

In the New Rules of Sociological Method *you say 'there is no way of justifying a commitment to scientific rationality rather than, say, to Zande sorcery, apart from premises and values which science itself presupposes' [1976, p. 140]. Can you expand, and relate it to the Kuhn, Popper, et al., stream of thought?*

I would like to make two comments on this. One isn't so much to do with the content, as the context, of the remark. As I said before, I think there has in recent years been a tendency in social theory to concentrate too exclusively on this type of issue. I take a more reserved position with regard to these debates than many writers do, and I don't regard the core of social theory as to do with epistemological problems. I'm fairly sympathetic with the idea that the traditional aims of epistemology are perhaps suspect and that nowadays one can't have an epistemology in the traditional sense - that is, the theory of knowledge which can somehow be founded, can have some foundations that could be agreed upon. I'm fairly sympathetic to the movement away from epistemology in that sense. But as regards the grounding of science and justification of belief in science I'm afraid my views are fairly conventional. I'm inclined towards a realist position, in the sense of the 'new realism' so-called. I think there are mechanisms to be described in the world and that these can be described accurately. The criteria of describing them, the modes of testing out empirical descriptions, are basically fairly stock and orthodox - that is they're to do with describing things in a way which others can interpret, criticise, repeat if necessary. I take these to be quite compatible with all the emphasis upon the hermeneutic components of social analysis that I also make.

(...) Right, a different question. With Mick Mann I was talking about history and sociology, and he was saying that rather than sociology being, you know, the handmaiden of history if you like, sociology was 'the queen of the sciences'. In that vein how do you see the relationship between philosophy and sociology?

I see philosophy as a resource which anyone interested in social and natural science can use and can contribute to. I see social theory as a core of concerns with human actions, social institutions, social change, shared by all the social sciences. Social Theory is not peculiar to sociology. And I think of the social sciences as logically and methodologically unified, that is I don't think there is any separate logic of history for example which separates history from sociology. I take I think a very radical view on that. I think that the two are the same logically and methodologically; there is no such thing as historical sociology.

(...) So it's just an institutional or academic separation?

When you are talking about 'history' then there are all sorts of interesting problems raised about time and temporality. We tend naively to think that history is about change. That is manifestly not right. History is about time, and time is about stability as much as change, you could write a history of stability as it were. All these issues are intrinsically social theory because you couldn't have 'social order' without some kind of persistence across time and space.

(...) In your book Sociology *[1982a] you say that sociology 'necessarily has a subversive quality'. Now I know you go on to talk about its critical faculties, but when you say 'subversive' what were you thinking of?*

What I was thinking of was the phenomenon which we were discussing before. That is, when you study social life, you're not studying independently given phenomena which exist apart from the knowledge people have of it. Therefore, when you contribute new knowledge or you claim to do so, you're claiming in principle that the world can be different.

One of the definitions of sociology that I like is Norbert Elias's; sociologists - like other scientists - 'are destroyers of myths' [1978, p. 52], or is it more than that?

Yes I think it is more than that. That's a bit like what you might suppose natural science does. Natural science shows you that, whereas one might

121

think that the world is flat, it isn't. Social science can show you that the beliefs that people have about society are wrong. But I think that there is something more fundamental. When you make a claim that a certain state of affairs is the case it has implicit consequences for what actors do. That isn't the same in the natural sciences - atoms don't read text books about themselves. In the social sciences the most interesting theories are ones liable to be picked up and acted upon by the very people they're about. If you just think that the role of the social sciences is to just demystify then accomplishments are limited. If you see the role of social sciences always as a dialogue with what it is they're about - that is people's beliefs and activities - then they are much much more fundamental.

That's fine. You talk about the sociological imagination, using your terms rather than C. Wright Mills. You say the sociological imagination is related to several forms of sensibility, these forms of sociological imagination are historical, anthropological, and critical sensitivities. I know what historical and anthropological sensitivities are concerned with. The third one is interesting for me because you say it 'concerns the possibilities for the future', then you expand and say 'as human beings, we are not condemned to be swept along by forces that have the inevitability of the laws of nature. But this means we must be conscious of the alternative futures *that are potentially open to us. In its third sense, the sociological imagination fuses with the task of sociology in contributing to* the critique of existing forms of society' *[1982a, p. 26] - is this what you've been saying?*

Yes that is exactly what I've been saying. I was a bit hesitant to use the term 'sociological imagination' because it has became a banal term with over-use. I do think when you make a claim about what the social world is like you disclose a possible mode in which it could be different. When you do any interesting research you disclose a possible form of life which could be lived and which might be discrepant from the lives people live at the moment. Rather than repressing that, like orthodox science does, and saying this is a bit of a nuisance that people get to know about what we write about them and react on it, we have to treat it as essential to what social science is about. It is a claim to know better than people already do why they act as they do, that's why it has this 'political' power, this constitutive political power, not just demythologising political power.

Okay. You say 'I think it's important for critical social theory ... to outflank Marx from the left' and that 'there seems to me to be four further sets of questions leading to human emancipation which are inadequately analyzed both in Marx's and Marxist texts [1982a, p. 169]; so the four areas where Marx is to be outflanked, the problem areas are: the need for ecological radicalism, the problem of racial and ethnic aggression, the problems of sexual aggression, the problem of state power and its association with the propagation of violence. So do you see critical sociology as something which can outflank Marx? What would it look like as a theory?

I don't think there is a thing called 'critical sociology' because I think the moment of critique to be logically implied in social science. I am cautious about all such terms as 'radical' or 'critical' sociology. A lot of nonsense is written under those labels.

So sociology is then potentially a more powerful intellectual critique than Marxism?

Yes. Well particular versions of it anyway.

Okay tell me which versions. Also what would sociology lead to in terms of the transformation of, or the emancipation of society?

Well that's very difficult because it's such an all embracing question. Going back to the four things you mentioned, first of all one needs an account of industrialised countries and their relationships to the Third World which recognises that these issues can't be treated in a class-reductive fashion. For me that means an essentially post-Marxist standpoint, if you like. Second, in order to cope with them one needs a fusion of analysis with critique in the sense of having a more effective and embracing concept of *exploitation* than is available in Marxism, which again tends to be class-reductive. I don't think I've made that much progress towards working that out. However in the third volume of *Contemporary Critique* I'm seeking to elaborate a concept of exploitation that allows us to cope with various institutional forms of domination while not reducing exploitation to some kind of valueless formula ... Third, I think that in our times you no longer can suppose that there is a single agency of change producing a satisfactory type of social system. We have to recognise the modern world is both highly unified and highly fragmented and it's a world in which survival is the first premise in my opinion (...) some of the most under-analyzed areas of the social sciences are to do with the control of the means of violence, with territoriality, and the emergence of the modern nation state. I think Marxism is as deficient as traditional liberalism in dealing with these issues. Yet we live in a world in which there is just this fantastic escalation of violence. It's a world which I think is very remote from the world which sociologists portray in text books, which rarely give war and violence the role which they manifestly play in modern history. I try in the second volume of *Contemporary Critique* to produce an account of the origins of the nation state, and the significance of control, the means of violence in the hands of standing armies - of how it came to be that we live in a world which is so different from the nineteenth-century world, because that goes right back to the beginning of what we were talking about ... neither Marx nor Durkheim, and to a limited extent maybe Weber projected a world which is like the world in which we live, one ridden between nation states and superpower blocs with unbelievable military power. This also bears on normative political theory. We must pose the question 'what would a society in which there was democratic control and means of violence look like?' as a counterfactual question that sociology can investigate ... It's an extremely difficult issue. One can see some sense in nineteenth-century scenarios about reforming industry: that is, returning the control of the means of production to workers. Workers' self-management with all its defects, makes some kind of sense, and modern technology could in principle relieve people of the worst kinds of oppressive labour. But there are no direct parallels with regard to the control of weaponry. To suppose you can return control of weaponry to the populace is a fantasy now, but in the nineteenth-century it was a characteristic idea Marx really believed - the arming of the workers. No one can believe in that any longer as a means of controlling the escalation of the means of waging war. There's an asymmetrical relationship between the traditional political theory which we have inherited and *the* fundamental political problem facing the world - the escalation of military violence in the hands of the nation states.

(...) What I was going to ask you, this is a narcissistic question ... obviously you've been influential, but how would you like your influence to be used? What would you like to be influential about?

Yes, I suppose I'm fairly ambitious and seek to be influential in the three areas where I regard my writing has been concentrated ... I would like what I've written on the history of classical social theory to be taken seriously as an attempt at a scholarly re-examination of what we regard as classical texts. I still think of myself as having scholarly interests in the past development of social thought. I'd like to develop, much further than I have done, an account of the main institutions of industrialised countries, and that is why I am writing this three-volume *Contemporary Critique*. Traditional concerns with capitalism and industrialism need to be complemented by other things which we've talked about. Third I hope the general account of social science that I've provided in structuration theory does actually provide some illumination for people who think about theoretical issues and also who attempt more basic empirical research. I think it's important to make connections with the people that sociology is supposed to be about. That is I do think it is important to write little introductory books and to do the sort of work as you said earlier that people would dismiss as 'pop sociology'. I'm very much against the protection of social science as a kind of restricted discourse (...)

5 Howard S. Becker

Professor of Sociology at the University of Washington, Seattle and formerly MacArthur Professor of Arts and Sciences, Northwestern University, Evanston, Illinois, Howard Becker is a sociologist of wide interests and abilities, although he is normally associated solely with 'labelling theory'.

Born in 1928 in Chicago, the city which so moved Weber when he first visited the USA in 1904, and of which he spoke of (in Gerth and Mills, 1970, p. 15)

> the Greek shining the Yankee's shoes for five cents, the German acting as his waiter, the Irishman managing his politics, and the Italian digging his dirty ditches. With the exception of some exclusive residential districts, the whole gigantic city, more extensive than London, is like a man who skin has been peeled off, and whose entrails one sees at work ...

Becker fused his abilities as a jazz musician and a sociologist in his first paper, published in 1951, 'The Professional Dance Musician and His Audience' (*American Journal of Sociology*). True to Chicago tradition, his approach has always been that of symbolic interactionism and indeed in 1980 he was awarded the Charles Horton Cooley Award, Society for the Study of Symbolic Interaction.

In 1961 Becker published with Blanche Geer, Everett C. Hughes and Anselm

Strauss *Boys in White: Student Culture in Medical School*, and two years later *Outsiders* (1963) in which he developed 'labelling theory'. Downes, commenting on *Outsiders*, argues that 'this central organising principle - "Deviant behaviour is that which is so labelled" - superficially a banal and even trivial assertion, caused an explosion in the petrified forest of criminology' (1979, p. 3). Some of the consequences of the approach were that of taking the viewpoint of the actor, an examination of the *reaction* to crime, and the taking of sides, invariably that of the underdog. Labelling was criticised from both left and right, but surely Plummer is correct when he asserts that 'the labelling perspective constitutes neither theory nor proposition, but is a useful series of problems designed to reorientate the [former mainstream] study to the consideration of the *nature, emergence, application* and *consequences* of deviancy labels' (1979, p. 88). The consequences of partisanship, or taking sides, led to both another Becker publication 'Whose Side Are We On?' (1967), and a public dispute with Alvin Gouldner.

The question of 'values and sociology' is of course a vexed issue and one which has received considerable attention from Weber's initial value-free position (see Turner and Factor, 1984). The dilemma, of course, is that we have got to accept as 'though they were observation statements about the world, descriptive statements which are full of meaning and value', and moreover the fact that the 'question of what is problematic in the world depends upon what states of affairs one sees out there' (Rex, 1975, p. 11). Gouldner in an oft-quoted article 'Anti-Minotaur: The Myth of a Value-Free Sociology' (1963), argued that if sociologists 'ought not to express their personal values in the academic setting, how then are students to be safeguarded against the unwitting influence of these values which shape the sociologist's selection of problems, his preferences for certain hypotheses or conceptual schemes, and his neglect of others. For these are unavoidable and, in this sense, there is and can be no value-free sociology' (orig. 1962, 1963, p. 51). An earlier 'classic' position on the matter is contained in appendix two of Myrdal's *An American Dilemma* where he asserts that (1944, p. 1043)

> There is no other device for excluding biases in social sciences than to face the valuations and to introduce them as explicitly stated, specific, and sufficiently concretized value premises.

There is no doubt that this issue of the 'limits within which value commitment can be allied to objective methods of study' (Halsey, 1982, p. 175) has continued to trouble sociologists, and it is in this context that Becker wrote his piece. He began by arguing that it was a false assumption to imagine that it was possible to do research 'uncontaminated by personal and political sympathies. I propose to argue that it is not possible and, therefore, that the question is not whether we should take sides, since we inevitably will, but rather whose side are we on' (orig. 1967, 1971, p. 123). He concluded that *he personally* was on the side of the underdog and - in a vein not dissimilar to Myrdal (1971, p. 134) - argued that we should

> take sides as our personal and political commitments dictate, use our theoretical and technical resources to avoid the distortions that might introduce into our work, limit our conclusions carefully, recognise the hierarchy of credibility for what it is, and field as best we can the accusations and doubts that will surely be our fate.

Gouldner was unhappy with Becker's arguments about taking the side of the underdog and in his article 'The Sociologist as Partisan - Sociology and the Welfare State' (orig. 1968, and in 1975) he argued that Becker viewed the underdog as mismanaged, not as someone who suffered or fought back. And moreover that Becker was directing his anger at the caretaking institutions who do the 'mopping up job' rather than the 'master institutions that produce the deviant's suffering'. Gouldner concluded that 'Whose Side Are We On?' had given birth to (1975, p. 49)

> the first version of new establishment sociology, to a sociology compatible with the new character of social reform in the United States today ... It is a sociology that succeeds in solving the oldest problem in personal politics: how to maintain one's integrity without sacrificing one's career, or how to remain a liberal although well-heeled.

This, of course, is quite a different way of saying what Taylor, Walton and Young felt about the labelling perspective, namely that it 'ignored the structure of power and interest' (1973, p. 170). Becker wisely decided not to comment on Gouldner's accusation.

Of course another element of Becker's work, and again in keeping with the Chicago tradition, was his interest in methodology. For example in his informative introduction to Clifford Shaw's *The Jack-Roller* (1966) he notes that attention today is turned away from local ethnography, 'from the massing of knowledge about a single place, its parts, and their connections'. Instead, he notes, we emphasise 'abstract theory-building more than we used to ... and a great loss it will be' (1966, p. ix). Finally, a more recent development in his work is in what can loosely be termed the sociology of art, and indeed in 1982 he published *Art Worlds*, a brilliant and wide-ranging account of art as 'collective activity'. In addition he has regularly exhibited photographs including 'Six Sociologists' in New York, 1976, and more recently 'Exploring Society Photographically' at Evanston, in 1981.

Could you tell me a little about yourself?

I was born in Chicago in 1928 and went to elementary school here in the city of Chicago. I went to high school for two years and then entered the University of Chicago College which you did at the end of two years at secondary school. I went there for three years; I was playing piano by that time, which I started doing professionally when I was about fifteen. So all the way through graduate school, especially, sociology was a kind of hobby, because what I *really* was doing was learning to play the piano and playing piano in taverns in Chicago. I was twenty-three when I got my PhD, and there I was, I always liked to say I was the most educated piano player on 63rd Street. And the question was what line of work I would get into.

What was the PhD on?

On Chicago school teachers, which I published as a series of articles. When I got my PhD I realised maybe there was something serious about this, after all. I hadn't really taken it terribly seriously until then. I was really planning to go into English Literature, but the spring before I went to graduate school I read *Black Metropolis* by Drake and Cayton [1945]

130

and I thought that was terrific. I was really taken with the urban anthropologist or something like that. So I went into sociology. I didn't know any more about sociology than my grandmother.

Can you talk about 'Chicago sociology' at the period when you began?

The people I studied with were Everett Hughes, Herbert Blumer, Louis Wirth, Ernest Burgess, Lloyd Warner. The people I worked closely with were Hughes and Warner. I didn't realise until much later how much I'd been influenced by Blumer but it was very substantial. What a lot of us picked up at Chicago was a combination of Blumer's explication of Mead, Park, *et al.,* and Hughes' practical approach to research. And they both, after all, were students of Park so there was a fundamental harmony in their approach.

And then?

I finished my PhD in 1951 but I didn't have a job. I was 23 years old and people could hire a grown-up for the same price, so there was no point in having a child. I found it quite difficult to get a teaching job. In fact, I didn't. I was making a hundred dollars a week playing the piano, which was more than most of my colleagues were doing from teaching, and then the sociology convention - the ASA convention - was in Chicago that August and I met some people and talked myself into a job at the Institute of Juvenile Research [Chicago] doing what turned out to be my marijuana study. That was a half-time job; I did that, and then the winter of that year, during the Christmas vacation, a Chicago streetcar fell over during a storm onto a car driven by someone who was teaching the Social Science II course at the University of Chicago and they suddenly needed a new teacher. Social Science II had been organised by David Reisman around his interests in 'culture and personality' and there were about 25 people teaching it. There were two lectures a week by various people (we all took turns) and we each had sections, so I taught a couple of sections in that class. I did that for three years. The second year after I graduated, they hired me half-time in the Sociology Department to teach Hughes' fieldwork class and other things while he was on leave.

I did that for two years and then I got a post-doc in Urbana at the University of Illinois. I went there for two years and did work on occupational identities. In the middle of my second year there Hughes called me up and said I should meet him in Kansas City the next day. He said 'there is a possibility of doing research in the medical school here', and I ended up doing that. I was there for seven years working for a non-profit research organisation called Community Studies Incorporated. It was wonderful, just great.

Most people I'd been to graduate school with were a little older than I was, they all got teaching jobs and were busy teaching. I couldn't get a teaching job so I was forced to do research, my job was to do research and write it up and I did. After seven years I'd done a lot of research and written it up. Many of my friends used to feel sorry for me because I didn't have an academic job, but I was really better off. I left Kansas City and went to Stanford for three years in a research institute. I've been at Northwestern since 1965 as a professor, so I avoided all the miseries of the early part of an American academic career, which is terrible.

What was significant about the 'Chicago School', so-called?

I don't think it got to be called the 'Chicago School' until well into the 50s, and then it was to distinguish it from some of the newer programmes. When it was the only school, in the 1930s and 40s, it *was* sociology, Robert Park, Ernest Burgess, that was sociology. There were a few other people. In the 30s, eventually, Parsons trained that generation of Merton, Kingsley Davis, and Robin Williams, they furnished the next generation. After World War II a number of departments became major centres of graduate training. Michigan became competitive with Chicago, Columbia certainly, Harvard. When you've only got one school it didn't have to have a name, when you've got six schools then people see differences, theoretical differences, and methods too; the alternative to the Chicago School came to be viewed as survey research. There was plenty of survey research done at Chicago and Sam Stouffer had been in some sense part of the Chicago thing. There was a bitter dispute between Stouffer and Blumer which you can find in the journals. Blumer was very critical of survey research and Stouffer believed it was the way to the future, and there was a terrible moment at one of the ASA conventions when Blumer read a paper that was very critical of survey research, and Stouffer was the discussant and accused Blumer of being the 'gravedigger of American sociology'. That is, not allowing it to fulfil its potential by being so critical of what *he* regarded as the most important thing. So it got to be called the 'Chicago School' and became identified in the long-run, I think, mainly with Hughes and Blumer as the living representatives of it, because Wirth who would have been another one was dead.

Could you talk a little about qualitative methods?

I really am, in some sense, a student of Park's. I trace my lineage from Simmel-Park-Hughes. Park understood there was a difference between quantitative and qualitative methods but it wasn't either/or, you did whatever seemed suitable and that's always been my position. I don't think you have to choose between those at all. The main advantage of so-called qualitative methods is that you get to change your mind. When you do a quantitative study you're pretty well committed when you design your instrument, that's what you're going to do. You can't, except in the series of studies, profit from anything you learn. If you're half-way through a survey and one of the questions isn't working, you're worried, what are you going to do? You can't change it. Whereas if I learn today something useful from my field research, my observation, I can go out tomorrow and use it. You lose the advantages of standardisation and you gain the advantages of flexibility, it really is a trade-off.

The question of scientific validity ...

The way I treat the questions of validity and reliability, is that I say to myself and to my students: supposing you decide, okay I've done my research, I know this. Now imagine someone who really does not want to believe your conclusions and would prefer very strongly that it not be that way. He says to you, 'I don't believe you', and you say 'why not?', and he says 'because ...'. When he says 'because you have a lousy sample', or you didn't do this or you did do that, what are you going to tell him that will counter that criticism? When you think of what you're going to tell him, then you have to ask yourself if you have the information that will allow you to say that. If you do, you might as well put it in what you write right now.

133

In my view the object is to do your research and write it up in such a way that even someone who does not want to believe you has to say 'Well, I guess you're right'. If somebody says to me 'So you went there on Thursday, they only act that way on Thursday, if you go on a Friday, you'd see something different'. I'd want to say 'No, it wouldn't make any difference, and the reason I know it wouldn't make any difference is ...'. Then I show them.

(...) How influenced were you by Blumers' symbolic interactionism?

The term 'symbolic interactionism' really did not exist when I was a graduate student. Blumer did not use the term until quite late and I think he was a little bemused by the whole thing. But to me, fundamentally, the presumptions that you start out with in Blumer's system are really the basic presumptions of almost any sociology ... things like that people are acting organisms, not reacting organisms, and that the basic thing we study is collective activity, that's what it's about. *How people do things together* (...) Most of these things are not fundamentally different from any other sociological view. I think it's less sectarian than most, which is not to say there isn't a sectarian school of symbolic interactionism, there is. It goes heresy-hunting like all the other schools. The influence on me, was what you got at Chicago when I was there. There was Blumer telling you what the basic theory was in this very abstract way -how collective activity was accomplished, what capabilities had to be imputed to human beings in order for that to happen, what the character of social interaction was, and so on. What you got from Hughes was how you went about studying things, which was a specification of all that in terms that were devised in order to relate to the details of what you observed. And that's right out of Park.

And the best way to learn about sociology is to do it?

Right. The question is whether the point of sociology is to understand what is going on in the world or to make a better theory. Now obviously both are very important, and you might say that the question is one of emphasis; do you make the theory in order to understand the world better, which is what I believe, or do you try and understand the world in order to improve the theory, and there are people who feel that way. I really don't. To me theories can be in conflict and contradictory, up to a point, and I'm certainly not concerned with devising a theoretical scheme that's watertight, error-free, I'm much more concerned with fixing something up which will help me understand what I've been doing. I don't have time for theoretical hair-splitting, I mean I'm just not interested in that.

Have you read much Giddens?

I've read some of Giddens' stuff, not much. I have not read Althusser at all. I read Foucault's *Madness and Civilization* [1967]. I didn't feel I was learning anything I didn't know. The test I apply to theoretical works now is, if I accepted the argument that's being offered here would I have to do something different in my subsequent work? If the answer is no, then I'm not going to bother with it, if it's not going to change my work. I do read things occasionally that make me think I can't do that anymore or I better keep that in mind from now on. But it's more like I find something and I say 'Hey, I can use that', an idea that I can use, incorporate. I once asked Basil Bernstein who I knew knew a lot about linguistics, and this was when Chomsky was getting very big, and I said 'Basil do I have to read Chomsky?', and he thought for a moment and said 'no, nothing he's writing about has anything to do with anything you're interested in, it won't affect you in the least'. That's it.

(...) Erving Goffman. How do you evaluate his work?

That is very hard, because Erving's work in some ways was quite restricted. He was not writing about all of sociology or all of society, he was writing about a certain territory that he'd carved out, the details of interaction. I always thought his work was very useful; take one of his papers which isn't cited often now, 'On Embarrassment' [1972], it focused on what happened in embarrassed interaction. He also specified the conditions under which that would occur, which made it possible to use the existence of embarrassment as a kind of diagnostic tool. If you see embarrassment then you'd better look for this kind of social situation. He didn't much study those organisational situations, except when he did the hospital [*Asylums*, 1961] because that's pretty straightforward old-fashioned ethnographic sociology, it *is* organisational but most of his work wasn't and he would

135

rather take a lot of the organisational stuff more or less as given and then work within that. So I never thought of Erving's work as something that you bill as sociology all by itself, it was just a part, in the same way that you would study the city. I've always thought that his work on *Behaviour in Public Places* [1963], was tremendously important for understanding the character of contemporary urban life, because when you don't know people well enough to know what it means when they do certain things in public then you're well on the way to developing the kind of large-scale paranoia that affects the middle-class in many large cities. I don't think that Erving felt that you had to choose between, let's say, the organisational level I work at and the less-organisational level that he worked at, it was two different parts. I believe he thought of his work as very specialised.

(...) Could you talk a little about sociology and science?

'Science' is a kind of rhetorical device. People will say to you 'that's not science'. I first got onto this from watching people in photography who would say to each other 'that's not photography', which translated, means 'you can't have a job in our department'. It's a kind of political statement, a way of excluding people. I think that the idea of science that I adhere to, because I do understand there's a difference between that and other kinds of enquiry, is that it's like commonsense only more so. You can hear all the basic criticisms made in the course of a scientific discussion in any bar-room argument: sampling, reliability, all the rest of it, it isn't put in our language but it's obviously - 'you only talk about those guys over there, come over here and see something different' - sampling. The thing about scientific work is that it's designed in such a way that many of those criticisms aren't applicable, you get rid of those obvious errors.

Could you talk a little about how British sociology looks to you?

Looking from the outside and knowing very little about it, British sociology by virtue of being so much smaller than sociology in the United States seems much more subject to wider swings of fad and fashions; it's relatively easier for a fad to sweep thirty departments than it is for it to sweep 500 departments. In American sociology there's an enormous middle-ground of people teaching in universities and colleges all over the country who are relatively unaffected by those kinds of things. It's kind of hard to move 2,000 departments in any particular direction.

Can you talk about how you see Marxism in American sociology?

(...) Well, what has happened to Marxism, like many other waves of thought that were designed to totally change American sociology, to revolutionise it, so that all American sociology would be different, is that they have become subject to what someone called ...

... partial incorporation?

Yes, something like partial incorporation, neutralisation, co-optation. What happened with all of them is that they get to be another speciality. In American sociology there is an amalgam of dozens and dozens of different specialities, organised in different ways, and Marxism has become another one. In this country it is also very tightly tied to two or three areas of subject matter, such as the whole business of the dual-labour market.

Okay. Your views of Marx, Durkheim and Weber.

I think that it is unfortunate that any trio of thinkers got enshrined as *the* three people you are supposed to deal with, when there are literally dozens of people who have thought interesting things that might well be the basis of a system of sociology. You could just as easily have a trio of ... Veblen, Simmel and Park, that would be just as interesting.

But American sociology is touched by Marx, Durkheim and Weber ...

Yes, but the difference here is that it gets shunted off into another speciality called 'theory', so that students learn to make a kind of obligatory deferential bow to Durkheim, Marx and Weber, then they go about their business, it has very little to do with the research they do.

137

Is sociology simply what sociologists do?

You have to distinguish between sociology as an organisational phenomenon and sociology as a way of thinking; the two do not necessarily go together, there is not a one-to-one correspondence. A lot of people who are part of the organisation of sociology do not think particularly sociologically ... No names please! ... and, conversely, there are a lot of people, and I became very aware of this when I was doing *Art Worlds* [1982], there are many people who have professional titles like 'professor of literature' or art historian or musicologist, who, from my point of view, are doing sociology, thinking the same way as I do. In that sense it is not true that sociology is what people called sociologists do, but in an organisational sense clearly it is true.

What then is distinctive about sociology?

I have finally come to a simple way of putting it, in the hope that it will stifle questions like this, which is, 'sociology studies how people do things together'. The emphasis is on doing it together, on the co-operation, which could be an antagonistic co-operation; fighting is a form of co-operative activity, struggle is a co-operative activity. In classier language, it is the study of collective activity, which is the way that Blumer would put it, and you may have noticed the title of the book of my papers, which was published in Brazil, *A Theory of Collective Action [Uma Teoria da Acao Coletiva,* 1976].

Something you wrote with Irving Horowitz; 'it is the purpose of a meaningful sociology to demonstrate how it is that society and its institutions are on trial, and how it is that society and its organisations are undergoing crisis' [1972, p. 63]. Could you expand?

Some people were treating sociology as something in crisis, saying that sociology was on trial. The point of those remarks was that sociology, after all, is not that important. Society has crises not sociology, and a further implication is ... a lot of people have the idea that if you could only clean up sociology everything else would follow, to clean up the categories of sociology is to clean up the world. Well, you are not going to get rid of oppression by figuring out what Marx meant. That is the whole point of the quote, it is in opposition to that view ... which is very peculiar. You know here we are in the late [1960s] in the middle of this 'radical revolution' in sociology and what many of the allegedly most radical thinkers wanted to do was to fix up sociology. It somehow seemed foolish.

In the same essay you say that only 'good sociology' can be 'radical sociology' ...

Irving Horowitz had a wonderful example of this, which is if Che Guevera had been a better sociologist he would still be alive today. If he had not tried to export a model of the conditions under which revolutionary activity would be successful to a place where it did not apply, he might not have been killed in Bolivia. In that sense 'bad sociology', sociology that produces false factual conclusions cannot possibly be radical, it just leads you astray. The point we wanted to make was that if you really do sociology according to its own precepts, if you really do it, really find out the answers to these questions, you cannot help but be radical, because you are going to violate all sorts of established pieties. It is just that simple, even with statistics; if you gather statistics honestly you are going to find out all sorts of terrible things. I will give you a beautiful example, a paper [Everett] Hughes did on the German statistical system during the Nazi regime. Do you know this paper?

No.

These German statisticians lost six million people, somehow, in this 'infallible' system of statistics, because they were not good statisticians. If they had been they would have exposed something the Nazis did not want exposed. It is just that simple. So to do a decent workmanlike, journeyman's job of statistics in that situation would have been revolutionary.

Alvin Gouldner talks of you and others as the 'second wave of Chicago sociologists' and that your identifications are with 'deviant rather than respectable society'; it's a school of thought, he goes on to say that 'finds itself at home in the world of hip, drug addicts, jazz musicians' and so on [1975, p. 29]. Do you recall that quote? Did he simply misunderstand?

Yes. That will teach you to ask a leading question! One of the first things I tell my class is 'don't ask leading questions, that can be answered yes or no'. Yes, he did, you would have to ask him why. A lot of people just did not read the original documents, they would read something like you have just quoted and not go back to the originals. They only knew the ideas second-hand, through a very misleading interpretation of what went on, because the same group of people also studied physicians and lawyers, and governmental agencies and so on.

Gouldner, discussing your 'Whose Side Are We On?' [orig, 1968], argued that it had given birth to the 'first version of new establishment sociology ... a sociology of young men with friends in Washington ...' [orig. 1968, 1975, p. 49]. What do you make of that?

I am not going to be able to answer questions about how Gouldner came to say those things or why he said them; he was a guy who mixed his own personal ideas up in his own life, that characterisation applied very well to him. Al Gouldner lived very well himself. I do not know what went on that led him to that characterisation.

How do you see 'Whose Side Are We On?' in terms of, say, the Weber value-freedom debate?

You have to distinguish two things. One is that you want to do your research in such a way as to make it as likely as possible to find out that what you would deeply like to discover is not true. You want to leave yourself open to finding out that you are wrong, like Che Guevera. *That* part of the research you have to make as value-free as possible; you do not want to be counting people in the wrong category because it would be nice to think that it came out that way. On the other hand, every way of picking a problem, defining a problem, defining what things you are going to look at and what you are going to leave out, involves some kind of value choice. Furthermore, you cannot come to a conclusion that will not be taken as having some kind of import for some value-laden issue. My favourite example is: 'how many junkies are there in the City of New York?' Truly a statistical, demographic, count 'em up question, no values involved there and you certainly want to get the right answers. You might as well know how many there are as make one up. On the other hand, every answer you get to that question would turn out to be important for all sorts of organisations, institutions, groups in society. If you wanted to prove that the police were doing a good job, ideally what you would want to show, I think, is that there are still a lot of junkies but fewer than there used to be since the police have been at work. The ideal would be to show a large but declining number. You might periodically want to show that the number was increasing. If you ran an agency that wanted to show that more funds were needed for the treatment of drug addicts, then you would want to show a large number. If you wanted to argue that the trouble with the world is that there are too many black people in it, that *they* are all junkies, *etc*. Every one of those numbers had some kind of importance for somebody's position politically. It could be an abstract political consideration about whether oppression and poverty causes drug addicts, or something practical like how big the police budget should be for the next year. The most value-free objective sociologist in the world would inevitably find himself embroiled in political debate whatever answer he came up with, and then he would have to realise that the number you came up with would be a function of how you chose to define terms, and what procedures you used to count them and that you could get a large number or a small number, depending on how you wanted to do it. So that what seems like a truly technical question is a big political question. In that sense there can be no value-free sociology.

John Goldthorpe was [once] saying to me that it annoyed him that while survey-type research, or quantitative research got hammered, ethnography never did. Well, what you say about participant observation in Sociological Work *is that the 'technique consists of something more than merely immersing oneself in data and having insights' [1971, p. 38]. Could you expand on that?*

As far as I can make out, every faction and specialty in sociology considers itself oppressed and mistreated by other factions, because of course most field-work sociologists or qualitative sociologists would feel that it is just the opposite of what Goldthorpe says. Some years ago Blalock, the inventor of path analysis, published a little article in which he complained that

141

methodologists were not taken seriously, were treated like shit, could not get jobs, could not get their articles published, the whole litany of complaints and he obviously meant it, and probably had had such experience. Lots of other people, of course, thought they were being oppressed by the likes of Blalock. I think the truth is that nobody is in a position where they don't feel somewhat mistreated in that way. Goldthorpe is undoubtedly right and the opposite of that is true also!

Okay, participant observation. It is the hardest, most tedious work. If I were lazy, I would do survey research; because when you do field work you are not just immersing yourself in the data. That's shorthand, what you really do is to go to various places, very often inconvenient (people do not come to your office), you go there at the hours when it is convenient to them, not when it is convenient to you, when they are doing whatever they do whenever that is and for as long as it takes them to do it, and when you are done watching and listening and talking to people, you have to go and write it all down. Every last word that was said, everything that you saw, so you have double the work. When I studied medical students, for instance, I might go to the hospital at 7.00 in the morning, stay there till 3.00 or 4.00 in the afternoon, then go home and write field notes. That is quite difficult both physically and emotionally, quite draining. Then you have to analyze all those notes systematically, in the ways that we described in *Boys in White* [1961], which is a very elaborate procedure. It is much more difficult than the analysis of quantitative data because it takes more handling of the data, which has to be coded and re-coded. Having 'insight' is shorthand for the systematic assessment of all these materials that you have gathered in a variety of ways to establish a variety of specific empirical points and then to amalgamate them in some larger argument. It is a hell of a lot of work. Jack Katz, who did a study of lawyers, has written this long piece where he argues - it has to do with the validity of field data - that someone might object that, after all, you could make it all up. He makes a lengthy argument which says that it would be infinitely more difficult to make it up, it is much easier to go and see it and write down what you saw than to invent the same material.

What are the benefits of participant observation?

First of all, it is really rigorous research. You can see empirically all sorts of propositions that would have to be taken on faith with less rigorous forms of research. When somebody says to you for instance, 'I got such and such yesterday', you are in a position to check with other people who were there yesterday to see if he really did do that. You may well have been there yourself so that you could have observed what he did, so you have multiple sources of information on that single point. In that sense, it is much more rigorous, you really have a great deal more information on each point that you deal with. That is one advantage, a very sizeable one. Another advantage is that the procedure is very flexible, you can take account of what you have learned on day one when you do your work on day two. I would like to make a distinction for you here between a research plan and a research design. A research design, you could say, is a fixed design that you adhere to, like a sampling design, in order to get the benefits that come with that design. If you follow a strict sampling design you get to make certain kinds of inferences on the basis of the theory that was associated with designing it that way in the first place. The problem with that, is, supposing you learn part-way through your research that some of the premises on which you based your design were not true. If you change what you do from then on, you lose some of the advantages of the design. A research plan is what you make every day when you set out to work. You can vary what you do on day two depending on what you learned on day one. So that you can say, well, since Bob Mullan told me yesterday about the sort of corruption that was going on in city government, today I had better go and speak to so-and-so, so I can get their point of view on it, explore new avenues, get more data, maybe I should look at certain records, the archives, and so on.

In your preface to Clifford Shaw's The Jack Roller, *you say attention is turned away from local ethnography, and rather towards 'abstract theory building' [1966, p. ix]. That was 1966, is it still the case?*

I guess so. I was talking about the confluence that you got in Chicago during the 20s and 30s, where all this research was focused on the same place. It was not just in sociology. The University of Chicago was a hot bed of social research. There was a great deal of local history being done. Political scientists studied local politics in Chicago, economists studied the economics of the region, everything fed into everything else. In other words, if I was doing a sociological study, the demographic information

143

about the area I was studying was right there. I only had to turn to the *Local Community Fact Book*, which was published every ten years, after the US census. I could lay out the historical statistics for a relatively small area of Chicago if I wanted to. If I want to look at the area that Harvey Zorbaugh wrote about in the *Gold Coast and The Slum* [1929] I can do that, I can get statistics for that area of the city every ten years from 1920 on. It is wonderful to have that resource available. That was largely Park's influence, he was the kind of person who got people to do what he wanted. He got the political scientists interested in local government, he got the economists to do things, all those people ...

When was the demise?

I don't know, you would have to write a history of sociology to do that. The nearest you would get to that today would be, I guess, at Michigan, where they have the Detroit Area Study, where they have been doing these survey studies in the city of Detroit over and over, year after year, as a training device for their students, but also gathering information about conditions in Detroit. I don't think that they have used it that way particularly, and certainly they have not combined it with other kinds of research. Also, the rise of the survey method as the major method of doing research tended to pull you away from local ethnography, although it need not.

On the issue of generalising from one interview, you used the analogy of reconstructing from archaeological remains in an unpublished taped interview you did in 1980. Do you recall?

You can make a generalisation on the basis of anything, archaeologists do all the time when they find a coin. If that is all you have, you do it. Historians inevitably, and archaeologists especially ... I think it is a wonderful case because whatever they find *that is it*, and then they have to infer as much as they can from that. I habitually ask students to do that. I say, 'You have done your first interview, now suppose something happened and you can't do anymore. But one interview is more than anybody else knows about this subject and it is worth knowing, so what do you know? If they were all like that what would you know?' The point of that is not

144

that that would be a wonderful finding, but under the circumstances it might be the best you can get. But if you treat your first interview that way then you have a generalisation that you can try to test on your second, that is the way you develop your hypothesis from interview to interview.

Have you anything to say about the problems of access in sensitive areas of research? Are sensitive areas always worth exploring?

They are always worth exploring just because they are sensitive, because something the people involved consider very crucial is being threatened.

Relatedly, do we spend too much time researching underdogs?

There is something to that. Sociologists, by and large, have imagined more barriers than there are to the study of elites. Paul Hirsch has been doing a study of corporate takeovers in this country, interviewing the directors of major corporations. You would think that would be something that would be quite hard for a sociologist to do, to call up and say 'I would like to talk to you', but, on the contrary, they talk their heads off. We once had a graduate student who decided he was going to study the social elites of Boston; there is no more prestige-conscious city in this country than Boston, and here is this working-class Jewish kid, who decided he was going to do that. He went out and bought himself a suit at the Salvation Army for seventy-five cents, went to Boston and soon he was talking to all these upper-class patrician types, they were all delighted to talk to him.

It is a lot easier in some ways than you imagine. I don't suppose Ronald Reagan and Margaret Thatcher are going to have sociologists sitting in doing studies of their cabinet meetings. But then you usually have other sources for things like that, people involved in those things generally talk their heads off in print shortly afterwards. You have all the problems historians have of the one-sidedness of these accounts, when you cannot check them out with an aggressive interrogation. But of course a lot of work has been done on elites.

Plummer argues that 'methodology is not a thing to be endlessly pontificated

145

about, rather is simply done with a firm problem in mind' [1983, p. 1].   Is this your position?

I don't know whether you have to have a firm problem in mind, but it is certainly not done for its own sake, in other words you wouldn't want to develop a method just for the fun of doing it.   But I must say that since I have got involved with my Apple computer I have discovered the machine part, like when I took my first photograph.   I have suddenly understood in a way that I had not before how someone feels who has learned to do path analysis and wants to do it to everything!   Because once you have learned to make photographs then you naturally look around for things to make photographs of.   And there is a certain sense in which you develop the craft almost independently of what you do with it, it is not completely true, but there is something to that.   But I have no patience for *endless* debates, and I have no patience with the notion that we have to settle those questions *definitively* before we can go on to the research, because for me the research is what it is about.   What we are supposed to be doing is research, and we'll learn what's wrong with our theories and methods by doing the research and seeing where we have trouble.   I have done a lot of theoretical and methodological writing, almost always as the by-product of some research I was doing.   I would find some concept I did not understand well, but wanted to use to explain something I had data on.   It didn't make sense, so I had to work it out.   The neatest example I can think of is the paper I did on 'commitment' [1960], where I found myself saying that, but realising that I did not know what the hell I was talking about, 'what do I mean by that?'.   So I had to work out what that concept might mean.   And the same thing with procedures of research.   Blanche Geer and I developed all the elaborate things we did in *Boys in White*, because we found we had certain problems with the data we had collected: how to present them, how to deal with them in such a way as to say what we wanted to say.

(...)   Plummer notes that 'sociology and photography could be dated from the same year -1839 - when Comte published his key work, and Daguerre made public his method for fixing an image on a metal plate.   But over the past 140 years the two have rarely contacted each other' [1983, p. 11].   Could you talk about this?

I've had a lot of fun with sociologists by pointing out that every major so-

146

called hard science used photographic material. After all, you could not have astronomy, you could not have particle physics, without the use of photographic material, you could not do biology, you could not do any of those things that are done in the natural or physical sciences without the use of photographic material. It is only the social sciences, as usual, that are lagging behind, failing to use the devices characteristic of contemporary science. It is a matter of catching up. It is perfectly clear that to rely on the written word means that anything that is difficult to describe in words is going to fall through the net of our data gathering, we are not going to be able to talk about it. It is just obvious, things like gesture. If you want to talk about gesture the way Goffman and others do, you cannot do that. In principle, you *can* do it in words, but it would take a highly developed style of description that is quite difficult for most people, and uneconomical. It is much easier to show a photograph of a gesture than to describe it in 5,000 words.

How would you stop that from ceasing to be sociology?

A camera after all, is just a machine, you might just as well ask the same question about a typewriter. How would you keep what you wrote from being just writing, instead of sociology? It is the same question. The camera is just a device for describing something, making it permanent, that's all. The fact that it is not words or numbers does not mean it is not something being described. We are just very slow in figuring out those things. By the way that has to go both ways. A lot of my interest in photography has come from dealing with photographers, not sociologists, while photographers know how to make pictures they often do not know what to make a picture of, and they do not know what to think about what they are making pictures of. You can argue that photography really is a conceptual art, because you cannot make a picture without having an idea and a theory. Everything that is in the frame is by way of some kind of ... sometimes a causal statement, sometimes a narrative statement, a statement equivalent to the kinds of statements we make with other data.

(...) You have complained that 'sociologists habitually use twenty words where two will do' [1982, p. 3]. And recent trends in sociology compound this?

Some of these fields have their roots in German scholarship and the translation from German to English, apparently there are things that make sense in German that do not when they are translated. There are other fields of science which have a conventional language. Part of the mystification of sociological language has been importing terminology from other fields where it has a history and everybody knows what it means, and bringing it into our field where nobody knows what it means, because we have not learned it. A lot of people will throw in a French term or a German term now and then, because those are the languages of scholarship. What if I were to throw in a Portuguese term, wouldn't that be fun?

(...) 'Relativism', is a term that is sometimes associated with your work. Are you aware of that?

How could I not be? I'll give you an example. When I first started working on *Art Worlds*, I was asked to give a talk to the faculty of the College of Arts and Sciences at Northwestern. I gave a talk on the basic ideas of *Art Worlds*, talked about the collective character of art work and so on. When we were through, the dean - who was a philosopher - asked the first question, quite visibly upset: 'But Howie, what about Mozart? After all, is not he a genius?'. I have been asked the same question about deviance. Just after *Outsiders* was published, I gave a colloquium at Berkeley and Philip Selznick asked 'But Howie, what about murder? Isn't that really deviant?'. What lies behind those questions is this. I do not build into the analyses I do judgement that the kind of music Mozart produced is somehow really *really* better than the music the Beatles produced, or *vice versa*, for that matter. I do not build the idea that some things are really evil into my deviance theory. It is as though you said 'We are going to analyze these chemicals. Now let us divide these chemicals into evil, rotten chemicals, and good, beneficent, helpful, wonderful chemicals.'. Now any damn fool knows that it all depends on how they are used. I can't see what is added to the description of something as evil - which is a moral judgement, I'm perfectly willing to make and do all the time - or that Dizzy Gillespie is a great trumpet player, or that Mozart wrote terrific music, I don't see what's added to that by making it a sociological distinction. Supposing I say that murder is somehow *really* evil. Now you want me to say, in addition, that it's deviant. I want to reserve the term deviant for an interactive process in which someone calls something a bad name, whether or not I agree with that

148

bad name. What's added to the description of it as evil, or rotten, or nasty, by calling it deviant? As far as I can see, the only thing that's added is the notion that science has proved it's nasty. There are substantial advantages in not making those judgements as part of the analysis. The advantage is that it allows you to see that the act of judging is part of the process you're involved in.

Downes, talking of Outsiders, *argues that 'the central organising principle - "Deviant behaviour is that which is so labelled" - superficially a banal and even trivial assertion, caused an explosion in the petrified forest of criminology' [1979, p. 3] ... How did you see it?*

I guess it had that effect, it was widely taken up. But the book almost didn't get published because people thought it wouldn't be interesting. Ned Polsky was an editor at the Free Press and he got them to publish it for an old buddy of his, they didn't think it would be a big thing. I didn't think it would be a big thing. And it all happened very gradually, so the image of an explosion ... I mean, what happened was that there was a kind of convergence, a lot of people were thinking things like that - Kitsuse and Cicourel came to that from one direction, really via Lemert, Kai Erikson came to it from another direction. I think what I did was to say it more clearly than anybody else.

Well tell me again clearly the fundamental principles ...

I now see it in the light of the kind of language I use now, as collective activity: deviance is something that people do together, in the sense that everybody involved in so-called deviant activity is part of making it deviant. So it does not do to just focus on the person who is supposed to have done the bad thing. You need to study the whole organisation, including the people who try and stop people like that from doing bad things, the people who define those things as bad, and all the rest of it. That is the phenomenon. It is fairly obvious; I mean murder, it takes a judge and jury to figure out whether it was a murder or not.

Downes points to the importance, following Outsiders *of taking the viewpoint of the actor, looking at the reaction to deviance, partisanship and so on. Is that how you see it?*

I don't like that language, it is the language you get out of Lemert, of 'societal reaction'. One of the chief things that happened was that it got to be more interesting and more justifiable to study agencies of social control as part of the phenomenon. One of the clearest things that happened was the increase in the studies of the police, judges, and courts. Those had other roots, there were other reasons why people would do that, but that got to be a much larger business. 'Taking the viewpoint of the actor,' that is tricky too because ... I think Blumer's line on this is right. Blumer says we are *always* talking about the viewpoint of the actor, the only question is whether we know what it is, or invent it out of our own subjectivity. When people wrote about, say, drug-users, it is not that they did not take the point of view, they took it, they attributed to drug-users a certain point of view. What they attributed to them was a kind of pathological obsession with drugs, the desire for perverse pleasure and the like. What I did was not to bring in the viewpoint of the user but to ask is that true? Is that their viewpoint? Is that why they take these drugs? It is taking the point of view of the actor to say that the actor had a problem reaching a certain goal and that the means were not adequate to it, and therefore eventually hit on the solution of using an illegitimate means, that is also taking the point of view of the actor. The question is whether you actually study that and at least check it out to see if that is true or not. In Lindesmith's study of opium addicts [1968], he gave a homely, everyday understanding of why addicts took opiate drugs regularly. What do I do with marijuana is kind of classic in that respect, because the imagery that went with marijuana-use in the lay public was right out of De Quincey, *Confessions of an English Opium Eater* [1822], exotic, oriental pleasures. People who had never used marijuana themselves and had never talked to anybody who did, imagined that some sort of indescribable perverse pleasure led people to use marijuana. My contribution to that debate was to say 'Listen, if you want to talk to marijuana users they never mention anything like that, they talk about much simpler matters' (...) If you understand taking the viewpoint of the actor into account that way, it is not to say that you believe what the actor said necessarily, but you believe it subject to all kinds of checking out that you might do, because people lie.

(...) Plummer also notes that labelling theorists, particularly yourself, were criticised from both right and left [1979, p. 88].

I take that to be a good sign, you have to be doing something right!

Take the criticism from the left, that you have tended to ignore dimensions of power and so on ...

That is patently not true (...) In general, there is not a whole lot of emphasis on class. There is a kind of generalised emphasis on power in the sense that it is clear that some people are more in a position of influence than other people and *vice versa*. But I do not know what the history of all that is ...

It could be that Marxist styles of thought were becoming relevant. You have to think about the history of Marxism in relation to sociology. Not that nobody read Marx up until about 1960-1965; that is certainly not the case. Although you will not find much reference to Marx in, let's say, Alvin Gouldner's earlier work, it is not because he did not know about it. A lot of sociologists in the 30s and 40s were probably involved in various kinds of political groups, and many of them kept it secret (in the US for good reason), and then felt it was safe to come out of the political closet; so that they revealed a knowledge of Marx that they had been unwilling to espouse openly before. All that happened and then they may have looked at likely places of likely things to study. And deviance was a very popular area in the 1960s.

Gouldner argued that you focused on the caretaking institutions who did the 'mopping up job', rather than the 'master institutions' [1975, p.49]. How have you countered that accusation over the years?

I just ask people to read the original documents.

(...) Could you tell me how you came upon the notion of 'labelling'?

That book [*Outsiders*], was written about the time I was doing the marijuana

151

research, about ten years earlier than its final publication. I wrote probably thirty or forty pages, it was kind of mixed up, I was not quite sure what to do with it, but most of the basic parts were there. Some years later Irwin Deutscher said 'Why don't you write that up', so I started working on it again. That is how it happened that, for instance, I was unaware of Lemert's work, because I had not worked in that field, most of my research was in the area of education, except for the marijuana stuff. That is why it is reasonable to say that it was a direct outgrowth of this kind of sociology, because it came right out of that; I said to myself 'If you apply the kind of sociology I have been doing about schoolteachers to this thing, what would it look like?' So you might say it is really an occupations and professions point of view as applied to deviance. As somebody said about *Art Worlds*, 'Hey, that is not the sociology of art, that is occupations and professions applied to art.' That's right.

Have you ever seen 'deviants' as 'proto-revolutionaries' as some theorists have?

No. That's romantic. I knew those people, the idea of a junkie as a revolutionary is a joke. A junkie has no time to do that, a junkie is running around trying to score drugs. There is a kind of Laingian sense of revolution in that they see the world differently. That is true, it is a very radicalizing experience for some people to discover that things they thought were terrible are not. A lot of people had that experience, especially with things like marijuana, because they had been told the whole story by the rest of the world about what a terrible thing this was, and then when they found out from their own experience that it was not - 'they've been lying to me' - it can have the influence of consciousness raising, making people aware.

Were you ever harassed when you did your marijuana study?

I had a notion that I was going to be harassed by the government because they had harassed Lindesmith who had written about drugs, so I was sitting around waiting for a knock on the door for years, but it never happened. I decided, it's not going to happen. I think British researchers operate under a much heavier set of conditions than we do here, we don't have the equivalent of the *Official Secrets Act*, but god knows Reagan and co. are

152

trying to legislate something like that. The result is that you're relatively safe, at least you're not going to be leaned on in the legal way, you may get harassed in other ways, but that doesn't happen much.

How exactly does Art Worlds *fit in with your other work?*

If that were a book about schools, and how people get educated and how schools are organised, nobody would ever raise that question. What I did there was simply to treat the production and consumption and distribution of art works as something that is done *via* the organised life of societies, the same way that you would study anything else. People raise that question because they think that art is something different. The same question arises with respect to the sociology of science. It is nothing special, art is a kind of work, it is done like all other kinds of work in institutional and organisational settings. What people do is, in large measure, a function of the organised settings that they have to adapt to or to create. It is the circumstances they work under. Every artist knows that, and they would be fools if they did not; a composer knows that you write music having in mind the instrumentalists that are there to play it, or if you do not then you will have to pay the price, which is that it will not get played. That is the same kind of analysis you do in any other area of sociology.

So it is demolishing myths?

The book is not organised to demolish myths; it takes the myth as demolished, it starts with that. What argument there is about that comes much later in the book, because later on I talk about, for instance, aesthetics, not as philosophical justification that we need to take seriously, but rather as something people in art worlds do in order to provide justifications for their activities. The reason people find it difficult to see what I am up to, which seems to me to be so obvious, is that there is a field which is called the sociology of art, and I in effect said 'This is not part of that field' (...) The official name 'sociology of art' kind of belongs to the Frankfurt School, Lukacs, like that, which I take to be a kind of school of aesthetics, a philosophical school of thought not concerned with the problems I am concerned with.

Not sociology then?

I would not think of it as the study of collective activity. Lukacs wrote about novels, in a way I don't find terribly useful. And Adorno ... I stopped taking Adorno seriously when I read his piece on Jazz, an early piece, which was fairly racist, he does not quite say 'Jazz is a nigger music and therefore we need not pay any attention to it' but he comes pretty close. I figured that anybody who can write that really does not have to be taken seriously. That may be too harsh. But a lot of people said to me 'Look, you are not dealing with the sociology of art'. So I said 'Well, okay, I'm not going to argue about the word, what do I care'. I wrote it carefully to say 'I'm not going to get involved in those discussions, it's not what I'm writing about', and people still said it's as though if you're a sociologist and you write about anything to do with the arts you must deal with this material even if to show why you're not going to deal with it. I couldn't see any point in that kind of thing, it's a student exercise in literature review. Plenty of other people have dealt with it ...

(...) And your current research ...

This is a project to study different ways of representing knowledge about society. It's very similar to the *Art Worlds* thing. It's a matter of treating the production of everything that is a vehicle for presenting ideas about society in the same way as I did in *Art Worlds*. The kinds of things we'll be looking at are such things as the 'problem play': one of the classic examples I have before me all the time is Shaw's *Mrs Warren's Profession* [orig. 1902; 1925], a tremendous vehicle for the analysis of the problem of prostitution. Maps, mathematical models, tables and graphs, ethnographic descriptions, novels, Hollywood feature films, documentaries, whatever, life histories, all of those things. To compare them and understand how each way of doing it has evolved in relation to the social organisation in which it's done.

(...) How influential do you think you have been, or would like to be?

I don't know! A lot of my work has been influential with respect to specific areas of study. I certainly have been one of the people who have kept alive

154

and made kosher the use of fieldwork techniques, but not the only one. It works two ways, one is you write something and it goes out and people read it, and abuse it, and use it. That's happened quite a lot (...) Becker, Matza, Lemert, for example, those became more and more cited over the years in deviance theory. It's clear in that area, again not just me but that whole movement, that the kind of questions that were investigated changed. And the ways of being investigated; the whole ethnographic study of social control agencies on the one hand, and the people they dealt with on the other, became a kind of *genre* which was very well known and legitimate. I think the work that Hughes and Geer and I did on student culture [*Boys in White, 1961*] has had quite an impact again in a generalised way but lots of other people were working with similar ideas (...) The other side of it, though, is the work you do with individuals, students, people you work with, people you get to know, read their work and criticise it, help them find a direction for it. I've done a great deal of that. It's not that I put my stamp on them, but they rubbed up against me, they argued with me, they learned something from the classes I taught ... and that has a generalising influence (...)

Would you like to see any particular developments in sociology in the future?

(...) I really honestly am very eclectic about a lot of this stuff. I think it's just fine that people do all sorts of other kinds of work than I do, because who knows where the next good thing is coming from. If you'd said to me five years ago that I was going to be interested in microcomputers I'd have laughed at you. If you'd asked me 'Should we encourage the use of microcomputers in sociology?' I would have said 'God forbid'. That was based on the foolish mistaken notion that computers are only good for doing statistics with, but I know better now, and so people who were monkeying around with computers twenty years ago, I now see that as a good thing, I'm glad they did. I think that British sociologists really need to understand the difference [that] scale makes. British sociology *is* relatively small, relatively few institutions giving money out for research, and here there are thousands ... but any damn fool knows that anything anybody wants to do can be done, and is being done, and there's no way to stop that.

And it's okay?

It might as well be. I mean, is it okay with me if it snows? What would anybody do about it? In Britain it would be possible for somebody, let's say, who is influential on the SSRC [ESRC] or the Nuffield Foundation to really make a dent, really stop people from doing things, they just cut it off (...) Here you can have money for anything, you just have to look at the journals and the books being published, and every kind of thing can be done, it can be published, and qualitative research has been published all over the place by major presses, the University of Chicago Press in the last couple of years, for instance, published Doug Harper's book *Good Company* [1983] about tramps and hobos ... not just qualitative, it's one long narrative of how a tramp socialised himself into that world and is accompanied by a large portfolio of photographs that Doug took. There's no sense in anybody saying you can't do that kind of thing, he did it. Could he get a grant to do another one? I don't know, what's the difference? I think it's a bad mistake for social scientists to get that involved with money; some kinds of research cost a lot to do, if you're going to do national sample surveys and all that it's going to cost you, on the other hand to do an ethnography involving one or two people really doesn't cost that much. Probably the biggest single expense is secretarial help and once you've got your computer you don't need that (...) I've been in this business thirty years now and so I've seen all the 'right ways' come and go. Like in the 50s, when the Ford Foundation first got going, the 'right way' was the propositional inventory, that was the 'right way'; we'd done all the research that ever needed to be done and all we had to do was to get all these propositions in order and sort them out and get them connected with each other. That was the way, a lot of money went into that. And where are those propositional inventories today? Then there were various subject matters - mental health, and many of those of course were scams, in the sense that you always had that kind of scam in scientific funding; 'we'll call it cancer research, we know what we are studying is the basic physiology of the liver', 'we'll call it mental health, okay we know what you're going to do is the social organisation of schools', there was a lot of that kind of thing going on, that's normal (...)

6 Laurie Taylor

Journalist and broadcaster, and formerly Professor of Sociology at the University of York, Laurie Taylor is best known as co-ordinator of the now defunct National Deviancy Symposium (NDS) from which sprouted 'radical' theories of deviance, the 'new criminology' and ultimately political economies of crime. A great admirer of Georg Simmel and Erving Goffman, he has also written books reflecting the approaches and insights of the aforementioned thinkers, and also books traditionally termed as being within the sociology of deviance.

Born 1935 in Sutton Coldfield, he had many occupations including acting, before turning to psychology and sociology. He soon learnt to appreciate Goffman and in 1968 concluded a piece on Goffman arguing that 'what started out as an extended commentary upon the mannerisms of individuals in social interaction has become over the years a disturbing vision of humanity' (1968, p. 837). Ever provocative, Taylor also observed that (1968, p. 835)

> Sociologists have been described as licensed voyeurs. But not many of them exercise their professional rights, being too busy talking in each other's washing to have time left over to examine anyone else's. Erving Goffman is a notable exception. For ten years he has been out bugging everyday human behaviour. While others were compiling the grand theory, he was to be found peering through cottage windows in the Shetlands, enjoying a smoke with catatonics in a closed ward or making the scene in Las Vegas.

In July 1968 Taylor, together with other similarly minded people, formed the National Deviancy Symposium, held meetings at York, and began researching deviance in a new and non-positivistic manner. Not that everyone saw the NDS in a completely favourable light. Rex, for example, noted that much of the most 'provocative sociology of recent years has been produced by those who study deviance, because they are in some degree deviant themselves ... [and] ... on the whole they are a small group of middle class children who have lost faith in their parents' culture or have simply been given the possibility of deviance by their indulgent and liberal seniors' (1974, p. 232).

In the early stages of the NDS what was crucial was seeing the deviant act from the actor's perspective, hence the keen adoption of the labelling perspective, symbolic interactionism, and the like. For example motives and meanings were sought for industrial sabotage: 'in our researches we have been told by Woolworths' sales girls how they clank half a dozen buttons on the till simultaneously to win a few minutes rest from "ringing up"' (Taylor and Walton, 1971, p. 219). Some other themes of the NDS were those of connecting with the public; seeing deviance as a process; the political implications of studying deviance, and so on (see Cohen, 1971). Ian Taylor, Paul Walton, and Jock Young's *The New Criminology* (1973) emerged from the NDS, which included some elements of previous thinking, but was much more concerned with the wider structural origins of the deviant act, the political economy of social reaction, and indeed viewing the 'whole process' as one of politics.

Laurie Taylor meanwhile was not on the 'new criminology' bandwagon and in 1976 together with Stanley Cohen wrote *Escape Attempts* in which - amongst other things - he claimed that he clung on to an 'ideology of bourgeois individualism', and concluded the book pointing to the 'fundamental pessimism of the sociological tradition' (1976, p. 224)

> Destiny is social destiny, there is no reality other than that to be found within the density of social life. This is the same pessimism as Freud's: the desire to escape the self is part of the sickness. There is nowhere to go, either in society or in the mind.

The first thing, is just very briefly - unless it is significant about why you ended up doing sociology - is background, you know, where you were born, what you did ...

Yes, yes okay. Although I always try to pretend I was born in Liverpool because it had a great deal more street credibility when I was adolescent, in fact I was really born in Sutton Coldfield, which is near Birmingham but I've always managed to geographically and eventually ideologically - transplant myself to Liverpool, until I now actually believe that I came from Liverpool. I also believe much of the time that actually I came from working class parents in Liverpool but in fact I came from lower middle-class parents in Birmingham, and went to live in a middle class suburb in Liverpool.

In the 1940s ?

Yes that's right. I was a Catholic for years and I went to a Catholic boarding school. I was originally going to be a priest, that is what I wanted to be most of all, most of all I wanted to lay down moral standards for other people and so when I was between the ages of seven to eleven or twelve I went to a very, very, claustrophobic religious institution, in a place where you went to mass four or five times a week, it was a community of ... they were called 'Priests of the Sacred Heart' and it was a community of these people ... there was a considerable amount of homosexuality of varying degrees of explicitness. In fact my best friend, I mean I use the word 'homosexual' carefully, my best friend who was called Michael, was expelled at the age of nine for being a homosexual: the youngest homosexual I ever knew! We used to fiddle around a great deal with each others' cocks, all of us, but a whole drama developed with little incestuous, familial, details, you know romances and stories of attachments to Masters, all bound up with confessions and church and incense and prayers and penance and the Stations of the Cross, the whole Gothic thing ...

(...) You said [earlier] that you were going to study English ...

This is like at seventeen or eighteen, yes at school. I went to an interview at Birmingham University, and I can remember the moral of that funny interview at Birmingham University where I was interviewed by, I think, a

159

very astute professor of English who said to me, 'who's your favourite novelist?', or some such banal question you know the way we ask questions now such as 'what are your hobbies?'. I said 'well Charles Dickens really', so he said 'well, why Charles Dickens?', and I said 'well you know the realism' so he said 'what do you mean the "realism"?' so I said 'you know the poverty and the rough streets and crime and that sort of stuff, you know *the realism*' and he said 'who else are you studying at the moment?' and I said 'Jane Austen', and he said 'why don't you like Jane Austen?', so I said 'well you know it's not real', so he said 'what do you mean it's not real?', so I said 'well there's none of that stuff of poverty and the mill', and he said 'is the only reality of the world poverty and the working class, and mills and factories, isn't there a reality of the upper middle class, a reality of the upper class life as well?'. I have often encountered this view of realism afterwards; people here at university talk about going out into the 'real' world and I think they have some notion of a Dickensian ghetto beyond the university into which they can disappear.

(...) So what did you do then?

Well I didn't get into university because I did so badly at 'A' levels that I wasn't allowed into university and couldn't get in, so I just went to work for Littlewoods' Mail Order stores and where I suppose, if I had any valuable experience it was learning about the peculiar bonus system which operated there. The bonus you got paid there at the end of the week depended upon the number of items that you successfully shifted from the ground floor of the warehouse to the second floor of the warehouse ... the items varied between an ironing board in one case - that counted as one item - and a stairclip which came in packets of six dozen, so that I can remember standing with about fifteen or sixteen eager people outside the gates because it was believed that the lorry which brought the stairclips was coming and there was the exciting possibility of having your bonus enhanced by getting a couple of truckloads of stairclips ... it was an amusing place.

(. . .) [Then] you trained as an actor?

Yes, I did three years and trained as an actor. Yes that was a marvellous place, the whole thing was like a play in itself. A great sweeping melodrama. I mean I described the Catholic boarding school as claustrophobic but this was very similar, the emotional state was just as intense: they weren't concerned about ultimate salvation but more about their virginity or the possibility of playing Ophelia on the West End stage within the next couple of years but it was still a hothouse.

(...) Okay, so we'll move on. After drama school did you go straight to do psychology?

I did a bit of professional acting for like five to six months for Joan Littlewood at Theatre Workshop then I thought I'd go to evening classes and I went to Birkbeck. I thought what subject will most help me to show off at parties, and I thought well - psychology, so for four years I did a psychology degree at Birkbeck, a very tough-minded behaviourist degree which I did with a sort of crossword mentality. I was determined to master this system, I didn't bother to question its assumptions. I arrived [at Birkbeck] at the particular point at which the professor of psychology, a man called Summerfield, had replaced the bust that he had of, I think, Plato on his desk with a model of a rat *'Rattus Norvegicus'* in a case, because I suppose he believed the experimental rat could tell us far more than any philosopher about the nature of human experience. (...) I really knew all about behaviourism and when I occasionally hear first year students saying of course behaviourism is wrong, well I just say ...

Read Skinner properly ... ?

That's right I knew all that ... Hull, Tolman, and Thorndike, and Skinner the lot. I could do Hull's mathematico-deductive system of learning now for you on the blackboard (...) I did two years of sociology and that was marvellous because I did it with Ron Fletcher, and if I have to talk about the next influence it'd be Ron Fletcher, who was of course the first professor of sociology here at York. I can see you now sort of nodding about Ron Fletcher. There is something ... perhaps I should say this off the record ... I disappointed Ron Fletcher, I should imagine, because he brought me here to York, he liked me, we got on marvellously well at the university because he introduced me into ways of thinking and notions about society that I had never dreamt existed I mean ...

161

An example?

Well a very good example would be one of the books that I shall always remember Marc Bloch's *Feudal Society* [1961]. I still think that I would have to put that amongst my five or six books which produced a completely different shift in my ideas about the world because that conveyed to me a vision, a version of a life, a way of living, which I never got from anything else that I had ever read. I mean when Marc Bloch produced those accounts of people living in their isolated villages, the marauding Viking ships, it's years and years since I read it last, his description of their fear of God as a potent social force, people expecting the world to end in the year 1000 and the problem of not knowing when the year 1000 would arrive, their notions of time, the imminent sense of death, the brevity of life, the failure to know anything which lay outside your own village. That vision of a different way of thinking.

(...) Did that shift you from psychology to sociology?

It did, it did absolutely.

(...) If a student said to you - what is the difference Professor Taylor between psychology and sociology? Is there an easy answer that you could give them?

In the first year I talk about the difference between psychology and sociology because I think it is a nice potent area to work on. I mean I love working with the idea of paradoxes. I like to talk about the study of the individual ... I say what can the psychologists have, what can we allow the psychologists, what is not social about the individual, how does a concept for example like role distance in Goffman, all those conversational asides, all those tones of voice, all those little subversions which accompany all the role performances, how much they too are truly social.

Does that mean you rejected psychology?

Yes ... really psychology as conceived in this country, I mean the fact is that one of the people that I still enjoy reading very much is William James and if we are talking about a William James type of psychology which was concerned with questions about the reality of everyday life or about realms of reality, I think that *The Varieties of Religious Experience* [1902] is a splendid psychological book and it is one that I return to a great deal, and indeed his *Principles of Psychology* [1890]. Now that sort of psychology is something I'm very interested in, but I think that psychology in trying to divest itself of its philosophical and non-experimental trappings threw away so much that little valuable was left. I 'did Freud' in a course called 'theories of personality' at London University in which four weeks were devoted to telling me that in fact none of his theories could be proved ... experimentally tested. So it was an absolute delight to me to come back again to Freud and the way that I came back was really quite amazing ... I came back through Lacan, which is really like returning to Cole Porter via Schoenberg (...)

In both Psychological Survival [1972] *and your paper with Stanley Cohen in the Bell and Newby book [1977] you discuss a number of methodological issues, particularly those concerning 'taking sides' and problems of access. Could you talk little about this?*

I feel strongly about this area because of the Becker-Gouldner controversy, in which Gouldner chose to attack Becker for betraying the secrets - for selling out the culture of particular disadvantaged groups. I felt very strongly about it because I saw, if I can talk historically, that within the National Deviancy group ...

We'll come to the National Deviancy Symposium later ...

Okay, well let me take it another way. I sympathise with Becker because it doesn't seem to me that he is in any way necessarily betraying the secrets of the group, that in this sort of research you ever get to know what the real secrets are (...) but it is extremely important as a sociological exercise, as a human exercise, to be able to convey the story of one culture to another, to show that all sorts of apparently irrational behaviour has some sorts of meaning, that these people do have some sense and are as coherent and rational as members of other enterprises ... the whole of anthropology is about that (…) I've seen people deterred from going out and studying groups which they belong to, of which they were members, because they thought that by doing so they might betray that group. Now I don't think that is necessarily the case. At the moment I'm doing work on professional criminals. I don't find really very much difficulty in separating out those aspects of those people's lives which can be talked about and told, and which do justice to their view of the world and their reasons for engaging in behaviour, and those parts of their world which if I brought to the attention of the authorities might lead them to being caught or arrested or indicted. I mean I just don't find this so difficult … but when Gouldner puts it down it looks as if this *is* difficult, and when Becker says 'who's side are we on? We've got to take sides', he is not being patronising, he is giving a methodological injunction. He is saying, look in order to be able to find out you have to, in some ways, show the people who you are working with that when occasions occur you will pay them back for what you have taken from them. So it seems to me that when I can write an article defending a particular criminal who's on a charge that he shouldn't be on (…) when I know that particular sorts of injustices have been going on in prisons, then I should say so. I think that's important to do, there is a paying back to be done and I do object to people who just take and scurry and run. But with those provisos I think that Becker is right and that Gouldner is wrong about this, and I find that Gouldner's high-minded moralism …

Presumably you agree with Gouldner's other arguments elsewhere [1963] about there being no value-free sociology?

Yes. I'm pleased to see that the debate has in a way receded - 'where are your values?', *et cetera* - it's receded in a way because, from time to time a whole number of committed people arrive who are very anxious to rescue and present the case for a previously devalued group. These people really shake and rattle so many existing ways of viewing the world, and they do it from a highly value-laden position. Here are people setting out with the view that, say, women have been discriminated against in every possible area. They start with a straightforward belief that women have been discriminated against in every possible area under consideration, including sociology. Proceeding from that point they tip over the whole apple cart, they upset the whole bag of tricks. That's delightful. And value-loaded.

164

What methodological lessons have you learned from studying say, prison?

I think that you never exaggerate the problem of access. It's always possible if you're talking about research, to strike up local bargains, it's much easier to get into places than people think it is. We [Stanley Cohen and L.T.] found numbers of sympathetic people, people said look you can come in here, you can do this, there are governors that I know, there are people who ring me up and tell me things, so I think it's important to establish a little insider network. It is a bit like spying, I think you do have to bring the techniques of spying, I think you do have to cheat in some cases in order to get the sort of access that you want (...) I'm afraid sociologists have got to be prepared on occasions to sell official people out a little, they've got to say to people I'm doing this research for this and for this reason, and when they get it they've got to scuttle back and tell it how it is, however unpopular they might be. I would like to see far more people who work inside institutions doing research; there are people at the moment working within institutions, the Home Office, the army, who could be doing valuable research, who could be saying all sorts of things about what's going on. We've just had Simon Holdaway publishing his book [1983] on the police, an excellent thing, he did it while he was inside, then he came out and told the story. But there are many other people who are inside who could do much more ... Secretly, if necessary.

What about the argument that (you) could be, if you like, 'fouling up the patch' for subsequent researchers?

Well there is that, but I think that is always over-stated. I can remember when *Psychological Survival* was published someone wrote a review of it in the *Prison Officer's Journal* saying that we'd set research in prisons back twenty years, and we thought '20 years ... that's like going back to well before Morris's *Pentonville* [and Morris, 1963]', and then Terry Morris rang us up and said 'It's funny that you should have had this statement made about you. When I did *Pentonville* I was also told that this would set prison research back 20 years, that puts it back about 40 years ...'

John Rex told me that he had great hopes for the National Deviancy Conference Symposium (NDC), he thought that there would be communication between sociological theory and deviancy theory, but rather deviancy became 'a little slick paradigm of its own'. Can you tell me a little about the Symposium?

I mean the committee of the NDC, as you well know, was a diverse committee which at the beginning didn't realise exactly how diverse it was. It consisted of Jock Young and Paul Walton and Mary McIntosh and Stan Cohen and Paul Rock and David Downes and Roy Bailey and a couple of other people I've probably forgotten. The point was that we initially had an object to attack - orthodox criminology - and we also had good weapons at hand with which to attack it, the writings of people like Becker and Lemert and Matza. And what's more, we had an attractive lifestyle to go with it, and of course I think that the peculiar fortuitous convergence - well not entirely fortuitous, that would be unsociological - of the 60s lifestyle together with the ideological support for this culture of diversity was a quite surprising combination. I mean *literally,* one had a situation in which people who were at that moment exploring alternative lifestyles, who were growing their hair for perhaps the first time, who were perhaps allowing themselves to be publicly homosexual, who were experimenting with certain sorts of drugs, who were 'dropping out', who were taking on aspects of the 60s culture, trying on these different identities, were the same people who were simultaneously using things like Becker and Lemert and Matza as intellectual arguments against the orthodox, positivist, criminological 'truths' of the time ... I was conscious that I had a *social* contribution to make, I felt that I was good at keeping these people together, and I was aware of how much the lifestyle helped me keep these people together, they would have gone off in separate ways if the *only* parameter had been the intellectual one. Now when the lifestyle began to disappear when the hippies and the beads and Hendrix, whatever ... as all this departed as the great rush of 60s expectations drifted away, then people were suddenly exposed holding in their hands what turned out on inspection to be rather different ideological versions of the world, there were the interactionists, and the labelling school, and the phenomenologists, and there were the much harder-line Marxists with their concerns about the State, with their concerns about repression, their involvement with the working-class, their Trotskyist version of the world. Those two groups really were fundamentally incompatible; it took us a number of years to find that out, but of course now they have gone their separate ways and they hardly meet.

(...) What were the fundamental *differences between the Becker, Lemert* et al *approach, and the later 'political economists' of deviance?*

The *fundamental* differences *were* first of all what seemed to us on that labelling-symbolic interactionist side far too greater readiness on the part of that left to recruit deviants for proto-revolutionary activity. That was one critical difference. The second one was the socialist utopia, the idea that crime and diversity were *somehow* related in some sort of firm fixed way to capitalist society and were not likely to be features of other societies. We saw this as having totalitarian overtones and we found it difficult to imagine the society where there wasn't diversity and deviance - how they might be managed interested us, but we didn't look forward to some sort of socialist utopia. And I think that thirdly we objected - this was well before Foucault - to the versions of power which were put in terms of social control in some sort of global blanket way. *The* state, various arms of social control, you know *the* judiciary, *the* police, *the* social workers and probation. The word social control was used so loosely and many of us wanted to talk about the ways in which that social control worked, the mechanics of power at the micro-level, and it was interesting later on that many of us would derive legitimacy for that concern with micro-power from Foucault, because Foucault himself as you know ... one of his starting points is to attack that Marxist emphasis upon power being located as it were within the state and power being something which is imposed (...)

Was The New Criminology *[1973] of Ian Taylor, Paul Walton and Jock Young simply an outgrowth of the NDC, or was it one of the two wings?*

No *The New Criminology* was really the break. I thought *The New Criminology* was a splendid book, you see if you want to see how confident this deviancy group had got *The New Criminology* is an example - I mean this in a nice way - it's an example of megalomania in action. Here were three people, all quite young sociologists, who casually bestrode the universe of criminology and the sociology of deviance and produced lengthy chapters criticising everyone, putting everybody down, everybody was wrong. The 'giants' of the criminological tradition were casually taken on and despatched within a couple of pages, then a 'new criminology' a brand new theory of criminology was articulated, which was to have considerable influence. This was a fine grand sweep and at the time I can remember that many of us were very jealous, I was actively jealous. The popularity of the book meant that I didn't actually read the whole thing for about eighteen months but simply went around cultivating negative opinions of it which I could relay to other people (...) Of course there were *real* things wrong with it ... It's interesting to see Jock Young later on referring to it, caricaturing it, as 'left-idealism', using E.P.Thompson's phrase in order to refer to himself and his former colleagues. This 'left-idealism' which refused to examine the *particularities* of social power, which put the courts, and the police, and the educational system and psychiatry together and called it all social control. Which refused to consider matters like civil liberties, which refused to consider how the police *actually* acted because the police were simply forces of repression.

(...) I'll read you something from the conclusion of The New Criminology; *'for us, as for Marx and other new criminologists,* deviance *is normal - in the sense that men are now consciously involved (in the prisons that are contemporary society and in the real prisons) in asserting their human diversity' [1973, p. 282]. I find this amusingly naive ...*

Well I think you're right to be amused by it. Although I said I meant 'megalomania' kindly, there are certain passages where I think I'd use the word cruelly. There's also a statement in *The New Criminology* which talks about theft being essentially the redistribution of private property, you know ... these are statements which are far too grand, rhetorical flourishes which are a bit meaningless.

(...) Some commentators refer to the impact of labelling theory as being like an 'explosion' ... how do you remember it?

I can't remember, I learnt about Becker later. I was late in on the scene and I went to see Stan Cohen and he explained all about it to me, but you've got to remember that in a funny sort of way crime had never been taken on board by sociologists before, and I think that this was a way in which it suddenly became sociological and really the noise that was being made was the discovery of a new area, and whenever that happens in sociology, there's that sudden moment of excitement. I've no doubt that it happened with the beginning of ethnomethodology. I can't think of the equivalent statement that was made by Garfinkel, in *Studies in Ethnomethodology* [1967], but I'm certain that ethnomethodologists could tell you that 'when I read that Garfinkel said this' ... I can't really use the term paradigm shift, but that moment when suddenly we switched on to the notion of deviance as negotiation ... in a country which had for years and years treated a crime as a thing, an event, a statistic, a clear-cut concrete rock which you could look and consider its causes and why it occurred in the first place, and I think the sudden idea of negotiation within the context of deviancy ... The other important thing, and it has to be said, it always got blurred in these early days, was that there was this sudden new interest in other negotiable things like mental illness ... for example Goffman's [1968] statements and references to the relative arbitrariness by which people were labelled mentally ill

(...) Can we talk a little about your own politics . . . you were in the International Socialists weren't you?

Yes I was in IS for many years with excellent people like Peter Sedgwick, Bob Looker and Nigel Harris and so on. It was very important to me. I certainly read a great deal of literature and material then, and more than anything, Victor Serge's *Memoirs of a Revolutionary* [1963]. I loved that book, because it seemed to me a magnificent picture of a person moving between different cultures, never being caught up in one culture, always arriving somewhere and then moving on, always somewhat uncertain of his own identity and mission. Yes, I was in it for a time. I even wrote an article for *International Socialism* years ago with Ian Taylor called 'We're all deviants now', it was a time when we were trying to interest International Socialists in people like criminals, in the mentally ill, and attempting to say that it was about time that the left paid rather more serious attention to these groups ...

But you were in IS because you believed in Socialism and the revolutionary route?

Yes, in the past I had been in things like the Labour League of Youth, I'd been in the Communist Party for a time, I'd spent a great deal ... I mean when I was young in the Merseyside Unity Theatre. I was in 'the left' in an artistic almost aesthetic sort of way rather than in a political way, it just

169

seemed to me that the literature I read, the things I liked, were much more likely to be written by people on the left, that the good plays came from the left, the good novels came from the left ... the best histories, Trotsky's *History of the Russian Revolution* [1967 edition] the full excitement of the exploration of the world, the demystification of the world, was done by people on the left. But I found however I couldn't swallow the organisational aspects of International Socialists, their almost mystical belief in the potentiality of the working class to create the revolution, their certainty that history was on their side, their sectarianism, (...) this was the Catholic Church all over again and the doctrinaire nature of these meetings was losing what seemed to me what I wanted to purchase. I later came to think, which I still think now, that the success of these factional left groups in being able to appropriate certain issues has had important repercussions for politics in this country. I think that the Labour Party has found issue after issue taken over by radical groups ... they've been left with rather a thin menu ... the left groups have always had the sexy items to discuss and talk about, and be sectarian about.

(...) *How would you define sociology?*

I'd have to put in the word 'demystification' straight away. I mean the demystification of conventional social and cultural beliefs and arrangements. That suggests as it should, that there is always a job to be done, that always at all times reified structures and belief systems are growing, *and* they're also growing within sociology. And the demystification of sociologists' practices and beliefs is just as important as the demystification of other people's.

So you'd agree with someone like Norbert Elias who says that all scientists including sociologists are simply 'destroyers of myths' [1978, p. 52]?

Yes I think that that is their main job and if what is being said by a sociologist doesn't produce some sense of *surprise* somewhere amongst its readers then something is going seriously wrong.

Does sociology have a scientific *status?*

No I don't like the ways in which that phraseology has been traditionally used, the way in which it suggests, as it were, a mark and a tick can be put on certain sorts of pieces of work, against those that can be declared to be scientific when compared to others. You might well prefer one piece of research to another on all sorts of grounds, but to simply say that it's scientific whereas the other isn't, begs all sorts of questions (...) what I am delighted about in the sociology of science at the moment, is its demystification of scientists' claims to be acting according to the ways in which they claim to be acting. So that if sociology is busily demystifying science, it is hardly appropriate for it to try to apply the word science to its own efforts in other areas.

(...) *Is Erving Goffman a 'one-off'?*

Well I think, and it will come as no surprise to you, he is exceptional. He is exceptional. It's just that on a simple thing I am still so *surprised* by what he has to say. I mean only two to three days ago I was re-reading a small section of *Frame Analysis* [1974] and was suddenly delighted by a small extract that he had there in which he described in perfect detail the mere activity of an air-hostess on a plane pouring out coffee for a gentleman and indicating there was not enough to fill his cup. Little things like that emerge all the time for me from Goffman. I don't read it for a bit and I go back and I find there is more there. I don't think he's unique. I think there are a few other people who Goffman would have found it difficult to write without them having existed ...

George Herbert Mead?

Mead certainly. Mead was very, very, important, but I think probably more than Mead I would turn to someone like Simmel. You see there are two surprising things about Goffman, one is what he chooses to look at. I turn the page and there he is looking at a radio programme, at the way people walk up and down the street, at the expression on a poker player's face, we forget how many things that he made us look at, how many elements that are all around us that he made us look at. Now the second thing is his *style,* in order to be able to write about those matters which are so close to us, which almost touch us, language almost has to run inside our belief systems and

171

almost sort of prise them out, prise these elements out which have been for so long implicit and then hold them up for our inspection ... the prose has to be brilliant in order to do that. It really has to creep around inside our own belief systems and dig these elements and objects out and present them to our gaze. That's a most difficult job for language to do (...) so style and content, the originality of the content, and the ability to have a style which as it were does justice to the subtlety of what he wants to say. Now if you go back to Simmel ... Simmel again has the most surprising content, I mean, you open Simmel's theoretical works and there is an article on 'the ruin', a magnificent piece. Why does he take 'the ruin'? ... because he always loves those elements which vibrate at the edge. If we are talking about demystification, you always have to find a vibrating example, you always have to find something which won't quite fit into neat categories. When he talks about 'the ruin', he explains that we are so attracted to it, because it represents a peculiarly ambiguous item ... something which is man-made or has been man-made and yet which is about to become nature, it exists between the two, it draws our attention to both ...

I was going to say David Frisby looks at Simmel's loathing of methodology, and argues that of 'all of his contemporaries who have attained "classic" status, Simmel stands alone in his contempt for methodology' [1981, p.68] ...

Yes, and Simmel too said when asked about what is method, he said he thought method was rather the same thing as style in art, and I think that that is an excellent thing to say. It's not an empty vacuous phrase at all, I mean that if you talk about Goffman's method, you have to talk about Goffman's style, and when people say 'just a minute how did Goffman arrive at this?', well he arrived there by the variety of rhetorical devices, but those rhetorical devices are the only possible ones or almost the only possible ones which could produce that particular demystification of 'taken-for-granted' reality, you know that is a splendid achievement.

And what would, in a nutshell, be Mead's importance to Goffman ?

Well I suppose, I think that the particular ... if I have to pick one image from Mead, it's where he's talking about children playing 'hide and seek', and about the fact that the very young child doesn't have an image of the 'seeker' doesn't know quite how to hide, he goes to hide and then reappears shouting 'here I am' as it were ... that little passage about learning to take the role of 'the other', beginning to form an idea of the other person's mind (...) ... now one of the *a prioris* of sociation which Simmel talks about is that necessity of typifying others because of our inability to comprehend their full individuality. Now it's that which Mead is talking about as well, the necessity of typifying others' response because of our inability to comprehend their full individuality. This also obsessed Goffman. In one of his last books *Frame Analysis*, at the very end, in the last bit of it, is a wonderful quotation from Merelau-Ponty in which Merelau-Ponty gives a phenomenological description of what he sees of the other person, their voice coming from them, the sight of them, where the words are coming from, where they're located, the awareness that the person in front of you is just 'darkness crammed with organs' but somehow they're responding to you, and then Goffman says 'reverse it'; that is, think of you representing that and being that to them. It is always that running backwards and forwards between subject and other. It is there in Mead, where he has that lovely symbolic sense of backwards and forwards in his notion of self, it is there in Simmel in his paradoxes of sociation, it's there throughout Goffman in *The Presentation of Self in Everyday Life* [1969] and particularly in that lovely transformation in Goffman's writing between the notion of the dramaturgical metaphor in *The Presentation of Self in Everyday Life* to his realisation in *Frame Analysis* that it wasn't a dramatic metaphor at all, in fact ... the only reason we can understand plays is because our lives are already dramatisations, we are in plays all the time.

What are Mead, Simmel and Goffman actually demystifying?

They are demystifying the individual, they are demystifying the coherence of the individual, they are all talking about the self as something that has to be socially achieved and managed and constructed and brought off.

(...) Is Goffman political, albeit in an implicit kind of micropolitical way?

Where he talks in *Asylums* about the way in which the self is created in the interstices of institutions, created against them, well of course that is what started us off on *Escape Attempts* [Cohen and Taylor, 1976]. We were interested in 'escape attempts' because we wanted to talk about the notion that in order to feel fully individual, people have to set themselves *against* existing and conventional arrangements. We wanted to take this further on and say that unfortunately the co-option which can occur in contemporary society meant that all these attempts to resist the pull of reality and to convince oneself that by resisting one produced a solid sense of self, were doomed because of the institutionalised and conventionalised ways in which these escape routes were now offered and controlled (...) I think that you can find in Goffman a situationist impishness ... When I'm teaching Goffman I often start off talking about such notions as men opening doors for women, talking about what he calls in *Relations in Public* [1971] using Hobbes' phrase, the micro-government and taking up Hobbes' idea that the density of these arrangements might be the most important thing, and that those who talk about the possibility of a revolution to use [Raoul] Van Eigem's famous phrase 'he who talks of a revolution without talking of a revolution in everyday life has a corpse in his mouth' ... it's not a phrase Goffman uses but it's a nice one.

(...) I think you say about Goffman, that he's always anxious to assure the reader that his speculations are only a preliminary stage, a 'spying out of the land'. That suggests that after all this field work and observation there is going to be some statement; has he made 'the statement'?

No, he's never made the statement because ...

Is that what you mean by the way ?

Yes, he was always racing on to the next statement. For Goffman there was always so much to be said, he was always so excited by sociology, ... he was always fascinated by the *density,* the absolute density of social life ...

Which entraps us?

Yes I met him once, and I spent an evening with him and throughout the evening he was as obsessively concerned with social arrangements and objects and events as one would have hoped that he might be, I mean he was

174

saturated (...) He was overcome by the social architecture, by the scaffolding of social life: it was as though he continuously saw the cobwebs, the tracery, the lines, the connections between people, it was almost as though, what would be a metaphor to describe it ... almost as if he forever saw wires stretching between simple bits of behaviour and simple actions. And because he saw all this as *moral*, that was the other thing about it, it was the moral density of this social life which obsessed him, the fact that people felt that this was the only possible way they could go about doing the things that they were doing.

What I was going to come to, is that you said that 'what started out as an extended commentary upon the mannerisms of individuals in social interaction has become, over the years, a disturbing vision of humanity' [1968, p. 837]. What's disturbing about this vision?

I think that Alan Dawe captures it rather nicely in his article [1973]. When he tries to suggest that Erving Goffman has moved from a mild anthropological curiosity about social arrangements to a paranoid vision of America under seige ... the disturbing vision is this; that this psychological view of Goffman's does parallel in certain ways the increasingly privatised bourgeois world of contemporary America and of this country as well: it fits nicely with Richard Sennett's notion of 'destructive *gemeinschaft*' in which we insulate ourselves in the home, shut the door against the night, close the outside world off, because of our fear of the burglars, the murderers, the rapists, the muggers ... because of all those public horrors that Goffman talks about in *Relations in Public*, the urban underpasses, the 'dangerous areas', the possibility of contamination, all the insults that can come to self in these public places. So we retire from them and we lock ourselves away within private homes in a private world. But Goffman hasn't finished tightening the screw - because in that story 'the insanity of place' rather like in *Straw Dogs*, there is within this private room - even when we've shut the door against the night - there is an insanity within the private arrangements, lurking and waiting for us.

(...) Alan Dawe argues that 'in Goffman's basic assumptions, one finds a view of the social world almost totally lacking in some of the central features of that world: power, class, conflict, political domination, purpose, moral

commitment and so on'. Dawe says we smile at his observations, 'it renders the tribute due to the sociological jester whose jokes always contain a shrewd observation on social life - but also a caricature and a denial of the real substance of that life' [1973, pp. 247-8]. How do you see that?

There *are* times when the business of reading Goffman can be an arid affair where you feel that his fascination with the frames and the brackets of analysis does leave you without any sense of humans being around. But I think that Alan Dawe at that time might have been going through 'the John O'Neill phase', a romantic over-humanised sociology, so that I think that he overstates the case slightly. I think that you do need antidotes to Goffman, I think that a complete diet of Goffman is probably very bad for the soul, I think that it *is* a dehumanising process, and I think he is infatuated at times with his own cleverness, and that is why I like to turn to other writers and to other places when in fact I want sociology to be more compassionate, more concerned, and having more detailed involvement in practical dilemmas, problems and circumstances.

Gouldner in The Coming Crisis *argues that Goffman's work is without a 'metaphysics of hierarchy'; that it dwells on the immediate and episodic; and that for Goffman tact replaces moral codes as the major constraint of behaviour between anonymous others [1970, p. 379]. Do you think that's true? It's all a case of making your way, shuffling around, and managing ...*

Yes a lot of it is indeed about that, but I think that questions of morality are often settled within those local small areas. There's a lovely moment in an Alan Ayckbourn play where one of the characters turns to another and says 'could we have a serious conversation now about really important matters', and the joke is that all their conversations about eating tuna fish and whether to have extra cups of tea are already about the real matters. The real matters of their existence are phrased in terms of cups of tea, and turntaking, and going through doors, and getting up for breakfast and I accept the potency of that. I think there is a tendency for sociologists who go on about, say, stratification to believe, as it were, that the world is lived out in terms of those preoccupations (. . .) There are of course real people suffering from malnutrition, who die younger than others, who are the victims of massive discrimination, the great facts and features of human inequality and existence. And there are sociologists, some excellent and brilliant ones, who deal with these matters. But I would also say with Goffman that there are different sorts of imaginations about social issues and although it is possible for my imagination to be exercised about institutions, about say prisoners, and about prisoners' rights and about that area, there are other areas where I find that I cannot respond imaginatively in the way that I should ... but the thing that has saved me, preserved me if you like, or has helped me to preserve some sense of a radical version of the world is Foucault.

(...) Foucault for a lot of people is very difficult ... what do you think his central message is for social theory? What can he tell us as sociologists?

I started on Foucault with the greatest ...

Why did you start?

Really in the same way that I started with Lacan because I just didn't understand what was being talked about and by teaching a course on Foucault I thought I might actually understand a little bit more than by simply sitting down and reading the books (...) Like so many of my intellectual interests it started out as straightforwardly pretentious, well I thought 'well this is something else that hardly anybody else in the department seems to know about. I can put on a course on Foucault, and keep everyone else away', it was rather like why I chose to do psychology in the first place, it sounded good. But I love pretention, pretention is nice, people trying to be more than they are, they're always the more interesting people aren't they? It's so boring if people just go on being the people who they are, but if people adopt airs and have delusions of grandeur, you know splendid, that's fine. They are splendidly vulnerable. What I find in Foucault is the wonderful element of surprise and excitement. I mean this morning for example, I have been doing a most difficult two-hour seminar, not difficult I hope because I made it difficult, but because the material *is* difficult. What we were considering was the way in which Foucault in *Madness and Civilisation* [1967] talks about changes occurring in the dramatic depiction of madness. In particular the depiction of madness which appears in *King Lear* and the comparison between this and the depiction of madness which can be found in the final scene of Racine's play *Andromache*. Now it's a very very important distinction for Foucault in *Madness and Civilisation* because, as you know, he wants to say that with the arrival of the classical period, one begins to see the development within societies of institutions, the houses of confinement, the workhouses, in which the mad together with all the vagabonds and the poor are to be put on one side. They are geographically, socially, physically, to be separated. Then he turns and asks how can this separation of madness, the sense that madness no longer has anything transcendental to say about the human condition, how is that represented on the stage. Now he's already talked about *Lear* where madness appears centrally in the play, where when Lear is mad he has something to say, all the people observing Lear listen attentively to his mad reason. The mad person is the tragic hero, the tragic hero has something to say about the human condition. Now when you move to *Andromache* and Racine, when Orestes goes mad in the final scene of the play *his* madness is presented as an hallucination. He goes into the darkness as Foucault puts it into unreason, into delusion, into hallucination, into an obsession with Hermione who produced this particular madness - it's the last play if you like of the Renaissance theatre, the last play in which the tragic hero does go mad, but it's also the first play of the classical era in that he goes mad in terms of delusions and unreason and is ushered off the stage. *Just as all madmen were ushered off the stage into the houses of confinement.* Now that to me sets off so many reverberations. It is so good to be talking about Racine and Shakespeare, and the same time talking about such definite historical events as the founding of the *Hopital General*, (...) Now it may well be that Foucault gets it wrong - I read many people who say that he doesn't quite get it right, the houses of confinement didn't quite develop in the way that he said it did, what about this play that doesn't fit. But if I am talking about sociology as an imaginative exercise, one which has to be placed alongside literature, in its capacity to transcend conventional understanding, then it's splendid ... When Foucault's talking about the archaeology of knowledge he's talking about it in almost geological terms, about sort of sinking a shaft down through the core of our present consciousness, going down through the layers of our present consciousness to discover the different epistemological arrangements of different ways of thinking which are possible compared with what we take to be for granted at the moment. I love that. Foucault is profoundly exciting. In his *History of Sexuality* [1979], what a marvellous reversion that is to suggest that the whole repressive hypothesis about sexuality is the wrong way round, that really far from the nineteenth early twentieth century-story being one in which people are trying to repress sexuality, it's one in which sexuality is actually being constituted, in which ideas of sexuality are being set within children and within the family, and then surveillance systems in order to monitor them are being set up which once in place are very effective ways in which power, micro-power can operate (...) I could go on for hours, I still find Foucault exciting, when I read reviews of him, criticisms of him, I get angry, if they don't do justice to the excitement ... the way in which he's recreated a sense of history in sociology is so important, real history.

(...) Is he merely a very good historical sociologist or is he doing something quite new?

I think his attempts to determine the conditions of possibility for particular discourses in particular times and particular ages has to be said, in a way, to be new. I think that it is not historical in many ways - although I've said it reintroduces history - it is the history of the present and I always teach it as the history of the present, so I talk simultaneously about Laing, about Sartre, about Artaud and about people like this at the same time that we are considering the seventeenth century. I mean to take Foucault seriously you must simultaneously consider the present and the past. His history is the history of the present. It is there for the present.

And it's still sociology because of its unmasking nature?

Yes, because at every turn, in every paragraph it's engaged in demystifying. I mean you couldn't have anything much more demystifying than that book on sexuality, or the final paragraphs of *Discipline and Punish* [1977] where he suddenly says that the main point about prisons is of course that they don't work. Their failure is in fact the most important and significant feature of prisons. That's a lovely thing to work with, to start with, that upsets in a few pages whole legions of criminologists and armies of sociologists of deviance. It puts them on the defensive, they've got to do something about statements like this, in the same way that he has all the psychiatrists on the line in *Madness and Civilisation*, in the same way that in *The History of Sexuality* he has all the Freudians concerned. And in *The Order of Things* [1970] when he talks about Marx *swimming* with 19th century economic thought like a fish in water, when he talks about Marxists, when he talks about the epistemological nature of Marx causing no more than a few ripples

179

in a paddling pool of 19th century economic thought. I mean it's splendid to find Marx and Freud being taken on in this way. Demystification is, as I said much earlier, not just about the demystification of the world but also of sociologically accepted things, accepted truths.

What to you is 'ideal' sociology?

I would only say that I look for surprise; anything enthusiastic, stylish, surprising, demystifying, subversive.

What sociology do you think tells the obvious then?

I think cumulative empirical sociology, you know in which it says x and y have discovered a and b, but supposing we consider another variable and see if it holds still in the case of c. I mean that is the idea of continually building by doing yet one more similar study in the same area. In some cases I know that it has to be done, I mean if you're doing something like studies of poverty it quite clearly is important to index the various social groups and occupations to which that might apply, but you know all those dreadfully dreary things which we used to be confronted with (...)

Can you think of such a sociology today?

You mean that I dislike intensely?

Yes, if you want.

No, not dislike, but I suppose I'm *bored* by certain sorts of sociology more than others. I mean the sociology of education - I have just little prejudices - the sociology of education has always seemed to me a difficult area to feel enthusiastic about, and the sociology of the professions. I think what it is, is those people who've set up little study groups where they're concerned with a small area of sociology, and in the way that John Rex was characterising to you the sociology of deviance, actually *that* sociology was a bit broader than he allows, but there certainly are groups, obsessive, incestuous, professional groups operating within one particular narrow area. Just one special topic area which they obsessively patrol ... it often seems to owe much more to promotion and to publication than to intellectual curiosity.

And presumably politics?

Yes politics, and I can't understand how anyone who is absolutely committed to intellectual understanding and knowledge can possibly spend most of their life going to meetings concerned solely with the sociology of the professions.

(...) So what's the 'baseline' for sociology then?

What would count as sociology? I'd like to think that sociology is one of those disciplines within a university, and philosophy should perhaps be another, where that question is less permissible than anywhere else.

Have you a vision of what the 'good society' would look like?

No I don't have a vision of the 'good society'. I don't at all. I wish that life was considerably more public, more than anything else it is the privatisation of life which I object to. I long for a return - perhaps I'm being unrealistically nostalgic - but there are times in your life perhaps when you're adolescent when you're eighteen, nineteen or twenty-one, when you live publicly. You know where public places are your own; where you feel at home in the city centre, in bars and in clubs and at football grounds and cricket grounds, you feel that these places are very much part of you, you don't experience them as public or alien, and I regret most of all those people, my parents and other families that I see - and I see it in myself as well - who become frightened of the public life. If I had an ideal society it would have bits and pieces from elsewhere, it would certainly have the public politics and public entertainment of somewhere like Italy. I am still staggered in Italy to turn round the corner and find an open air political meeting of the Communist Party in which large numbers of people are publicly debating, there is an open arena for that sort of public debate. I mean I still like the idea of festivals and I'm an aged hippie to the extent of feeling that those large gatherings of people at rock festivals, and demonstrations - I still regularly go on demonstrations not solely for neat political reasons, but because the sight of all those people there, united for a particular purpose but still with their individuality I find very moving.

Do you take such notions like 'equality' for granted?

Yes. I hate the cynicism and the brutality of the present political arrangements and its philosophy as much as anyone else. I hate in particular what seems to be the totally cynical ideology which exists at the moment. I think there are brands of conservatism which lack that sort of cynical search for personal and class advantage but I see now a cynicism and a determination to corner resources and a readiness to bankrupt the country and to bankrupt the spirit of particular groups in the country for the sake of personal class advantage which is as naked as at any time as it has ever been, so I mean I hate that (...) And yes, I am a believer in the possibility of sociology saying something socially relevant.

(...) Do you think you have been influential and in what way? You see I asked someone, 'what would you say if you were going to see Laurie Taylor?', and he said, 'is he ever going to do anything serious any more?' ... also what are you doing now?

I've nearly finished writing a book which is called *In the Underworld* [1984].

With John McVicar?

No. I'm not writing it with John McVicar, I'm writing it by myself now, and it's on professional crime which is again back to the sociology of deviance, and about the coherence and moral density of a particular culture. It's rather nice that you said that somebody said when is Laurie Taylor going to do something serious again. I would like to think that I could, in twenty or thirty years, and at the end of it people would still be asking the same question.

7 Michael Mann

Michael Mann is best known for his short yet influential *Consciousness and Action Among the Western Working Class* (1973), as editor of an encyclopaedia of sociology (1983), and his three-volume project on the 'sources of social power'.

Born in 1942, and educated in modern history at Oxford, Mann is Professor of Sociology at the University of California, Los Angeles. In *Consciousness and Action Among the Western Working Class*, Mann argues against both Marxist approaches and 'end of ideology' theorists, and asserts that 'we must reject both rival claims that the capital-labour relationship contains an inherent tendency toward either revolution or harmonistic stability' (1973, p. 68). On the working class Mann is particularly pessimistic in terms of their role as agents of change; 'whatever the *objective* possibility that they might be the bearers of a new principle of social structure - collectivism - they themselves either do not perceive this or do not know how to translate it into action' (1973, p. 69).

Discussing the 'boundaries' of stratification research, Newby observes that there are signs of a 'growing rapprochement' between historical sociology and sociological history (mainly following the demise of functionalist sociology), and that this has also encouraged sociologists 'increasingly to take account of the historical antecedents of contemporary processes and relationships' (1982, p. 63). Mann himself would concur, and points to a weakness in sociology, arguing that it is noted for its 'lack of historical depth', and that 'much contemporary sociology is essentially a-historical'

(1984, p. 67) . Abrams, in his posthumously published *Historical Sociology*, adds that there is 'no necessary difference between the sociologist and the historian', and further argues that 'sociology which takes itself seriously must be historical sociology' (1982, p. 17). This is also Mann's position.

In the *Sources of Social Power* (1986, 1987, 1988), Mann attempts to provide a history and theory of power relations in human societies. He claims to have arrived at a distinctive, general way of looking at human societies which is 'at odds with both usual explicit models of society dominant within sociology and usual implicit models found in detailed historical writing'. This Mann terms, in a manner not dissimilar to Rex, as 'structural symbolic interactionism' (1984, p. 1). Mann argues that we can 'never find a single bounded, demarcated society in geographical or social space', and that, in fact, *'societies are constituted of multiple overlapping, intersecting socio-spatial networks of power'*. He continues that (1984, pp. 2-3)

> Systems theory, Marxism, structuralism, structural functionalism, normative functionalism, multi-dimensional theory, evolutionism, diffusionism, and action theory all mar their insights by conceiving of 'society' as an unproblematic, unitary totality.

Mann concludes, quite candidly, that 'it may seem a funny position for a sociologist to adopt, but, if I could, I would abolish the concept of society altogether' (1984, p. 3; see also Urry, 1981).

For Mann, history does not repeat itself, but rather precisely the opposite: 'it is only through historical comparison that we can see that the most significant problems of our own time are actually and totally *novel*' (1984, p. 68). And, historically speaking, for the past two centuries for sociology, Mann correctly observes, the 'basic yet elusive issue is that of ultimate primacy or determinancy' (1984, p. 5).

Could you tell me something about your background?

I was born 1942, in Manchester, lower middle class background. My paternal grandfather was a bank clerk all his life, my father started out as a salesman, worked his way up always within the same big industrial company, Turner and Newall, to being sales director of the asbestos side of the industry. As he worked his way up, I remember while I was at home there was a kind of constrained lower middle class background 'keeping my back straight', 'getting on in life', 'eating one piece of fruit a day', 'thinking what I liked but being careful about what I said', and then coincidental with my leaving home to go to University my father got a major promotion to be a sales director of the asbestos company and so that in late middle age they became reasonably prosperous. They valued education very highly, and obviously I was quite bright and I went to Manchester Grammar School and then went on to Oxford, read history though I started out reading law because he wanted me to be a lawyer ...

You changed ...

I changed after three weeks because I found it rather dull. I realised that ... I worked in the law libraries, saw the immense cases and realised that I didn't particularly enjoy that and perhaps it was a conservative reaction on my part going back to history which I knew and had done at 'A' level. So I read history. Mind you I was never terribly stimulated by it, and spent a lot of time doing other things at Oxford. I was active in politics and started out as a Liberal as the town I came from, Rochdale, had a strong Liberal background and my own background was constant with that, but I changed and joined the Labour Party in my second year as a student, and played rugby and did a variety of other things. I was an average student, got a second-class degree. I wanted to stay on a year in Oxford because I was involved with a girl, and so did the Diploma in Social Studies with the vague intention of helping people and being a probation officer more specifically. And so I did my first sociology course, and Peter Collison, who is now professor at Newcastle, taught me and I got on very well with him and he was very helpful to me, and in the course of the year I think I was probably showing a much greater interest in academic things than before and so I was offered a chance of doing research which I took instead of being a probation officer, and that was my thesis research.

Workers on the Move?

Yes, *Workers on the Move* [1973a] in which I spent most of my time doing fieldwork, empirical research, going into this factory ...

Was there any influential book, or person(s) that made you want to do sociology?

No, I don't think so. No. I think I was interested in society and, I mean in the empirical world around. I certainly was very theoretically undernourished for a long time ... never read any Weber, Marx, except for the *Communist Manifesto* for other reasons.

Was Workers on the Move *closely related to the D.Phil?*

Yes.

So you hadn't read Weber and Marx when you wrote the book?

That's right. Well I'd read Marx on 'alienation' because that obviously came out of mainstream industrial sociology and that's as far as I got.

In Consciousness and Action Among the Western Working Class [1973] *you talk about the 'end of ideology' thesis, Clark Kerr, Daniel Bell, and so on. Ten years on what are your views on this? Do you still think the thesis very weak?*

I still think it's very weak, in fact my historical research has shown me how absolutely absurd the notion is that societies cohere because of value consensus in some way, or indeed that they're torn apart because of value dissent, that that is an important dimension is nonsensical in any but a politically democratic society and the idea could only gain currency because of the kind of dominant ideology of political democracy, and it's so much at odds with social reality ...

... Further in the book you say that whatever the 'objective *possibility that*

they might be the bearers of a new principle of social structure - collectivism - they themselves either do not perceive this or do not know how to translate it into action' [1973, p. 68]. Could you talk a little about your remark?

If I think back to the terms which I used in that book, and one of the four dimensions of class consciousness was 'totality', the question is 'how are workers to get a grasp of the total society in which they're involved, which they might want to change'? Well, by and large, when we're dealing at the level of the national state, most workers are not significantly involved in the totality of the national state, their conflicts with their employers are more normally settled at a local and industrial level, and therefore their situation is not one where they view conflict in terms of total social processes, and so they cannot develop a coherent notion of society as a whole and I think that the evidence shows that they don't have a harmonistic-consensual image of the society as a whole but nor do they have a kind of alternative vision. Now where they *do*, and indeed there are quite a lot of processes of settling of industrial relations and also other aspects of class relations and areas of consumption, where they do develop, rather where, in a way, they are objectively implicated in the institutions of the national state, as for example they have been increasingly doing with such corporatist tendencies as there are and incomes policy and the like. What's happened is that capitalism has simultaneously moved beyond the national level to the international and that therefore it doesn't really matter what they do at the national level unless they're capable of grasping the transnational operations of capitalism ... then they will not objectively be able to do anything and the first stirrings of movement towards something else will be undercut by international pressure, and it will show them that factually they cannot change the situation, and they get dispirited, and say 'well we can't do anything about it so we've got to settle for much less'. Even the Callaghan Labour government and the Wilson government, such movements as they made towards more social welfare policies were undercut by international capitalist pressure. I see no tendencies whatever for there to be an international or transnational working class movement, and at the moment whatever the tendencies within the national state - and there are national states which have stronger labour movements than ours, in their different ways Sweden and France, they too are undercut by international pressure (...)

This could lead to extreme pessimism about social reform, but I think that two things are possible. I think that more limited achievements are possible for people interested in redistribution and developing possibilities for working class people developing more control over their lives in minor ways. The other thing is that I think that the labour movement has in a sense to be told all this and to be told 'you can't get anywhere unless you attack the international level'. And so, I've become more aware of a political role for this kind of sociology.

(...) How have you seen the 'Braverman debate', or the 'de-skilling debate'?

At the time I was scathing about the book. I didn't regard the thesis as proved and regarded the empirical substance of it as flimsy. I felt that to establish it you would have to look at areas which you might think were actually being in a sense re-skilled, that is newer industries and the like and compare the two and see how significant they were. In the last few years I think that the Cambridge group of sociologists [Stewart, Prandy, and Blackburn] have found another major defect in it which I hadn't thought about until they did the work. They pointed out the difference between jobs and people, and that in the area of lower white collar work the jobs may have become de-skilled over the twentieth-century. Whether they have or not is difficult to establish, they probably have since about 1880 ... but it has very few social consequences because the people filling them have changed through the period, and they note that there are three very different kinds of clerical worker and that the most important group of them are women who are entering that area of the labour market for the first time and they haven't been deskilled as people. The second group are young men who are moving up and for them the career, the life trajectory is what matters and so they too are not being de-skilled. The third group are sideways-promoted manual workers who become checkers in warehouses and a lot of other jobs that are classified nominally as non-manual, but for them it's a normal part of their work life, it's the sideways move when your strength starts to fail. Even if these jobs had been de-skilled it would have very little significance. I would also say I don't think you can explain all that much about the working class from what's called the labour process, I don't think you can explain the development of the working class movement and numerous other aspects of social structure just as a result of what happens in the workplace. I think that is a result of taking these words 'relations of production' at a far too literal level and assuming that class relations, economic power relations, are reducible to what happens in workplaces. I don't think that's so at all.

Many people talk these days of naivete surrounding the study of the state. Would you like briefly to talk about that, and in connection with, say, the Miliband-Poulantzas debate?

Well that concerns such a narrow aspect of ... well I've always had the difficulty with sociology that it seems to me that the theoretical debates that we get ourselves into represent a tiny fraction of the sociological theories that are possible and plausible, and that doesn't just apply to this area. There are lots of ways of thinking about the state which people have had over the last hundred years. If one thinks of the kind of tradition of Gumplowicz, Oppenheimer and Hintze [see Mann, 1984a], that is one tradition and way of looking at the state. Another tradition of looking at the state is provided by the kind of political and legal theorists who developed notions of sovereignty and that has been resurrected in the contemporary world by people who study the international political system and the notion of relations between states being very important. There are people who have thought of the state as an ideological process, people like Clifford Geertz. Now what is very striking is the way that these different ways of looking at the state stay in their compartments, they're different types of research, and yet they're all obviously relating to real social processes. A genuine theory of the state would certainly combine all of those that I've mentioned as well as the Marxist tradition of states having some relevance to social classes. Now what was curious about the Miliband-Poulantzas debate is that it was not only looking at reducing states to social classes, but it was exclusively concerned with contemporary capitalist societies, that it appeared to put on enormous blinkers in not even thinking about the Soviet Union as an alternative form of state, that it was always talking about *the* state as if there was *a* state in a relationship with capitalism instead of there being many states with a hierarchy between them. Therefore the American state has very different roles from the British state. The American state is concerned with the defence if you want to call it, of capitalism as a whole, though I wouldn't really, whereas the British state is not as significantly concerned and the West German state has virtually no defence role at all. All of these issues never ever figured in it (...) Miliband and Poulantzas were going at each other over such a narrow range and I never regarded it as a terribly interesting argument. What I got from Poulantzas was at the level of metaphor; the metaphor told me that I had to raise my vision and I had to try and think about classes and states and ideology in some more systematic way and that I couldn't carry on with the commonsensical, empirically based tradition of research in which I'd been. But when Poulantzas actually said anything specific I disagreed with it fundamentally. I disagree with Miliband fundamentally too. It's ridiculous to reduce the British state to the needs of the capitalist class. The main limitation is not the pluralist kind of limitation, but rather that it's a national state existing within a world of states and therefore it organises social groups which are different to capitalism, they're spatially different, they're socially different. I began to see that at the time of the Miliband-Poulantzas debate and have worked on that problem ever since.

(...) In Newby's review of the stratification research [1982], he stresses the important yet neglected area of gender division. How important is such a relative omission?

There would be two possible justifications, I mean once the feminists made their charge and said we'd been neglecting gender, which we had and obviously everyone has to accept that, there'd be two - no, sorry - one possible justified reaction to that. One would be to say well gender is very interesting and of course yes we should study women and their relationships with men but that is, as it were, a separate dimension of society and of stratification, and therefore we can carry on with the traditional theories of stratification without considering gender as affecting their internal form. We would then add on a separate gender dimension. Well I don't think that's true; however it has a semi-justified position historically which is now fading away. In most preindustrial societies the relationships between men and women have remained very largely unchanged throughout recorded history, I mean that's an astonishing generalisation but the major forms of what feminists I think rightly call patriarchy were established by the time of the first historical records, and we can find some changes in the relation between men and women through historical periods. One can note, as Keith Hopkins does in Egypt, that relations between men and women in ancient Egyptian society were *relatively* egalitarian, marriages were more like equal contracts, divorce was possible, women had property rights. Then the Greek and Roman conquests steadily took rights away and Christianity finished them off, and they ended up with the subordination of women with women not having property rights and with women having to promise to obey, etc., etc. Those are some variations, but nevertheless having said that there is throughout the recorded history that I can find one basic form which is that

190

public power relations - relations of political power, of economic power at the level of market relations or of expropriation of surplus, military relations, the nature of ideological institutions - are the relations between male heads of households, patriarchs, and that women are the subordinate part of each household and that's the important thing about patriarchy. So there is an invariance, and so curiously enough many of the theories that we have about historical stratification systems do remain fairly intact, and in that case we can add on as it were a separate dimension and we say 'yes, we've got to remember this is a household structure, a patriarchal structure and if we want to describe the whole system then we have to include this thing that has been neglected'. Of course, there are many different systems of the transmission of property and marriage systems and a body of research on that, but it doesn't fundamentally affect the nature of power and stratification as a whole. Because women have no capacities for collective organisation because they're all trapped within their households, there is no collective role for women. One can detect very slight glimpses of it now and then, in Ancient Greece and in the first-century of the Christian Millenium, but the latter case is one where we can see them clearly repressed. By 200 AD women are not in any positions of authority in the Christian Church. So that there is no collective movement. Then in the course of early modern history ... Parsons' distinction between 'particularism' and 'universalism' [1952] is a very valid one. We have the replacement of particular power relations, particularistic-kin-genealogical-local-territorial-based societies are built of aggregations of particular groups either kin or territory or class. But we have the emergence of three main universal elements in early modern society: Christendom and its notion of individual salvation, intensified by Protestantism, and the notion that the individual has some justification in the sight of God and therefore has an ultimate significance. The second element is the notion of individual citizenship, that gradually systems of power relations include too many people to be organised by particularistic networks, and the development of parliamentary systems, even if they're confined to classes, nevertheless the males within those classes are individuals and have individual rights, and we have the ideology of liberalism and citizenship. The third element is capitalism and commodity production and in that labour is just labour, and particularistic ascriptive categories make no ultimate difference. Now those are not in any particular order they're part of a general process; but they break up this particularistic system, the household and patriarchs diffuse social forces coming right into the family. Labour is labour whether it's male or female, citizenship is

191

justified in terms of an ideology of the individual which makes it difficult then to exclude women and Christianity also gives women a very important role and because of the role of the family in Christianity ... women actually end up with having a particularly important role in that, and so you get the combination of the importance of religion in the development of the first feminist movement and the problem of the transmission of matrimonial property. The problem of capital is an abstract force, it's not like land. You can transmit land safely, it's there, but you need good systems, different systems, to transmit capital, and therefore women acquire rights to acquire property as they hadn't any historically. And so the last two hundred years has seen a development of a system of stratification in which gender relations are not a separate dimension but have become integrated into it and so women as labour - as a reserve army of labour, largely unorganised, non-unionised, coming in and out of the labour market with lower aspirations, no capacities to force things out of their employers - start to be a very important collective group in affecting the conditions of male employees ... and they enter into the stratification system in all kinds of ways so that if we want to discuss stratification in the last two hundred years we have to integrate gender, the changing nature of the household, the changing nature of public-private relations into it. We haven't gone very far in that yet. I see it as analogous in many ways to *race* which again is not reducible to class, but it's analogous also to the problem of nation, that our theories of stratification are abstract, they apply interchangeably, to the conditions within any single nation state and they also apply to industrial society or capitalist society as a whole and frankly that's a false interchangeability and the notion that collective organisations who have a power relationship to each other are as likely to be ... to have a national identity (some have a national identity, some have a transnational identity) and that also has to be integrated.

(...) In retrospect how do you view The Affluent Worker *research?*

Well, I think it was a very important study though at the time I found a lot of faults in it in the way that one does if one's working in the same kind of area ... Nevertheless it stands up in certain aspects to everything that one throws at it and it was a sustained piece of empirical research which set the tone for a certain number of other studies. I think there's been less development in that kind of research than there should be and ...

192

In what sense?

Well [you mention] the Newby project, and recently I heard him give a paper on that and I was extremely disappointed by how the paradigm for that research is entirely *Affluent Worker* and that the notion that somehow or other if their main - the main problem of this paper whether it's the main problem of the research I don't know - but the main problem of the paper was the extent of the development of the consciousness of the working class, and that their explanation for it, that is that it was a combination of firstly work relationships, relations at work, 'the labour process' in the contemporary jargon, and secondly family structure, 'privatisation' and the like, seems to me extremely flimsy and I wouldn't seek to explain any aspect of the development of the working class movement in the last hundred years on the basis of those two things combined, and they seem to me to have left out all that has been made problematic by newer developments in the last ten, twenty years; the importance of the state - the nation state, the questioning of the centrality of production in economic life in general, the question of gender relations which are not the same as the family structure that they are looking at, and so I was rather disappointed by that, I mean so that ... well perhaps this raises the fact that I don't have an entirely negative view of the theoretical sectarianism of the 1970s, I think that though there are many aspects of it which are in a sense quite unnecessary, there are some aspects of it which are historically necessary like Donizetti. I can't stand Donizetti, but it's a kind of historical necessity, it gets to be much better opera ... and in this case, you see I think that when the Althusserians started hammering away - though they have quite other reasons for their hammering - we empirical sociologists working in certain areas did need hammering for certain things and that I would have thought that you cannot carry on neglecting political processes, you've got to generate a higher level of theory, one that deals with fundamental social structures of the contemporary world that questions the notion ... the *Affluent Worker* is a fine study but it doesn't equal class structure, its methodology doesn't equal class structure and that was made perfectly evident in the third volume. Survey research which is based on asking atomised individuals a number of questions can reveal something but it can't reveal a number of other things and so if one actually does want to discuss problems of class and class structure as a whole, one has to find other sources of information besides survey research and one has to go to macro-social processes and make some structural and historical study of them. What I find still lacking in most stratification research and most industrial sociology research is the willingness to diversify methods and to relate survey research and studying of people's concrete industrial experience and family experience and other experiences they have with larger social processes (...) I also think there is one other aspect of the *Affluent Worker* ... the orientation and 'action approach' [which you mentioned], I assume, in fact I think I know was very much John Goldthorpe's contribution to that; well that's not something that appeals to me, it's not that I am as it were a structuralist versus an action theorist but I think that the whole dilemma is a false one for sociology and I'm just bored with these books which go on and on repeating the same old dilemma in more and more sophisticated and unintelligible ways ...

(...) Do you in fact see specialisation as helpful in the development of sociology?

Well I would not like a single item of the total sociological budget to be diverted from empirical specialised research, there isn't enough of it done, and therefore I will answer no it's not too specialised because empirical research is the basis of sociology. What I would like to see is resources diverted from what is laughingly called theory - which is substandard social philosophy. No I wouldn't say substandard, just social philosophy, as all social philosophy is substandard. What is generally called theory is to my mind not theory. I regard theory as being substantive theory about the development of real societies and what Marx, Weber and Durkheim did and what major sociologists did until 1920 was worry about the way that the world was going, their contemporary world generally ... it doesn't have to be the contemporary world, you could do comparative and historical research but most of their theories developed from the way they thought their world was going. From 1920 onwards sociological theory hasn't been that, it's been abstract ...

(...) In a recent article John Rex [1983] talks about the 'philosophisation of sociology', and Anthony Giddens' attempt to 'rewrite sociology'; how do you see Giddens' contribution?

Well I don't really know what I actually do think, I don't understand a great

194

deal of it. The middle-period books where he's very much concerned with action versus system I don't think anything comes out the other end, I don't understand a lot of what goes on in the middle, he doesn't convince me that I should read all of the people that he discusses. The earlier phase was fine and I assumed he would be developing . . .

. . . you mean on the 'founding fathers'?

Yes, I assumed that he would be developing further. The latest work is interesting but he never stays long enough in one place to actually do anything sustained. A lot of the things he says are good but they're underdeveloped.

(. . .) Is the kind of work you approve of like W. G. Runciman's work on Ancient Rome [1983a]?

Well I disagree with the thesis of that paper, I don't think Rome *was* 'capitalism without classes' but I approve very much of the kind of enterprise that he set himself and to some extent, yes.

(. . .) Philip Abrams describes historical sociology as 'the attempt to understand the relationship of personal activity and experience on the one hand, and social organisation on the other as something that is continuously constructed in time. It makes the continuous process of construction the focal concern of social analysis . . . [and] . . . there is no necessary difference between the sociologist and the historian' and (secondly), that 'sociology which takes itself seriously must be historical sociology' [1982, pp. 16-17]. What did you think of that argument?

Well, I think there's *no necessary difference* between history and sociology. I agree with that, there's obviously a great difference between the practitioners and perhaps there's nothing necessarily wrong with the division of labour . . .

Could we be clear on this; you're saying history and sociology are the same thing?

I believe with August Comte that sociology is the queen of the social sciences, the human sciences and that the more specialised disciplines like that of history are in a sense parasitic upon sociology, that is upon the general theories which sociology can develop. Most historians embody usually implicitly the kind of conventional social theory of their own time and I think it's helpful to them if they actually try and make it a little more explicit, think about it a little bit more systematically. On the other hand, I'm not saying that sociologists are great and historians are piddling. The question of who does good work is quite different from that and I wouldn't claim any peculiar professional disciplinary superiority so that I wouldn't say that I necessarily have some advantage over, let us say, William H. McNeill, you know *The Rise of the West* [1963], and *The Shape of European History* [1974]. He's a historian who likes to generalise about the development of social structure and he does brilliant work which obviously has a very different centre to the kind of work that I'm trying to do, but which ... He's a historian by training, he has difficulty in coping with the notion of social structure but he has other capacities which I probably lack (...) In most of the historical periods that I've been looking at, the capacities of those specialists to *understand* the social structure of their time is extremely limited. For example Assyriologists, people who study Ancient Assyria, serious scholars who study the texts and the archaeological remains ... and they emerge with statements like 'the Assyrian army was 150,000 strong in this particular campaign' . That is sociologically impossible. The capacities of that form of society to assemble a body of men, to point them in a single direction, to have some minimal discipline among them, to supply them for three days on the trot, makes the maximum possible Assyrian army 20,000. Now I am a complete outsider, I am dependent upon what they tell me for the empirical details of that society, but I know that they're talking bullshit. I know that scholars of Ancient Egypt have an extraordinary exaggerated view of the power of the Egyptian state and of the importance of ideology in cementing that state because I have a much better developed sense of social plausibility, of what human beings are generally like, of how you can pass messages amongst them and control people, what kinds of social structures are appropriate. Actually in that case they will be more likely to agree because the contemporary view amongst Egyptologists is that they have somewhat overdone the ideology and the state in the past. Similarly in many different areas of social experience, because they don't have enough of a comparative frame of reference they are usually scholars who are much more detached from their own society than we are, so they have a lesser understanding of people, they receive peculiar currents so that, for example, people who study early Christianity or the Middle Ages have ... they very often are religious people and they are religious people in twentieth-century terms, and their views of the nature of religion are greatly coloured by that. They just don't have enough of a comparative knowledge of societies nor do they have enough knowledge of their own society. Whether people who do this are going to be from the profession of sociology doesn't matter, but for the tradition of comparative study of societies, some knowledge of your own society bestows a sense of social plausibility.

One of Abrams' conclusions is that the 'project of historical sociology involves us in superimposing structure on history with a view to recovering the way history superimposes structure on us' [1982, p. 335]. Is that how you see it? I've a feeling you don't.

I have a difficulty with those two things being separate, structure and history, the way that ... now having just about finished the first volume of my work which is on the development of power in pre-industrial societies, the way that has developed is not ... at the end of it I have emerged with some kind of general approach, I mean it's not a set of law-like propositions but nevertheless it contains some important generalisations, but I've in a sense derived that through a continuous process of immersion in historical and comparative detail, and have not started with a clear notion of structure which I have then imposed upon history. I think there is much more of an empirical interplay between the theoretical notions that one starts with and the way in which things develop. For example when I started I had exactly the three (well in my case four) dimensional theory of stratification of Gary Runciman. One could write general descriptions of society and social change in terms of the interplay of four different dimensions of power. I've abandoned that and although they continue as ideal types ... real social forces are always merged forms of power. I have developed very different sets of theoretical structures as a result.

If we can talk about the Sources of Social Power [1984]. *On the first page you say you have 'arrived at a distinctive general way of looking at human*

197

societies which are at odds with both usual explicit models of society dominant within sociology, and usual implicit models found in detailed historical writing'. You then call it, or you say some people would call it 'structural symbolic interactionism' [1984, p. 1]. What exactly does that mean?

There's no such thing as a single unified social structure, there's no such thing as 'society' as a total entity. Human beings, including us, are involved in various overlapping networks of power relations, it should be obvious enough in our own contemporary world in that we are obviously influenced by international capitalism, we're influenced by the nation state, we're influenced by the military alliance of NATO, we're influenced by various different cultural elements including Christianity in its various forms, and more secular kinds of western liberal culture. All of these power networks have different boundaries, they do not add up ... our social experience is not summed up at any uniformed sets of social structure. These things, and I've only picked out what I conceive of as the most important networks, have an influence upon us. But they tell us to do different things. What capitalism tells us to do is different in certain respects from what the nation state does, and it's different from what NATO tells us, which means that both individuals and social groups have to confront contradictory social processes, socialisation processes. We make decisions about them, there's an active sense of this, we're never passively socialised by 'society' not because as individuals we refuse it or as individuals we have some autonomy from 'society' as a whole, but because 'society' does not exist as a whole. And as rational human beings we have human needs including human needs for order ... we have to constantly make decisions and orient our action in the face of contradiction, which means that there is an active agency. But the only active agencies that count in significant terms are collective ones where groups realise they are confronting the similar kind of contradiction and find a *temporary* solution in a particular way. I'm interested in trying to create structures where none actually exist; that is, if one dispenses with the notion of a single total society then our notions of structure are then *always precarious*. But one imposes in order to understand, one imposes structures as ideal types which the empirical world approximates to and they're useful heuristically in developing our notions; for example, to explain major aspects of modern society in terms of the interplay of capitalism and the national state makes a great deal of sense and we can get a long way with those two notions of social structure which are competing. On the other hand what the symbolic interactionists saw about - unfortunately they always called it 'mass society', it's always micro, it's always the notion of the individual who is always a member of occupations, has hobbies, has many different life worlds and there is a constant interplay between these, that's what I take from symbolic interactionism, the kind of creative interplay of these things at the main level which they always relate to individuals, because they're deeply individualistic. I would wish to transpose it to collective social processes and to develop that. But the metaphor is ... perhaps a mistake on my part because in a sense I'm trying to bypass a great amount of traditional social theory ...

You add that 'we can never find a single bounded demarcated society in geographical or social space ...'. Could you elaborate, with examples?

Well if I ask 'which society do you live in?' what do you reply? ... Many of the social processes that affect us emanate from the national state, which in our case is the United Kingdom, and there's a real boundary at that level for many of the things that do affect us. So that there is for example authoritative redistribution of economic resources within that unit between different age groups, between different regions, between men and women, between social classes, and they stop there and there is then a clear boundary and of course our citizenship is an important and constraining force upon our lives. There's many things that we are implicated in that perhaps we would not wish to be implicated in, but we are, forcibly. It's quite clear the national state is a society in Durkheim's sense as exercising constraint over us. It also has certain sacred elements, it's again as Durkheim expressed it, the notion of 'the nation' and of having a national identity is an important aspect of most of our lives. But as well as that we are affected by the economic system of capitalism and there are many aspects of that economic system which are significantly transnational, that is which transcend the boundaries of state, there are other aspects of it which are international, that is, that the capital is, as it were, a committee composed of the different representatives of national capitals. Now those two elements, the transnational and the international, are well exemplified for example in the International Monetary Fund (IMF) which consists of bankers who are the same kind of person ... they have the same kind of rationality, the same belief as to what is real in society, whether they're British, American or Swiss or whatever. But there are other aspects where the United States is the main force in the IMF, and Britain and West Germany, France, and the others constitute a significant European interest in that, so that's an example of how the force of capitalism has a different social and geographical location to the nation state. Then we are a member of a military alliance NATO, which is in a confrontationist situation with another military alliance, the Warsaw Pact, and whose struggle may well end the world in the next century or two if it continues; and that is not reducible to either the interests of capitalism or the national interest of the United States, though of course the United States is the most important power agency within it. Similarly the cultural aspects that we carry around with us, some people are fervent Christians which may mean Catholic or it may mean Protestant or it may be a small sect, their networks may be therefore larger than the national state, that is they may look very much to Rome for certain aspects of their lives, or they may look to a very small sectarian group located in the celtic fringes of the United Kingdom. Now ... and many of us are members, or consider ourselves as members of a kind of European-centred-liberal-humanist tradition which has certain values, some of which are liberal, some of which are socialist, social-democratic, and all of these different social relationships have two things; they have a great impact on our lives and they are all an important part of our identity. The second characteristic is that they are all differently located in social and geographical space. They relate us to different sets of people, different sets of power relationships.

(...) You talk about the distinctive methodological implications of your approach, that you operate at the social, spatial and organisational level. What's so distinctive about all this?

Well I think there are two main differences. The one that's easier to understand is that I approach power and social control from the standpoint of *logistics*: how is it actually possible to pass messages, human beings, and resources over given distances? How is that capacity to pass messages, human beings and goods ... how has that capacity changed through time, and trying to identify the points of time in which it jumps, that is when there is an increase in the capacity of human organisations to extend their control, when that happens what is it due to? And what I note is that there are four ideal typical ways of controlling people, territories and goods; control can flow from either possession of economic power resources, or from military force, or from possession of the state which I don't equate with military force, or from ideology. Now what I am then trying to do is to look at all four of those as organisational techniques of controlling people in order to achieve collective, or sometimes private exploitative ends ... and so the kind of empirical substance of the history therefore, is trying to see at what point in time the capacity say to pass messages - communication - greatly increases. Obviously that is connected with things like the development of literacy and the development of extensive networks of urban trade, and the development of religions which are universal religions in their claims which don't relate to a particular experience of a locality or a tribe but claim to say something about human beings in general ... the world salvationist religions ... and try to explain why these capacities increase at different points in time, and to say what they're due to. So that I give in a sense a narrative history of the development of the capacities for control, stopping the narration every now and then and saying okay here we have a major jump, what is it due to? What I find in ...

What do you find which may be, if you like, surprising?

Well I find that there is a kind of unevenness about the process, that in contrast to most sociologists who generalise greatly about historical processes and about theoretical matters for that matter, I don't find a continuous set of relationships between let's say the economy and ideology, the economy and military power, and the like. I find that the way in which human societies do develop their capacities has changed very greatly through different historical periods and that in particular the characteristic of early modern society which dominates sociological theory, that is the emergence of industrial capitalism, that they're not found very broadly in earlier history ... by which I mean that neither economic power relations nor social classes have the kind of dynamic role in history that is generally attributed to them in say the Marxist tradition and indeed in some other traditions.

(...) Presumably related to this is your comment that 'through historical comparison ... we can see that the most significant problems of our own time are totally novel' [1984, p. 68]. Is that another difference in your approach?

Yes I think it is different. There's never been a multi-state system in which there was mass participation in each state (through the nation). There has never been a situation in which warfare between the most advanced powers

201

is totally and utterly incapable of achieving any precise human purposes because of the destruction of the weapons themselves. There has never been a situation in which gender is *potentially* dissoluble from its normal historical role, I mean it might have been so before the agricultural revolution but we really know so little about gatherer-hunter societies, it's quite unclear. So that there is a definite uniqueness about contemporary society, and our very survival depends upon our working out some kind of understanding of it. There's another thing which is ... I find it very difficult to express in a very brief way, but by looking at the sources of power as organisational means I appear to be breaking with some of the main traditions of sociological thought. Perhaps the most important one of them is the traditional dualism between idealism and materialism. So what I appear to be finding are cases where ideological movements do attain a massive historical force and are able to structure human societies. The most overwhelming example to date is the emergence of the world religions ... and the ones I focus on are Christianity and Hinduism and their powers to create new societies. Christendom was a society which was not dependent upon particular states, it was something that carried a notion of civilisation through a period in which states had very puny power and in which economic development occurred *through* the agency of Christendom and not as a separate thing ... and one could develop similar arguments for Hinduism in some ways. One explains that enormous power of Christianity which traditional materialism totally failed to come to grips with, one explains that not in terms of idealism but the need of human beings to find meaning in the world. Durkheim's theories, Weber's theories, Clifford Geertz's theories, Robert Bellah's theories, all of the people who seriously tried to explain religion, they have universal theories and so they cannot explain why religion played this role in this particular point in time and space, and why it didn't before, and why it hasn't since. So one cannot explain it in terms of a universal propensity to find meaning, so the way I try and explain it is in terms of the development ... if one doesn't start from the notion of a single society but starts from the notion of overlapping networks of interaction, the interstitial development of one of these particular networks which cannot be confined within the structure of the (in this case) Roman Empire, it is the networks of urban trade, artisans, in which certain peoples, the Greeks and the Jews, are particularly important, in that they create a new social world for sub-groups within that society who try and struggle to understand the new situation in which they find themselves ... they don't find much help from official Roman ideology which excludes them from the state, they develop a new form of social organisation which can give them a sense of community, a sense of normative solidarity *and* of understanding, and that because of the importance of urban trade develops a power which is able to withstand the decline of the Roman Empire and is able to transmit the notion of society through into the Dark Ages and into Medieval Europe. Now that's a case of where I have in a sense given a social explanation of religion, that is I've explained it in terms of the nature of Eastern Mediterranean society in and around the time of Christ, and so it is a traditional sociological, social stroke materialist explanation, not merely in terms of the economy but in terms of social structure, but once developed it is *emergent*, it has emergent powers and in a sense that's one of the most important things that Durkheim produced for sociological theory ... that once developed it has a power which is then irreducible to the conditions which produced it in the first place and in this case has an amazingly powerful role in social transformation. Later I give it quite a role in the explanation of the emergence of capitalism for example.

You say that in the 'last two centuries for sociology, the basic yet elusive issue is that of ultimate primacy or determinancy ...' [1984, p. 5] . Presumably you're *also looking for the ultimate primacy?*

I think that perhaps you're asking a bit more of me than I can deliver there (...) I'm not too sure what the totality amounts to yet. I'm quite clear at the next level down, the next level down is 'what are the general relationships between different forms of power, economic, political, military, ideological and the mixed institutions that they generate?' and that's the next level down theoretically. Now the next level empirically down is 'how do we understand the relationship between in the contemporary world, capitalism, the national state which is now the monopoliser of military force and therefore one doesn't need that independent dimension any more, and the kind of ideological legacies that we have, some of which actually encourage us towards solutions to some of these problems and they don't imprison us totally within these' ... Now in a sense those are the two things I'm relatively clear about, I know all I'm arguing about is the relations between economic, political, military and ideological power, I think one cannot talk about the primacy of one in any ultimate sense as there just isn't enough of history for us to be sure of that, but one can periodise according to different conglomerations of these forms of power. Similarly in the contemporary world I think I'm able to try to explain the contemporary structure of power better than other people because I'm willing to take these different historical inputs into contemporary society all seriously, and by and large that is not done within contemporary social science, by and large people either elevate capitalism or industrial society or they elevate the sovereign state ... So the next level above that is, in a sense, 'what does this all amount to?' I don't know ...

I don't want to sound simple-minded, but isn't a lot of your work an attempt at a 'refutation' of Marx?

That's how it started, but you see I've become equally interested in refuting what has come to be known as Weberian idealising in sociology. I find sociology astonishing in the way that its different traditions stop short at particular points, and that for example in the debate between materialism and idealism, that one can find constantly published books which just restate the primacy of one or the other. I mean Rheinhard Bendix's *Kings or People?* [1978] published a couple of years ago, which has a lot of useful stuff in it, but the theoretical structure which underpins it just says 'ideas are autonomous'. Well they're not! But nor is material production primary, and what I find absolutely astonishing is how few sociologists have been willing to actually attempt to try and put them together, indeed if you start to do it then there are traditional words of abuse, eclectic is the main one.

(...) You say that the 'empirical test must be a historical one' [1984, p. 64]. Is that also for work other than your own?

(...) One can mean different things by history. I mean my work starts in 10000 BC, right now I'm not remotely claiming that many people have to do that. I think that any social problem, however micro ... if you're doing an ethnographic study of the interaction of a small number of people, you have to include in that notions of their life trajectories. And if you want to stay with that as an interesting piece of ethnography, fine, that's perfectly acceptable, but if you then want to try and explain more of it you obviously have to go back a bit further and ask 'okay they're coming into this interaction as social beings, what are the things that produced that?'

Is there a difference between your approach and comparative sociology?

Yes, I have become increasingly sceptical of comparative sociology, that is, the enterprise of comparing societies as units, across different times and spaces. If I try and explain our society, if I try and say why are things as they are, I find there isn't a very general explanation across the world, I mean our contemporary society has got certain baggage, historical baggage ... capitalism is never something that completely swept across society dominating it, it came to terms with the things that it found already. Two of the most important things are the national state and gender relations and it fitted itself into them. This isn't a general social process, it's the only time it's ever occurred ...

Where does quantification come into your research?

Well wherever it can ... wherever, which is not very often. The most sustained piece of quantification is in the analysis of state finances, and I have in fact published an article on English state expenditure from 1130 to 1815 trying to work out the functions of the state, what it spends its money on [1980]. And though expenditure doesn't tell you everything about functions, because some important functions don't cost much, it nevertheless is a very precise way into some traditional theoretical problems. I try and do that also with the Roman state though one can only find spotty data for it. I tried to artificially create a quantification by trying to ask 'how far is it possible to march an army unsupported in different historical periods?', 'what are the comparative transport costs of land and sea transport?'. Classical scholars have worked on them (...) the structure of the Roman Empire say ... another thing that sociologists tend to neglect, we've inherited this dichotomy between industrial and pre-industrial societies and the notion that there were very complex, highly stratified differentiated historical societies existing, and somehow they'd forgotten. The Roman Empire is tremendously important, it's a very well documented agrarian empire, and I tried to work out rather carefully how far the Governor can make this Writ carry ... and so I'm all for quantification, I think that one can get insights from all kinds of means, but in order to develop them and say who's right and who's wrong if people are arguing, unless one is dealing with universal properties of society, one is dealing with tendencies which conflict with other tendencies and the most precise way one can establish their interrelations is to quantify them.

How would you like to see sociology develop?

I'd fire almost all epistemologists. I would like to seek to remove the fetters of government on research which have grown over the past few years so that empirical sociology didn't mean 'official' ... problems defined by officialdom.

What is sociology anyway? The science of society?

Yes if you mean by science, systematic knowledge, reasonably systematic knowledge, organised knowledge, then yes. The Greek word from which it derived doesn't imply Comtian notions. I'm trying to understand the world in which we find ourselves (...) It's the world of course with all sorts of theoretical preconceptions, and it helps to make those explicit. But one should do that, I think that where theory means both epistemology and continuous scholarship on what Marx, Weber, and Durkheim *really* meant ... they're the two greatest hindrances (...)

8 Ann Oakley

Born Ann Titmuss in 1944, Professor Ann Oakley works at the Institute of Education, London, and is the author of nearly a dozen books including the recently published autobiography *Taking It Like a Woman* (1984). In addition she has written literally over one hundred articles and papers.

She is known for at least two contributions: to feminism and for detailed imaginative empirical studies of under researched areas like housework and childbirth. However in addition she has much of importance to add to discussions of methodology, and her work can be understood in terms of her attitude towards 'theory' which she argues can 'be dangerously close to religion in its creed-like qualities' (1981, p. 340).

Quoting Jessie Bernard, Oakley notes that types of methodological procedures reflect traditional gender stereotypes, and accordingly methods like participant observation are seen as 'feminine' and have 'less academic prestige' (1974, p. 21). On interviewing, Oakley argues that in the 'text-books' the motif of successful interviewing is 'be friendly but not too friendly', which she sees as humane manipulation of interviewees as sources of data (1981a, p. 33). She argues it is considered that 'getting involved with the people you interview is doubly bad; it jeopardises the hard-won status of sociology as a science and is indicative of a form of personal degeneracy'. She adds that, for her, the difficulties in interviewing women in her childbirth research were of two main kinds: firstly *they asked her* a great many questions, and secondly repeated interviewing over a considerable period of time and 'involving the intensely personal experiences of pregnancy ... established a rationale of personal involvement I found it problematic and ultimately unhelpful to avoid'. Oakley considers that personal involvement is more than a 'dangerous bias' it is the 'condition under which people come to know each other and to admit others into their lives' (1981a, p. 41, p. 42, and p. 58). It is worth quoting in full Oakley's example of the 'dilemma' facing the feminist interviewer (1981a, p. 48)

> The dilemma of a feminist interviewer interviewing women could be summarised by considering the practical application of some of the strategies recommended in the textbooks for meeting interviewees' questions. For example, these advise that such questions as 'which hole does the baby come out of?' 'does an epidural ever paralyse women?' and 'why is it dangerous to leave a small baby alone in the house? ' should be met with such responses from the interviewer as 'I guess I haven't thought enough about it to give a good answer right now', or a head-shaking gesture which suggests 'that's a hard one' (Goode and Hatt). Also recommended is laughing off the request with the remark that 'my job at the moment is to get opinions, not to have them' (Selltiz *et al)*.

Her absolutely fundamental contribution to the sociology of housework is precisely seeing the occupation *as work*. One of the possible consequences of this reality for the workers themselves is, as Oakley puts it, that the 'deconditioned' housewife is 'thus a potential revolutionary' (1974, p. 197). On childbirth, obstetric practices and attitudes, Oakley's research reinforces the growing belief that the male-controlled system of reproductive care has a 'tendency to treat women not as whole, responsible people but as passive objects for surgical and general medical manipulation' (Oakley, in Mitchell and Oakley, 1976, p. 54; see also Arms, 1975).

Could you tell me a little about your background?

I've got an autobiography coming out in January, *Taking It Like a Woman* [1984] ...

I know but I need a little here ...

Well, I was born in 1944 in London. I went to a girls' school, I think that's probably important. I went to a single-sex school from the age of 6 to 16, then I left in a fit of anger and I went to a Polytechnic and just spent the first year painting. I took the Oxford entrance examinations because my father, who was a socialist, had a rather secret ambition that his only child should go to Oxford. So I took the entrance examinations for Oxford, and I actually took them in his room at LSE because Chiswick Polytechnic didn't have facilities for people to take entrance examinations for Oxford . My father's secretary kept coming in the room to make sure I wasn't looking at *Incest in Scotland* or any of the other interesting books (...) I had an interview at Somerville, and they told me I'd failed every paper except the general paper which was the best one they'd ever seen. On the strength of that they offered me a place, and they discovered I hadn't any 'A' levels so I went back to Chiswick Poly and I took 'A' levels there (...) So I went to Oxford and I did politics, philosophy and economics. In my last year they introduced sociology as an option (...) Looking back on it, and considering my interests, I think I would have been better doing a straightforward sociology degree, but I didn't want to go to LSE. I didn't want to be in London (...) At that time I wanted to be a writer, a novelist in fact, but I was advised not to do English at University as if you wanted to be a writer that was the last thing you did. So I think PPE was perhaps the most congenial degree offered at Oxford.

So very little sociology for you at Oxford?

I didn't do very much sociology [there]. I had I suppose eight tutorials with Bryan Wilson ... he was terribly nice to me and I certainly enjoyed that term and the other term I did with Halsey; Halsey did inspire me, there's no doubt about it, he did. The first essay I did was on Dahrendorf's *Class and Class Conflict in Industrial Society* (...) That was important given that I'd spent the previous two years doing moral philosophy, political theory, etc, subjects which actually in their own way could have been very exciting but just are not. The way they were taught made them seem an irrelevance to the modern world and the way in which the world actually worked.

209

Can I ask you about your father? Did he affect your motivations and interest in (say) social problems and sociology before you went to University?

Parents always have an effect on their children. They don't need to sit down with them and take them through something, the theory of something or whatever ... I think that I was influenced in the sense of hearing particular issues discussed in the household and of there being people like Richard Crossman and Tawney and people like that who came to the house. It was the atmosphere. Politically he certainly influenced me; and I don't think I would have been a socialist without that influence. As it was he wasn't a sociologist, he described himself as a 'student of society' because he left school at 14 and he didn't have any formal education after that (...) Clearly he was interested in social processes and relationships and clearly I was too. But he didn't ever attempt to influence me directly in terms of what I was going to do, in fact both he and my mother gave me a rather double standard about what I should do in my adult life, in the sense that clearly, I felt, they expected me to achieve in line with the male career model, but also expected me to get married and have children. And nobody ever made it clear to me how these two things were to be achieved. Neither they nor the schools; that was a common experience for women then, and probably still now.

In the beginning of the Sociology of Housework *you talk a lot about the 'invisibility of women' or their inadequate representation ... One thing you say is that 'the discrimination against women in the academic domain' is 'particularly true in sociology, the "science" that studies social reality' [1974, p. 1]. Don't you think it's a science?*

I think it's as scientific as any science. One of the things I've realised over the last few years is that the physical sciences, and medical sciences in particular, are really not superior to social science ... that was written ten years ago and I wasn't aware then how inadequate the basis of much physical science was ...

'Sociology is sexist, purely because it is male-oriented' [1974, p. 2]. Presumably over the last decade you think that's changed to a great degree?

Obviously in some ways yes, it has become less sexist in that there's more awareness of the problem, people write articles and books about it, there's a big literature now; and women's studies courses, but these are not necessarily fundamental changes. I notice on your list that you've got one token woman, there are other women you could have interviewed ...

(...) You disapprovingly quote Giddens who argues that 'given that women still have to await their liberation from the family, it remains the case in the capitalist societies that female workers are largely peripheral to the class system' [Giddens, 1973, p. 288, in Oakley, 1981, p. 281]. Why do you think sociologists continue to argue such things?

Because they're men! Because ... the dominant view of women in our society is still unchanged, and it's easier to participate in that view than to challenge it. When sociologists do a study of social mobility they only look at men because they make the assumption, and it's not articulated, that social mobility for women is not important, or if you study social mobility you study men first and then you perhaps go on to study women (...) So the basic pattern of behaviour that sociologists study and that people think about in this country is men's behaviour and that hasn't changed.

In Subject Women *you note that there are, at least, three definitions of social class: the official, the sociological and the Marxist. And you add that each 'has difficulty with the case of women' [1981, p. 281]. Could you summarise?*

The 'official' definition of social class is the one based on male occupations and therefore by definition doesn't include the position of women ... some people do fiddle around with things like women's education - attempts have been made. I think I am depressed at the very little progress there has been in the last ten years towards sorting out a different way of looking at these problems (...) The Marxist one is problematic in a somewhat different way because the criteria are taken from the relations of production and the different contributions of men and women to production and reproduction ... I mean that problem is not dealt with, not well articulated or dealt with.

(...) You also talk about the 'founding fathers' of sociology and . . .

211

I was very much criticised for that, particularly the bits that I put in about their domestic lives, it was said that it was totally unfair.

Do you think it's unfair?

No I don't think it's unfair.

What you said was that the 'so-called "founding fathers" (an appropriate phrase) lived and wrote in an eminently sexist era', and that, for example, the 'prototype of many a wife, before and after, was Marx's wife Jenny' who [1974. p. 22] 'dedicated her whole being to his life and his work. It was an entirely happy marriage. She loved, admired and trusted him and was, emotionally and intellectually, entirely dominated by him. He leaned on her unhesitatingly in all times of crisis and disaster, remained all his life proud of her beauty, her birth and her intelligence ... In later years when they were reduced to penury, she displayed great moral heroism in preserving intact the framework of a family and a household, which alone enabled her husband to continue his work' [Berlin. 1939. pp. 78-79].

The people who read the manuscript and other sociologists, publishers and so on, said 'it's not done' in sociological circles to criticise people on professional grounds from aspects of their life which are personal. I hadn't worked it out sufficiently myself at that stage, but there *is* a very close association between people's personal experience and what they do in terms of their area of work, their interests in that, and the methodology that they use (...) It's part of the male bias within sociology to make this big separation between self and work, not a separation that has made much sense to women and indeed women sociologists who have any kind of feminist perspective ... So I don't regret saying that, no. I heard that sometime after I got a grant from the SSRC [ESRC] that they didn't really want to give me the grant, because although they had no objections about the work I did, they didn't think I treated my husband very well (...)

You say that Marx 'provided the bones of an analysis of marriage as female domestic slavery, although he was personally something of a rearguard romantic' [1974, pp. 21-22]. Meaning what exactly?

212

What I meant was that there is a contradiction between what he says about marriage, his theoretical point of view, and the way he lived his life. And he wanted women to be his darling little slaves...

(...) On the question of values you argue that it 'must be noted that in sociology (and elsewhere) a feminist perspective appears to be polemical because it runs counter to the accepted male-oriented viewpoint - a viewpoint which is rarely explicitly articulated', and hence 'feminist values stand out like a sore thumb'. You add that 'conventional male-oriented values are buried in the very foundations of sociology and have to be dug up to be seen (but not believed)' [1974, pp. 2-3]. So do you think that we all have values and biases and that these simply must be made explicit?

I think we all have values. To have said in 1974 that the 'founding fathers' of sociology were sexist was a terrible allegation to make, because once again the canon of sociology and academia was not to make any sensitive remarks about personal experience (...) I think a lot of sociologists have not applied their professional insights to themselves, they don't look back at themselves and think 'how is my perspective on this affected by my position in society? The fact that I'm a man, the fact that I have a wife at home who cooks me dinner every day, or whatever', it seems to me that their eyes are actually blinkered.

So the traditional-male-conventional sociologist studies such things as power, domination, authority, and so on ...

Yes, if he - and we are talking about men here - if he tried to answer the question as to why he was only interested in certain areas he would see it was because of his background and position. That these areas like domestic work, or reproduction, or intimate relationships or whatever, these things are not interesting to him because he has been channelled or conditioned to think in another way. It doesn't mean that they're not interesting, it doesn't mean they're not relevant, and it certainly doesn't mean that you get a good picture of the way a society works by ignoring them, because you don't.

(...) In an article on research techniques you say that in textbooks the 'motif

of successful interviewing is "be friendly but not too friendly"', which you consider to be the humane manipulation of interviewees as sources of data. You add that so-called 'proper interviews' owe more to a masculine sociological vantage point than to a feminine one [1981a, p. 33 and p. 38] ...

I think men are brought up to do so [to be manipulative], and more inclined to do so in research.

You say that the 'lack of fit between the theory and practice of interviewing is especially likely to come to the fore when a feminist interviewer is interviewing women' [1981a, p. 32]. Why?

Because I think that a female interviewer who is interviewing women and who is aware of the way in which women are treated and the position of women, is going to be aware of this contradiction between what the textbooks say interviewing is all about and how a feminist feels she should treat other women.

Okay, you've seen two main difficulties in interviewing women; firstly, they asked you a great many questions, and secondly that over time you felt that 'personal involvement with interviewees was problematic and ultimately unhelpful to avoid' [1981a, p. 42] ...

They asked questions which they hadn't been able to ask or have answered *by doctors*, things about pregnancy and so on and I think I say in that piece the most extreme question I was asked was by a woman who asked which hole the baby came out of. She had been to the hospital, to classes, but they didn't deal with those sort of questions and so she asked me and according to the textbooks I should have said 'well I guess that's something we can talk about later', or 'go back to the hospital and ask them' and I felt it was absurd to say that questions like that should not be answered. They asked me questions they couldn't get answered elsewhere, they were also asking me things because they knew or suspected that I had personal experience of these things and they were interested in my personal experience. I think this is particularly a problem - if you want to see it as a problem - in *repeated interviewing*, it's much easier in a one-off interview to behave like the textbooks and say 'I'm not going to tell you anything about me because that's not what this interview is about' (...) I was dealing with intimate relationships at a crucial time in their lives and you need their co-operation, and you really cannot - it's inhuman - ask for somebody's co-operation with this kind of thing without giving them something in return. I think it's unethical, but I also think it doesn't work. I mean if over a long period of time you're asking people to divulge information about themselves and every time they ask *you* something you shut up it just isn't going to work; they're not going to give you the kind of feedback that you want. It's the ethical and the pragmatic. It's surprised me in a way that nobody else who's done a lot of interviewing has written - has come out of the closet as it were - and said 'interviewing isn't like this'. I've talked to people like this, but to put it down in print is a challenge.

Despite personal involvement and so on, presumably you felt you were getting, as it were, impartial accounts as well?

Well, I was interested in *their* accounts and *their* experiences so I wanted partial and subjective answers as it were ... I think they told me the truth as they saw it. One relevant contrast here, is the contrast between the kind of information that I knew I got in those situations and the kind of information that I knew was on the case notes ... I've talked to women about termination of pregnancy and so on, then I've gone and looked at the case notes and there's nothing there - people don't like to give information about themselves to somebody they don't know, and therefore they feel they can't *trust*. There needs to be, I think, the trust and it is difficult to trust a person who isn't giving you anything back, who is behaving like an automaton.

(...) Can you tell me a little about how you obtained your 'sample' for the housework research [1974: see also 1974a] ?

I took the forty names from the practice lists of two general practitioners, one in a middle class area and one in a working class area, so the first twenty names in each one, of women with at least one child under five. And then I knocked on their doors.

You said your approach was new as it looked at 'housework as a job and

215

seeing it as work, analogous to any other kind of work in modern society'
[1974, p. 2]. How was it looked at previously?

As an aspect of family life, or an aspect of the psychology of femininity (...)
I didn't have a perception of housework as work before I came to do it
myself, I suppose I did call myself a housewife, I'd always 'worked' in
some capacity, but for years I had the rather typical experience of being at
home with two children and being responsible for them and for the
housework. And I remember dusting my husband's bookshelves and picking
up Blauner's *Alienation and Freedom* [1964] and looking at that and looking
at women in the index and finding Blauner making a statement something
like 'it's not possible for women to be alienated in factory work because
their major satisfaction is at home'. And it occurred to me that what women
were doing at home a large part of the time was actually quite possibly the
same sort of monotonous work that was being done in the factory. And when
I looked around a bit, and went back to the LSE to the library I couldn't find
anything about housework apart from books on marriage and the family ...
So that's what I decided I was going to do. Now that in its way was also a
very selective view, because I was going to take this perspective rather than
the other one which you need to do to correct the bias that was there (...)

In respect of under-researched areas, what would be your priorities in terms
of future sociological research?

Well, I think there are other areas of unpaid work within the family that we
haven't yet looked at ...

Like child care?

Yes, and looking after elderly relatives. What's that like, and that's a burden
that very often falls on women. I think the area of relationships between
parents and adolescent children is something we don't know much about. I
don't think this is an area that's been covered anywhere. I think that sociologists have the same kind of model that's 'out there' that having children is
about having a baby; it's actually about having a seventeen-year-old
unshaven youth who comes home at two o'clock in the morning or whatever.
It ends up being about that, and it ends up by being in a way a very much

216

more challenging process ... for the parents. I think that relationships between men and women have not been researched ... people have concentrated so much on marriage, marriage is the legal term for a form of relationship between men and women, but that the whole area of intimacy between men and women the extent to which men and women can or cannot get on because of their different social positions and backgrounds ...

(...) In terms of dissatisfaction with housework you say your findings 'lays to rest the idea that only a tiny minority of women are discontented housewives' [1974, p. 182]. Could you elaborate?

Well I think there's plenty of other research which suggests that ... I would return to the basic distinction that I made in *The Sociology of Housework* between how women feel about being a housewife and how they feel about housework. The percentage of women who dislike being called a housewife and dislike that role is probably small ... the majority of women, I think, are content to see themselves in that way, *but* the percentage of women who dislike housework in one way or another is very large.

You mention the fact of 'loneliness' ... meaning what exactly?

You can be very lonely with small children, as anyone who has looked after them will know. I mean obviously there is constant interaction and a constant level of demands flowing one way, so there are very few opportunities afforded actually to talk about the things one is bothered about with small children. The social contacts in the life of someone who is at home with small children have to be created, they have to be sought after, they have to be pursued, it's not a ready made social situation (...) and if you have the personal resources to do that that's fine, but I think many people do not. I mean the whole business of creating social relationships that are congenial to one is actually difficult.

One of the positive findings is 'autonomy' which is a highly valued dimension of housework; isn't that tinged overwhelmingly though with the negative findings?

Well the balancing-act between 'does the autonomy outweigh the disadvantages' is probably different for different individuals. It depends on particular circumstances ... I must say though that being in control of one's work is an aspect of *my* work that I like and that's one reason why I haven't pursued a teaching job. So it's not just in housework.

So in the 'perfect world' what would be the division of labour vis-a-vis childcare?

Well I think in the 'perfect world' children are not brought up within small families. I think it's a process that makes them too vulnerable to things going wrong in individual families ... I think it's better for children to have as many parents as they can get and that means more than two and I think that in the long run the only solution is some kind of collective childrearing.

In your research the range of the houseworker's working week was between 48 and 105 hours, with a 77 hour average ...

A couple had full-time jobs, I didn't select the sample on the basis of whether or not the women were employed, my starting point was that *all* women who have children, are married, are housewives in the sense that they are given responsibility for the housework that being in a sense the definition of a housewife (...) the opposite extreme were women whose lives seemed to revolve around their husbands, they just simply did a lot in terms of washing their curtains every week.

You say that the 'deconditioned' housewife is 'thus a potential revolutionary' [1974, p. 197] ...

Well, I think that oppressed people who are aware of their oppression and try to do something about it *are* revolutionaries, and that's what I meant by saying that the housewife who is somehow 'deconditioned' and aware of the cultural baggage which makes her into this person who has to do all this housework, she becomes aware of that ... then there is a potential revolutionary. Whether or not it manifests itself in terms of political action is much more a question ...

218

Would the first step be 'wages for housework' campaigning?

That would be one step ... though I actually think that's not a good idea (...)

Why precisely did you get into researching into childbirth?

My reasons for becoming interested in childbirth came directly out of the housework study. I saw that the point of transition in women's lives was not marriage as it used to be but having their first child, and clearly for that reason if no other this is an important transition .... and when I began to look at this I saw that there clearly wasn't in some sense a social transition at all, it had become a medical transition and medical experience, so what I wanted to look at was that particular aspect of it ..... If I were a man I would be much more indignant than many men are about what happens to their babies in pregnancy during labour, delivery and immediately afterwards. Although people have fewer children, the children that they do have are incredibly important, and the fact that children are brought up in nuclear families and the fact that parents have an enormous influence on children's lives - these are all reasons for being interested in how it happens and why it happens the way it does. And I think that we have quite a lot of evidence to show that the way pregnancy, labour and delivery is managed can actually have a long term effect on the mother, father, child and the family.

Examples?

For example there is some evidence that high intervention rates in birth and delivery are more often followed by post-natal depression. We can go into what post-natal depression is - but it is something negative, so if obstetricians are handling birth in such a way as say 50 per cent of women are having forceps delivery or 20 per cent of women are having caesarian sections and it *is* as high as that, higher in some cases, as you know, then what they are doing isn't simply confined to the management of birth it is having a profound impact on the experience of motherhood for that woman. If she is going to be depressed afterwards, this is going to affect her entire relationship with the child, the child's father and the people she lives with or whatever, and perhaps the child's development as well. These things may be difficult to measure, and obstetricians certainly haven't been especially interested in looking at these sorts of measures, what they have been interested in is perinatal mortality. They need the sociologists to convince them that the other kinds of outcome are a) important and b) measurable ... we've got to find the right way of measuring them, we've got to start somewhere.

(...) I'm going to come on to some comments on feminism, and then we will come on to your present research. Dale Spender in Men's Studies Modified says that we have been able to construct knowledge about women and that the task 'leads us directly into the area of the politics of knowledge. We are changing the rules' [1981a, p. 8]. What do you think she means by that?

Dale is sometimes rather hard to understand, could you read it again?

Knowledge about women leads us into the area of the politics of knowledge and we are 'changing the rules'.

Well what I think she's saying there is - she is querying the basis of knowledge, what she is saying is that knowledge comes from experience and it comes from the experience of personal relationships as well as from scientific data-gathering or whatever.

Okay. Helen Roberts in the same book says 'one of the strengths of the development of feminist analysis within sociology has been the active participation of many feminist sociologists within the women's movement' [1981]. Is being in the women's movement necessary?

No, I don't think it is. I think many feminists in sociology have had a period of activism in the 'women's movement' - I had, but I haven't for some years, and I don't think it is a necessary requirement, of being a feminist and having a feminist perspective to have been politically active in the women's movement. Perhaps Dale is saying it is hard to understand what 'consciousness raising', for example, is all about and what kind of effect it has on people if you haven't participated in it, or at least found out about it as directly as you can.

Sheila Rowbotham has argued, or so I believe, that patriarchy is not a useful concept as it suggests the fatalistic submission, which allows no space for the complexities of women's defiance. Do you still see it as a very useful concept?

I think it *is* a useful concept ... because we need a concept that expresses the power that a male dominated culture has over women. I don't think using that word, defining it and using it means that you can't talk about the way women are able to defy it, or the various forms of resistance there are to it or the interlocking with class oppression, I don't think that the use of the concept rules those things out, we do need a concept of that kind.

Well that's what I was going to ask you related to that. What are your thoughts about the issue of feminism and Marxism. Stuart Hall, for example, when I asked him about feminism and Marxism, said that the black issue, black oppression and so on, is interwoven with class but fundamentally it is class, and he says it is the same with gender. You don't see it that way do you?

No, I think fundamentally it is gender. I don't know, I mean one can play around with this comes first, that comes first, a lot of all this can be reduced to commonsense. Quite obviously there are at least three forms of structured oppression; black versus white, women versus men, and there's class, and anybody can be located within these three structures, and there's going to be some situations in which one of those structures is dominating and in another it will be different. But I don't think the subjection can all be reduced to a matter of class, unless you are using class in the sense of gender class.

Does it generally depress you, this over-theorisation of Marxism and feminism?

I am not generally keen on theory, and I know I have been accused of being atheoretical, and not developing theories. But I have found very few theories that actually help me to understand the world. I think if theories do help you

221

to do that, then they are a good thing, but I don't believe in theory for theory's sake, and I believe that a lot of the debate about which of these things come first, and what is 'radical feminism', and what is 'Marxist feminism', I think is dull, I don't think we need it.

(...) What interests you in contemporary sociological theory?

Not a great deal (...) There is only one reason why I would describe myself as a sociologist, there's only one reason why I do research and that's to find out about things *in order to make them better*. I can't make this divorce between an academic activity which bears no relation to the real world, and the real world as it exists and how one would like it to be, and that is why when I do research I think a very ignored part of the research process is communication of research findings. That's something that I always try to do and that means writing articles for *Mother and Baby, Woman's Own* as well as for *The British Journal of Sociology* and *The British Medical Journal* or whatever, and I put them all on my c.v. and I won't take them off, even when I see some people's hackles rising when they see *Mother and Baby* or *Cosmopolitan* written on there. I think this is important.

Sure. (...) The other kind of feminist discussion is like The Sceptical Feminist *[1980]. I've never been particularly interested in philosophy anyway but it seems to me that in her view it is all about reasoned debates with individuals to help them see the error of their ways. Have you got any interest at all in that approach?*

Well Janet Radcliffe-Richards did rather a nice review of *Subject Women* after which I felt that I hadn't paid her book enough attention. I started out by doing philosophy at Oxford and being launched into the most arid philosophical debates about the meanings of words, and so on. I have quite a lot of scepticism for that particular approach, and there's another thing here when we are talking about feminism there is a very profound cultural divide, which has got men on one side and women on the other, science on one side and nature on the other, and it has got reason and emotion in there somewhere, and to me feminism is at least partly about valuing emotions, valuing feelings and valuing those ways of perceiving the world that are not reasoned debates or whatever. I think there is absolutely nothing wrong in being guided by feelings. And I think the association between women and feelings is the same sort of thing as housework really. We have undervalued a whole dimension of human experience.

Right. Subject Women. *You talk a lot about the importance of 'sisterhood'. Can you just explain why it is so important?*

Well I'm saying, that embedded in the concept of sisterhood is the idea that relations between women are important and that is an idea which runs counter to the culture, and which says relations between men are important. I've run into trouble with what I have said about sisterhood ... Juliet Mitchell and I wrote a preface discussing the concept of sisterhood which said too many women, particularly feminists used this concept uncritically. You can't hide all sorts of errors, mistakes and ommissions under the heading of 'sisterhood' (...)

But it is still important?

Yes and I think one of the ways it is now emerging as important is in the relationship between mothers and daughters. I think people in all sorts of ways are beginning to see this as incredibly crucial. I saw it as important when I did the housework study, not *before* I did it, but out of the interviews came this very close association between the way women behaved with respect to housework and the way their mothers did. This identification with mothers, is a theme that has been undervalued in all sorts of ways, for example, daughters' choices of jobs, daughters' reproductive careers: there are a whole lot of links there.

Okay. You say that the main division in feminism is between socialist feminists and radical feminists and you argue that 'while the former implicate capitalism as the perpetrator of women's oppression, the latter accuse men of being its prime movers and beneficiaries' [1981, pp. 335-38]. If feminism is about putting women first, presumably you've no objections to any feminist perspective, if it is a feminist perspective. Do you in fact see it all as helpful?

Well if I said it was *all* helpful I would be contradicting what I said earlier,

223

that not all theory is helpful. So I think that in so far as feminist theory is grounded theory it is helpful, but some of it just degenerates into very arid concepts.

So, if the theories are wrong, it is because the empirical world doesn't look like the way they say it does ... is it as simple as that?

I think it is that people get carried away by theory and they lose sight of the *point* of the theory.

One thing you say is that there is a problem of not being able to directly examine the evidence about the conditions in which the universal oppression of women came about. What kind of evidence are you talking about - just historical evidence?

Yes, before the advent of capitalism were things really equal? How did men behave? Is the oppression of women due to their biology or is it due to this particular economic system? Those are actually empirical questions, which we can't answer because we don't have the data. We do have some data in the form of looking at preliterate societies, small-scale societies, and I think that some of that evidence is interesting. And to me what it shows is the absence of a standard pattern.

Having said that, do you think therefore, that it is pointless pursuing that avenue?

Yes, because there is also the question of 'alright we may know how we got here but how do we get out of here', and understanding the history does not necessarily help one to formulate a plan of action which is going to solve the problem.

(...) What would the 'good society' look like?

I think the good society for a feminist would be one in which one wasn't aware of the biological sex of an individual and it wasn't the most salient factor in the way it is now, and people were seen, treated, and valued for their individuality for their individual ability, resources or skills or whatever and not because they happened to have one set of chromosomes rather than another. I have just been to China and that was quite an instructive experience in that my feeling about being in China was that very often one was not aware of the sex of the person, and that's partly because they tend to dress the same, they tend to wear dark blue, dark grey - the men and the women, I went to a conference of obstetricians and quite a lot of the obstetricians in China are women and they had short hair, and unless you were paying a great deal of attention you wouldn't notice whether it was a man or a woman speaking and nor was that fact relevant, you did not need to know it in order to understand their work position, their family position, why they were at the conference and why they were saying what they did, it just did not have that degree of importance that it does here. It does not mean that there aren't inequalities. I had some very interesting discussions with people from the Ministry of Health in China about social class! I gave a paper on social class and pregnancy and they had just begun to look at some pregnancy outcomes within an analysis of women's occupations and of course what they were finding was that different women's occupations *did* differentiate in a way which they don't here, and the reason why they do that in China, is because women's occupations aren't all bunched in the middle like they are here ... It was interesting to be in China and to know that this was a communist society where people do not have freedom of choice and in this area the degree of control that is exercised over people's reproductive lives is enormous, and on one hand it is terrible, but on the other hand to have this sense that here is a society in which the tremendous social importance of gender has been played down, as a deliberate political action and to feel comfortable with that is good. I mean I left my hotel in Shanghai at 4 o'clock in the morning and walked down the streets and there were lots of people, thousands of Chinese out at that time and I had absolutely no sense of fear, about being out in the dark in a strange place. And then on the way back from China I went to Hong Kong and I immediately started counting my money when I bought things and looking around me when it was dark and the experience of being a woman in China that was really quite different.

(...) *How do you see feminism advancing now?*

225

(...) Well I think your question isn't really about feminism, but about how the position of women is going to change. I mean feminism is only interesting in so far as it relates to the position of women. I think it's a bad time for them now and it will be really for the next few years, with the Conservative government, the economic recession and so forth. I'm sure this is the standard answer you have had from everybody, but I can't see that things are going to get better. I think if anything they are going to get worse.

Have you ever thought about how your ideal of a 'good society' - where gender is played down - how it could be brought about? Is it an educative process?

In my books I have said that I think it is a process of long term education for everybody and I think that it is, I also think, obviously, that it requires a political commitment on behalf of the state.

What kind of degree of political commitment?

Well a damn sight more than what we have got now.

(...) You are not in any sense a revolutionary ...

I *am* a revolutionary in that I believe that what we need is a revolution. I'm not good at revolutions; I think that my skills are better developing the sorts of things that I'm doing, trying to change people's attitudes. I wouldn't be any good at organising a revolution.

Okay. The last couple of questions. How influential do you think you have been, which is halfway answered, so put another way - if you have been influential, why would you hope that to have been the case?

I don't know if I've had any influence. (...) For example, I have a curious status now I think in that I get invited to speak at 'important' conferences within the social science field and within the medical field. I have obviously

226

become 'the woman', 'the consumer', 'the social scientist' who can come and do this sort of thing, and be trusted not to be too outrageous. So what I have developed is a style of delivering, I think, radical thoughts, but in what I guess is a more conventionally feminine manner. I think this is a formula which I have found that has worked for those sorts of audiences and I am aware of doing it very consciously ...

What kind of influence would you like to have, how would you like people to see your work?

I think I would be satisfied with having done a bit of what [you have described], in terms of making a few basic commonsense points about private areas of life and women's lives being socially important and undervalued, both socially and sociologically, getting people to change their focus of interest somewhat, getting people to do research in these areas, getting students to be aware of them in a way that they weren't before ... and I think I have tried to change the stereotype of feminism too, but I think that is important.

Two things before we go on to the future, have you also wanted to help people get away from theory, per se?; *the other thing is also linked to what you said earlier - that you want your work to have some kind of practical importance - it is not enough just to say 'here's a book', it has got to have a sense of it changing things? Yes?*

I don't know. The point of writing books about research is that your books are about the empirical world and not essentially first and foremost theory-building exercises. It is not that I haven't developed theories: I actually think my most important book is *Women Confined* [1980] which has got in it a quite complicated theory about post-natal depression, and the experience of loss, social, medical and biological, and that really has not been picked up by other people and I have a feeling that that is the kind of thing - theory - that is only going to be appreciated much later. It's as though when I do theory people don't recognise it, but the theory comes out of the research because that is the way round that I see it ... and the question on wanting things to change for the better?

Do you hope that the research not only makes people want to do research but also to do research that has practical implications?

Well I can only say yes.

What can we expect from you in the future, and incidentally why did you write the autobiography?

(…) I had various reasons for writing it, one of them was this constant battle I feel I'm engaged in … I guess to be taken seriously, and not to be reduced to simple formulae like 'here is somebody who hates men, who hates doctors, who is out to get back at the world' … so it's a protest against simple reductionism of feminism like that. And it's an attempt to *partly* answer the question of what makes people into feminists, where does feminism come from (…)

9 Peter Townsend

Described as the Fabian sociologist *par excellence* (Inglis, 1982, p. 159) Peter Townsend is Emeritus Professor of Social Policy at the University of Bristol, and author of possibly one of the most extensive surveys in the twentieth-century, *Poverty in the United Kingdom* (1979). Born in Middlesbrough in 1928, Townsend has spent his career promoting social reform both intellectually through his research and writings, and practically with, for example, the Child Poverty Action Group (CPAG).

As a sociologist he has aimed to 'derive practical recommendations for policy from sociological evidence' (1957, p. 227), and more specifically he states the following (1973, p. 9)

> I work as a sociologist. I should like this to mean that I explore and write about present day society so that others may understand it better. I should like it to mean that I spend a good deal of time observing and interviewing small cross-sections of the population before writing detailed reports which aim to keep human beings to the forefront. Above all, I should like it to mean studying very carefully the life of the poorest and most handicapped members of society.

Often Townsend's work has been criticised for being *only* empirical, but this is clearly an inaccurate assessment, and his own views on the matter are most informative: 'theories and data are, of course, interdependent. Bad theories may not just be the consequence of bad data, but also give rise to the collection of bad data, or at least the failure to collect good data.' (1979, p. 45). It is not of course only the poor Townsend has been concerned with, indeed following his early research into communal homes for the elderly in England and Wales, he was able to write in 1962 that the homes 'do not adequately meet the physical, psychological and social needs of the elderly people living in them, and that alternative services and living arrangements should quickly take their place'. For Townsend this 'profoundly depressing conclusion' threw doubts on some of the 'basic values of modern society' (1962, p. 430).

Townsend began his studies of poverty - initially with Brian Abel-Smith - in order to demonstrate the persistence of poverty in affluent, post-war Britain. Indeed by the mid 1950s a number of studies had appeared in Britain showing that despite post-war social reform, high taxation and low levels of unemployment there was poverty among old people, fatherless families, the unemployed and the sick. Across the Atlantic Michael Harrington's *The Other America* (1963) argued that one fifth of the population was living in poverty.

Townsend's *Poverty in the United Kingdom* (1979) has been described as a 'bible' for the poverty lobby (Donnison, 1979, p. 24) but it has nonetheless had little effect in terms of reform, which would not greatly surprise Townsend but merely disappoint him. Published in 1979 the actual national surveys of 2,500 households were completed in 1968 and 1969. Townsend notes that according to the state's definition, nine per cent of the population are in a state of poverty, while taking his definition twenty-six per cent are. His 'relative' definition of poverty, as opposed to an 'absolute' one, is as follows: 'Poverty can be defined objectively and applied consistently only in terms of the concept of relative deprivation ... The term is understood objectively rather than subjectively. Individuals, families and groups in the population can be said to be in poverty when they lack the resources to obtain the type of diet, participate in the activities and have the living conditions and amenities which are customary, or are at least widely encouraged or approved, in the societies to which they belong. Their resources are so seriously below those commanded by the average individual or family that they are, in effect, excluded from ordinary living patterns, customs and activities'. (1979, p. 31)

Of course, as with any set of ideas, there have been criticisms of his

230

conception of 'relative poverty', including, for example, problems of definition - what are 'ordinary living patterns'? - and of course the argument that there should be an absolute as well as a relative definition (see Wedderburn, 1981, p. 278; see also MacGregor, 1981). But who can deny that we need graphically reminding of the pathetic lives some are consigned to live (Townsend, 1979, p. 314).

> The house was the worst the interviewer had ever seen in his life. It consists of four small rooms and a tiny kitchen. There is a WC in the yard outside, no bath and no cooker. There is a cold tap but no wash basin or sink. It has every structural problem imaginable. Even with a coal fire in the back room it is cold. The roof leaks, there is loose brickwork and plaster and decaying floorboards. The doors fit badly, the plaster is cracked. When the back door is closed, the vibration causes other doors to open. The larder is of rough stone, which is black and cold. There are said to be rats, mice, bugs and cockroaches. The rat catcher came a few weeks ago when, after demolition started near by, the number of vermin increased, but said he could not put poison down because of the danger to the children. Upstairs, both bedrooms are cold and damp. The wallpaper is peeling. The ceiling is giving way and they have stuck paper over it to delay a fall. Beds have to be covered with plastic sheets to keep the damp off them. In one bedroom, husband and wife sleep with the two youngest daughters. In the other, two sons sleep in one double bed, and two older daughters in another. The carpets downstairs have to be kept rolled up because of the damp. Mr and Mrs Mulligan are fearful of the house literally blowing down in a gale. The whole environment is dismal. The house next door is empty and in an advanced state of dilapidation. Tramps sleep there. The air in the neighbourhood is so smoky 'it looks as if a big fire is always burning'. The children have nowhere to play indoors and nowhere safe nearby.

The first thing is, could you tell me a little about your background?

I was born in Middlesbrough in 1928 where I lived for only a year or two because my mother separated from my father and brought me south to London where I attended elementary schools as they were called then, first in Pimlico and then in Hampstead and got various scholarships to grammar and independent schools at the age of 11. My family origins lay in Yorkshire and were of very mixed class. My mother was on the stage, she was a kind of embryonic Gracie Fields and she had some quite distinguished parts. She worked for ENSA in the war, and was the leading lady to Sid Fields at the beginning of the War in 'New Faces' which was a quite famous musical. She was a distinguished singer in her own right but had, as one might expect with a woman in that sort of position, a double problem. First of all she was the breadwinner and I was brought up by my grandmother who lived with us, and my mother had the experience that a lot of people, women on the stage have, of not being wanted after the age of about 40 and that certainly touched considerably my life as a young and middle aged man.

Did you go to University straight from school?

I was in the era when people went through conscription. I was misplaced in the Royal Army Service Corps because although I am not mechanically minded, as everyone will testify to you, I had played as a child with mechanical puzzles like bent nails which are supposed to be detached from one another and they gave me a set of these IQ tests and found I scored a 100 out of a 100 and they automatically assumed I should be allocated immediately to the RASC. From which I graduated to the Royal Army Education Corps and did certain teaching during that period, so I had a couple of years' break really before going to Cambridge in 1948.

And that was neither enjoyable nor not enjoyable, just something you had to do?

I regarded being in the Army as a waste of time and had a slight feeling of guilt because when I went in I was not yet a pacifist in the sense of what I then became.

What did you go to read at Cambridge because presumably there was no sociology?

I read philosophy which was then called moral sciences and ex-service people could get degrees in two years so I read moral sciences which was a mixture of four subjects, of psychology, elements of philosophy, logic and ethics and opted to stay on for the third year although I needn't have done to read part II of Social Anthropology (...)

(...) *Two things you said in the* Social Minority. *Talking about the Second World War, that you had a 'real kind of sense of "human nature"' and also a 'prevailing mood of self-denial' [1973, p. 3]. I mean did you really feel that you saw from the War a vision of what people could be?*

Well I'm very acutely conscious of how common it is for people to idealise the circumstances of their youth and early adulthood by comparison with their middle or old age. And yet even allowing for that I think it is true. There was a genuine collectivism within the war years, a kind of mixing up of classes and an acceptance from all political points of view of what later was called Butskellism after the war, but which of course was a genuine consensus politics of recognising that you had to provide orange juice and free milk to young mothers with babies even though you were producing ammunition for war, and there were a lot of decisions at that time which later one looked back at and realised were operating really as agents for equalising conditions in the population - rationing, utility clothes, and the rest. There were things which I think did greatly modify class structures and not just for the war period because they were continued subsequently for a time until, as some of us have called it, there was a kind of middle class counter attack. Opposition to high taxation and the supposition that they weren't benefiting from the welfare state and processes of economic growth allowed those in power to put more of a distance between themselves and the poor.

(...) *Okay. What happened following Cambridge and anthropology?*

I emerged from Cambridge and went to Berlin. The summer before I left Cambridge I was editing the undergraduate newspaper *Varsity,* and I was invited to some European jamboree in Berlin at the time of the Youth Festival organised by Eastern Germany. I went across the border and that was quite a traumatic experience visiting East Berlin. During the course of

233

this brief visit as a kind of representative of western student journalism I met the Registrar of the Free University of Berlin which had been set up under exciting conditions as a breakaway movement from the old Humboldt University of Berlin which had been left in the Eastern Sector. I was invited to be one of the first bunch of scholarship holders from Western countries who could do postgraduate work at the Free University. So I went there with my wife - I was married at 21 - and we were intending to stay for the full academic year but quite frankly couldn't afford to and she was having a baby in the latter part of the year ...

(...) And when you returned, did you get a post?

When I came back, I can't remember the exact sequence of this but I did apply for an advertisement for a post in *Political and Economic Planning* which is now the Policy Studies Institute, and I think it was largely my student journalism which got me the job. I remember being interviewed by, among others, John Edwards, Labour MP, Angus Maude, Conservative MP, Richard Goodman, the Director, and Francois Lafitte, who was leader writer on the *Times* and later graduated from journalism to academic life. There were a number of others like Lafitte, Rudolf Klein is an example. Lafitte graduated from journalism to a Chair in Social Administration at Birmingham. I had the post of Deputy Secretary of a Social Policy Committee which was producing broadsheets or pamphlets and I produced about six during the next two years before I went to the Institute of Community Studies.

(...) In The Social Minority *you said, and it was in 1958, that there were not enough research sociologists, that 'the graduates are not much employed on surveys of everyday life' [1973, p. 10]. Have you come to have a more definite idea of what sociology is?*

I have become clearer as I go along. I'm becoming more confident about what it should be and how it relates to policy which has been of central interest. I think you have to remember here that my empiricism derives more from a kind of intellectual process than one which was pure experience. It was through social anthropology. I have touched on the fact that I was doing social anthropology for about a year, but it made an indelible impression upon my early life. I formed an entire respect for the comprehensiveness of the anthropological approach. It was to understand an entire society and to live within it and actually pay methodological respect to getting below the surface of social relations so that you could explain them. I've always taken the view that sociology is not merely a reputable discipline but one which ought to be a dominant discipline, perhaps the dominant discipline of the social sciences. I don't take a Comtian view about the grandiosity of sociology but I do take the view that it deserves much more serious recognition within it, I mean among its participants, as well as outside.

(...) So if you have to define empiricism, or if someone said 'I want to be an empiricist sociologist', what would they have to do?

Again I think this should be something which is the stock in trade of all good sociologists, that they should be simultaneously empiricists and theoreticians and that obviously one has to select because one can't do everything, but the two are so intimately related. I could give lots of examples. In order to develop any theories about social behaviour sociologists have to have intimate knowledge of what they are talking about. This means intimate knowledge of organisations, it means intimate knowledge of the roles being practised, of structures and the rest. I think you can only get that by either living in as anthropologists, as it were, or making repeated sorties into the experience of different classes and into the behaviour of different organisations. How one gets that sort of empirical authority is another question. But you do have to have empirical authority.

(...) Do you actually think the study of social policy is anything without sociology?

I don't think it is very much, I must admit. I think that it really informs and makes worthy of respect the whole solidity of the concept of social policy. After all, what I'm concerned with are the conscious measures by which a society, through its institutions and the practices which it adopts, maintains or changes social structure, to put it very crudely. And if one is concerned with that, then one is concerned not just with government policies in the administrative sense but the underlying implications of the authority structures of industry and bureaucracy and of the professions and of the

Church. This does of course, widen the subject inordinately but allows a good focus on the more conscious strategies that society is adopting in order to manage its structures.

(...) Donald Macrae, quoted in a paper by A. H. Halsey, states that 'empirical research is easy, as well as quite often being genuinely useful. Most of it, like most natural science, could be done by well designed mechanical mice'. [1982, p. 166]. Why do you think that this ...

That's an arrogant statement which should be totally derided.

Why do you think that people, not only like him but other people, decry empirical research? Why do you think that is the case when we know there is a great tradition in British sociology of empirical research?

I suppose the concession one would make is that many people engaging in social survey work in particular, and also individual case studies, have disregarded the motivation or causes of behaviour and have taken for granted the structures within which they are seeking to do their work. That means they are adopting a position of subservience to existing structures and authority in government ... and that is what one has to get away from. That is of course just a mealy-mouthed kind of empirical sociology where all you are doing is being directed by government to do this or that piece of applied work to enable them to administer things more efficiently and there's a lot of that still going on, of course.

(...) The Institute of Community Studies. What was the kind of feeling like there about doing sociology and actually working at Bethnal Green?

Well it was brilliant improvisation on the part of Michael Young. He invited the other two of us [PT and Peter Willmott] to join him in spelling out what the extended family was like in London city, and because of my brief anthropological background and my own personal relationship to my grandmother I needed no introduction to the values and functions of kinship. There was the opportunity to do something which anthropologists frankly hadn't done in this country before, which was to look at the implications of the extended family and to what extent kinship still applied even in working class urban Britain and to relate this to policy to a problem-oriented realistically-oriented, as I would see it, interest in old people and pensions and the Health Service and the rest. The first piece of intellectual work I did after leaving university, I should point out, was a pamphlet on *Poverty ten years after Beveridge*. The intentions are expressed in the title, and that has remained with me. I've been extraordinarily lucky in having that kind of continuity in my career.

When was this period, Peter?

The pamphlet was 1952, then from 1954 through to 1957, I shared the first three years of the life of the Institute of Community Studies. It was established first of all in Oxford House and then moved to a house in Victoria Park Square in Bethnal Green. Originally the three of us were going to do three separate books, one on childbirth and infancy and the young family - one on the established family, children growing up and perhaps leaving home; and mine on old people. Michael Young and Peter Willmott combined in the course of their work. I'd drawn up my proposal which was submitted independently to the Nuffield Foundation, which granted the money. All three of us were caught up in the excitement of revelation - what other people didn't know, didn't appear to believe in, which was the existence of very strong kinship relations within the working class. Obviously this applied not just to Bethnal Green but to many other parts of Britain too. I felt that the work was well worth doing, a great excitement, a new way and I think a more comprehensive way of approaching social policy in a theoretically oriented way within the process of social development to look at policy. I was able to study social policy in relation to sociology which allowed me then to go on to the University of Essex. That has to be pointed out. What is also perhaps important to call attention to in our conversation is that I've always believed that the Institute of Community Studies did not then go on to consolidate that early work on kinship in British society which it could easily have done. I mean such questions as what marriage means to the population. That has still not been researched adequately in my view, especially in relation to kinship structures. There are all manner of other possible follow-ups ... the relation between kinship and power, political power, business power. There *is* a little sociological work on these themes but it is extraordinarily superficial about the inter-connections between the directorships of different companies and tends to stop there. It doesn't go back and say 'no you must not start with a few stray records of stocks and shares, but you must go back to wealthy families and try to discover what part kinship has played in the maintenance of inequality and the perpetuation of power in our society'. That really hasn't been done.

Why wasn't it done at the Institute?

It was partly I think Michael Young's talent for innovation without necessarily consolidation. I mean that with all respect. Many people can't do either of these but he has a certain sense of impatience with subjects he knows a lot about already or leaves others to do it when in fact others haven't yet had the kind of immersion in the subject to care about it sufficiently. There was an element of grievance on the part of some social anthropologists at their territory being invaded by the 'uninitiated' and that I'm afraid had unfortunate results in two ways. First it caused some social anthropologists to reel away from the subject because they thought it wasn't theirs, and it caused some sociologists to feel, as I think they still do, that kinship and community studies are perhaps more in the area of social anthropology than in their direct interests and I don't think they realise the value of that area of work in relation to class and power.

(...) So you then move to Essex. As a professor or a lecturer?

Well there was an intervening period which I ought to explain from the Institute of Community Studies, when I took a deliberate personal decision I looked around and said 'who can I learn from?' which is important to the kind of work I believe in and I took the calculated view that Richard Titmuss was such a person. Remember that sociology was tiny, in fact so thin on the ground that when I went to Essex I think I was about the seventh or eighth professor of sociology appointed in this country, and that was in 1963. Before that it was really LSE and nowhere else as far as sociology was concerned, and many of us felt antipathy towards the form of sociology as practised at LSE (...) philosophy plus a kind of mechanistic empiricism concentrating on population or demography.

David Glass?

You need the force of numbers, but it *is* true that the attitudes adopted by the leading forces at the London School of Economics, including Morris Ginsberg and David Glass but also others, was first erudite and philosophical, and where it was empirical rather mechanistic. It was very elitist in the sense that it did not particularly foster and proliferate anxious scientific work elsewhere in the country and certainly looked down its nose at any amateur attempts to undertake sociology. I think these were among the reasons which some of us got to know quite well during that period of the early fifties and mid fifties. That kind of sociology had no attractions for me. It seemed insufficiently related to the major problems of society. It did insufficient to *explain* why we had such class inequality, poverty, and poor relations between races as we were already then having. A lot of these urgent things LSE was not equipped even to discuss let alone follow up in its research.

So Titmuss. You decided to meet someone ...

I took a conscious decision that the Institute of Community Studies was not the place to undertake uninhibited work on social policy or develop the kind of ideas about the kinship network and power that I favoured. I was successful in going back to the Nuffield Foundation to say 'please, having done one study of old people in the community, please could I have money to do a study of old people in institutions?' ... because during that early work I had one experience (in gathering information for the *Family Life of Old People*) of following one poor old person into a former workhouse. There was to all intents and purposes, a Master, who wore a velvet dressing gown and had servants obeying his every whim. This was in Stepney. I went back to this workhouse and was shocked by what I saw. I then asked 'who has written about this? Why hasn't somebody told me that what Nye Bevan said in 1947, with the passage of the *National Assistance Act* that the old *Poor Law* was going to be abolished, that in fact it hadn't been abolished?'; I was fascinated by that. I decided that that was worth putting in a bid to do research. I put in a bid to visit a random sample of nearly two hundred local authority and voluntary and private institutions around the country. I then wrote it up as *The Last Refuge* [1962].

239

So is this where you became acquainted with Titmuss?

When I got the grant I said in the application that I wanted it to be established at LSE with Richard Titmuss as a kind of counsellor, and that was approved. Incidentally Michael Young put in an application at the same time for me to have a grant at the Institute of Community Studies which wasn't what I wanted to do - two competing claims for my time, as it were. And then at LSE I was full-time on research for the first two or three years but then was persuaded by Richard in 1960 to take a full-time lectureship. I held a lectureship in Social Administration and managed to complete quite a lot of research.

I've read Titmuss and been most impressed, particularly with The Gift Relationship *[1970]. What was the impact of him on you, and do you think he's had any impact on sociology as opposed to social policy?*

He hasn't ... there was a lack of coherence about his sociology. He was learning, he was improvising, but he had an enormous talent for asking both the searching and fundamental questions and writing about the paradoxes which captured people's imagination as betraying symbolically the issues which had to be confronted by capitalist society. Take *The Gift Relationship* and altruism and the giving of blood and what implications that work has for the relationship between the public sector and the private sector and privatisation today. It is the most important bit of reading that I give students to learn about privatisation and the whole management of the monetarist or neo-monetarist economy ... and much the same is true of his arguments with the Institute of Economic Affairs. That exchange still provides much the most penetrating debate about the relationship between social values and social objectives and economic management. That is the thing which inspires a lot of my work today: the relationship between economic management and the pursuit of social objectives through the analysis of social policy and theories of social development. This is one reason why his work attracted me although I would be the first to say, on the one hand, that he lacked a kind of overall theoretical perspective which explained the different parts of his work and moreover as a direct inevitable consequence I came to find in his final years that he was much too inclined to identify with the Wilson establishment than he should have done, had he had that coherent sociological perspective.

(...) At the end of The Last Refuge *you say 'the evidence' is by no means complete. How much evidence would you need?*

The answer is very simple, that one ... I suppose I've grown up in so many kinds of critical contexts, self-critical contexts, that I'm acutely aware of how the individual perceptions can be structured by virtue of the position he or she holds in society. I am conscious that what I say and write about equality or poverty partly derives from my position in society and I'm forever catching myself out in unguarded moments of betraying my arrogance or my authoritarian position within society and I think people are always unable to escape social position. They can take all kinds of counter-vailing measures to try to correct or balance it but it means that you can never entirely rule out self interested perceptions or behavioural ones.

So the collection of data is to do with self criticism. Scientific reliability ?

It's partly ... what that means is selection, perception. Perception is selection. We have to recognise that means there will always be observations which didn't occur to us just as there are important policy issues which are not recognised by anyone in society today but which may be recognised subsequently. If you look at the recent history of the recognition of inequality between the sexes, it has reached levels of fundamental research which were not anticipated during the period of the suffragette movement. If you look at child abuse or baby battering, or wife battering, they weren't on the agenda politically or socially twenty years ago. They weren't mentioned by anybody anywhere. Even if you pursue science, and try to collect data, there will be the perspectives of subsequent generations, and observations which will be made by somebody which are new and which will have a relevance to the observations made hitherto.

(...) You've stuck firmly to studying the working classes, or the poor and old people and sick people. What are the methodological lessons here and the kind of values we must have when we are looking at this? I mean, someone might say, we know too much already about working people and so on and so forth ...

241

Well this is perhaps an indirect answer to you but it's the most important thing I ought to say - it is that I have detected a change, a slight shift, in the emphasis of my own work. I think right at the beginning you can see that I tried to reflect an interest in, for example, I can give you a precise example which can be checked, the occupational pensions of the rich, the private pensions of the rich as well as of the poor. But it *is* true to say that a lot of the interest that I've had, a lot of the work that I'm doing has shifted in both its theoretical and its empirical direction. The work on poverty, I would call it one of the most original features, was the material we collected about the rich. Here I'm referring to one of the only sources of data in this country since the War - not just evidence about how much wealth the rich have, and with all that it implies about accumulation and inheritance but also the ways in which the rich influence definitions of poverty and therefore standards of need which are adopted in the social services. They do this by the positions they hold in professions and in management, and in positions of power politically. They shape the very styles of living, underwrite what start by being the new fashions but which become the ordinary customs of society. They actually are reproducing and recreating patterns of need. It's not merely that they are plundering more than their fair share of the resources which might be commonly available, it's also that they have too much power in organising the kind of life we lead and hence the needs that we feel we've got to fulfil.

(...) What methodological problems are specific to, say, the study of the poor? Or is it obvious?

Oh no, it's certainly not obvious. There are problems of contact, styles of language, putting questions, which inevitably derive from middle class conventions which both those who design questionnaires and those who carry out interviews have to be more sensitive about, have to be, the more that one can begin to recognise ways of translating these conventions into working class and underclass equivalents, the better (...)

(...) Okay. Well to move on and on to Poverty in the United Kingdom *[1979]. Do you see any relationship of your work to, say, Rowntree and Booth?*

God forbid. These were entrepreneurial philanthropists. One of the ironies about Rowntree is that he carried out three studies of poverty in York and that city has remained one of the low income areas of the country, partly because of the low wages paid by his particular company. That is an extraordinary paradox in the whole history of the study of poverty. They were more preoccupied with converting conventional opinion, they were like the 'wets' among Tories at the present time. That is a bit unfair to Seebohm Rowntree, I realise, who had strong views about the liberalisation of company management, but in some respects what they were concerned with was to persuade people on the political right of their time that many people were poor for reasons other than their own fault and that state action had to be taken to remedy matters. Now that was their policy objective and it's not one which we find objectionable ... However my objectives were rather different in doing some work on poverty. Both Brian Abel-Smith and myself at the LSE had collaborated together on different work and we formed the ambition to do a national study. We'd done some secondary analysis already but we formed the ambition to do a major national study of poverty which would, we hoped, provide some of the answers to the problem of controlling what were the structures of inequality in society and the new ways we might think up to remedy them.

People say the importance of your book, your whole work in poverty with Abel-Smith and so on, is that people were surprised by the 'rediscovery of poverty' in the 50s. What closed their eyes so much because it is quite clear from your book that poverty was just not a small scale thing. Why were people so surprised in the 50s?

It followed the War years ... you see if you remember that the Coalition Government of the War had established full employment, high rates of taxation and welfare state legislation which was confirmed by the Labour Government immediately after the war. People thought that represented those three things, represented the abolition of poverty and I've given in print a number of quotations from reputable sources showing that this belief was very widely shared. Then research workers at the margins of the social sciences, not central to the tradition of sociology may I point out, made a number of discoveries - that the conditions of the long-term sick, widows with young children, and especially of old people had not improved as much as had been supposed by the War and the immediate post-war generation, even under a Labour government. There were 'pools', as they were called, of poverty, or there was 'residual' poverty still in society. Secondly there were social workers, especially connected with the Family Service Units of the Quakers who knew at firsthand that their families were in poverty rather than mismanaging their affairs. These two groups - of researchers who had done occasional scattered studies of minorities, and social workers who knew families at firsthand - came together to found, for instance, the Child Poverty Action Group in 1965. Before that some of the research workers said 'let's check through secondary analysis how much low income or poverty exists', and had found that it not only applied to some of the minorities I have spoken about but also to the low paid in full-time work who had dependent children, had two or three or more dependent children. So this was the basis of the revelation that the post-war welfare state hadn't done all that it had been supposed to do.

The cycle of deprivation thesis ... is that just politics or is that sociology as well?

Well it's a version of ... the rebirth of the eugenics movement of the 1920s and of the so-called extravagancies of sociobiology of applying too narrowly genetic theories. One can trace this through the work of - the fraud of - Sir Cyril Burt and others and the whole history of the measurement of intelligence, but it also applied to interpretations of the culture of poverty which were within sociology as well as the cycle of deprivation to refer to the term which was taken up by Sir Keith Joseph in the early 70s. So we were victims already of those who were applying biological ideas to society, to social structure ... and social anthropologists who were applying too sweepingly the case studies of particular individual families to society as a whole and in effect implying that bad habits in bad areas were passed on to the children and therefore there are origins of popular beliefs about 'blaming the victim' to be found within sociology, certainly within social anthropology [see the work of Oscar Lewis].

(...) T. H. Marshall, in a somewhat disjointed review, makes the distinction that for you inequality is not poverty as inequality ignores deprivation [1981]. What does that kind of thing mean?

Yes T.H.Marshall did not quite comprehend what I was trying to argue, partly because some of his views on citizenship and welfare claimed there had been far more social progress than my theoretical approach was prepared ever to allow. He was a liberal pluralist in the central tradition. But he was quite right that I did try to distinguish poverty from inequality, in that not only does the concept of poverty apply to the lower end of the ranking by inequality, as it were, but also poverty seems to me to be of serious scientific interest only when one is conceiving of criteria of deprivation applying to people as a consequence of their low income or low resources. I'm interested in the thresholds - the criteria by which one can distinguish people in society who are in need quite apart from those who are living way above or well below average in that society or have a position which is way above or well below average. They are in need when they are in poverty for what I argue to be social reasons and not just physiological reasons and here I have to say, very briefly, that the old way of looking at poverty was to argue that it was a condition experienced by people by virtue of the lack of the physical necessities of life and that among other things, is highly individualistic ... but people are not Robinson Crusoes. The fundamental point about them - which is highly sociological, centrally sociological - is that people are social beings before they are anything else. And as social beings they have social needs. If they have social needs we are envisaging criteria of poverty where at some level of income they are unable to behave as members of society in some significant sense. That's what I'm interested in and would regard as the threshold of poverty.

(...) Just keeping within the context of British society, aren't we being restrictive by not asking at the same time the question about the materialism, the gross consumerism of our society. Aren't we in danger of forgetting that?

Ours is a materialist society and also an acquisitive one. Even in political debate we use examples of the possession or non-possession of a TV set or a video as criteria of affluence and of progress. That steers attention away from social values and objectives which should be central to political debate and social analysis.

So although you say that people are poor, relatively speaking, if they cannot do things that other people do, you are nonetheless saying at the same time that a lot of what other people do is not what we would really want them to do anyway but that's just something we have to accept?

There is a two-stage level of analysis whereby, first, the structural conditions which determine people's needs within the society of which they are members, are identified and have to be accepted. Second that does not mean one cannot deplore or question those conditions. The construction of life within any particular society is not the *only* form of construction which is available within the historical experience of humankind.

That's fine ... Your two concepts of 'style of living' and 'people's resources' obviously broaden out completely our previous discussion but they are difficult in the sense that they are not neat. Can you just say something about how you manage that problem?

It arises from the life we lead, or rather the social content of that life. If we are asked to describe what we are or what we do, then we can adopt the customary treatment of sociological 'role'. The idea of role is that people are an amalgamation, a bundle of roles which they play as parents, children, brothers, comrades, fellow workers, and citizens. Or we can look at the relationships and the customs in which people participate. In understanding what people need, we have to understand who they are and how they behave so we have to look at the roles they play and we have to look at the life-styles which they indulge in and the customs that they share in. That is complex and we require an appropriate terminology which will foreshorten or generalise such complexity so that we can explain structures of need. I suppose what I'm asking for is the empirical content of social norms. We can convey this partly by describing and analysing legislative rules, and partly by describing and analysing shared behaviour and expected behaviour. The problem to be posed is how to describe normative behaviour and experience with which to compare individual experience.

Of course one problem is those people who are clearly in poverty, as we know it, but refuse to acknowledge it to themselves. Which is obviously a practical, a political problem. How do you conceptualise that in your own mind when you look at these people?

It is a form of false consciousness. But its importance may be exaggerated. We found a close correlation between subjective interpretation and objective position in society. This seems in part to be a result of careful methodology. But there are still quite a few exceptions and this takes us back to the ways in which structures and earnings are legitimated. What are people's reference groups? To explain the lack of fit between subjective and objective deprivation remains a fascinating conundrum.

Okay. Something that Suzanne McGregor said about your work was that 'the conclusion must be ... that the emphasis on the redefinition of poverty has been a disservice to the poor ... Many people began to think there was no longer any real poverty, that poverty was just a relative matter of whether one could afford a holiday in Spain or not', and that your 'insistence on seeing poverty as relative deprivation has the effect of draining the term poverty of its concrete, objective content and [has] inadvertently contributed to the view that poverty no longer exists in our society. Why did he do this?' [1981, p. 76]. Can you comment?

(...) One answer to these commentators or critics is to point out that our version of the meaning of poverty is as applicable to poverty in the Third World as in Britain and what's at stake ...

Because you say you talk about the relative within a context so the context can be anywhere, Yes? Third World? That's what you're saying isn't it?

Yes it is the only scientific position. People tend to assume that the 'relativist' is opposed to the 'absolutist' version of the meaning of poverty and that only the latter can be scientific. I think the opposite is in fact the case. In practice the approach to the definition of poverty as 'absolute' poverty is a kind of undercover relativistic view. People conceal from or deceive themselves into thinking that it isn't relative, and what I'm trying to do is to bring that relativism out from under the wraps so that it can be properly scrutinised and justified in scientific measurement ... What's at stake here is the standard which people need to live at to be full members of the societies in which they are engaged. I would argue quite sharply with such people that what they're up to is to depreciate the needs of the poor both in our own society and the Third World. I'm against them because what they are failing to do is recognise the full income, the scale of the income required in order to be full members of that society or the scale of the resources required in a Third World context to be full members even in *that* society. We have to choose between a minimalist view of how the poor of any society or of the world are to be treated and a much more generous standard (...) Kenya is a country I have visited recently. I'm hoping to complete a study of poverty there ... You cannot measure poverty in Kenya by taking some historical standard of what was happening before Independence. It is now a different society which is expecting new things of its citizenry, new standards of education, new standards of involvement in work, and in social activity. You can only apply those new standards to that population. If you do apply those standards to that population - and not only so-called 'absolute' standards of food, shelter and clothing - which are physical rather than social - then you will form a view that very many more people in Kenya are in an impoverished state and especially those who haven't yet had access to some of the new developments of that culture. This produces a different perspective about social change. One is then becoming much more sensitive to the modern integrative mechanisms of that society - a kind of participation in development - as compared with being fobbed off with some of the residual questions of what share in the remains from the surplus over and above meagre subsistence should the poor be allowed. Now that's the kind of sharp implication that this argument, and I hope it's a very vigorous argument, about conceptualisation leads.

In your conclusions in the poverty book, you make the point that 'none of this is going to be easy', and your recommendations include things like abolition of excessive wealth, abolition of unemployment and the important smaller things like the reorganisation of professional practice ... taking into account the fact that you said it would be difficult, can most of this or the majority of this be achieved through parliament?

Logically and rationally it's the only way it can be achieved, I don't mean through Parliament only. It isn't parliament as an institution which is the key vehicle for a society adopting structures which are more egalitarian and which defeat poverty. If you adopt principles of revolution by violence or seizure you are condoning the acceptance of principles which you are then going to have to reject in the kind of society which you may wish to establish. Once having embraced selfish and arrogant and authoritative principles it is very difficult then to abandon them. One has to look realistically at a process of change. The process of change demands that sooner or later enough people in that society have to be persuaded or educated to want to live like that. Those are the only criteria which I would want to operate. If you are tempted to adopt means other than to change those which contradict the principles on which you stand, then you are lost.

Fred Inglis, in his Radical Earnestness *talks of the importance of books to Fabians, of knowledge and education and reason, and he makes the point that 'the so-called "rediscovery of poverty" by the Labour government of 1964-70 was made by Titmuss, but it was recently made clear with philistine callousness that this rediscovery was limited to a few explorers when the Secretary of State dismissed the classic new work of Titmuss's pupil Peter Townsend,* Poverty in the United Kingdom *in terms which vividly recalled Titmuss's own worst enemies named in the 1959 essay' [1982, p. 153]. Does it disappoint you ...*

I am very conscious of its shortcomings. I also think that something as ambitious as that does have reverberations which many people don't like. But it appears to go on being discussed. You raise the question of being a Fabian socialist. Let me reflect on personal history. I happened to be invited to write a Fabian pamphlet with Brian Abel-Smith entitled *New Pensions for Old* in 1955. We had a bright idea about a new pension scheme and then the Labour Party got interested in some of the same things. I stayed in the Fabian Society although I didn't much like the representation of socialists that I found within that Society. Perhaps my enthusiasm falters from time to time but it does at least accord with the kind of perspective that people like Tawney adopted. Tawney was far more left-wing than most of the Labour Party in recent years - as I've argued in a new preface to his book *The Acquisitive Society*. He was a fundamental restructurist. I like to regard myself as a devoted pupil in that I do see that social change cannot be brought about without transformation of the existing structures of wages, industry, bureaucracy and the professions, and that we do have to recognise and work towards that because we've lived for too long with the Butskellite philosophy which has served us badly.

(...) It's quite clear that your values are about a more fair society and that's

249

reflected by what you decided to do in sociology. John Rex described you as a radical and courageous, but he added that with others like David Donnison, you assume that you are part of the government, that there are mandarin assumptions in your work, that somehow the working classes do not come into it. Is this a misunderstanding of your work?

I'm a friend of John Rex but I think that's a misrepresentation. Unlike Donnison, unlike Titmuss, I did not join the Labour Government as adviser, and after 1965 when the disastrous *White Paper on Immigration* was published I refused to participate in any formal sense in Labour's administration . So from that early period I detached myself quite comprehensively from participation in that administration. But that doesn't mean to say I wouldn't talk to or didn't allow to have presented to Labour ministers summaries of my work and I sought to do that through a variety of channels.

His idea that the working class aren't somehow in the scheme of things ...?

If one listens to poor people because it's important to represent their views and their experiences, I don't think it can be argued that I haven't tried to do that ... We live in a very unequal structure of power. In order to embarrass and make uncomfortable some of the people in positions of power you have to try and educate them and tell them what poor people are experiencing as a result of their decisions. One does have to report things in that way. Okay, you may not be able to get very far just with embarrassment, and exposing their discomfiture at the evidence and arguments that can be deployed against them. Obviously what is also important is to raise the consciousness of poor people. Here it is important to speak and write about industrial democracy, constituency parties, pressure groups, and organisations of the poor. I've tried to work with a number of them.

On values, is your position that you do scientific work but the values only come into it because of what you choose to study?

Which is chicken and which is egg is very difficult to decide but the values, I think, are reinforced by the reality as one sees it.

When you talk about Tawney in Sociology and Social Policy *you say he warned against the 'corrupting influence of a false standard of values, which perverts, not only in education, but wide tracks of thought and life. It is this demon - the idolatry of money and success - with whom, not in one sphere alone but in all, including our own hearts and minds, Socialists have to grapple' [1976, p. 290]. That was his kind of moral vision. What would your good society be?*

It would be one where power was very much more devolved than it is to local communities. But ... there is a major problem of relating national to local standards of conduct. There has to be a major tension, where you make clear what are the guiding principles and how national resources are allocated from the centre of the society but that must leave a great deal of power to adapt to local situations and conditions. I certainly do see a good society as one which is refashioning local community. It would involve a lot of restructuring, with emphasis on universal education compared with specialised professional training. It would require much more of a parcelling out of property and land than in the past. The ways in which both a geographical community but also a non-geographical community can be developed are of deep interest to me currently. My hesitation comes from knowing that this is an almost impossible dream but one which we have to care about. I've always been very uneasy about the Marxian dismissal of the *lumpenproletariat.* I think the tendency is to be relatively dismissive or indifferent towards a section of the population - whether they are called an underclass or a dependent minority or whatever - they comprise today in Britain around a quarter of the population. Their situation seems to me to be of great importance. A very sensitive body of services and occupations for them, whether disabled, whether old, whether in one-parent family, or other situations has to be constructed.

Are there any models that you've seen in the world or history that you can draw upon this vision?

Like many people I draw in a kaleidoscopic way on particular observations or experiences and point to examples in other countries. It isn't possible to say, there in history or there in todays's world, that's the kind of model I'd want to establish. I can only point to conditions in Scandinavia or conditions in central Europe, like Austria or Hungary, where they don't have as much unemployment, where there aren't as many poor or where there are not conditions of such deprivation or inequality as prevail here.

(...) Finally, do you think that your work has been influential and in what way, and if you could get people to do certain things, what would you like them to do within sociology?

I know the answer to the second question better than the first.

Go and study poverty in Norwich and everywhere else?

No, indeed not. I'm absolutely clear about the second question. I think that sociologists and those in social administration who are working on social policy partly because of the way in which the availability of information is structured in our society - look too little at the construction and reproduction of wealth, the social causation of industrial change and the social causes of the internationalisation of trade and consumption. I'd like sociologists to look more at the mainsprings or origins of present day structures than at the outcomes.

What about your own work. Do you think it's been influential, and in what way?

It's very pleasant to find that people are, whether they agree or disagree with certain propositions, actively interested and concerned and take up some of my propositions in their own work. On the other hand direct influences are very hard to trace. Most work has a very indirect effect on others which in the long run is unmeasurable. All that it is possible to say is that there have been a few minor policy decisions where I can at least say I wrote x or y shortly before they were made. A minor example is the history of the attendance allowance for people with disabilities I contributed to that history. The State Earnings Related Pension Scheme is another example.

What about within sociology? Do you think your type of work has been taken up?

252

I'm optimistic about that. There has been a movement within British sociology towards policy analysis as the key in constructing theories of social change and towards that generalist sociology which my work represents. That's a source of encouragement. Sociologists are much more concerned with inequality and policy motivation for inequality than they used to be.

10   Stuart Hall

A Marxist and Professor of Sociology at the Open University, Milton Keynes, Stuart Hall has written widely on politics, the media, deviance and cultural studies. Born in Jamaica in the 1930s, and educated at Oxford, he has always been involved in socialist writing and campaigning, and indeed was the first editor of the *New Left Review* in 1960.

The first issue of *New Left Review* (Jan-Feb 1960) was overseen by an editorial board consisting of such luminaries as Doris Lessing, Norman Birnbaum, Alasdair MacIntyre, John Rex, Edward Thompson, Raymond Williams, and Peter Worsley, to name just a few. Contributors to the first issue included Richard Hoggart and Arnold Wesker, and Hall's editorial asserted, amongst other things, that the 'purpose of discussing the cinema or teenage culture in *NLR* is not to show that, in some modish way, we are keeping up with the times' but rather that these are 'directly relevant to the imaginative resistances of people who have to live within capitalism'. He concluded, and in retrospect a comment tinged with irony, that 'our hope is that *NLR* will bring to life a genuine dialogue between intellectual and industrial workers' (1960, pp. 1-3).

Hall's writings on the media, culture and ideology often vary from being direct and political, to more sophisticated attempts at essentially redefining Marxism. For example in his *Drifting into a Law and Order Society* (1979), Hall talks of the 'ventriloquists of the popular press', who give voice to the 'silent majority' representing it in its most 'virulently traditionalist and authoritarian disguise without a single memorandum passing from Whitehall to Fleet Street' (1979, p. 4). On other occasions he talks of the media 'sometimes deliberately, sometimes unconsciously' defining and constructing (say) race in such a way as to 'reproduce the ideologies of racism' (1981, p. 28). Indeed he refers to 'inferential racism', that is when a liberal broadcaster is talking honestly about 'a problem' of race relations (1981, p. 37).

Hall directed the highly imaginative Centre for Contemporary Cultural Studies (CCCS) at the University of Birmingham for the period 1970 to 1979, and it was there that much empirical work was undertaken in the area of cultural studies. What is so striking about Hall, particularly as a Marxist, is his insistence on *taking ideas seriously*. Ideology for Hall, provides the framework within which people define and interpret social existence, hence there is 'a struggle over a particular kind of power - cultural power: the power to define, to "make things mean"'. Hall notes that (1982, p. 12)

> To this struggle the radical right have devoted themselves with conspicuous success. In the categories of commonsense, 'freedom' has not only been separated from but has effectively *displaced* 'equality'.

The same cannot be said, argues Hall, for the left. For example, within the realm of ideologies, Hall notes that 'what we know collectively about' the tactics and strategy of a popular anti-racist struggle, 'would not fill the back of a postage stamp' (1981, p. 51).

In 1978 Hall and his colleagues from CCCS published *Policing the Crisis*, a book which Bridges called 'one of the most important books to be written on race relations in Britain' (1978, p. 193). The book is about *mugging*, an old crime, but with a new societal reaction, namely a moral panic. Hall *et al.* located 'mugging' in the politics of the ghetto and the racism of British society. More profoundly Hall *et al.* saw mugging as one aspect of a crisis of hegemony and the emergence of a 'law and order' society. Hall, elsewhere, argued that 'the police now form a sort of vanguard in the drift towards the disciplinary society' and more generally that 'we are now in the middle of a deep and decisive movement towards a more disciplinary, authoritarian kind of society ... [we are heading] ... towards some sort of interim climax' [1979, p. 17 and p. 3].

Can you tell me a little bit about your background?

Yes, I was born in Jamaica in the 1930s, I went to school there, my parents were from a sort of lower middle class background - middle class coloured background. It was not an intellectual one, not an educational one, my parents ... my father was an accountant, but trained himself, etc., my mother never worked. My brother did go to the States to university, but rather late after the War. So I suppose in a sense I was the first ... I was a kind of scholarship boy, you know, I went to a big secondary school and then came to university as a result of having scholarships, and the first sort of intellectual person in my family in that sense. I could have gone, I suppose, to the University College of the West Indies as it was at that time, it started when I was in the fifth form at school, but my parents were fantastically upwardly mobile for me, as it were, I was going to do it, do it for the family etc., which is a source of enormous cultural and psychic tensions. It explains for instance why I really was never going to go back home when I arrived in England, although I had no notion that that was the case - I didn't understand that until about ten years later - but actually I couldn't have gone back home because I was in flight from everything that I'd stood for. But nevertheless I was sort of encouraged to try for the scholarships that allowed you to go to university abroad rather than home, and I got a Rhodes scholarship which pleased me enormously. I can't imagine I was who Cecil Rhodes thought he was going to send to Oxford to be properly educated! I mean Rhodes scholarships in the old days used to go to the sons of local white Jamaican families, and then as political changes occurred there so that changed too, so, for instance, Michael Manley's father, who was one of the early Prime Ministers of Jamaica when it became independent, was a Rhodes scholar. So it sort of came down the colour scale as Jamaica has gone on, and so a whole stratum of people who'd never have had Rhodes scholarships before got one. So I got one, to go to Oxford, and I wanted to read history. I was persuaded that the Oxford history school was terribly precious and required you to know Latin and High German and so I think wrongly that I was advised to read literature instead (...) and went to Merton College, Oxford, deposited by my mother and I nearly died for about three years. No, that's not true, I nearly died for about a year, when I felt I was deeply deracinated there.

(...) Were you interested in politics at the time?

I was interested in politics, I'd always been interested in politics. I was very much a kind of nationalist, West Indian nationalist, because that's the kind of phase of politics that Jamaica and the Caribbean were going through at that stage. I wasn't, I don't think a socialist.

(...) *What were the early influences on you?*

I read Freud very early on. Just, I mean, as a figure I started to come across in reading and decided to read at the public library. And I quite decided at that stage I wanted to be a psychoanalyst. And then my sister had an extremely serious nervous breakdown, which nobody in Jamaica had the slightest clue about and I kind of understood what was going on, and understood it as a product of my own family culture, of the tensions of my own family culture.

(...) *Intellectually, so there's Freud, who else was particularly important?*

There's Freud, yes, but very early on ...

And Marx ...

And Marx. And the anti-colonial ... identification with anticolonialism and those sort of historical arguments.

And did you leave literature behind at some stage?

No, no. At that stage I didn't. At that stage I suppose I was more, I looked intellectually more interested in literary criticism than I looked like a serious scholarly historian (...) Well, at Oxford, my main formation there was the resistance to the view of literature which was held, namely, you know, divorced from society, not a serious study, *belles-lettres*, you know, the things of cultivated men, good talk, etc. And so I became a fierce Leavisite; not necessarily because I ever subscribed, I don't think, to the kind of elitism of Leavisites. I was always worried about the small elite of the cultivated sense of sensibility; but because he took it seriously. It did matter, and it was connected with real things, this was about social change, and it was about how culture was shifting in a time. So I picked up *that* side of Leavis, and that's really what carried me through ...

(...) Just ... because there's so much ambiguity, what do you mean by culture?

Yes, I mean it's stupid to hesitate because that's what my work has been about. And yet I don't have a really clear conception of it. I mean ...

We'll come to that later.

Yes - but certainly that's where I started, I mean that's to say, in the formal reading in the social sciences. I began in anthropology, not in sociology. I began in stuff about African culture, and I began the whole thing about West Indian culture and its relationship to Africa and to the West, and syncretism ...

Black Jacobins *[James, 1963]?*

Yes, exactly. And a lot of things about creole culture. An interest in the cultural mix of the Caribbean, with its Spanish and English and African and Indian influences and so on. Because it's a kind of political question. I should say that at that stage I also became much more directly explicitly interested in politics. I had been interested in, principally in West Indian politics in the early part of the fifties. In the latter part of the fifties I decided to make a more direct engagement with British politics, on the left. And I can almost date it, because it's the point where I resolved to go to what was called a Socialist Club meeting. The Socialist Club was a front for the Communist Party. It was where the Communist Party and other fringe people on the left met, in the discussion about class. And I'd started to read Marx again, and I went to make the point that you had to recognise the ways in which modern capitalism's class structure had changed, and that this did not necessarily invalidate the concept, the Marxist concept of class. And I've been talking about that ever since.

(...) Mannheim suggests that the best people for doing sociology are those on the outside, or displaced persons, or immigrants or whatever. Has that any significance, that comment, for you?

Yes. Yes it does. It does have a lot of ...

I mean, in the sense that British people take Britain for granted?

Yes, it is. I am tremendously interested in the things which give people or groups a particular shape of which they're not aware - I mean the unconsciousness of culture, the habits, rhythms, which they just think are themselves or how things are, and being outside it does give you a shaft of insight into that because you see it as a particular formation. On the other hand I'm convinced you have to be close enough to experience it; I mean it's not just the New Guinea syndrome, you know, you wander in and aren't they funny. So I feel very close to England and the English language, you know, I was educated in Jamaica in those things - I knew English flowers, I don't know any Jamaican ones because I read Wordsworth!

(...) Okay, before I come on to New Left Review *(NLR), which I should probably do next, but just something before that. I just want you to talk briefly about Perry Anderson's 'absent centre'.*

Yes.

(...) John Rex said to me, maybe tongue in cheek but I think he meant it, that the the reason there's an 'absent centre' is that there's too many Perry Andersons, and that Oxbridge historically has denied the development of British sociology. Do you think that has any significance at all?

Well, I think in one institutional sense, its very absence as such from the disciplines recognised by Oxford and Cambridge for ages and ages and ages is a very important and telling factor in British intellectual life, because those institutions do have the setting of the imprimatur on what is to be learned and what is not to be learned. So all the time that I was at Oxford there was no sociology. There was nobody called a sociologist. A few people lived in

260

Nuffield you know, and were a funny new breed only related to graduate students. There were no sociology courses. You took sociology through history, or through politics, or through political theory, or through PPE, so I think that has a lot to do with it. Secondly, I think that sets a particular kind of amateur but also philosophical stance in relation to sociology; that's to say once sociology was recognised and you got Oxbridge people as well as others coming in to it, I think they still brought a particular spirit which was not the route through the *science of the social* in the way in which it exists in France.

What did they bring with them?

Well, I think they bring a much stronger ... they regard analytic philosophy for instance, as telling them almost all they want to know except the facts. If somebody tells them facts, it's really in order to order that - it is the philosophic mind.

Facts are dirty things that sociology can deal with?

Yes, sociology can do that, and it will empirically grub and bring you the thing; but if you want a synthetic movement, well someone trained in PPE or somebody with familiarity of the classical greats, you know it's much more likely to give that stamp of integration to it, so I think that has been a very important factor. But I want to say that I also think that in the social investigation line, which I think is an indigenous English cultural contribution, yes, a really strong, investigative - in which I would place the Fabians and the Titmuss group and Townsend - that's a genuine tradition. It isn't the high tradition of social science, but it is a genuine tradition of social investigation. But that has also been weakened by its lack of philosophical and historical sophistication. It means you get a funny kind of split in which the very bright men are principally philosophers of a certain kind using social science data, or on the other hand very empirically minded social investigators, with a deep suspicion of theorising. So I think there is, I think Perry's right, there has been an absence of what I would call theoretical sociology, and that *is* a genuine absence which you don't find in other cultures ...

It's just an accident?

No, I don't think it's an accident. Partly it has to do with the nature of those institutions like Oxbridge, and their centrality to English academic and intellectual life; secondly it has to do with the deep individualism - I mean I think that's really what ... If I wanted to go to somewhere culturally, I would say that it has something to do with the whole individualist liberal tradition, which I think makes it very difficult to think sociologically. That's why if you ask me who's the most important sociological figure in the strict tradition I would always say Durkheim, not Weber, because I think it's Durkheim whom the English find it impossible to understand, because they don't understand the social as such.

(...) New Left Review, 1960, volume one, you're the editor. When you look at the editorial board, some of the members, Doris Lessing, Norman Birnbaum, Michael Barratt-Brown MacIntyre, Rex, Saville, Edward Thompson, Peter Worsley ... And then the first issue - writers like Hoggart, Williams, Arnold Wesker and so on. Can you just tell me what it was like then; my impression was it must have been a very exciting time, and, you know, a period of optimism ...

Well, the really optimistic time is from 1956 to 1960 rather than 1960 onwards, I think. That's the period of the formation of the New Left; 1956, Suez and Hungary, which I mean, people talk about those two as symbolic, but they do between them define something, because it was those people on the left who were not prepared to support, covertly support Stalinism. And 1956 and the Hungarian revolution and the invasion clearly revealed all that side of the Stalinist thing which had been coming out ever since the 20th Congress. On the other hand was the notion that therefore what we have, British consensus, was okay; and some of us said it's perfectly possible that this country's going to lurch into an imperialist thing again, because all the dynamic of an imperial capitalist society is not exhausted, and Suez revealed that. And that gave a space for a kind of independent socialist voice. We were still at university or just leaving university then, and that's when we formed the *Universities and Left Review*, that's the precursor of *NLR*, which had later joined up with *New Reasoner*. And that's the period that feels to me like a period of enormous exhilaration and expansion ... we felt unconstrained about taking up quite wild, or rather irresponsible ideas, about that, you know - is it really, perhaps it is the end of capitalism! (...) It's the period when Raymond [Williams] is writing *Culture and Society* [1958], revaluing that English tradition, and it's the period when Hoggart's writing *The Uses of Literacy* [1957], and one's beginning to get a kind of insight into changes and shifts in working class culture; it's part of the Titmuss group ... exploration of Britain. It's latched to a question: what is modern capitalism?, what is the working class in modern capitalism?, what does socialism mean in the second half of the twentieth-century? Those are the problems, and the journals are ways of developing a political movement and developing a debate about that. The *NLR* then is put together out of those two traditions in 1960. I'm made the editor, really because ... well people who should have been editors like Edward Thompson were so exhausted by their inner Party struggle between 1956 and 1960 that they couldn't have done it. I was very, very inexperienced in terms of contact with the British Labour movement, I was about twenty-four, so I don't think I was a very good choice. And, round about then, the possibility of the New Left becoming a really big movement began to go, although there was CND, which a lot of us were involved in in the early phases. So there was a great deal of political activity, and it felt politically exciting because there were opportunities - opportunities for a new kind of politics, I think. It was intellectually exciting because a lot of people who I think were not naturally in politics at all, were in that period in a political debate. And therefore for instance, in Birnbaum and Rex and Worsley, I got my first image of what it would be like to be a professional sociologist - they were the first professional sociologists I knew, because after all I wasn't taught by a professional sociologist. They were politically engaged, using sociological insight and imagination and I read Wright Mills in that context, not in the context of academic sociology but as somebody interested in the New Left who was also a sociologist. So I got a very exciting sense of what sociology was like, eventually I discovered it was there all the time - a way of combining political analysis and intellectual rigour and seriousness.

Okay, I'll move on. In your first editorial, you say that 'our hope is that NLR *will bring to life a genuine dialogue between intellectual and industrial workers' [1960, p. 1]. Was there a real attempt or was there always difficulties in trying to engage in a dialogue between intellectual and industrial workers?*

There always was a problem. There always was a difficulty ... and I think there always is a difficulty in Britain, because I think those cultures are - I mean I think the division of intellectual labour is massively advanced in Britain, and I think for very many good reasons the labour movement is deeply suspicious of intellectuals, since they've betrayed them many times ... you know, it's quite right to be ... I attribute a great deal that's wrong with British socialism to the Fabian tradition. Who wants another generation of Fabians squaring up to the popular demands and giving it, you know, their particular rationalistic, administrative stamp?

(...) *In* The Battle for Socialist Ideas in the 1980s *you say that 'in spite of all the traps which lie in wait for the attempt to restore the question of "party" to socialist politics today, the fragmented political scene continues to be haunted by the absent ghost of not the party (there are plenty of those), but of "party" in Gramsci's sense' [1982, p. 4]. Could you just explain that, briefly?*

Yes. First of all, what I would call the *moment* of organisation, that is to say the moment where the instinctive feelings of people who are at the bottom of the heap, who I don't think you can ever say are in false consciousness, because they know they're at the bottom of the heap, yes, I mean they're not stupid, so they know that. But that doesn't produce socialism, socialism is only one of the ways of politically encapsulating that. And therefore I don't think - you can't move without that, that mass tendency of resistance and opposition to exploitation. But that alone, without the attempt to organise it and develop it, to transform consciousness - I don't believe socialism is a natural product of working class experience. So you can read it different ways. Therefore you need that moment of organisation. Now, the moment of organisation is also in Gramsci's sense, the one which enables people who have been punctuated into different social strata by the division of labour, like intellectuals and non-intellectuals, to come together and, because they share larger goals to a movement, to an ideal, to an organisation, the things which really divide them do not so *divide* them that they can't speak to one another. So they have to find a language in which intellectuals can talk to non-intellectual people because they have a task to do, they have a place to capture. I know all the reasons why the sixties and seventies have been unable to either find or reconstitute a party of that kind; socialists cannot forget Stalinism, the terrors of the vanguard party etc. But without it we are

264

fragments, and what we do is to try to reconstitute that unity through the membership of ten different things, so you know, we try to become worker intellectuals in the universities, and ... you know what I mean? We have the party inside us, in the ten different things we do - a lot of people, on the left.

You make the point that we must understand the clear line that divides socialists from people who'd like to see society more humanly governed ... In other words 'socialism without all that bother about the working class'. And you say that that kind of socialism, without all the bother about the working class is the dominant tradition inside the Labour Party itself. Do you want to talk briefly about the Labour Party?

I mean that there's nothing essential about socialism, in the sense of transforming the structures of capitalist life and culture. I would say that if you wanted to find a political form that is more, *natural*, reformism is. It perfectly expresses the difference between us and them (...) That's a much more natural kind of politics. And actually I think that has been a long political tradition in Britain for all kinds of historical reasons, and that's basically the kind of institution the Labour Party is (...) It *is* a reformist organisation, reformism is a form of working class politics.

(...) In the Battle for Socialist Ideas *article you talk about the radical right's success in taking ideas seriously: 'They actually do believe that you have to struggle to implant the notion of the market; and that, if you talk about it well enough, effectively, persuasively enough, you could touch people's understanding of how they live and work'* [1982, p.12]. *Can you talk about that?*

Yes. Well, what I mean by that is ... slightly to repeat a point I made a moment ago. Those things don't initially just come out of ideas that float around, they have to be real experiences, of which the ideas allow you to conceptualise. Now, in people's experience in Britain, in the experience of the majority of the popular classes, the working class, there's *both* the experience of the market *daily*, you know, people live in one sense only through the market. How else could people live? The wage, consumption, buying the shopping, having enough to go round. I mean they're dominated by the actual experience of the market. So to believe that somehow, because the market became a bit unpopular during 1968 when there was a kind of 'anti', you know, the brightest and best of our undergraduates don't go into business because it's not a nice thing to do - to believe that somehow the reality of the market had disappeared then was entirely illusory. So it's not that the right didn't have anything to work on. In the same way socialism - it can only depend on what type of people are dependent on one another, and all of them can't climb up the same ladders and so on, that gives a reality to the conception of equality which socialism then tries to conceptualise in a political programme. So what I'm saying is that the roots of both those visions lie in the experience of people. But there is that crucial moment where those things are formulated so that people begin to grasp them, and I think the right did at a moment in the mid-70s understand that the tide had shifted against that so far they had to give people an actual vision of what it would be like if you let the market define life. I don't think socialism has ...

When you say - well, this is what I can't understand. When you say socialists therefore have got to understand the strategic role of ideas, haven't they always done that? I mean hasn't the WEA, the Fabian Movement, the Open University, books for working men - Penguin books, in a sense?

No, I don't think so. I think those things are extremely important. But I would say they're what we have *instead of* a truly political education. I mean, let me put it another way. You can be a life-long member of a trade union, and give your efforts to keep it going and be a really solid member and never understand what trade unions are about, what the history is about, when last the state was driven to legislate in that area, how important it was that it was moved out, how crucial it was ... Do you understand what I mean?

Okay. In your Drifting into a Law and Order Society, you say 'we are now in the middle of a deep and decisive [my emphasis] movement towards a more disciplinary, authoritarian kind of society, and [we're heading] towards some sort of interim climax' [1979, p. 17], I mean when you say decisive movement, decisive in what sense, and what's the kind of interim climax?

Well, what I mean by decisive is something more than the normal backwoods of a Tory Party enjoying the day out at a conference where they scream for hanging and whipping and so on. And sometimes that gets a little bit more of an echo in society and sometimes it doesn't. But I think those are kind of ebbs and flows around a point, and I think as between the 1950s and the 1970s the point shifted. So although there's still a lot of fluctuation around, it's around a greater acceptance of the need for social authority and discipline. I think, what I would call the liquidation of the sixties, Britain punishing itself for getting into that consumer boom, pleasure, permissiveness ... you know, free-floating, swinging. I think we're really in a different time, a different epoch - in that sense I do believe in epoch.

So what would the interim climax look like?

What I meant by the interim climax was this. That's written against a background of research that we did in the 1970s, which is in *Policing the Crisis* [1978], which started as an interest in crime and race and the state, and eventually became a kind of book about the whole crisis. Now, people forget that that book was written in 1977, still in the middle of Labour government, so when we talk about authoritarianism in *Policing the Crisis* we are not talking about the *current* situation, we're talking about the middle of a Labour government. And our sense was that that was by no means the furthest point at which authoritarianism would go, and we've seen many forms of it. But what we wanted to say was there's a huge shift, and now we may find there's a kind of 'Callaghan' authoritarianism, you know, Callaghan, populism, Callaghan stood and said aren't our police wonderful. That's one moment - it's very different from a kind of Leon Brittan short-sharp-shock moment.

(...) You say that this 'drift' has its roots in the structural backwardness of the British economy. Could you just expand on that? Is it a kind of 'losing empire' - is that the kind of thing?

It's not losing the empire - it's the crisis of imperialism itself. I mean, I think the British world turned between the 1880s and the 1920s, I think it's as decisive as the turn in the industrial revolution. And it's that post-imperial crisis which establishes, you know, an economy which is enormously

267

dependent on overseas exports, on the role of the City, on the relative backwardness of manufacture, on the relative depression of the British economy even in comparison with the more advanced ones, at the very slow rate at which Britain becomes an advanced industrial capitalist economy, and its forms of organisation, and its mentality. And ever since then, I think that is what I could call a structural weakness ... and it's crucially related to a whole evolution which crested in the first stage of imperialism, and which then set institutions in that mould.

I'll come specifically to Policing the Crisis *later, but one of the things you say is that the police now form a sort of vanguard in the drift towards the disciplinary society ...*

Yes. What I think about the police is partly what I think about law, and I've changed my view about law, I suppose, since a kind of simple notion that the law is really bourgeois etc., etc. I don't think anybody can think that any longer, and I don't think the experience of actual existing socialism allows us to think that any more. I mean I can't conceive a socialist society without some form of law, so it can't be the law itself, and once you say law you mean degrees of enforcement, however that is done. So it's not an argument that one doesn't need the police ... how could it possibly be? When you look at the fact that such an enormous amount of crime happens within the working class itself, sections of the working class ripping off other sections of the working class - what in God's name is progressive about that! - when you look at the need that working class people have to be secure about the few possessions they have, why should they lose them, when thousands of other people who have amassed fortunes riding on the backs of others are sitting luxuriating in them. So, I mean, I have never been in quite that extreme romanticism of the deviant, you know, because they're criminal they're proto-revolutionaries. On the other hand one understands precisely how law and how any social force that has the legitimate excess of power at its disposal, one understands the intrinsic threat that it always is to exploited or dispossessed people. It's an instrument for enforcing the will of the powerful on the powerless. So, we're going to have to be fantastically careful in this area. Now, one of the things that I think that *does* go back to a kind of notion of a social contract is that there are limits within which, in spite of all the things that they - working people - have had to suffer from the police, and the use of the police by the ruling powers, that nevertheless

268

there's a kind of contract within which they think they can be reasonably and decently policed. And it does have to do with the acceptance by the police of the requirement that they themselves must function within limits. That's why the British didn't want them in the first place because they thought they would never control them and that's exactly how it has turned out. So, in addition to the problems that black communities have in being over-policed and aggressively policed, in certain instances, I have a particularly strong revulsion against a force like that appearing as an openly politically campaigning force. I can't describe to you - I don't know exactly where it comes from, but something of a pure civil liberties kind rises in me when a Chief Constable tells me what to vote. You know, when he tells me that I ought to vote for hanging for my own safety, I want to say 'you are out of line! Your function is as an officer of the political power, and the point at which you put an advertisement in a newspaper on the eve of an election to tell me to vote Conservative because they are going to give you more money, is the point where you have become ... you're out of any control. You've broken a kind of contract. The contract that gives you the power to arrest me depends on *your* discipline not to step out of legal line.' And it's the point at which I just think that's becoming more and more the case, and so they should tell us ...

Okay, I found your review of Lord Scarman very interesting. Again it's about race, but it's about other things as well again it's about reform or revolution. You say: 'Scarman provides a sort of test of many of the cosy assumptions of the left, which now require to be more openly debated ... The forces of law and order did not like Scarman one little bit' [1982a, p. 66]. Could you tell me more?

Well, the thought that lies behind it is this. It's neither that the Scarman programme is the solution to the problem because the Scarman programme is in some ways classically English in the kind you talked about earlier on, in that it makes mechanical adjustment to a structural problem and thinks that the two will sort of correspond to one another. So it's not a case for Scarman. On the other hand, it's a case against what I think is the deepening isolation of the left from the only raw materials in socialism we have which is the experience of ordinary working people. And I don't see any alternative in a non-revolutionary situation like we clearly are in in Britain and have been for a very long time, I see absolutely no alternative but to using every

269

opportunity to build on and transform what exists to take you to the next stage. Therefore you can't say we don't need any police. Because who does that connect with? I mean what mass of working people who could in the end provide the motive force for a change in British society ever believe that? They just think that's utopian intellectuals who've never been in a real situation talking. So one has to recognise what it is *they* recognise, in the problems of blacks and policing, open up the possibilities - I mean push the line of progressive reform in Scarman beyond the limits, but be sure that you have people with you while you do that (...) But on the other hand, it's a reformist strategy in that it never thinks it can take three steps forward without taking a hundred thousand more people than it took to make the last step. So you have to be in touch with their contradictions - sometimes racist, sometimes fearful, you know, sometimes deferential thinking - you have to touch those roots and show that they can go somewhere to take control of their own lives, in a way which they at each stage recognise as real ... The one thing they're not about to do is set up vigilante squads and police themselves - it's just not around at the moment.

Not the Bristol riots, but you know the riots of 1981 - did it all come as a surprise to you?

No, it wasn't, although I didn't predict it at that stage, at that moment. I think you would have to have been closer to some of those communities than I was to actually predict the moment of it. But I have never thought that we could get through the seventies into the eighties without an explosion of that kind. I just didn't think so. You see, I don't think it's just poverty or unemployment that does it, that obviously doesn't always lead anywhere. What I do think is that if you were in touch with those problems as we were beginning to be from about the mid-seventies onwards, you could see that the combination of the objective - the worsening of objective circumstances - together with the positive counter-identification of blacks was an explosive mixture. I mean, a passive population that is being de-industrialised and driven into poverty quite often can't get itself together to turn around, but some sections of blacks that do have really positive, even utopian, even millenarian ...

I was going to say ... how important were Rastafarian ideas? I mean were

270

they a crucial set of ideas?

Well, I would say that Rastafarian ideas are not crucial in the actual tinder-spark of riot, but that they're the cultural pre-conditions for that.

The cultural pre-conditions?

Yes, yes, yes. And I mean that, in no sense in terms of the committed, religious Rastafarian ...

Bob Marley?

Yes, I mean cultural Rastafarianism. Which already has played *the* most fantastic role in Jamaica (...) Cultural nationalism and cultural Rastafarianism in Jamaica are the same. It happens ten years after formal independence. When formal independence goes, the test case of what Jamaicanness is still is something very anglicised, very middle class, very respectable. And it's another ten or fifteen years before the cultural test of the roots of nationalism are really in the backyard - in the roots.

Why Rasta then?

There's a kind of political movement that leads to formal independence, on the back of a sort of nationalism, Jamaican nationalism which has no cultural content. Now what's that cultural content going to be? It has to be a cultural content which draws on the mass experience of the people. Now, where is that available in forms, in cultural forms? Well, one of the places where it's available is in Rastafarianism.

(...) I'm interested in your perceptions and attitudes towards the race relations industry and, in particular, academic sociological research into questions of race ...

Yes. Well, let me say something about the race relations industry to begin with. Surprisingly, I didn't get into that area at all by that route. I

271

specifically decided to keep out of it. I mean I thought it was just too predictable, for the only thing that a black academic could ...

Politically or creatively?

Both. Creatively I didn't have anything particular to say about it, and also politically I felt a kind of requirement not to falsely bridge an inevitable division that exists between somebody who comes my route into the intellectual middle class, and guys who've lived all their lives in Brixton or Moss Side, a completely different experience. So I didn't come into it in that way at all. I came into it by 'deviancy', and by those kinds of questions. I would say that Rex is by far the most serious sociologist functioning in that terrain. And I think one has to be very careful indeed about transferring simple political arguments one might have with him, into a kind of simple minded view of what he's contributed to the area. I've always thought of him as a very serious, very engaged sociologist. I've known him from way back, I've known him taking radical political positions in times when nobody else did. I've known him in periods when he in his relations with his students had a much more democratic dialogue than most people had in traditional academia. I know his long concern about African, and anti-colonial movements, so I just think that a lot of the stuff that is said is kind of politically reductionist. But I think *Policing the Crisis* does differ from the analysis that he offers, in three ways. First of all it continues to be concerned about the interpenetration of race and class, and I don't know but I think he would feel easier if he can *separate* rather than have to work with and across the complexities of those issues. Secondly I think it does suffer from some of the problems of the race relations industry in general, and from many of the responses of the black radical left, in disaggregating the race problem from the problem of the British social formation as a whole, and the one thing we wanted to do in *Policing the Crisis* is not about blacks, it's about a crisis, it's not just a crisis of racism, it's a crisis of a whole social formation of which racism has an internal, complex set of internal relations. And thirdly, I think now, a bit of what Rex says is disfigured by his experience of simplicities from the left, you know, a certain kind of entrenched anti-Marxism, because if a Marxist says it, it has to be wrong, and I think that is actually disfiguring his own much more complicated argument. And I've said that in public (...) So I take Rex intellectually as a most important adversary.

272

(...) I know it is incredibly complicated, but if you had to make it simple, what is your position on the relationship of the concepts of race and class?

What I think about it is this. That there are no relations, no sets of social relations, which in our society are outside of the fundamental structure of class, and therefore whatever you do however you study it, you have to study the way in which it is shaped by and locked into the class system. However I don't think any longer that all the major social contradictions arise from the class contradiction: I think there are social contradictions which historically pre-date it, and I think each of those social contradictions have their own specificity, so they have a history which is different from that of the history of class relations. They have effects, in other words, some of the pre-determining structures are different from the class ones, and consequently the experiences and resolutions have their own distinctiveness. And therefore someone can actually be obliged to live out all the disabilities of a class relation, but because in addition to that they live out the specific disabilities of being black in a society which is racist, their consciousness of what you might call class, or their consciousness of social divisions and social inequality, will be organised round the experience of race rather than around the experience of class.

Would black politics take that form?

Yes, I think the forms of their politics do reflect those differences, I think they do, and they give priority to political issues which are not the same as the white working class.

But presumably you're saying that being as there is no contemporary vehicle, organisation, organ for the white working class anyway it doesn't matter. In fact you just have to do your politics wherever you do it, but still thinking about class?

Well, yes, that's a consequence of the earlier question, the thing we talked about, about party. Just in the same way as you need political organisation to bridge the distinction between intellectuals and non-intellectuals, so you need it to bridge the differences between specifically different social contradictions. And to develop politics which both addresses why it is that you could have a socialist revolution and the society remain racist, or why it is that you could have a socialist revolution and the society remain sexist. They can't be the same thing, if you can transform the one without transforming the other, as is patently the case. I just think that socialist politics is going to have to live with complexity, because that's the real situation. The real situation is those things *are* different.

(...) Some of the papers in The Empire Strikes Back *[CCCS, 1982] particularly concerning Rex and others* seem *to be about the impossibility of doing research on race relations because they were not black. Is there any point to their argument?*

Let me put it this way. I really don't believe in racism, *I really don't*, that's to say I don't think it's the pertinent social division or line of closure to organise around. Therefore it follows logically that I must believe that ideas have no colour. And therefore the fact that you're black, and a researcher, does not guarantee you either the correct analysis or the 'right-on' political position. Now that's a generous statement, because obviously in the process of doing research, sensitivity, trust, understanding, basic commitment, access, all those things matter in the logistics of research, and there are some political moments, yet I'd make the distinction between the general case which I hold to, that there are no black ideas, no feminine ideas, just good ideas or bad ideas, and some men have some good ideas and others. But tactically, I do think one has to think about the circumstances in which research is done. That's why I didn't get into the race relations business: not because I didn't think race was important, but that there was a political moment when I just thought - 'it is wrong, the thing to do now is not to add another project on what the blacks are thinking, it's just the wrong moment', and sometimes some people can do it and sometimes they can't. I think one has to clarify what are the criteria for the tactics: why is this the wrong moment for Rex to be in Handsworth? Why is that the wrong kind of question for him to ask just now? And that's a different thing from saying that no white researcher will ever be able to understand (...) *The Empire Strikes Back* is by no means only, certainly not researched and thought through, by an entirely black group ... [but] I think in that appreciative sense, they are able to get close, and they have a kind of way of affirming that and understanding its importance, which I think a lot of other people

274

haven't. I think a lot of researchers haven't even attempted to explore that level, that kind of racism ...

(...) Say you had to give an inaugural lecture here [at the Open University] and you had to say what sociology was, what would be your quick answer?

Well, I mean I did have to give an inaugural lecture, and it was mainly about two points: it was around the use of the sociological imagination or insight into social processes to question the obvious - I think the sociologist's question is always 'it looks exactly like that, therefore it cannot possibly be - how is it really?' Demystification, yes. So I think the critical edge, I think sociology is by definition the critical edge, even to its own assumptions, its own positively constructed things. That's one thing. And the second thing that I said, which may not have come across very clearly in things that I've written, I think it's a discipline much more like history than like chemistry or physics. Very close to history.

(...) And if historians do sociology that's fine, but historians can do other things as well which are not sociology?

Historians can do other things as well. It's that conception of the social, which I do think then both functions much more like historians, or historical reality, does. I think a lot of sociology is really like trying to write contemporary history. And I think sociology without a sense of history is nothing. But then obviously there's a difference there between the attachment of the unique particularity of any historical circumstance, and the interest that sociology has in tentatively generalising its laws. However, I'm not a positivist and never have been. I think that those - that the laws at the level of positive science are almost all (a) unprovable or (b) uninteresting. I mean they're at such a level of generality, they don't give you insight into any particularity at all. Therefore I would always want, as it were, to bend the twig of sociology back towards that historical sense of what is particular and concrete.

A bit soft?

Yes, it is soft. Absolutely, there's no question about it. And I think that we're in trouble with Sir Keith Joseph and the media interviewers and the public because we did get tied in the sixties in the period of institutional expansion, into making promises about predicting trends, you know, telling what the future was like, how to get Britain out of the deep, which we never knew how to do, and is not in the line you know. What we could do is sensitise every decision, every argument taken, to dimensions of what is not obvious about the structuration of our society; and our decisions, our politics, would be more deeply informed by that. I think in that sense sociology is principally an educative mode, rather than a predictive one.

Okay, next thing. Is Marxism just a form of sociology or are they incompatible approaches?

What I would say is that to a certain extent they share the same territory, but they're not coterminous with one another. That is to say, I think sociology is basically analytic. And it is not prescriptive - you might go so far as to say, not quite in Weber's sense, that it tells you what the options are, it informs you what the options are. Certainly it informs you what the causes of patterns are, but never within itself adequately, partly because it's been so wretched at dealing with questions of the distribution of power. If you have a science which is not organised around the concept of power, you have a science which is essentially intrinsically depoliticised. Now Marxism I think obviously shares terrain in that I believe that unless it does function as an adequate way of either analysing or helping you to begin analysing the way in which modern societies work, what has it to say? It's another religion. So it shares with sociology that interest in analysing social structures and relations.

But it necessarily goes beyond ...?

Of course, it necessarily goes beyond, because it *does* say that because that is so, or because that is so and you would like it to be so, those are *the* agents, powers, constraints, which might help it to become so or not.

Should one choose between them?

276

I don't think you have to choose between them, because if you put it as a simple choice, you would suggest that you can be a sociologist without getting into those arguments, and I think you never can. I don't know any sociologist who is outside of the value question ...

That's what I am coming to next. Does the value debate - I'm thinking of Weber, Myrdal, Gouldner and so on - have any relevance for you?

Well I don't believe it any more. I never did actually. But I was wary about it at the time when I didn't think I knew. What I think is that practically no great sociological insight has ever come out of a value-free position. I think it always comes out of having already seized for some political or ontological reasons on a set of 'givens', and then, it seems to me, where the sociological imagination comes in then is the sense that you're not satisfied with just having stated it, you're not satisfied with finding the world exactly as that, as your 'ought' or your 'desire' would like to bring it about. It's the willingness after that to face the difficult case, or to be genuinely surprised. But not in its foundations. And I think the same is true of learning. I think students don't learn from somebody who has said, 'I of course have no presuppositions, I tell you what that is, and that is, and that is ...' On the other hand I don't think people learn well either from saying 'I'm a Marxist and therefore the world can only work in this way', I think it works from saying 'That's my take on the world, that's my grasp of the world. Now, I do want it to be the *best* theory, the *best* way of producing knowledge within that framework, and if you show me something else I'm willing to test mine against that, and I'm willing to borrow from it if it improves the thing I have' ...

We'll just accept that all knowledge is soaked ...

In the social. Knowledge of the social, I don't know a thing about science. Knowledge of the social is I think soaked in the taking of positions. I don't know actually what knowledge is if it isn't the knowledge about something from some position.

All right. If we just go back a minute, you said a lot of sociology is contemporary history. Well, that suggests that it is history ...

Well, I think there are different sociological styles within it, and I'm not exclusivist about that. My own style is very much more a kind of literary-historical kind of work. I don't for that reason think that somebody who is more into testing hypotheses in a more systematic way, that that's necessarily bad work. You see what I mean? I'm not opposed to decent quantitative work, at all, which I think a lot of people think, well, because you're anti-positivist you must be. What I'm desperately against is the fetishism of methods; I don't give a damn what the method is, the method is just a good way of knowing and finding out, and if you can't find out the best way you find out the next best way, and the next best way. So it's the confusion of methods with substance that I'm opposed to. That's to say I can tolerate and learn a great deal from a variety of sociological styles, but I do think that intrinsically if you want to say to someone, 'it's a science', well in what sense is it a science. I would want to say, 'well it's like a historical science: it's systematic knowledge, it's serious knowledge, it's critical knowledge, it's knowledge which is aware of its theoretical presuppositions, and so on, it's self-conscious knowledge, it's organised knowledge, so it's not just common sense, but it's knowledge in the sense in which a theoretically informed historian would work, not quite the knowledge of atoms, or the stars'.

Okay, Giddens, and what Rex calls the 'philosophisation of sociology'. What are your thoughts on Giddens?

Well, I've learned a great deal from Giddens. But I suppose the two things that worry me are ... I think there's a difference between an interest in theoretical questions - and I'm deeply interested in theoretical questions - and what I think you're calling the philosophisation of sociology. I think those two things are different. The second is I think an over-preoccupation with epistemological questions, with how do we know anything at all, and that so preoccupies you that ... Now Giddens is not quite like that, but there's a touch of that about his work, about what I would call the translation of concrete problems, the wrong kind of translation of concrete problems, into a sort of socio-philosophical articulation. And that I do think just renders the work, gives the work a feel in general, of being much less concerned with concrete historical and political and social questions, than I think he actually

278

is ... I think there's probably a way of reading Giddens to grasp what it is he's really puzzled and bothered about, but the writing doesn't come across like that, it comes across as a work of rather detached synthesis, intellectual synthesis, and that I think is a kind of discrepancy between where he is really at and how the work appears ...

Why do you think Giddens and his apparent influence has appeared at this moment in time?

Well I think it goes back a little bit to what I was saying about Oxford. I think *that* is what the English understand by theory. I think the English understand by theoretical sophistication, a kind of philosophical reflexiveness, whereas I don't think theory's like that at all, I think theory's about the logical connections of propositions about substantive problems. And therefore I have no time for philosophical reflection in sociology, but I've all the time for theoretically informed concrete studies. I think there is a difference between those two.

(...) Something which John Goldthorpe has written I find interesting and I wonder whether you could comment: 'intellectuals seek to exert not only a cognitive, but also a moral and a political influence; and what historicism offers them is in effect a tempting shortcut from one to the other' [1979, p. 17] ...

Yes. Well I mean I think that is ... not in a Weberian way, but nevertheless an attempt to divorce sociological knowledge from its inevitable moral underpinnings and political consequences (...) And I'm not interested in short-circuiting the links between those two, as I've said before I think it's impossible to divide them ultimately. I don't think there's any shortcuts between them. I'm certainly not interested in moral takes on the world which produce the right answers, I mean which produce acceptable answers politically but ones which don't explain anything.

Presumably you're either a Marxist or not, he would say ... What he means presumably is basically a belief that the working classes are morally better than other sectors. I mean for the Marxist, you believe that to be the case?

Yes, you believe that to be the case. And you hope that the knowledge that you bring to bear, that you produce, and the policies or strategies which develop out of that are which advance those causes. Where we share, is, that if investigation provides knowledge which does not suggest that's an easy route, or a necessary, or an inevitable route, that's knowledge which we really need.

(...) On to television. If someone said to you, the question of who are the ruling classes is a really difficult one, say, how, why is TV so determined, I mean ... how controlling is it? How do we start to think seriously about it without being conspiratorial?

Well, I'm sure the simple notions won't do in the sense that a conspiratorial view of history is simply not adequate. That does not mean that no conspiracies exist incidentally ... It just means that you can't account for the structuring operation of the whole field simply by who is in whose pockets, or what Gramsci would have called 'dirty Jewish interests' (...) In fact coming back to something I said earlier on, in fact the unconsciousness of ideological structures, the degree to which ...

Say inferential racism ...?

Yes, the degree to which people who sustain ... Now, perhaps I should say what I think about this (...) That it is less the specific content of any ideological statement and more the ideological categories and the logics which connect statements.

Can you give me an illustration of that?

Yes. It's when you map the economy out in terms of value for money, say. Now, I mean you don't have to be a monetarist, you don't have to be anything at all. In a sense it's irrelevant what you are, you could be a raving Trotskyist. But if every time you think to ask a relevant question about the economy you have to say, 'but, you know, it's ...' Do you understand what I mean? So people very much go to the bias in terms of the answers that are given, when you are already inside the game, when you think, if you have

280

the classic buying system ... and therefore I'm interested in the way in which television, with the wide variety of voices ... so the pluralist account genuinely accounts for something. And why the conspiracy theory doesn't hold, because people who live in the media and really know it, know it's not monolithic. It's got all kinds of voices - ex-Trots, libertarians ...

Is the unconscious in the viewer and them?

Well I think very often so.

So, in other words, these kind of media people who are SWP maybe, still cannot see what they're doing?

Well it is quite difficult. But remember that you can't say that although those structures are shared - it isn't, I mean the old Marxist question of who has the principal means of setting the thing in motion, have a very important role to play in the re-confirmation of that existing map, so although you and I share it we don't share it in equal dialogue, equal weight. I mean I propose the statement and you make the qualification within it. I say, it's a problem of numbers, and you say, there're not so many of them. Then we have an argument about whether three million is enough, or is one and half million enough. The underlying thing has already carried the implication: the unstated implication that numbers of blacks are a problem. And it is really at that level it seems to me that the media 'structures consciousness' by providing the kind of grids within which understanding occurs, rather than slewing each statement that way.

This question might be difficult. What would democratic, popular, free communication look like?

Well, let us not talk about what it would look like in the ideal socialist society. Let's talk about how it might look like if the existing structures began to disintegrate. It would look like ... like ... like a hundred flowers. That is to say that the true professionalism of the broadcaster, like the true professionalism of the policeman, would then emerge. It has nothing to do with pre-determining the outcome.

Is that in any way possible?

No, of course in the ideal sense it's not possible. But it is possible that a broadcaster could see his social role as facilitating the most important discordant voices from making the most articulate statement they could.

So fundamentally we would still have a situation in which there'd still be agenda setting, but we'd just be reducing it ...?

You would be aware of the agenda setting. You'd have to be aware of the agenda setting. And I would have to say, look I'm going to give you an obviously kind of Marxist view of the world - you don't have to buy it. But you do need to know that I'm not a lunatic, I'm not outside the discourse of reason in order to see the thing that way; and that's how I see it, and I don't take a simple-minded view ... And that's what that view looks like. That's who the Marxists are, that's what they think. And that makes an extremely good programme, and it exposes the constant play of presuppositions which is what the dialogue is really about. The problem about it is that the dialogue is masked. Nobody says, 'those are the presuppositions', or 'those are the limits to voices that have access to the dialogue'.

Cultural Studies *[1980]. You discuss Hoggart, Williams and Edward Thompson ... Could you tell me why Hoggart's* The Uses of Literacy *was so important?*

Well, remember when it occurs. It occurs in the middle of that argument about embourgeoisment, has the working class disappeared? What is the modern working class? And therefore it had a real concrete historical reference to what is in fact some aspects of traditional working class culture in the thirties, and it made sense, it made a kind of sense of what had happened to those things in the period between then and the fifties. So it was recognisable; it matched one's perceptions, namely that you could still see where it was, but its dynamic was different from Leeds in the thirties. So it really gave an account of the change from traditional working class culture from before the War to the period afterwards, which allowed one to recognise it as it was, and it provided an alternative image to the image of the 'embourgeoisifed' worker. Where I think it was misleading was that we didn't understand - I don't think he did at the time - the degree to which the picture then drawn of the fifties pulled not so much on experience and observation but very much more on some of the quite abstract propositions of American mass culture. And if you go out and read them now, they're little vignettes of what de Tocqueville would have said if he'd been in a 1950s Elvis Presley milk bar. They're not really observed, in any other way, but there's a kind of concreteness to the language. So I think it's very very perceptive about the nature of working class culture - empiricism, pragmatism, fatalism, you know, that love for the concrete, which he describes fantastically. And I think that those are really distinctive values of that culture.

(...) The founding of the Centre for Contemporary Cultural Studies ... It was attacked by some sociologists at the time wasn't it? Can you just, briefly ...

Essentially positivistic. Essentially social psychologists saying ...

Did they think it was going to become Marxist, or did they think that it was going to be just loose and woolly and vague ...

Loose and woolly and vague, yes. They thought it was going to be kind of Hoggart, Orwell stuff.

You said that 'it may be hard for us - confronted as we are now by the immense disarray of "mainstream" sociology - to recall a time when British sociology was so confident in its claims and proprieties' [1980, p. 21]. Okay ...

Well, you know what I mean. I mean they took us on as if sociology was - we all knew what that was and its proper scientific procedures and the positive knowledge it produced and here are these people dreaming to tell us anything at all about how society was going. And I can't imagine anybody, even distinguished professors coming on so strong with what sociology is and isn't nowadays.

You mentioned funding, and some difficulties you had. Have you got any strong feelings about this?

(…) It wasn't a problem of funding in the political sense for us. It was much more in the sense of kind of opening unorthodox methods of research not in a centre of excellence, not with professional sociologists heading it, it was those kinds of considerations. And the truth is that we struggled and struggled and struggled to get resources, because the way in which we were trying to do the work at CCCS did require us to have a critical mass of students in place with a lot of time to spend on it, because we were doing all sorts of things as well as producing their theses. So although we were short of that, the fact is that the sixties did allow us to do that - we did eventually get quota students. And it's a terrifying prospect now, because a place like that simply could not have happened, it would never have happened now.

Before the 'second decisive break' in cultural studies, you talk about the ongoing tension between experiential accounts and larger accounts of structural and historical determination, which have been pivotal. And then you talk about the second decisive break, 'the break into a complex Marxism', and [these studies] 'returned to the agenda the key question of the determinate character of culture and ideologies - their material, social and historical conditions of existence. They therefore opened up a necessary re-working of the classical Marxist question of "base" and "superstructure"' [1980, p. 25]. Well, that is the one that constantly bothers me … And obviously, the question I've got here is, 'Stuart Hall takes culture seriously and what are the consequences for Marxism?' Can you just talk a bit about that?

Let me just say, this is what - the base/ superstructure problem, for which culture is another name, really, it's that aspect of culture that we've been concerned with, that's at the root of the CCCS work. That's one of the problems that I started with. One of those problematic questions that I was concerned about. And it really arose out of literary studies. If you don't want to study literary forms in the abstract, in an aesthetic sense, and you want to relate them to the social. On the other hand you don't want to simply say this is a progressive novel and therefore it's revolutionary, and that's not … or the novel form is bourgeois etc. Well, how do you understand the relationship between cultural forms and social relations? So that's what interests me. Now, it's a different interest from being interested in culture as such. And I used to say at CCCS, that what we're doing, but don't mistake that for the most important problem in the world, it's not the only important problem in the world.

It happens that that is an area that Marxism is relatively underdeveloped in, or doesn't give us the right answers in, or it's a very complicated set of problems, and we've chosen to specialise on them. So my specialism is culture. But I don't think culture runs the worker, you see, I want to make that perfectly clear ... there are lots of other very important things. And in any case, if you're interested in it from a base/superstructure perspective, you can't be interested in the internal relations of culture alone, so you're really (...) I think all struggles have their ideological-cultural dimensions. But I think there's a species of cultural studies which really replaces culture for the economic determination by the cultural in the last instance, and I don't believe in that either . So it's never been a project to supplant a crude materialism with a crude idealism. So, having said that, then take the question of hegemony. What I think Gramsci says about hegemony is, that there's no hegemony which doesn't deal with the question of dominant relations in the sphere of the economic. On the other hand, to dominate in the sphere of the economic is not to construct hegemony . So it's one of those - you can't do it without, yes, necessary but not sufficient conditions. You have to then construct the social and ideological and political conditions of leadership and ascendancy which enable you not just to get people back to work, but positively to organise that in relation to some project of restoring that level of capitalist profitability, which does not depend only on technological or managerial questions: it depends on attitudes and beliefs and hopes and fears and ideas and coercions and so on, yes?

Yes. Look, let me put it another way, 'the problematic of cultural studies thus became closely identified with the problem', the one that's worried us all for years, 'the relative autonomy of cultural practices'. Paul Q. Hirst has said that things are either autonomous or they're not, they can't be relatively autonomous [1977, p. 130]. Has he a point?

He's got a point if you think structures work logically, but social structures do not. I think that is one of the problems that arise from what I would call the 'over-epistemologisation' of sociological enquiry, because I do think that one can see the degree to which the state, for instance, functions in all kinds of ways in a relatively autonomous way ... generates its own momentum, has different loci of struggle within it which don't simply correspond to class fractions outside, and yet if you say 'what is this thing doing in relation?', it's obviously not functioning outside of the social relations.

It's about unevenness?

It's about unevenness, it's about specificity. It's about the fact that something can have a specific effect within its own sphere on a structure on which it is nevertheless dependent. The state cannot drive capitalism where it wants to go, and yet where capitalism goes is crucially dependent on whether the state can get this or that policy off the ground.

(...) Do you see Policing the Crisis *as somehow an example of how to do empirical work plus holding on to structural notions?*

Yes, I mean I tried to - it wasn't designed like that.

There seems to be a good case for it ...

That is how I like to work, for myself ... I'm not going to make it a prescription for other people. I don't like to work on purely theoretical questions without concrete examples. On the other hand I think the critique of a kind of stupid empiricism which Althusser has made is perfectly right.

(...) Yes, but I think he painted too pure a picture, a pure picture, which was ...

Well, I think that's true. You know, the work of the Centre was influenced by Althusser, some people would say infected by it, because it became very sensitive to not making an empirical statement which wasn't theoretically underpinned. And I had the experience of that being extremely inimical to research. People couldn't put pen to paper because since they didn't have the

286

answer to the riddle of the universe, you couldn't say anything! You couldn't say anything at all because you couldn't account for how it is you said it and why you knew it. And I think that was extremely damaging, and I learned enormously from Althusser because I'm interested in a non-reductionist Marxism, and at the same time resisted theoretical practice, the excesses of theoretical practice. I never subscribed to that, the notion that kind of revolutionary practice occurs in the purity of one's logical categories. I don't believe that.

Why Althusser? I mean was it the kind of revolt against socialist humanism, more than an academic exercise?

Yes, I mean, Althusser then had an effect on a lot of graduate students in sociology and on sociological knowledge itself, which was a pretty academicising impact. But as you can see we were already into many of those arguments without the benefits of Althusser's insight. If you were wanting to know about base/superstructure, and how you could hold some of the anti-idealist positions which base/superstructure allows you to think, without reducing one thing to another, without being stupidly economistic about it. And therefore humanism just simply didn't do anything very much about that. It sort of said, you know, there are these hard structures, then there are people. You know, there's a flow of good feeling ... And so we wanted something which was intellectually tougher than that. And whatever else it did, Althusser did offer us the ways of beginning to think about determination without being reductivist. It was that inspiration which ...

I mean also it sharpened people up I think ...

Yes it did that. But don't forget what that looks like in excess. It looks like a kind of stupid dancing on a pin exercise, between who can be more rigorous than whom. And it led people to take out rigorous positions today, which they as soon as the poor student's caught up with it and struggled to understand and fell into line with it, it was changed equally rigorously in the next book! So there was a lot of rubbish connected with it, and a lot of 'over-scientism' which went into it. But nevertheless it did make people aware of the requirement for theoretical rigour.

287

(...) Would you, without being accused by everybody of over-simplifying, say gender is like race when you analyse it?

I think it raises the same kind of problems. Yes. I know feminists don't like that, when one says it. I think ... it raises the same kind of problems, in that it is a form of social relations, social division, of strategic political import-ance in different societies, which are *never outside* of the structure and feel the force of class relations, but which are not reducible to them. Once different tensions arise, or class tensions are translated or deflected by their existence, you have to develop a politics that answers to the specificity of each of those contradictions.

(...) Okay, yes. What did you mean when you talked about the CCCS's 'intellectual practice'?

Well, we felt, that sociological research, or social science enquiry, was predicated on a model of a separation between intellectuals and non-intellectuals, and on the private appropriation of knowledge - you did your little thesis, and you had a relation, usually unsatisfactory, with one other superior. And these seemed to be to us the relations of production of knowledge in most traditional universities. And we were lucky enough to have the circumstances in which we could try and do something about that. CCCS is in part an exploration of the problems and difficulties of unlearning one method of producing knowledge and trying to learn another. And of course *Policing the Crisis* is a long and rather discursive book, because it's written by five people, it really *is* written by five people - we wrote each other's stuff. Now if you just think what is required by graduate students and the Director of the Centre, to research together and to have one another's sentences taken apart, and really to struggle through to, well, what are we prepared to say about this. Well it's a big effort, and it occupied a lot of our time at the Centre, and it led to the encouragement of people to publish before their PhDs, it led to the notion that a lot of PhDs can be based on an early stage of collective research. So it was an attempt, in post-1968 really, to change the internal intellectual practices, and make them more collective.

(...) How would you see your work as having been influential? Or what would you like of your work to be influential? Just all of the things you've

talked about, about methodological freedom, the importance of stating one's position, theoretical plus concrete research, all those things?

Yes, yes, it's no different from all that. I don't think much about the question of influence. I mean I suppose I think that CCCS was, it's a big moment, you know, because it's when one tried to institutionalise that. It wasn't just 'high work', one did try to generalise it as a practice and to make it more democratic. And I think that did have an influence. I mean the establishment of those questions, they're not questions that we raised alone, Raymond [Williams] and many other people have raised them, but we tried to work on them within the framework of an educative practice (...) In CCCS it ['1968'], translated many of the questions which had previously been posed outside of universities inside universities, the questions of hierarchy, and intellectual leadership and academic responsibility and status in the hierarchy ...

Has that disappeared now with the drift towards the 'law and order society'?

Well it has disappeared a good deal. I mean I think that I would say 'was' for two other reasons. One is that I think a great deal of what happens now in the social and moral and educational field is an attempt to recoup what people thought they had lost in 1968. I mean I think sociology is still being punished for 1968. When Sir Keith Joseph gets on his high horse, you know, it's the moment of 1968 that he has in mind when he's doing it. So I think it's a long memory, a long course of revenge that's going on. But the third thing is that I think sixty-eight was an anticipation of the new forms of struggle of certain new kinds of political tensions which we don't understand at all. And in many ways the revival and return to a more traditional industrial relations, class parties, the Conservative enemy, has entirely obliterated the memory of this phenomenon ... It looked like a traditional festival of the revolution, and yet, made by Tariq Ali and the LSE - I mean what is that? What was that? We don't understand that. I think sociologically it's an extremely teasing problem, which we've entirely forgotten about really, it's kind of past.

(...) I think you've answered this already, but if you had to write an agenda for sociology in the 1980s and 1990s, I mean presumably it would be about

289

researching and thinking about the drift into the law and order society, popular authoritarianism and so on?

Well, it would be about those questions and it would be about the centrality and importance of the domain of ideology, which are traditional things that I've worked on. But I think it would be much more now about the state, than it was ... I was coming towards that, historically, at the Centre by the time I was leaving.

Would you want to try and make sociologists more and more aware of their political role?

... Well, my hesitancy is because I am afraid of an over simple politicisation. So I don't want sociologists to become propagandists of the classroom, I really don't, and that's something that the Open University teaches you. When you have to teach students who are not academically very sophisticated, but who tomorrow are going in as responsible adults into all kinds of jobs around the world you cannot get away with a simple over-politicised view of the world. So I don't want sociologists to be that. I really don't believe in one-sided polemical teaching because I don't believe in one-sided polemical societies! But I do believe that sociologists need to be aware of the intrinsic political pay-off and dimension of social thinking and social matters.

If you wanted people to follow a good sociological practice, would it in fact be the work of people like Raymond Williams, Richard Hoggart ... I mean to say not particularly 'professional' sociologists?

A question I haven't thought about really. I think probably now I'm more aware of the weaknesses of the *Uses of Literacy* than I would have been at the time. I still think it's a very important and exciting book, but it's terribly subjective; and I'm aware of the traps which that sort of uncontrolled, undisciplined subjectivism can lead you into. Quite unconsciously I don't think Richard himself knew the degree to which he was actually borrowing from a range of images in order to see his own world. I like Raymond's books a lot, and I get a great deal out of them. And I have a funny relationship with Raymond, in that although we are very different people from very different

290

backgrounds, he and I have found - I have found myself intellectually and politically worrying about very similar things to him at very similar times, without - you know, we've never been in constant dialogue, he doesn't know where I'm going next. And that's been true; I was interested in what you might call *Culture and Society* questions, at the point where Raymond said ...

It's a pity you see because of the institutionalisation, the professionalisation, the specialisation of sociology, people like Williams are considered to be Marxists, not sociologists, and simply may or may not be taught. I mean is anyone breaking that down or not?

Well, I do think that something can be done about that, and what would have to be done about that is an awareness of the kind of varieties of forms in which sociological insights occur, and I think that's true as much of the past as the present. There was profound sociological knowledge and insight before sociology arrived on the scene. I mean, the science of the social doesn't start at the point at which people call themselves sociologists. And therefore I think that is one of the things that people could do, something could be done about. The professional sociologists who understand that could begin themselves the de-professionalisation of the next sociological generation, by not drawing the lines like that, by showing the degree to which Weber is also a magnificent economic historian, by showing the profound sociological insight of Hobsbawm, or Saint de Croix in ancient societies. I mean who cares about the labels - what one wants is the knowledge and the understanding! In that sense I have nothing, no vested interest in the preservation of sociology as a professional area.

Okay. You mention Raymond Williams; in Towards 2000 *[1983] he becomes extremely mellow in the last few pages, and one thing he says which sounds to me a bit like, you know, the 'personal and political' if you like, he says that 'the central element is the shift from production to livelihood, from an alienated generality to direct and practical ways of life' [1983, p. 66]. It sounds like growing vegetables, in a sense, you know what I mean? 'These are the real bases from which cooperative relationships can grow, and the rooted forms which are wholly compatible with rather than contradictory to it, are the major areas of interest' [1983, p. 67]. And he talks about feminism, eco-politics, peace and all those things. So one, I'm interested if you have a vision of what the 'good society' would be like, and second, do you think people like Williams, I mean is this a kind of pessimism, or is this a new shift away from rigid class politics?*

Well, what I'm not into is very detailed utopian planning as it were, but I also think that without a vision you don't constitute a whole philosophy of life, you constitute incremental change without a vision, but you don't constitute a new order of life, without a vision. So I think that a utopian strain and strand ... I think also it is intrinsically Marxist, because the notion of respect for the constraint of conditions coupled with that which is still even while constrained to becoming something else - that tension between, yes, you fix it in determination and becoming-ness, which is what gives Marxism that dynamic, which is really what makes it *scandalous*. If it only remained fixed it would be perfectly absorbable within the hierarchies of knowledge, but it's the promise that even at that moment, you know, contradictorily it's becoming something else that makes it scandalous: that's the true scandalous nature of Marxism (...) And I think that Raymond's one of the few people who's able to write in that way. Now if you ask me if I have a vision like that I'd say that I've become much more aware in the recent years of the degree to which that has to do with democracy. I feel more, it's a positive word for me now, in a way in which it wasn't in my earlier political life ...

You mean before it was bourgeois democracy?

Yes, yes. But I think it has to do with the capacity of ordinary, unspecialised people to take charge of their lives and make something out of them.

And even deciding things that you don't like?

Even deciding things that I don't like. Because I think that is the leap both out of capitalism, and also out of social democracy which I feel has a deeply de-politicised, deeply undemocratic form, that form where the experts handle the real application of life, of things and knowledge ...

So I mean, this sounds naive, but it's a belief that there has to be genuine freedom, then let the people choose, that's what you want. Nothing else?

Yes. I mean obviously I would want to, I mean I can't even describe to you how deeply one would feel if that led to people saying, you know, give us hierarchy, give us power. So I think it is naive to put it that way because obviously I have built into what I'm saying the notion that people who have the capacity to make history themselves don't want anyone else to make it for them. What I mean is I'm willing to tolerate a variety of forms of that kind, I'm not interested in the imposition of forms of life, I am interested in the capacity of people who've been dispossessed from history to make history their own, to become history agents.

(...) The last thing. I've just found a quote which I think summarises your work actually, a William Morris quote: 'I pondered all these things, and how men fight and lose the battle, and the thing that they fought for comes about in spite of their defeat, and when it comes turns out not to be what they meant, and other men have to fight for what they meant under another name' [in Anderson, 1980, p. 17]. Do you think it summarises your work?

Yes I do. Certainly something that it accounts for - it accounts for the fact that actually my analysis of mainly the political prospects in the present, are pretty grim. But I don't feel put down by that.

No, well, it's either a struggle or it isn't.

Yes, yes. But in that sense you know, even when the best of your analytic prognostications don't seem to ... there's always more movement than you think, it won't ever happen quite in the way in which you predicted because history always escapes that final prediction, but that doesn't obscure the need to use the best course that you have. I'm very much a believer in tendency, I'm not a believer in prediction. But I am a believer in the kind of looser notion of lines of determination, and openings and closures, lots of lines of possibilities are closed off by history, but one still doesn't have just the predicted route, one has routes whose full consequences one can never actually quite get ahead of.

11   Robert K. Merton

Acknowledged by most as America's most distinguished and influential living sociologist, Robert Merton is still teaching the sociology of science at Columbia University, New York.

Born 1910 in a South Philadelphia slum, to Eastern European immigrant parents, Merton graduated in both philosophy and sociology from Temple University in 1931. With the help of a fellowship he then became a graduate student at Harvard and went on to 'establish a brilliant academic record under men like Pitirim Sorokin, Talcott Parsons, George Sarton and L.J. Henderson' (Hunt, 1961, p. 56). In 1940 he advanced in one leap from his instructorship at Harvard to a professorship at Tulane, where he became chairman of the sociology department. His tenure there was short-lived though, for in 1941 he accepted an invitation to join Columbia University as an assistant professor. The then divided sociology department had chosen Merton to please the 'theorists', following the appointment of Paul Lazarsfeld to please the 'empiricists' (Hunt, 1961, p. 58). Of their relationship Coser and Nisbet observe that 'Merton's students tended to be held back from undue flights of fancy by Lazarsfeld's earthy and rigorous methodological style, and Lazarsfeld's students, in their turn were reminded that the facts never speak for themselves' (1975, p. 7).

Merton is known for so many contributions to sociology, it is only possible to sketch a few here. One of his first - and lasting contributions concerned 'anomie and social structure', and particularly the nature of deviant behaviour. In a nutshell, Merton asked the question [orig. 1938, 1957, p.

139]:

> What ... are the consequences for the behaviour of people variously situated in a social structure of a culture in which the emphasis on dominant success-goals has become increasingly separated from an equivalent emphasis on institutionalized procedures for seeking these goals?

Another emphasis of Merton's is that of understanding the 'unanticipated consequences of purposive social actions' which he sees as a fundamental social process. Another way of putting this is that in the 'course of social interaction, men create new conditions that were not part of their intent', in other words 'short-run rationality often produces long-run irrationality' (Merton, 1976, p. 184). A related and important conception developed by Merton, grew out of an extension of W.I. Thomas's dictum 'if men define situations as real, they are real in their consequences'. Merton thus develops the process of the 'self-fulfilling prophesy' whereby 'fears are translated into reality' (1982, p. 264). As Merton explains (1982, p. 251):

> The self-fulfilling prophesy is, in the beginning, a *false* definition of the situation evoking behaviour which makes the originally false conception come true. The specious validity of the self-fulfilling prophesy perpetuates a reign of error. For the prophet will cite the actual course of events as proof that he was right from the beginning.

Of course in the 1950s particularly Merton was seen as refining the functionalism of Parsons with in particular his notion of manifest and latent functions, and in addition his argument in favour of theories of the middle-range in contradistinction to the 'grand theory' of Parsons . Manifest functions are those objective consequences for some person and intended, while latent functions are consequences which contribute to adjustment but were not so intended. Merton's additional notion of dysfunctions was introduced, and dysfunctional events are argued to lessen the adjustment of a social system. More recently Merton has developed his paradigm for 'structural analysis'. Some of the stipulations for structural analysis, according to Merton, involve the 'confluence of ideas deriving principally from Durkheim and Marx', and that social structures *generate* social conflict (1976, p. 120).

Merton is increasingly enthusiastic about his most recent work on 'socially expected durations' or SEDs as he calls them (1984, p. 265; see also Merton, 1982). Socially expected durations are 'socially prescribed or collectively patterned expections about temporal durations embedded in social structures of various kinds'. As Merton explains (1984, p. 266):

> Socially *expected* durations are to be strongly distinguished from *actual* durations. Indeed, the problematics of SEDs has to do in part with the behaviour and structural dynamics and consequences of interacting actual and expected durations. The expected duration of residence in a community, for example, has been shown to have social consequences, such as the degree of involvement in the organized life of the community, that is independent of the actually elapsed length of residence.

Merton argues that SEDs are 'ubiquitous in the social life of complex societies' and affect *'anticipatory social behaviour'* (1984, p. 266).

Over and above all of the aforementioned contributions Merton, quite simply, is the founder of the sociology of science in its modern form. And finally, and more generally, Merton's work has consistently and refreshingly always demonstrated close connections between theoretical issues and empirical evidence.

Could you tell me a little about your background?

No, for the simple reason that it is in print to the extent you could possibly have it. Have you seen a profile in *The New Yorker* [Hunt, 1961]?

Yes.

That tells you all.

In the Festschrift *presented to you, Coser and Nisbet argue that you were a 'stranger' in traditional American culture, and hence more open to outside, European influences? [1975, p. 4]. Is that how you see it?*

That is not my reading of the situation, but of course they may be profoundly correct and I may be superbly mistaken (...) At Temple I had the good fortune to encounter a young instructor, George Eaton Simpson, who had been studying not at the University of Chicago, but in those days, 1920s ... American sociology was essentially the sociology emanating from Chicago under primarily the influence of Park with the collaboration of Burgess and in the important background of the figure of W.I.Thomas and his work looming large - even though as you know he had been asked to leave the university owing to the simple-minded moralities that then governed such matters. I must have been a fairly arrogant youngster else why should I have decided by the time I was through the end of my junior year - that is the third year of a four-year undergraduate programme - that I knew all there was to know, all there was worth knowing of American sociology. was an omnivorous reader, very intensely engaged in this then still rather suspect enterprise known as sociology, and in truth arrogant, yes, but I probably was not far off the mark, there wasn't an enormous literature to digest and absorb. Furthermore, as an undergraduate I became aware of the work of Durkheim, Weber, of Pareto, chiefly through the appearance in 1928 of that extraordinary, treatise-textbook by P.A. Sorokin with the title *Contemporary Sociological Theories*. It was published I remember in 1928 and I began my undergraduate studies in 1927. I have never counted the actual number of sociologists listed in the index of the Sorokin volume, but I estimate it roughly something of the order between 600 and 1,200 (...) Some of his accounts interested me immensely, including sociologists that in fact never left an enduring impress on European sociology of the mid-twentieth-century or surely not on American sociology - Gabriel Tarde, Rene Worms (...) One made one's tentative choices on the basis of the digest in Sorokin and one's own differentiated response. The upshot was I had read some of Durkheim and some of Weber - none of it as I recall at the time had been translated into English, this was even before Parsons' 1930 translation of Weber's *Protestant Ethic* - but felt quite unorientated to the fundamentals of their thought. My instructors were not familiar with it, so my turning to the European streams of thought had been through various sources. Indeed when the time came for me to decide where I wanted to go to do graduate work I did not elect to go to Harvard, I elected to go to wherever Sorokin was on the grounds that he would be my 'open sesame' to these modes of interesting sociological thought. Now that is not quite the same reading as Lewis Coser and Bob Nisbet.

They added that they considered the most important European influences for you were Simmel and Durkheim. Again is that your reading? Or perhaps Weber was equally important?

Yes and no. I never adopted a Weberian outlook as an encompassing theoretical orientation that could contain my interests or my modes of enquiry. I drew upon Weber but I was in no sense a disciple - at a distance or anything of the sort . Of course when it came to my dissertation [published, orig. 1938, 1978] the influence to put it mildly, palpable . . . but as I tried to record in a 1970 preface to that study, it was not a direct application of a mandate from Weber that led me to the subject and the problem, it was rather Weber became activated as I was living in the seventeenth-century where I did live for some six or eight years, and, was struck by what then seemed to be the incredible, not synthesis, but juxtaposition of scientific commitments and religiosity. After all one had been brought up on the writings, the positivistic writings that said that the only relation between science and religion that was historically conceivable would be one of conflict with science undermining religion. Having made those observations stumbling on the fact - with Robert Boyle for example, one could go through the registry of scientists who were not all Puritans but the religiosity was astonishingly common - that activated the memories of Weber.

Alvin Gouldner argues that 'Merton was always much more Marxist than his silence on the matter may make it seem' [1973, p. x]. Does that mean much to you?

Let's go off the tape for a moment so I can consult the documents ... [long pause] ... I can *now* say with some assurance, indeed I know the passage well since I quote it on p. 128 of *Sociological Ambivalence* [1976] in my paper on structural analysis in sociology. He has it absolutely straight. I have been accused by (...) of having seduced bona fide young Marxists who came in my classrooms and led them down the garden path, or perhaps on the road to truth or something in between, of a more general sociological orientation, rather than a rigorously committed Marxian orthodoxy. The reason for that is that I was always persuaded and still am, that there are identifiable elements in Marxian thought - Marx to begin with and some, obviously not all of his un-numbered disciples - that were an integral part of structural analysis in sociology. Moreover that if one ignored the ideological conflicts and tried to penetrate to the cognitive substance of what was being pursued, that there was much more congruity between these elements of Marxian thought which were considered worthwhile and let's say the kinds of functional theory that initially interested me and which then turns much more clearly into structural analysis ... So that the interest that many of my students exhibited, many of them came straight out of Marxist doctrines ... Lipset, Daniel Bell, of course Alvin Gouldner, the list would go on and on. It is quite possible that one of the reasons why we had so much to say to one another [while they were students here at Columbia] was that, they had a sense of continuity and a sense of enlargement rather than remaining faithful to an ideology (...)

Yes I have always seen the functional and the Marxist analysis of religion as similar ...

Yes, and as you know nowadays there are whole currents in Europe and in this country where even the appropriate tags or inappropriate tags or labels have been introduced ... neo-functionalism, Marxian functionalism and so on, all of which may represent efforts at development but which scarcely came as a surprise.

Nisbet is 'tempted to say that for both Merton and Parsons if the other had not existed he would probably have had to be created' [in Coser and Nisbet, 1975, p. 5]. Does that mean much to you?

In truth I am not quite certain what Bob Nisbet meant by that, the old Italian quip from which he was drawing upon, 'if x did not exist it would have had to be invented' was one of the most marvellous lines that have moved down the corridors of Western thought, I appreciate that of course, but with regard to the substance here I am not at all clear what he had in mind (...) But I think a more appropriate response, appropriate for your purposes and mine,

300

would be for me to say a few words about the modes of intellectual influence that Parsons exerted. To begin with by way of a context that your students could not possibly know, or for that matter our students, I want to say a few words about my encounter with Parsons ... I remind you that for those of us who came to Harvard in the year of 1931 the first year of the new department of sociology there, none, literally none, could have come because of a young instructor named Talcott Parsons was there. He was totally unknown, he had published two papers, I think both in the *Quarterly Journal of Economics* ... he had no public existence. So that this first cohort of graduate students - and I will focus chiefly on just two of us, Kingsley Davis and myself - came to Harvard and it was surely not in order to study with someone who did not exist for us! By the same token, the moment we encountered Parsons in one of his courses we had an immediate, an excited sense that this was a mind reaching down into the bases of theoretical sociology unlike any we had encountered in print; the contrast between Sorokin's mode of treating prior sociological thought and Parson's was extreme. Parsons was far more analytical, far more orientated towards developing a *systematic* way of building upon the works of Weber, Durkheim, Pareto and the rest. So that in the first instance the excitement of proceeding into deep theoretical enterprises, efforts, was beyond measure. We instituted, we - the graduate students - instituted something that we, not he, described as 'Parsons' sociological group'. It met every two weeks or so for several years with Parsons, in which we generated problems and had very active discussions of how they might be theoretically developed. So in fact there was a kind of excitement and a kind of influence that rarely gets talked about at least in social science circles (...) the importance of the sense, the glow, the stimulus, of intellectual excitement, was by all odds a fundamental influence that Parsons exerted on me, and to some extent on Kingsley Davis. Kingsley, as you know, moved into the special field of demography very early and consequently the influence was not as direct and enduring, but nonetheless substantial. When it came to the substance of Parsons' thought, the influence was much more ... was filtered, screened ... he made it easy for us to express divergent opinions, and to question some of his interpretations and ideas - and we did. That excitement by the way, is what led to our sense, as graduate students beyond any question it was our mission, our fate not mission, *fate,* to re-do significantly parts of American sociology and develop it, because that was the scale in which we were experiencing ideas and intellectual agenda. That's a very important type of non-substantive influence. The more substantive influence was palpable too,

301

with regard to fundamental ideas ... Parsons crystallised rather than simply derived in *The Structure of Social Action* [orig. 1937, 1968] which I, like many others consider his most important work by all odds (...) The fundamental ideas of Parsons in which he was developing there have stayed with him. Perhaps the easiest was to see where the divergences began, would be ... I think it was 1947 when at the meeting of American Sociological Society Parsons gave a general paper on sociological theory and I was asked to provide the commentary.

Did structural-functionalism a la Parsons sweep American sociology for a period?

I believe it was diffused even in sociological circles (...) it was assimilated into various other modes of theoretical orientation and I think without a doubt it was a dominant orientation. To my knowledge I have never once used the terminology of structural-functionalism. I may have slipped once or twice and inadvertently used in a few sentences the term functionalism. These are all symbolic indications to me of a congealing of doctrines which I have found an anathema, but what I do want to emphasise is that there was a great deal of structural analysis in what was being described as functional that had not yet become sufficiently explicit, organised, developed and so on. That I think remains fundamental to most of the significant developments in theoretical sociology to this day.

John Rex in his Key Problems of Sociological Theory *concludes that functionalism 'tries to exclude subjectively formulated models of action' [1961, p. 77] ...*

Very simply to begin with the very notion of the analytic distinction between manifest and latent functions becomes vacuous unless one introduces the subjective component of the actor. Indeed I have an unpublished series of between fifteen and twenty-five lectures on one question which interested me in the 1950s, the question of 'what changes are introduced into social situations and social development when primarily latent functions become manifest, under what conditions do you get the reverse' which is rather rare? It seems at first thought a fairly simple notion (...) underlying all of it was not only the incorporation of the subjective component - the description let

302

alone the analysis of social behaviour and social structure and social change - but taking it so seriously that the notion of the agent or the actor was intrical to the whole analysis. Now I find that statement of [Rex] particularly puzzling when you consider that *The Structure of Social Action* was one of the foundation-books of the whole theoretical development.

But there was a period when 'functionalism' was ritually criticised ...

I don't know of any account of it that carries conviction, or provides understanding of it; for myself I think that there have been various roots, one, an offshoot of social change and ideological commitments which led to a very powerful impulse, collective impulse, to ascribe ideological commitment to any mode of functional interpretation, now *that* I find not merely questionable but gratuitous ... since when I published 'manifest and latent functions', [orig. 1949, but also Merton, 1967] I went to some pains to address the conditions under which this generic mode of analysis could become ideologically committed but to indicate what I considered its independence. Now this was raising the question from ten to twenty years before it became an endemic question - incidentally that paper which was published in 1949 was written in 1939, it was lectured on what I call 'oral publication' for ten years before I put it in print, and that by the way has been the pattern throughout (...) I used oral publication as a means of developing progressively new editions of earlier formulations.

In a new book on Parsons, the author states that 'Merton was probably correct when, in 1948, he described Parsons' aim of producing general sociological theory as doomed to futility' [Hamilton, 1983, p. 131] ...

I never said that, certainly it is not a direct quotation ...

He is referring to what other people thought you said, it's his quotation not yours ... and he goes on to say that Parsons' view never seems to have wavered that this strategy was the correct one to follow? Could you comment?

Well, there are two distinct observations. On the first, I would have to

303

consult the actual language. Certainly my intention, I trust my language as well, was to argue that an exclusive or overwhelming concern to produce here and now, or then and there, to produce general theory that had as its prototype, let's say Newtonian or for that matter Darwinian theory, was not merely premature but counter-productive. But the emphasis was on exclusive, that was my primary concern. It was not an argument that was *in principle* inconceivable. So much for my view. As regards Talcott's position, I may have it wrong, but I believe that in his piece he contributed to the Coser *Festschrift* he went on to say at some point that he saw ample room for the kind of orientation I had been devoting myself to ... I do not recall his language, but middle-range, and drawing from what was only a strong preference but a tacit recommendation that one does general theory or one is not doing sociological theorising [1975].

Can 'general theory' be developed out of theories of the middle-range?

I once thought so. I have not completely abandoned that thought, but it seems to me that I was overly-optimistic with regard again to a tacit schedule ... as you know, for some time, for several decades that the philosophy of science has been primarily under the influence of Popper ...

Can I return to that?

Yes alright.

If we talk about theories of the middle-range again. You say that these theories 'lie between the minor but necessary working hypotheses that evolve in abundance during day-to-day research and the all-inclusive systematic efforts to develop a unified theory that will explain all the observed uniformities of social behaviour, social organization and social change' [1967, p. 39]. Could you summarise for me the relations between middle-range theorising and empirical research?

I think so. The level of abstraction involved in middle-range theory is one in which it is possible to move from the abstract concepts to the indicators of that concept quite directly; that the concepts invariably are more general

304

than the specific empirical instances that are being explored; and that the merit of that level of conceptualising is that the reciprocity between observation and theorising becomes more intense, becomes more nearly cumulative. I think of the 800 to 1,100, that is my best estimate thus far, research papers that have drawn upon the concept of the 'self-fulfilling prophesy' in half a dozen of more departments of social life (...) through a whole series of domains that are ordinarily investigated in total separation each from the others. Then consider the model concept which has become quite differentiated, can be deployed in half a dozen or more empirical domains so that some of the findings in some of those domains feed back into and develop the theoretical notions (...) concepts, ideas, theories of the middle-range have been deployed in substantively diverse fields and yet have been found to deepen our understandings of those various substantive fields and to enable us to develop our knowledge further. So it is almost paradoxical, one has in fact been getting closer to a general theory by a middle-range theory than by starting with and confining oneself to very comprehensive doctrines ... a unified sociological theory.

Is it fair to say the 'structural analysis' as stipulated by you [1976] is the 'paradigm' for sociology?

In my sense it is an approximation to a paradigm ... structural analysis with its functional implications.

You argue that structural analysis involves, amongst other things, the confluence of ideas deriving principally from Durkheim and Marx [1976, p. 120]. Could you expand?

Well, again of course, as we know, Durkheim had no direct assimilation of Marxian thought, and I don't need to remind you of various descriptions of Durkheim as being anti-Marxist and not merely non-Marxist. But what I refer to there though is crystal clear to me. Starting with Durkheim, he had a largely tacit but so-often reiterated and developed kind of *structural* orientation, it laid the groundwork for later development. If we go back to his writings he does not have a serious programmatic statement of this, but drawing partly upon the anthropology of his time he took it for granted that his theoretical quest had to include, an effort to identify *types* of

305

relationships within collectivities or groups or communities ... and one gets back - it's not really the meta-theory of Durkheim - to such concepts of organic and mechanical solidarity - and that's a strategic one to take since it's one of his earliest theoretical formulations - one can say that what's going on there is an effort to identify structural patterns and to differentiate between them. Now solidarity is not thought of as structure in the sense let us say that kinship is. So too with his efforts in *Suicide* ... meta-theoretical about his four-fold classification . . . and he's dealing with notions of anomie and dealing with correlated notions of individuation, he is not thinking functionally he's groping for ways of characterising structural attributes of what's going on out there in society and culture. There are some extraordinarily informative works on Durkheim (...) If I was forty years younger I would be tempted to try my hand at a serious effort of a meta-theoretical treatment of the theories of Durkheim, and that's what would bring out explicitly what I have in mind when I talk about the con-fluence. On the side of Marx it seems to me far more articulate, far more explicit to begin with. When I take Marx to me I always mean Engels as well, and there's no question in my mind that Engels was regularly more explicit on the theoretical aspects of sociology than Marx was. That may be sacrilege but there's no question in my mind.

You then [1976, p. 120] argue that structural analysis has to deal successively with micro and macro level phenomena. I'm always reminded here of the difficulties with 'exchange theory' in this respect, so perhaps you could expand ...

Sociologists have independently confronted problems of macro analysis and micro analysis long before those terms came into common usage. I mention that because it is not clear to me, perhaps not clear to anyone, whether or not that terminology which gives a fairly clear conception of the difficulties of moving back and forth between micro and macro planes of enquiry derived from economics ... an explicitly direct intellectual diffusion, I rather suspect so but I don't know so. The economists to my mind have made great strides in clarifying the theoretical issues and the theoretical difficulties and in having criteria for assessing the theoretical proposals for moving from one to another plane of enquiry. I think we in sociology have had a much more diffuse almost tacit treatment of that until fairly recently where there is now ... again in part thanks to the work of types of economists, Mancur Olsen is indispensable here. What I was referring to in that 'declaration' was that for sociologists the macro level has characteristically been - irrespective of avowed theoretical orientations of one or another kind - institutional analysis, the great institutions of society, and our ways of dealing with the questions of social order and comparative analysis of total societies have been overwhelmingly on the institutional side, with a progressive effort to identify the distinctive modes of organisation within each institutional domain. It's also where there's more confusion these days than there was 30 or 40 years ago, it's also about cultural analysis, and the connections between institutional and cultural analysis. On the micro level the pronounced tendencies in contemporary sociology in the last twenty years or so has been the domain of detailed interaction enquiry, again of the various varieties - whether it's Goffmanesque or derived from Mead in the various forms of Blumer, or whatever. It's my conviction that the way in which one can move back and forth between the macro and micro levels is through the notion of social structure and individual behaviours, patterned individual behaviours within the constraints that structures exert. Of all the critics and all the commentators of what I've been trying to do for - too many years? - the one that had it most correct in my opinion is Arthur Stinchcombe in the Coser volume [1975]. He had it straight in many many many dimensions, but most of all in stating that I've been hell bent all through these years in trying to see the actor, the agent, behaving in terms of socially structured alternatives but not all alternatives are relevantly available, and therefore allowing both for individual variability rather than stereotyped monolithic determination. Individual variability which also has to be accounted for, is one of the most intriguing questions of micro analysis - at the same time such an orientation makes it impossible to think of individual negotiations or individual actions as being usefully abstracted from the structural context.

Finally - and I think this is where you may have been misunderstood in the past - you say that the analysis must include the notion that social structures generate social conflict [1976, p. 120]. Do they always generate conflict?

Always. *Always.* Now that's intended as a very strong theoretical claim, deliberately. The sense of disbelief that I've had over the years reading these imputations - I'll speak only of my own work - that there was no place or interest in social conflict, let alone analysis of ... a severe disbelief when I've read this. Of course I've made it almost a life-long policy not to write rejoinders, there's been three or four occasions when I've slipped from that policy (...) My disbelief arose from what I thought was the evidence ... it's not merely that social conflict happens to occur but from the standpoint of this mode of structural analysis it *must* occur and must be theoretically expectable, and that derives from just two components of social structure. One, the component of different statuses are assumed to involve to some degree distinctive interests and values as well as involving to some empirically ascertainable degree shared values with other statuses *or else* you would not have any interaction, let's say any possibility; and given that, that consequently the same phenomena would have differential consequences for people variously located in the social structure, and you put those two together and that's a recipe for social conflict. So it's not merely a *grudging* recognition that lo and behold the great empirical discovery of the ages there is conflict in human society ...

If the 'paradigm' then is structural analysis as outlined in your work, is the next step that it leads to discoveries, social processes, like the 'unanticipated consequences of purposive social action', if you know what I mean?

I've just completed a long long piece which I call a foreword to a volume of a student of mine ... Lewis Schneider was one of my students who took up an interest almost immediately about the pattern of unanticipated consequences of action. You will see a very detailed account of that in the paper (...) I don't know whether this is of any interest to you, but again it's not altogether publicly visible; my interest in UCPSA, that's shorter than unanticipated consequences of purposive social action my interest in that ... the first paper appeared if I recall in 1936, much antedated the structural notions which I was developing, such notions as status-sets, and role-sets, rather than statuses and roles - fundamentally different in the degree of structural complexity that is theoretically generated ... well this interest in unanticipated consequences was an effort to cope with the generic theoretical problem of purposive behaviour - there isn't a single word in that title that is not deliberate and designed to carry certain theoretical weight - it was one way of trying to think about the connection between purposive behaviour which given the tradition of economic thought typically, not Weberian thought but classical neo-classical thought, translated into rational; purposive became rational since the only purposes that were theoretically taken into account in economic theory were rational, on the one hand, and so to say the

308

nonrational bases of human behaviour, that was one. The second was, to the interests of UCPSA, was with regard to identifying modes of social change which are not confined to the intended outcomes. There is to my mind now a great recrudescence of interest, sociological interest, which Boudon who studies with us here at Columbia finds it fundamental, I find myself greatly interested in the work of Jon Elster (...)

You've argued that the 'self-fulfilling prophesy, whereby fears are translated into reality, operates only in the absence of deliberate institutional controls' [1982. p. 264]. How different is that from W.I.Thomas's dictum that 'if men define situations as real, they are real in their consequences'?

If you can convey the response to your question to your readers you will be performing a distinct service, in this parochial sphere. To begin with it is seldom noticed that W.I. whom I knew very well, introduced that sentence which I've often described as the most consequential sentence in modern sociology, in *one paragraph* of the book *The Child in America* [with Dorothy Thomas, 1928]. If one returns to that paragraph you find that what Thomas is referring to - which I called as early as 1938 the 'Thomas theorem' and I still think of it as a theorem but not in the mathematical sense but in a more general way - he is making a very important observation that subjective convictions invite behaviour that lead to objective consequences, *period*. The case he takes up in that paragraph is of a paranoid. Now the whole concept of paranoia over the decades has always contained that implicit notion, that paranoids respond as an extreme pathological or highly visible case, respond to *their* reading of the world around them and their behaviour is a response to that. That's all that W.I.Thomas ever had to say on that subject, he never reiterated let alone developed that idea. Now I mention that because the 'self-fulfilling prophesy' is congruent with that notion - that's why I went to great pains to introduce the SFP with strong reference to the Thomas theorem - congruent with it but it does not at all contain the specificity of the self-fulfilling prophecy which again has to do with what's still poorly understood ... the question of general theory and middle-range theory, the level of abstraction which directs actual observation. Now there's nothing in the Thomas theorem that speaks of the self-fulfilling prophesy, the case of a paranoid is indeed a case which leads to certain modes of behaviour which then have objective consequences. So that the notion that the self-fulfilling prophesy *is the same as* the other is, just on the face of it, totally misplaced.

Now [I've mentioned] the fact that on and off I've been writing this book which is stretched out here on the floor before you on the self-fulfilling prophesy and one of these days - one of these years - I'll publish it, and the gist will be a very considerable differentiation of modes and types of SFP. I restricted myself to a very special case in the original article, namely it has to do with erroneous prophesies, erroneous at the moment of their utterance or acceptance, and the transformation that that helps to bring about within the actual outcome of realising what was originally erroneous. That's only a special case, and I don't for a moment confine myself ... now I get to the sentence you referred to. One of the intentions of that sentence which I do remember well, the intent was to counter in advance the notion of total determinism *ergo* the lack of human controllability over *any* aspect of their futures, a direct indication that this was not a back-handed notion that suggested that planned collective action was totally impossible, that this would *only* lead to unanticipated consequences. Indeed the closing paragraphs of the piece on self-fulfilling prophesies are explicitly directed to that. It's almost as though I anticipated that some years later mis-attributions would be made . But that's the force of it; that if one understands these processes and mechanisms to some extent then in principle they can be brought under human control. At the same time in principle also and for fundamental theoretical reasons they will never result only in unanticipated consequences, and that is again a very strong theoretical statement not merely a remark which appears interesting.

I'm interested in your work on ambivalence, partly because such a notion is usually relegated to psychology, and you say that the 'sociological theory deals with the processes through which social structures generate the circumstances in which ambivalence is embedded in particular statuses and status-sets together with their associated social roles' *[1976. p. 7]. Could you expand a little?*

Well it's a very dense sentence, not in the sense of it being unintelligible, but it was contrived to summarise a great deal in one sentence ...

Well the crucial thing for me is how 'social structures generate the circumstances ...'

310

And that is indeed of course the fundamental distinction between ambivalence psychologically understood and sociologically understood. The fundamental idea there and I think in its way is fairly radical, intellectually radical not politically radical, is that social structures indeed do involve norms, rules, patterns, expectations which derive from understood or explicit rules, *but,* here comes the radicalness, in addition to those norms the effort to fulfil the purposes and functions of various statuses in action involves counter-norms as well again not as happenstance but as inevitable - and the counter-norms which will shift between personality and impersonality, are generated by the ongoing process of trying to achieve the objectives of the status (...) essentially that there can be too much of a good thing. Let's say that you have a linear development of certain modes of behaviour, of impersonality, that may be structurally required in order to get at a certain objective or task to perform. As it's carried beyond to a certain point it then becomes subversive, self-destructive and you need to introduce some more personal elements, and the generating of counter-norms is the result of the changing situation which derives from ongoing interaction ... and note this is looking at it in terms of meta-theory, meta-sociological theory ... back now to the mode of thought of social structure and individual negotiation within the structure, and the whole theme of the notion of sociological ambivalence is to differentiate structures in dynamic terms so that they are not (a) monolithic, all determined, (b) they are not static and the like (...)

In retrospect how do you view your paper on 'anomie and social structure' [1938]?

Perhaps the best response is to look at the fourth edition of *Contemporary Social Problems* [Merton and Nisbet, 1976] where I try to deal with the relationship between SS and A opportunity structure theory, labelling theory so-called and social conflict theory. In fact I would urge you to look at it and crib from it liberally ... you see I think that this kind of theoretical conflict is endemic in the field in large measure, not always, but in significant measure, the result of a failure of understanding the modes of connections between theoretical constructions, that I've tried to indicate in those few pages. Let us say, look at what is problematic in each of these three modes of theory regarding deviant behaviour, look at the types of proposals for dealing with the distinct problematics and you will see that in principle they need not only be contradictory, but in principle they are complementary,

311

each has to make its own way. (...) Has it ever crossed your mind how odd it is that in labelling theory from the very beginning, Lemert, Howie Becker and so on, that the self-fulfilling prophesy emerged as a fundamental concept and a fundamental pattern ... doesn't that suggest that perhaps the alleged conflict between labelling theory and SS and A theory may be more nominal than real; how do you account for this? Well one way of accounting for it is that I am theoretically incoherent, that I have developed a notion of social structure and anomie and opportunity structure, and at the same time have developed a notion of self-fulfilling prophesy and not realised that they are incorrigibly at odds in theoretical terms! (...)

The distinction some sociologists make, for instance Harry Collins [1983], is between the 'sociology of science' which is seen to be more USA based than the 'sociology of scientific knowledge' which is seen to be more European. Does that mean much to you ?

(...) I believe that there is an interesting interaction going on between on the one hand independent criticisms or responses to each of the 'social structure and anomie', even 'unanticipated consequences' (...) the literature is appalling, disturbing, to a whole series of papers in the sociology of science and so on. Each of these I think has independent life histories, sets of ideas, intellectual traditions, which always generate - if they're alive at all - new developments, some of which restrict, seem to subvert, reinforce ... I think that's gone on. Now *apropos* of your question, I also think that there is an interactive effect since they're attributed to the same person and then they're developed in shared imageries positive or negative, for or against, and in that sense I think there's an interaction, it's a second order (...) Ten or fifteen years ago a group of us devoted ourselves to something we called at *that time* the 'sociology of scientific knowledge' (...) who spent a year trying to devise a way of dealing with the sociology of scientific knowledge. The Harry Collins piece has heavy components of stereotyping, the degree of firsthand knowledge in the history of thought is so fundamentally important that with the best will in the world, people find it hard to avoid stereotyping because they're so remote ...

You've noted that the impact of the quite different *views about the philosophy of social science held by such people as Popper, Kuhn, Lakatos and so on, led some to herald the reign of subjectivity [1976, p. 114] ...*

For some time a good many sociologists seem to have taken the fairly diverse sets of ideas which have some overlapping components to be especially in the case of Kuhn - it devastated him - a mandate for the view that any set of ideas are as good as any other set of ideas, because in the end it's all subjective that there is no objective knowledge, that one cannot usefully as a working scientist adopt a notion of realities which are 'there' and variously glimpsed and variously conceived of and so on ...

How did you receive ethnomethodology?

Well the elements of ethnomethodology that I think had promise and have to some degree redeemed that promise are in direct line of continuity from the work of Schutz. The fearful elaborations of what's called ethnomethodology on the basis of diffuse and obscure imputations and modes of analysis that eventually ... led to very limited understanding, that I think has not got us anywhere (...)

(...) Nisbet argues, in connection with Paul Lazarsfeld, that your students, 'tended to be held back from undue flights of fancy by Lazarsfeld's earthy and rigorous methodological style, and Lazarsfeld's students, in their turn, were reminded that the facts never speak for themselves' [in Coser and Nisbet, 1975, p. 7]. Is that fair?

Well it is not incorrect. As you may know Lazarsfeld and I were brought to Columbia by distinct factions, self-described theoretical and highly empirical. We had never met before and we had the extraordinary collaboration over a 35 year period. We never had any difficulty, the two of us, in achieving mutual understanding. He was always a bit undecided about what sociology was up to but he was an intuitive sociologist of the first order. What united us was a shared conviction that intelligibility could be achieved and the movement back and forth between ideas - however generated - and empirical observations, the interplay between those, was not only feasible but indispensable, and that each could not only illuminate the other but feedback to develop the other (...) the 'history' of sociology like the history of any other discipline, is largely stereotyping, uninformed, premature cat-

313

egorisation. Now of course it's true that Lazarsfeld was quantitative, he was a mathematician by training, had a degree in mathematics, his interest was in empirical quantitative work, but the man *never, never* lost sight of the fundamental interaction between qualitative and quantitative research materials. It is most decidedly not accidental that the book directly behind you, a *Festschrift* for Lazarsfeld is entitled *Qualitative and Quantitative Social Research* [Merton, *et al.,* 1979] ... so the stereotyping is understandable but it is still stereotyping as Lazarsfeld as quantitative, or the worst dismal characterisation as a number cruncher is so far off the mark that one feels nothing but numb sadness at the forcefulness of the stereotype in what is ostensibly intellectual discourse.

In the new book C. Wright Mills, *Eldridge remarks that 'about Robert Merton there is a strange silence in* The Sociological Imagination' *[1983, pp. 105-6], meaning that although Lazarsfeld was attacked in the book you were not. Could you comment?*

Well he's right, but incomplete ...

How did you view Mills's contribution?

Well now you must not cut me short here because you have a real opportunity here ... but this will not necessarily be a coherent statement in the sense of being well organised. Here you truly have access to information I shall surely never write up, and which promises to get lost. I say it promises to get lost because you may have seen the full-scale biography of Mills by Horowitz [1983] ... now Horowitz pleasantly surprised me because all I knew of his perspective was that anthology he edited on people, power and politics or something of the like [*Power, Politics and People,* 1963] which was as you know sheer hagiography and the like. In this biography he makes a genuine effort to present a historian's even-handed and thoughtful account. Now he has again - he never knew Wright Mills really and so it's all second or third hand. The plain historical facts, and these are all documented in correspondence, so no one could have invented them and no one could have foreseen them. I became fed up with Harvard for various reasons as a young man and when I was given the opportunity to head up my

314

own department at a major university I seized it because it was in New Orleans one part of the country that was really interesting and remote from the north east where I was born and grew up. I never regretted that decision. There I was in New Orleans when I was asked to review a book by Becker, Becker, and Barnes; I did so and in the course of reviewing it I stated there's also a 'very interesting bibliographical appendix by C.Wright Mills.' Now C.Wright Mills was then a graduate student who Becker [BM; not Howard S.Becker] had asked to do this, and I had obviously responded to it. Well no sooner did Wright come upon this in print and I at once had a letter from him and then manuscripts and so on. After two years at Tulane I was asked to come to Columbia and decided that I had originally planned to stay five years but then I rolled the five into two and decided to go. The next thing I knew was Wright who did not yet have his degree, asked could he take my place, I was chairman of the department ... I think he may have published two or three papers by then, but you get the quasi-generational difference. [Mills got a job at the University of Maryland, and was there for four or five years.] Wright writes to me in desperation he 'must get away from Maryland', he was still not widely known though he had published somewhat more. I continued to be impressed, sometimes distressed, and so I mentioned him to Paul Lazarsfeld, who was director of our Bureau ... there were no posts in the department at Columbia. But Paul had a venturesome and wide-ranging mind, contrary to that stereotype, 'if you think he's interesting I'm willing to try it' ... so Wright's first post was at the Bureau of Applied Social Research. He and Paul never got on and that is a long story. In fact it was a very severe personal conflict and one thing that Horowitz does have right is that that was the history of Wright Mills throughout his life. His closest friends became his enemies. That never happened with Wright Mills and me. I felt that he had let Lazarsfeld down and I told him so, but he never defined me as being - as he defined a great number of people - as being dedicated to hostility towards him. And one of the more remarkable documents - I may even give you a copy of it - is a note from Wright Mills to me where Wright says something to the effect that '1 was appalled when I received your book', and the book was the 1949 edition of *Social Theory and Social Structure,* because it 'led me to realise how far I had strayed from serious sociological work'. Very private ... but that conspicuous silence which Eldridge notes is all a reflection of his ambivalence; on the one hand Wright was not given to pleasantries as his extraordinary note indicated a reluctant respect for what I was up to. On the other hand the feeling of lashing out at the universe around him wherever he

315

was. And in my case he resolved it by letting the two components of ambivalence neutralise one another ... it was not the case with Lazarsfeld and Parsons *though*, if one reads that tract *The Sociological Imagination* carefully, and reads it in terms of sub-textual analysis, what is between the lines, then contrary to the surface indications, he was also variously ambivalent towards Lazarsfeld and Parsons. In the case of Lazarsfeld the ambivalence was the reluctant admiration of the technical skills and inventiveness of Lazarsfeld despite the personal conflict and the principled objections. So too with Parsons, despite his lashing out at the obscurity and alleged pointlessness of Parsons' thought he still had a reluctant admiration of his access to deep sociological scholarship. Now in Parsons' case, you should know that Wright Mills never had any command of German despite the collaboration with Hans Gerth, it was all Hans and I had the whole anguished correspondence from Hans Gerth about how Wright Mills had exploited him and so on. So that, to recapitulate; Wrights' ambivalence with regard to my work and me ... he tended to merge personal relationships with the cognitive relations (...)

How did you see his work?

Oh, I thought it was exceedingly promising (...) I saw his early papers on the sociology of knowledge as indicating that [an interesting mind], and then like so many of his other colleagues became progressively disenchanted - as even in the *White Collar* [1951] book which he did at the Bureau - he began to merge ideology with uncraftsmanlike work. The irony of that appendix on craftmanship haṣ to be appreciated only in the context of his own dismayed self-description. He knew it, and what really shattered Wright more than any of the academic rejection, was when someone like Dwight Macdonald who represented the world of Manhattan intellectuals - which meant everything to Wright - when Macdonald reviewed *The Power Elite* [1956] with contempt as shabby, unanalytical work, that was devastating. So I thought for example the Gerth and Mills Weber volume *[From Max Weber: Essays in Sociology,* Gerth and Mills (eds), 1948] was magnificent, and what it has done ... it was all translated by Gerth, he was a deep-minded extraordinarily erudite man, but he could not convey or communicate what he had in mind, so that Wright Mills even though he did not know German, Wright Mills had an integral part in the edited version and that volume would have been a tragedy had it not been for his contribution. That was a very serious piece

316

of work. The book which I edited and had published in my series, *Character and Social Structure* [1953], well everything I said in that foreword is what I thought of it, I still think it is a remarkable piece of work. *The Sociological Imagination* I think is trivial and it tells something about the field (...) rather than recognising the long introduction to the Weber volume or *Character and Social Structure* or even parts of *White Collar*. So for me Wright Mills is a tragedy, he is a failed talent, nevertheless he produced enough, he was enough of a talent, so that the positive contributions make him one of the more interesting and significant sociologists of his generation. But the mythology contrived, understandably contrived, out of how the world *should be* ... even in the biography that appears in the biographical supplement to the *International Encyclopedia* [of social science] Horowitz wrote the entry on Robert S. Lynd and Helen Lynd and there I came across for the nth time a statement 'Robert Lynd brought Mills to Columbia', item ... Robert Lynd had never even heard of Wright Mills, how could he have, he'd never heard of him ... if anyone brought Mills it was Lazarsfeld and myself to the Bureau, and then the mythology of Lynd and Mills must have constituted an intrical view whereas Lynd regarded Mills as insufferable (...)

Was it his 'anger' that made Mills a hero?

Well yes in part, it was more than anger, he reached out, crystallised, politicalised - although as Macdonald pointed out, he was politically very naive and uninformed - but he represented a social protest, a social anger, and there was a good deal to rebel against.

What about Goffman?

He and I were remote rather than close personal friends. I was at first rather surprised at his going out of his way to express respect for what I was trying to do and interest in it. I read him religiously, there was not a book he wrote that I did not pick up immediately and invariably found it original and interesting, even I dare say enjoyable. I do not think either of us was in the least bit influenced by the other ... but immense respect. And indeed it was he, in what proved to be his last year when he was President of the American Sociological Association who led me to break a vow, a personal vow, I had vowed that I would never again take time out to write a major

317

paper for the professional association, I have paid my dues (...) Erving came to New York explicitly to say that the one session that mattered to him would be a session which would be exclusively turned over to me - any paper on any subject. I was so moved by that that I did it, and it was one of the best things he could ever have done for me because I would not have written that paper [1982] for a long time to come, since it was 40 years in the making (...) this, by the way, I consider possibly the most important piece of work I have tried to do since my 1957 paper on the sociology of science and the 'social structure and anomie' and the 'unanticipated consequences paper' (...) As for where I think Goffman stands? I think in a very strict sense, a unique figure, the reason that he has no intellectual progeny, is that in a very *positive* sense his is an artistic, highly personalised view of perceptions of human behaviour ... he never transmitted a base for others to go and do likewise. There are many sociologists deeply influenced by Goffman but they cannot reproduce the next phase, they can draw on him, they cannot develop, they cannot move on. One of the front page reviews in the *New York Times* on one of his last two or three books, I forget who wrote it, a brilliant review, but whoever wrote it captured it precisely in calling him the Kafka of sociology (···)

Part III

12 Personal postscript: The relevance of C. Wright Mills

It would be inappropriate to attempt either a summary or synthesis of the preceding interviews, particularly as it has been an aim of the project to demonstrate the healthy and necessary plurality of sociology. I do indeed think that the aim has been accomplished. However before outlining a little of the work of Mills, perhaps some general comments concerning the state of sociology should be made.

To begin with it is clear that as a reflection of both humanity and human society, sociology will remain 'as it is and always has been, a very disorderly and wholly provisional enterprise' (Hawthorn, 1976, p. 259). That should not concern us too much providing that we never lose sight of the fact that the *major* task of any sociology aims, in the words of Weber, to 'reveal the characteristic uniqueness of our times' (in Turner, 1981, p. 352). And as we have constantly observed, social life is inevitably complex, and each individual actor cannot know what is going on all of the time. Over and above this are the processes whereby social life is deliberately made complex. This is then where the second important role of sociology comes in; 'sociology is a subject whose insights should be available to the great mass of the people in order that they should be able to use it to liberate themselves from the mystification of social reality which is continuously provided for them by those in our society who exercise power and influence' (Rex, 1974, p. ix).

Following on from the demystification role is the focus for research. What

I would like to say, and it's been said before, is that not only are the sensitive issues always worth exploring, but that they *ought* to be explored; sociology has only just begun to investigate sociological problems emanating from the higher strata of British society. I might add here that the recent tendency to equate large highly-funded research with *necessarily* incisive or creative research is a dangerous one. It simply does not always follow, and besides it implies that there is a *real* way of carrying out research which, of course, is simply not true.

Turning to 'theory', it is so obviously true that theory as with methodology - is something 'simply done with a firm problem in mind', it is not something to be 'endlessly pontificated about' (Plummer, 1983, p. 1). Or as Weber famously put it: 'sciences are founded and their methods are progressively developed only when *substantive* problems are discovered and solved. Purely epistemological or methodological reflections have never yet made a decisive contribution to this project' (orig. 1906, in Goldthorpe, 1983, p. 1).

We ought to stay for a moment on this insidious 'boundary' between theory and research, as it is so important. Robert Lynd in his brilliant *Knowledge for What?*, first published in 1939, observed that social science 'contains within itself two types of orientation that divides it into two blocs of workers: the scholars, and the technicians' (orig. 1939, 1970, p. 1). The scholar becoming remote and even disregarding immediate relevancies with the technician too readily accepting the definition of the problems too narrowly. Lynd talks of the 'gap between the two' and points out that 'important problems tend to fall into oblivion between the two groups of workers' (1970, p. 1). More recently Menzies notes, quite obviously, that theorists ignore wide ranges of research and that researchers similarly fail to take theory seriously and concludes that 'rather than a creative tension between theory and research in sociology, there exists, if not a divorce, at least a separation' (1982, p. 188). Some people would, of course, consider such a state of affairs to be appropriate for a developing and professional science, but I disagree. Too much contemporary sociology is denuded precisely because both factions regularly ignore each other's contributions. *Both are absolutely inseparable and can only develop together.* If they do not the result is either the proliferation of surveys enumerating and collecting trivial information, or non-substantive theorising lurching at times into epistemological muddles. Another consequence of the distinction *currently,* is the elevation of certain theorists into gurus; only those with an understanding of French deconstructionism, postmodernism or *cafe* Marxism are allowed in. Besides all this, the distinction leads us away from our role as students of society; too often we seem to be only concerned with being students of sociology.

On the perennial question of the 'scientific status' of sociology what can be said, and what *is* clear, is that both the social sciences *and* the physical or natural sciences are being rethought. One conclusion already is - and here social science has been informative - that the physical sciences may not be as exact as once thought. What should be taken as 'scientific' is a rigorous and systematic methodology, with all of the process being publically visible. In addition there is surely no further need to try and collapse the two different types of science into one.

In summary; sociology, or more correctly social science is society's understanding of itself, it is about this contemporary social world and other social worlds; it attempts to define and discuss the characteristic uniqueness of the times it demystifies; it utilises a variety of methods appropriate to the *substantive* issue it investigates, while theory and research develop symbiotically; it attempts to analyse the possible unanticipated consequences of action and institutions, of processes and structures. Clearly there is much to be done.

Whilst stressing the importance of the historical dimension to sociology, Robert Lynd argued that the 'variables in the social scientist's equation must include not only the given set of structured institutions, but also *what the present human carriers of those institutions are groping to become'* (orig. 1939, 1970, p. 180). Like Lynd, C. Wright Mills saw sociology as a utopian venture. In his excellent full-length biography of Mills, Horowitz argues that the ideas contained in Mills' *The Sociological Imagination* (orig. 1959) are 'probably more relevant in Britain in the 1980s than they were twenty years earlier' (1983, p. 100). This is certainly true simply in the sense that sociology was only institutionally established in Britain twenty years ago, but more importantly sociology could indeed benefit from a brief re-visit to Mills' main ideas.

Charles Wright Mills was born in Waco, Texas on August 28, 1916, died in Nyack, New York on March 20, 1962, and in his forty-five year life fitted in a career in sociology. As Horowitz comments 'from the time he was twenty-five, [and] received the first medical report that he had a heart condition, to his fourth and fatal heart attack twenty years later, Mills worked at a fevered pace; he was a man in search of his destiny' (1983, p. 5). Despite completing a trilogy of major books on stratification, works on social psychology, pragmatism and, of course, Max Weber, not to mention *The Sociological Imagination,* Mills was and still to an extent remains a man of controversy. Daniel Bell sees Mills' work as 'vulgar sociology' and characterises it as 'rough in tone, discourteous towards opponents [and] impatient of syntax' (1980, p. 142). However the most well-known 'criticism' was that of Edward Shils in 1960 who asked the question (1960 P. 78)

> What does this solitary horseman - who is part prophet, in part a teacher, in part a scholar, and in part a rough-tongued brawler, a sort of Joe McCarthy of sociology, full of wild accusations and gross inaccuracies, bullying manners, harsh words and shifting grounds want of sociology?

Lipset and Smelser, in a footnote to an article on postwar American sociology (a footnote which Smelser later denied writing) argued that Mills had 'little importance for contemporary American sociology' and complained, amongst other things, that Mills recommended as the best books in 'sociology', books by 'non-sociologists' and an 'anthology of the writings of Marx and Engels' (1961, pp. 50-51). It is surprising to see that Horowitz agreed in that he argued that it is 'correct to note, as Seymour Martin Lipset did in a description of sociology during the 1950s, that Mills could no longer really be properly defined as being within the field of sociology' (1983, p. 87). This is simply an indictment of professional or institutional American sociology as it was in the 1960s. Again Horowitz makes a telling remark when he observes that American sociology after the Second World War, in particular, 'doggedly entered the path of professionalization, refusing to acknowledge individual or occupational explorations that strayed too far afield from disciplinary horizons' (1983, p. 2). And of course Mills did just that. He did not settle for a quiet professional definition of his role; it is also quite true that there has been a 'systematic attempt to denigrate and devalue' Mills' work (Rex, 1973, p. 81). Once again Horowitz puts it well when he observes 'that the boundaries of social science were often breached only led him to defy those professional structures rather than doubt his own moral and political imperatives. If we look back at the great utopians of the past, we find them uniformly breaking empirical barriers to create, in their mind's eye at least, a better future' (1983, p. 330).

For Mills, in the 'face of sociology nothing was sacrilegious', nothing had 'the right to stand above criticism', and he understood that intellect stood for 'stripping away secrecy; and for replacing the effect of secrecy upon impressionable "masses" with rational understanding upon a public' (Horowitz, 1969a, p. 56). And of course, as we have already noted, Mills uniquely stressed moral purpose in sociology .

Mills was considered the inspiration of what has been clumsily called the 'new sociology'; a quite difficult to conceptualise 'new paradigm' if you like. What was clear about it, however, was that it was about *criticism* of institutions and processes, and against a methodological view of any kind of social determinism; human action was to be considered significant and *relatively* free. Horowitz, in the final pages of his biography and discussing Mills' book on Cuba, *Listen Yankee!* (1960) argues that Mills the 'political ideologist ultimately betrayed Mills the social scientist' (1983, p. 301). What then were Mills' ideas on social science? *The Sociological Imagination* provides the answer.

The most well-known of his ideas are those criticising the trends of 'grand theory' and 'abstracted empiricism'. Grand theory, as represented by Parsons in *The Social System* (1952) is seen to have limited scientific value, unworkmanlike, abstruse, purposefully abstract in such a way that it avoids the issues of the day, and makes the 'Concept a fetish' (Willer, 1967, p. xvii). On the other hand abstracted empiricism (or certain forms of sociological research) makes a fetish of 'Method'. This usually takes as its data the set interview with a series of individuals selected by a sampling procedure. Abstracted empiricism is 'not characterised by any substantive propositions or theories' and is not based upon any 'new conception of the nature of society or of man' (Mills, orig 1959, 1970, p. 81). Mills did not see sociology as a developing science, but as an intellectual and humanistic endeavour not to be compared with the physical sciences.

Mills begins *The Sociological Imagination* - and we must remember that this was first published over a quarter of a century ago in 1959 - by stating that the 'facts of contemporary history are also facts about the success and the failure of individual men and women' and that 'neither the life of an individual nor the history of a society can be understood without understanding both' (1970, p. 9). The first lesson then for sociology is the 'idea that the individual can understand his own experience and gauge his own fate only by locating himself within his period, that he can know his own chances in life only by becoming aware of those of all individuals in his circumstances'. Mills adds that (1970, p. 12)

> We have come to know that every individual lives, from one generation to the next, in some society; that he lives out a biography, and that he lives it out within some historical sequence. By the fact of his living he contributes, however minutely, to the shaping of this society and to the course of its history, even as he is made by society and by its historical push and shove.

So the sociological imagination enables us to 'grasp history and biography and the relations between the two within society' (1970, p. 12). In particular sociology has to link 'the personal troubles of milieu' with 'the public issues of social structure' [1970, p. 16]

> Consider marriage. Inside a marriage a man and a woman may experience personal troubles, but when the divorce rate during the first four years of marriage is 250 out of every 1,000 attempts, this is an indication of a structural issue having to do with the institutions of marriage and the family and other institutions that bear upon them.

Thus in order to understand the changes of many personal milieux we have to look beyond them to the structural changes causing them, and the number and variety of those cultural changes increase as the institutions within which we live become more 'embracing and more intrinsically connected with one another' (1970, p. 17).

Mills argues, quite correctly, that the 'confusion in the social sciences' is 'wrapped up with the long-continuing controversy about the nature of science' (1970, p. 133). And on the natural or physical sciences, he argues that their 'cultural meaning' is becoming 'doubtful'. He adds that 'recent developments in physical science - with its technological climax in the H-bomb and the means of carrying it about the earth - have not been experienced as a solution to any problems widely known and deeply

326

pondered by larger intellectual communities and cultural publics' (1970, p. 22). For Mills it is important to pay attention to (say) matters of methodology but only *'when they are in direct reference to actual work'* (1970, p. 136, italics added). Similarly it is clear that only substantive theory would meet the approval of Mills when he argues that 'neither Method nor Theory alone can be taken as part of the actual work of the social sciences. In fact, both are often just the opposite: they are statesmanlike withdrawals from the problems of social science' (1970, p. 136).

On the nature of 'proof' he argues that 'verification consists of rationally convincing others, as well as ourselves' and to do that we must 'follow the accepted rules, above all the rule that work be presented in such a way that it is open at every step to the checking up by others' (1970, p. 141). Furthermore Mills adds that one must relate one's work to what has been done before and to other work currently in progress; that is, sociology is cumulative. In addition to his disapproval of the fetishism of concept and method, the apeing of the physical sciences, and the trend toward non-substantive methodology and theorising, Mills also condemns the determination of research by authority: 'In bureaucratic social science - of which abstracted empiricism is the most suitable tool and grand theory the accompanying lack of theory - the whole social science endeavour has been pinned down to the services of prevailing authorities' (1970, p. 144).

Substantively, sociology - or social science as Mills quite rightly calls it, with his healthy disdain for boundaries - is properly about 'human variety, which consists of all the social worlds in which men have lived, are living, and might live'. He adds that (1970, p. 147)

> These worlds contain primitive communities that, so far as we know, have changed little in a thousand years; but also great power states that have, as it were, come suddenly into violent being. Byzantium and Europe, classical China and ancient Rome, the city of Los Angeles and the empire of ancient Peru - all the worlds men have known now lie before us, open to our scrutiny.

> Within these worlds there are open-country settlements and pressure groups and boys' gangs and Navajo oil men, air forces pointed to demolish metropolitan areas a hundred miles wide; policemen on a corner; intimate circles and publics seated in a room; criminal

syndicates ...

The upshot of this is simply that 'to state and to solve any one of the significant problems of our period requires a selection of materials, conceptions, and methods from more than any one discipline'. Mills adds that a social scientist need not 'master the field' in order to be familiar enough with its materials and perspectives to use them in clarifying the problems that concern him. He concludes significantly, that it is in terms of such 'topical problems', rather than 'in accordance with academic boundaries, that specialization ought to occur' (1970, p. 147 and p. 15).

Mills believed there to be 'classic social analysis' which was a definable and usable set of traditions; 'that its essential feature is the concern with historical social structures; and that its problems are of direct relevance to urgent public issues and insistent human troubles' (1970, p. 28). And certainly the controversy surrounding Mills was much to do with the fact that his 'ethical perspective was more open to inspection than that of any other American sociologist' (Horowitz, 1983, p. 328). As Horowitz again argues Mills developed a notion that 'public performance and public worth were to become the touchstone of any social science'. He concludes that (1983, p. 328)

> If sociology lacked this active dimension it was worthless. Like psychoanalysis, which attracted Mills, sociology should make no bones about both its therapeutic goals for the individual and utopian goals for the society at large. A combination of therapy and utopia defined the work of social research, pure or applied.

Bibliography

Abel-Smith, B. and Townsend, P. (1965) *The Poor and the Poorest*, Bell, London

Abrams, P. (1968) *The Origins of British Sociology: 1834-1914*, The University of Chicago Press, Chicago

Abrams, P., Deem, R., Finch, J. and Rock, P. (eds.) (1981)*Practice and Progress: British Sociology 1950-1980*, George Allen and Unwin, London

Abrams, P. *et al.* (1981a) 'Introduction' in P. Abrams *et al.* (eds), *Practice and Progress: British Sociology 1950-1980*, George Allen and Unwin, London, pp. 1-12

Abrams, P. (1982) *Historical Sociology*, Open Books, Somerset Adorno, T.W. *et al.* (1969, orig. 1950) *The Authoritarian Personality*, W. Norton, New York

Adorno, T.W. *et al.* (1976) *The Positivist Dispute in German Sociology*, Heinemann Educational Books, London

Anderson, C.A. (ed.) (1972) *Varieties of Political Expression in Sociology*, The University of Chicago Press, Chicago

Anderson, P. (1969) 'Components of the National Culture' in Cockburn and Blackburn (eds), *Student Power*, Penguin, Harmondsworth, pp. 214-86

Anderson, P. (1974) *Lineages of the Absolutist State*, NLB, London

Anderson, P. (1980) Arguments within English Marxism, Verso, London

Anderson, P. (1983) *In the Tracks of Historical Materialism*, Verso, London

Arms, Suzanne (1975) *The Immaculate Deception*, Houghton Mifflin, Boston

Atkinson, D. (1971) Orthodox Consensus and Radical Alternative, Heinemann Educational Books, London

Bachrach, P. and Baratz, M.S. (1963) 'Decisions and Non-decisions: an Analytical Framework', *American Political Science Review*, Vol. 57, September, pp. 641-51

Bahr, H.M., Caplow, T. and Chadwick, B.A. (1983) 'Middletown III: Problems of Replication, Longitudinal Measurement, and Triangulation', *Annual Review of Sociology,* Vol. 9, 243-64

Banks, J.A. (1967) 'The British Sociological Association - the First Fifteen Years', *Sociology,* Vol. 1 (1), 1-9

Barnes, H.E. (ed.) (1948) *An Introduction to the History of Sociology,* The University of Chicago Press, Chicago

Barnes, J.A. (1981) 'Professionalism in British Sociology' in P. Abrams *et al.* (eds), *Practice and Progress: British Sociology 1950-1980,* George Allen and Unwin, London, pp. 13-24

Barrett, W. (1967) *Irrational Man, a Study in Existential Philosophy,* Heinemann Educational Books, London

Barron, J. and Black, V. (1984) 'Redefining the Boundaries: Feminism's Transformation of Sociological Theory', paper given at British Sociological Association Theory Group Conference, Hatfield Polytechnic, 4-5 January

Becker, H.S. (1951) 'The Professional Dance Musician and his Audience', *American Journal of Sociology,* Vol. LVII(2), 136-44

Becker, H.S. (1966) 'Introduction' in Shaw, *The Jack-Roller,* University of Chicago Press, Chicago, pp. v-xviii

Becker, H.S. (1967) 'Whose Side Are We On?', *Social Problems,* Vol. 14 (Winter), 239-47

Becker, H.S. (1971) *Sociological Work: Method and Substance,* Allen Lane, London

Becker, H.S. (1973 edition) *Outsiders,* Free Press, New York

Becker, H.S. (1974) 'Labelling Theory Reconsidered' in Rock and McIntosh (eds), *Deviance and Social Control,* Tavistock, London, pp. 41-66

Becker, H.S. (1979) 'What's Happening to Sociology', *Society,* August, pp. 19-24

Becker, H.S. (1980) Unpublished interview with John Cockburn 2 May 1980, *mimeo*

Becker, H.S. (1982) *Art Worlds,* University of California Press, Berkeley

Becker, H.S. (1982a) 'Freshman English for Graduate Students', draft April, to appear in *Sociological Quarterly*

Becker, H.S. (1982b) 'Inside State Street: Photographs of Building Interiors by Kathleen Collins', Chicago History, Summer, pp. 89-93

Becker, H.S., Geer, B., Hughes, E.C., and Strauss, A. (1961) *Boys in White: Student Culture in Medical School,* University of Chicago Press, Chicago

Becker, H.S. and Horowitz, I.L. (1972) 'Radical Politics and Sociological Research: Observations on Methodology and Ideology' in C.A. Anderson (ed.), *Varieties of Political Expression in Sociology*, University of Chicago Press, Chicago, pp. 48-65

Bell, C. (1980) 'Race, Less Community, More Conflict', *International Journal of Urban and Regional Research*, Vol. 4(1), 131-4

Bell, C. and Newby, H. (eds) (1977) *Doing Sociological Research*, George Allen and Unwin, London

Bell, C. and Newby, H. (1977a) 'Introduction: the Rise of Methodological Pluralism' in Bell and Newby (eds), *Doing Sociological Research*, George Allen and Unwin, London, pp. 9-29

Bell, D. (1980) *Sociological Journeys: Essays 1960-1980*, Heinemann Educational Books, London

Bendix, R. (1978) *Kings or People?*, University of California Press, Berkeley

Bendix, R. and Lipset, S.M. (eds) (1967 edition) *Class, Status and Power*, Routledge and Kegan Paul, London

Berger, B. and Berger, P.L. (1983) *The War Over the Family: Capturing the Middle Ground*, Hutchinson, London

Berlin, I. (1939) *Karl Marx: His Life and Environment*, Oxford University Press, Oxford

Bernstein, R.J. (1979) *The Restructuring of Social and Political Theory*, Methuen, London

Bilton, T. *et al.* (1981) *Introductory Sociology*, Macmillan, London

Blackburn, R. (ed.) (1972) *Ideology in Social Science*, Fontana/Collins, London

Blauner, R. (1964) *Alienation and Freedom*, University of Chicago Press, Chicago

Bleicher, J. and Featherstone, M. (1982) 'Historical Materialism Today: an Interview with Anthony Giddens', *Theory, Culture and Society*, Vol. 1(2), 63-77

Bloch, M. (1961) *Feudal Society*, Routledge and Kegan Paul, London

Bosanquet, N. and Townsend, P. (eds) (1980) *Labour and Equality*, Heinemann Educational Books, London

Bottomore, T.B. (1975) *Sociology as Social Criticism*, George Allen and Unwin, London

Bottomore, T. (ed.) (1981) *Modern Interpretations of Marx*, Basil Blackwell, Oxford

Bottomore, T. (1981a) 'Introduction' in T. Bottomore (ed.), *Modern Interpretations of Marx,* Basil Blackwell, Oxford, pp. 1-21

Bottomore, T. (1983) 'Sociology' in McLellan (ed.), *Marx: The First Hundred Years,* Fontana, London, pp. 103-42

Bottomore, T. (1984) *Sociology and Socialism,* Wheatsheaf Books, Brighton

Bottomore, T. and Nisbet, R. (eds) (1979) *A History of Sociological Analysis,* Heinemann Educational Books, London

Bottomore, T. and Nisbet, R. (1979a) 'Introduction' in Bottomore and Nisbet (eds), *A History of Sociological Analysis,* Heinemann Educational Books, London, pp. vii-xvi

Bottomore, T.B. and Rubel, M. (eds) (1963) *Karl Marx: Selected Writings in Sociology and Social Philosophy,* Penguin Books, Harmondsworth

Bridges, G. and Brunt, R. (eds) (1981) *Silver Linings: Some Strategies for the Eighties,* Lawrence and Wishart, London

Bridges, L. (1978) 'Review of *Policing the Crisis', Race and Class,* Vol. XX(2), Autumn, 193-7

Brotz, H. (1983) 'Radical Sociology and Study of Race Relations', New Community, Vol. X (3), 508-12

Brown, S., Fauvel, J. and Finnegan, R. (eds) (1981) *Conceptions of Inquiry,* Methuen, London

Bryant, C.G.A. (1976) *Sociology in Action,* George Allen and Unwin,London

Bull, D. (1979) 'Reflections on a Lifetime's Ambition: an Interview with Professor Peter Townsend', *Poverty,* No. 44, CPAG, December, 15-23

Cahnman, W.J. and Boskoff, A. (eds) (1964) *Sociology and History,* The Free Press, Glencoe

Cahnman, W.J. and Boskoff, A. (1964a) 'Sociology and History: Reunion and Rapprochement' in Cahnman and Boskoff (eds), *Sociology and History,* The Free Press, Glencoe, pp. 1-18

Calder, A. and Sheridan, D. (1984) *Speak for Yourself: a Mass Observation Anthology 1937-49,* Jonathan Cape, London

Centre for Contemporary Cultural Studies (1980) *Culture, Media, Language,* Hutchinson, London

Centre for Contemporary Cultural Studies (1982) *The Empire Strikes Back,* Hutchinson, London

Cheng, L. and So, A. (1983) 'The Re-Establishment of Sociology in the PRC: Towards the Sinification of Marxian Sociology', *Annual Review of Sociology,* Vol. 9, 471-98

Cicourel, A.V. (1964) *Method and Measurement in Sociology,*Free Press, New York

Clarke, T. and Clements, L. (eds) (1977) *Trade Unions under Capitalism,* Fontana, London

Cockburn, A. and Blackburn, R. (eds) (1969) *Student Power,* Penguin, Harmondsworth

Cohen, A. (ed.) (1974) *Urban Ethnicity,* Tavistock, London

Cohen, S. (ed.) (1971) *Images of Deviance,* Penguin, Harmondsworth

Cohen, S. and Taylor, L. (1972) *Psychological Survival,* Penguin, Harmondsworth

Cohen, S. and Taylor, L. (1976) *Escape Attempts,* Allen Lane, London

Cohen, S. and Taylor, L. (1977) 'Talking about Prison Blues' in Bell and Newby (eds), *Doing Sociological Research,* George Allen and Unwin, London, pp. 67-86

Coleman, James S. (1993) 'The Rational Reconstruction of Society', *American Sociological Review,* Vol.58, pp. 1-15

Collini, S. (1976) *Liberalism and Sociology,* Cambridge University Press, Cambridge

Collins, H.M. (1983) 'The Sociology of Scientific Knowledge: Studies of Contemporary Science', *American Review of Sociology,* Vol. 9, 265-85

Collins, R. (1975) *Conflict Sociology,* Academic Press, New York

Collins, R. (1980) 'Erving Goffman and the Development of Modern Social Theory' in Ditton (ed.), *The View from Goffman,* Macmillan, London, pp. 170-207

Coser, L.A. (ed.) (1975) *The Idea of Social Structure: Papers in Honor of Robert K. Merton,* Harcourt Brace Jovanovich, New York

Coser, L.A. (1981) 'The Uses of Classical Sociological Theory' in Rhead (ed.), *The Future of the Sociological Classics,* George Allen and Unwin, London, pp. 170-82

Coser, L.A. and Nisbet, R. (1975) 'Merton and the Contemporary Mind' in L.A. Coser (ed.), *The Idea of Social Structure: Papers in Honor of Robert K. Merton,* Harcourt Brace Jovanovich, New York, pp. 3-10

Crosland, A. (1956) *The Future of Socialism,* Cape, London

Cuzzort, R.P. (1969) *Humanity and Modern Sociological Thought,* Holt, Rinehart and Winston, New York

Dahrendorf, R. (1959) Class and Class Conflict in Industrial Society,Routledge and Kegan Paul, London

Dahrendorf, R. (1968) *Essays in the Theory of Society*, Routledge and Kegan Paul, London

Dahrendorf, R. (1968a) *Society and Democracy in Germany*, Doubleday, New York

Dahrendorf, R. (1973) *Homo Sociologicus*, Routledge and Kegan Paul, London

Dahrendorf, R. (1975) 'Review of A. Giddens *The Class Structure of The Advanced Societies'*, *Sociology*, Vol. 9, 134-7

Dahrendorf, R. (1976) 'Remarks on the Discussion of the Papers by Karl R. Popper and Theodor W. Adorno' in T.W. Adorno *et al.* (eds), *The Positivist Dispute in German Sociology*, Heinemann Educational Books, London, pp. 123-30

Dahrendorf, R. (1979) *Life Chances*, Weidenfeld and Nicolson, London

Dahrendorf, R. (1982) *On Britain*, BBC, London

Dahya, B. (1974) 'The Nature of Pakistani Ethnicity in Industrial Cities in Britain' in A. Cohen (ed.), *Urban Ethnicity*, Tavistock, London, pp. 77-117

Daniel, W.W. (1969) 'Industrial Behaviour and Orientation to Work - A Critique', *The Journal of Management Studies*, Vol. VI, 366-75

Davis, Tricia (1981) 'Stand By Your Men? Feminism and Socialism in the Eighties' in Bridges and Brunt (eds),*Silver Linings: Some Strategies for the Eighties*, Lawrence and Wishart, London, pp. 9-27

Dawe, A. (1973) 'The Underworld - View of Erving Goffman', *The British Journal of Sociology*, Vol. 24, 246-53

de Kadt, E.J. (1964) British Defence Policy and Nuclear War, Frank Cass, London

Ditton, J . (1977) *Part-time Crime*, Macmillan, London

Ditton, J. (ed.) (1980) *The View from Goffman*, Macmillan, London

Ditton, J. (1980a) 'Introduction' in J. Ditton (ed.), *The View from Goffman*, Macmillan, London, pp. 1-24

Donnison, D. (1979) 'Poverty and Politics', *Poverty*, No. 44, CPAG, December, 24-8

Douglas, J.W.B. (1964) *The Home and the School*, MacGibbon and Kee, London

Downes, D. (1979) 'Praxis Makes Perfect: A Critique of Critical Criminology' in Downes and Rock (eds), *Deviant Interpretations*, Martin Robertson, Oxford, pp. 1-16

Downes, D. and Rock, P. (eds) (1979) *Deviant Interpretations*, Martin Robertson, Oxford

Drake, St. C. and Cayton, H. (1945) *Black Metropolis,* Basic Books, New York

Durkheim, E. (1952) *Suicide,* Routledge and Kegan Paul, London

Eldridge, J.E.T. (1983) *C. Wright Mills,* Ellis Horwood/Tavistock, Chichester, London

Elias, N. (1978) *What is Sociology?,* Hutchinson, London

Emmet, D. and MacIntyre, A. (eds) (1970) *Sociological Theory and Philosophical Analysis,* Macmillan, London

Engels, F. (orig. 1845, 1958) *The Condition of the Working Class in England in 1844,* W.O. Henderson and O.Chaloner (eds), Oxford University Press, Oxford

Erikson, R., Goldthorpe, J.H., and Portocarero, L. (1983) 'Intergenerational Class Mobility and the Convergence Thesis: England, France and Sweden', *The British Journal of Sociology,* Vol. xxxiv(3), 303-43

Eriksson, Bjorn (1993) 'The first formulation of sociology,a discursive innovation of the 18th century', *Arch.europ.sociol.,* XXXIV, pp. 251-276

Eve, M. and Musson, D. (eds) (1982) *The Socialist Register,* Merlin Press, London

Fahey, Tony (1995) 'Privacy and the family: conceptual and empirical reflections', *Sociology,* Vol. 29(4), pp. 687-702

Feuer, L.S. (ed.) (1969) *Marx and Engels,* Fontana, Glasgow Filmer, P., Phillipson, M., Silverman, D., and Walsh, D. (1972) *New Directions in Sociological Theory,* Collier-Macmillan, London

Friedan, Betty (1963) *The Feminine Mystique,* Gollancz, London

Friedrichs, R.W. (1970) *A Sociology of Sociology,* The Free Press, New York

Foucault, M. (1967) *Madness and Civilization,* Tavistock, London

Foucault, M. (1970) *The Order of Things,* Tavistock, London

Foucault, M. (1977) *Discipline and Punish,* Allen Lane, London

Foucault, M. (1979) *The History of Sexuality,* Allen Lane, London

Frisby, D. (1981) *Sociological Impressionism: A Reassessment of Georg Simmel's Social Theory,* Heinemann Educational Books, London

Galbraith, J.K. (1967) *The New Industrial State,* Hamilton, London

Garfinkel, H. (1968) *Studies in Ethnomethodology,* Prentice-Hall, Englewood Cliffs, New Jersey

Garnsey, Elizabeth (1981) 'The Rediscovery of the Division of Labour', *Theory and Society,* Vol. 10, 337-58

Gavron, Hannah (orig. 1966, 1983) *The Captive Wife,* Routledge and Kegan Paul, London

Gellner, E. (1968) *Words and Things,* Penguin, Harmondsworth

Gellner, E. (1973) *Cause and Meaning in the Social Sciences,* Routledge and Kegan Paul, London

Gerth, H., and Landau, S. (1963) 'The Relevance of History to the Sociological Ethos' in Stein and Vidich (eds),*Sociology on Trial,* Prentice-Hall, Englewood Cliffs, New Jersey, pp. 26-33

Gerth, H.H. and Mills, C. Wright (1948) *From Max Weber,* Routledge and Kegan Paul, London

Gerth, H.H. and Mills, C. Wright (1953) *Character and Social Structure,* Harcourt Brace, New York

Gerth, H.H. and Mills, C. Wright (eds) (1970 edition) *From Max Weber: Essays in Sociology,* Routledge and Kegan Paul, London

Giddens, A. (1971) *Capitalism and Modern Social Theory,* Cambridge University Press, Cambridge

Giddens, A. (1973) *The Class Structure of the Advanced Societies,* Hutchinson, London

Giddens, A. (ed.) (1974) *Positivism and Sociology,* Heinemann Educational Books, London

Giddens, A. (1974a) 'Introduction' in A. Giddens (ed.), *Positivism and Sociology,* Heinemann Educational Books, London, pp. 1-22

Giddens, A. (1976) *New Rules of Sociological Method,* Hutchinson, London

Giddens, A. (1976a) 'Classical Social Theory and the Origins of Modern Sociology', *American Journal of Sociology,* Vol. 81(4), 703-29

Giddens, A. (1977) *Studies in Social and Political Theory,* Hutchinson, London

Giddens, A. (1979) *Central Problems in Social Theory,* Macmillan, London

Giddens, A. (1980) 'Classes, Capitalism, and the State', *Theory and Society,* Vol. 9, 877-90

Giddens, A. (1982) *Profiles and Critiques* in Social Theory, Macmillan London

Giddens, A. (1982a) *Sociology: a Brief but Critical Introduction,* Macmillan. London

Giddens, Anthony (1987), as discussant in Mullan, Bob (1987) *Sociologists on Sociology*, Croom Helm, London, pp. 92-114

Giddens, A. and Mackenzie, G. (eds) (1982) *Social Class and the Division of Labour,* Cambridge University Press, Cambridge

The Glasgow University Media Group (1976) *Bad News,* Routledge and Kegan Paul, London

Glass, D.V. (ed.) (1954) *Social Mobility in Britain,* Routledge and Kegan Paul, London

Goffman, E. (orig. 1959, 1969) *The Presentation of Self in Everyday Life,* Allen Lane, London

Goffman, E. (orig. 1961, 1968) *Asylums,* Harmondsworth, London

Goffman, E. (1963) *Behaviour in Public Places,* Free Press, New York

Goffman, E. (1971) *Relations in Public,* Allen Lane, London

Goffman, E. (1972) *Interaction Ritual,* Allen Lane, London

Goffman, E. (1974) *Frame Analysis,* Harmondsworth, London

Goffman, E. (1979) *Gender Advertisements,* Macmillan, London

Goffman, E. (1983) 'Felicity's Condition', *American Journal of Sociology,* Vol. 89(1), 1-53

Goldthorpe, J.H. (1966) 'Attitudes and Behaviour of Car Assembly Workers: A Deviant Case and a Theoretical Critique', *The British Journal of Sociology,* Vol. XVII(3), September, 227-44

Goldthorpe, J.H. (1972) 'Class, Status and Party in Modern Britain: Some Recent Interpretations, Marxist and Marxisant', *Archives Europeens de Sociologie,* Vol. XIII, 342-72

Goldthorpe, J.H. (1972a) 'Daniel on Orientations to Work - A Final Comment', *The Journal of Management Studies,* Vol. IX, 266-73

Goldthorpe, J.H. (1973) 'A Revolution in Sociology?', *Sociology,* Vol. 7, 449-62

Goldthorpe, J.H. (1974) 'Social Inequality and Social Integration in Modern Britain' in Wedderburn (ed.), *Poverty, Inequality and Class Structure,* Cambridge University Press, Cambridge, pp. 217-38

Goldthorpe, J.H. (1977) 'Industrial Relations in Great Britain: A Critique of Reformism' in Clarke and Clements (eds), *Trade Unions Under Capitalism,* Fontana, London, pp. 184-224

Goldthorpe, J.H. (1978) 'The Current Inflation: Towards a Sociological Account' in Hirsch and Goldthorpe (eds), *The Political Economy of Inflation,* Martin Robertson, Oxford, pp. 186-216

Goldthorpe, J.H. (1979) *Intellectuals and the Working Class in Modern Britain,* University of Essex, the Fuller Bequest Lecture

Goldthorpe, J.H. (1982) 'On the Service Class, its Formation and its Future' in Giddens and Mackenzie (eds), *Social Class and the Division of Labour,* Cambridge University Press, Cambridge, pp. 162-85

Goldthorpe, J.H. (1983) *Causal and Interpretive Understanding in Sociology*, unpublished paper

Goldthorpe, J.H. (1983a) 'Social Mobility and Class Formation:on the Renewal of a Tradition in Sociological Inquiry',*International Sociological Association: Research Committee on Social Stratification and Mobility*, Amsterdam, October 17-19, 1983

Goldthorpe, J.H. (1983b) 'Women and Class Analysis: in Defence of the Conventional View', *Sociology*, Vol. 17, 465-88

Goldthorpe, J.H., Lockwood, D., Beckhofer, F., and Platt, J. (1968-69) *The Affluent Worker*, 3 Vols., Cambridge University Press, Cambridge

Goldthorpe, J.H. and Bevan, P. (1976) 'The Study of Social Stratification in Great Britain: 1946-1976', *Social Science Information*, Vol. 16(3/4), 279-334

Goldthorpe, J.H. and Hope, K. (1974) *The Social Grading of Occupations: A New Approach and Scale*, Clarendon Press, Oxford

Goldthorpe, J.H. and Lockwood, D. (1963) 'Affluence and the British Class Structure', *The Sociological Review*, Vol. 11, July, 133-63

Goldthorpe, J.H. (with Payne, C. and Llewellyn, C.) (1980) *Social Mobility and Class Structure in Modern Britain*, Clarendon Press, Oxford

Goode, W.J. and Hatt, P.K. (1952) *Methods in Social Research*, McGraw-Hill, New York

Gough, K. and Sharma, H.P. (1973) *Imperialism and Revolution in South Asia*, Monthly Review Press, New York

Gouldner, A.W. (1963) 'Anti-Minotaur: The Myth of a Value-Free Sociology' in Stein and Vidich (eds), orig. in *Social Problems*, (1962) pp. 35-52

Gouldner, A.W. (1965) *Enter Plato: Classical Greece and the Origins of Social Theory*, Basic Books, New York

Gouldner, A.W. (1968) 'The Sociologist as Partisan - Sociology and the Welfare State', *American Sociologist*, pp. 103-16

Gouldner, A.W. (1970) *The Coming Crisis of Western Sociology*, Heinemann Educational Books, London

Gouldner, A.W. (1973) 'Foreword' in Taylor, Walton and Young, *The New Criminology*, Routledge and Kegan Paul, London, pp. ix-xiv

Gouldner, A.W. (1975) *For Sociology: Renewal and Critique in Sociology Today*, Penguin, Harmondsworth

Gouldner, A.W. (1980) *The Two Marxisms*, Macmillan, London

Gubbay, J. (1981) 'Capital and the State: Part 1: Welfare and Non-Capital Investment', *Sociology Discussion Papers,* No. 1, University of East Anglia, Norwich

Habermas, J. (1972) *Knowledge and Human Interests* Heinemann Educational Books, London

Hall, J.A. (1981) *Diagnoses of Our Time,* Heinemann Educational Books, London

Hall, S. (1960) 'Editorial', *New Left Review,* No. 1, 1-5

Hall, S. *et al.* (1978) *Policing the Crisis,* Macmillan, London

Hall, S. (1979) *Drifting into a Law and Order Society,* The Cobden Trust, London

Hall, S. (1980) 'Cultural Studies and the Centre: Some Problematics and Problems' in Centre for Contemporary Cultural Studies (eds), *Culture, Media, Language,* Hutchinson, London, pp. 15-47

Hall, S. (1981) 'The Whites of Their Eyes: Racist Ideologies and the Media' in Bridges and Brunt (eds), *Silver Linings: Some Strategies for the Eighties,* Lawrence and Wishart, London, pp. 28-52

Hall, S. (1982) 'The Battle for Socialist Ideas in the 1980s' in Eve and Musson (eds), *The Socialist Register,* Merlin Press, London, pp. 1-19

Hall, S. (1982a) 'The Lessons of Lord Scarman', *Critical Social Policy,* Vol. 2(2), 66-72

Halsey, A.H. (1981) *Change in British Society,* Oxford University Press, Oxford

Halsey, A.H. (1982) 'Provincials and Professionals: The British Post War Sociologists', *Archives Europeens de Sociologie,* Vol. xxiii, 150-75

Halsey, A.H. (1984) 'T.H. Marshall: Past and Present 1893-1981. President of the British Sociological Association 1964-69', *Sociology,* Vol. 18(1), 1-18

Hamilton,P. (1983) *Talcott Parsons,* Ellis Horwood /Tavistock, Sussex /London

Harper, D. (1983) *Good Company,* University of Chicago Press, Chicago

Harrington, M. (1963) *The Other America,* Penguin, Harmondsworth

Harris, M. (1969) *The Rise of Anthropological Theory,* Routledge and Kegan Paul, London

Hawthorn, G. (1976) *Enlightenment and Despair: A History of Sociology,* Cambridge University Press, Cambridge

Hay, Cynthia (1984) 'Sociology and History: No Man's Land Revisited', paper given at British Sociological Association Theory Group Conference, Hatfield Polytechnic, January 4-5

339

Hayek, F.A. von (1945) *The Road to Serfdom,* Routledge and Kegan Paul, London

Hayes, Bernadette C., and Miller, Robert L., (1993) 'The silenced voice: female social mobility patterns with particular reference to the British Isles', *British Journal of Sociology,* Vol. 44(4), pp. 653-672

Heath, A. (1981) *Social Mobility,* Fontana, Glasgow

Heath, A. and Edmondson, R. (1981) 'Oxbridge Sociology: The Development of Centres of Excellence?' in P. Abrams *et al.* (eds), *Practice and Progress: British Sociology 1950-1980,* George Allen and Unwin, London, pp. 39-52

Held, D. *et al.* (eds) (1983) *States and Societies,* Martin Robertson, Oxford

Hepworth, M. (1980) 'Deviance and Control in Everyday Life: The Contribution of Erving Goffman' in Ditton (ed.) *The View from Goffman,* Macmillan, London, pp. 80-99

Hesse, Mary (1981) 'Theory and Value in the Social Sciences' in Brown, Fauvel and Finnegan (eds), *Conceptions of Inquiry,* Methuen, London, pp. 309-26

Hindess, B. (1977) 'Review of A. Giddens *New Rules of Sociological Method',* *British Journal of Sociology,* Vol. 28, 510-12

Hinkle, R.C. (1980) *Founding Theory of American Sociology 1881-1915,* Routledge and Kegan Paul, London

Hirsch, F. and Goldthorpe, J.H. (eds) (1978) *The Political Economy of Inflation,* Martin Robertson, Oxford

Hirst, P. (1977) 'Economic Classes and Politics' in A. Hunt (ed.), *Class and Class Structure,* Lawrence and Wishart, London, pp. 125-54

Hobhouse, L.T. (1951) *Morals in Evolution,* Chapman and Hall, London

Hogben, L. (1938) *Political Arithmetic: A Symposium of Population Studies,* Allen and Unwin, London

Hoggart, R. (1957) *The Uses of Literacy,* Chatto and Windus, London

Hoggart, R. (1976) 'Foreword' to *Bad News,* pp. ix-xiii, The Glasgow University Media Group

Holdaway, S. (1983) *Inside the British Police,* Basil Blackwell, London

Homans, G.C. (1969) 'A Life of Synthesis' in I.L. Horowitz (ed.), *Sociological Self-Images: A Collective Portrait,* Sage, London, pp. 13-31

Hood, S. (1980) *On Television,* Pluto Press, London

Horowitz, I.L. (ed.) (1963) *Power, Politics and People,* Oxford University Press, New York

Horowitz, I.L. (ed.) (1967) *The Rise and Fall of Project Camelot*, MIT Press, Cambridge, Mass.

Horowitz, I.L. (ed.) (1969) *Sociological Self-Images: A Collective Portrait*, Sage, London

Horowitz, I.L. (1969a) 'Mind, Methodology, and Macrosociology' in I.L. Horowitz (ed.), *Sociological Self-Images: A Collective Portrait*, Sage, London, pp. 51-67

Horowitz, I.L. (1983) *C. Wright Mills: An American Utopian*, The Free Press, New York

Humphreys, L. (1970) *The Tearoom Trade*, Aldine, Chicago

Hunt, A. (ed.) (1977) *Class and Class Structure*, Lawrence and Wishart, London

Hunt, M.M. (1961) 'How Does It Come To Be So? (profile of Robert K. Merton)', *The New Yorker*, January 28, 39-61

Inglehart, R. (1977) *The Silent Revolution*, Princeton University Press

Inglis, F. (1982) *Radical Earnestness: English Social Theory 1880-1980*, Martin Robertson, Oxford

James, C.L. (1963) *Black Jacobins: Toussaint L'Ouverture and the San Domingo Revolution*, Random House, New York

James, W. (1890) *The Principles of Psychology*, H. Holt, New York

James, W. (1902) *The Varieties of Religious Experience*, Longmans, New York

Jones, R.A. (1983) 'The New History of Sociology', *Annual Review of Sociology*, Vol. 9, 447-69

Kent, R.A. (1981) *A History of British Empirical Sociology*, Gower, Farnborough

Kuhn, T.S. (1962) *The Structure of Scientific Revolutions*, The University of Chicago Press, Chicago

Kuhn, T.S. (1977) *The Essential Tension*, The University of Chicago Press, Chicago

Kurzweil, Edith (1980) *The Age of Structuralism*, Columbia University Press, New York

Laing, R.D. (1962) 'Series and Nexus in the Family', *New Left Review*, No. 14, 7-14

Lane, D. (1978) *Politics and Society in the USSR*, Martin Robertson, Oxford

Lawrence, E. (1982) 'In the Abundance of Water the Fool is Thirsty: Sociology and Black "Pathology"' in Centre for Contemporary Cultural Studies, *The Empire Strikes Back*, Hutchinson, London, pp. 95-142

Lazarsfeld, P.F. (1968) 'Measurement' in T.Parsons (ed.), *American Sociology*, Basic Books, New York, pp. 93-106

Leach, E. (1961) *Rethinking Anthropology*, Athlone Press, London

Leymore, Varda (1982) 'Structure and Persuasion: The Case of Advertising', *Sociology*, Vol. 16(3), 377-89

Lindesmith, A.R. (1968) *Addiction and Opiates*, Aldine, Chicago

Lindesmith A.R. (1981) 'Symbolic Interactionism and Causality', *Symbolic Interaction*, Vol. 4(1), 87-112

Lipset, S.M. (1960) *Political Man*, Heinemann, London

Lipset, S.M. and Smesler, N. (1961) 'Change and Controversy in Recent American Sociology', *British Journal of Sociology*, Vol. 12, 41-51

Lockwood, D. (1958) *The Blackcoated Worker*, George Allen and Unwin, London

Lockwood, D. (1966) 'Sources of Variation in Working Class Images of Society', *The Sociological Review*, Vol. 14,November, 249-67

Lukes, S. (1975) *Emile Durkheim*, Peregrine, Harmondsworth

Lundberg, G.A. (1939) *Foundations of Sociology*, Macmillan, New York

Lynd, R.S. (1970, orig. 1939) *Knowledge for What?*, Princeton University Press, Princeton

McLellan, D. (ed.) (1983) *Marx: The First Hundred Years*, Fontana, London

MacGregor, Suzanne (1981) *The Politics of Poverty*, Longman, London

MacIver, R.M. and Page, C.H. (1950) *Society: An Introductory Analysis* Macmillan, London

MacKenzie, G. (1974) 'The "Affluent Worker" Study: An Evolution and Critique' in F. Parkin (ed.), *The Social Analysis of Class Structure*, Tavistock, London, pp. 237-56

McNeil, W.H. (1963) *The Rise of the West*, University of California Press, Berkeley

McNeil, W.H. (1974) *The Shape of European History*, Oxford University Press, London

Macrae, D.G. (1956) 'Some Sociological Prospects', *Transactions of the Third World Congress of Sociology*, ISA, London, Vol. 8

Malinowski, B. (1944) *A Scientific Theory of Culture* University of North Carolina Press, Chapel Hall

Mann, M. (1973) *Consciousness and Action Among the Western Working Class*, Macmillan, London

Mann, M. (1973a) *Workers on the Move*, Cambridge University Press, Cambridge

Mann, M. (1980) 'State and Society, 1130-1815: An Analysis of English State Finances', in Zeitlin (ed.) *Political Power and Social Theory*, JAI Press, Connecticut

Mann, M. (ed.) (1983) *Student Encyclopaedia of Sociology*, Macmillan, London

Mann, M. (1984) *The Sources of Social Power*, mimeo

Mann, M. (1984a) 'The Autonomous Power of the State: Its Origins, Mechanisms and Results', to be published in *Archives Europeens de Sociologie*

Mann, M. (1986, 1987, 1988 forthcoming) *Sources of Social Power, Vol. 1: A History of Power from the Beginning to 1760 AD*, Cambridge University Press - *Vol. 11: A History of Power in Industrial Societies*, Cambridge University Press - *Vol. 111: A Theory of Power*, Cambridge University Press

Mannheim, K. (1963) 'The Ethos of American Sociology', in Stein and Vidich (eds) *Sociology on Trial*, Prentice-Hall Englewood Cliffs, New Jersey, pp. 3-11

Marshall, T.H. (1950) *Citizenship and Social Class*, Cambridge University Press, Cambridge

Marshall, T.H. (1963) *Sociology at the Crossroads and Other Essays*, Heinemann Educational Books, London

Marshall, T.H. (1981) 'Poverty or Deprivation?', *Journal of Social Policy*, Vol. 10(1), pp. 81-7

Marsland, D. (1984) 'Sociologists and Defence', Network, No. 28, Jan, pp. 13-14

Menzies, K. (1982) *Sociological Theory in Use*, Routledge and Kegan Paul, London

Merton, R.K. (1938) 'Social Structure and Anomie', *American Sociological Review*, Vol. 3, pp. 672-82

Merton, R.K. (1957 edition) Social Theory and Social Structure, Free Press, New York

Merton, R.K. (1967) *On Theoretical Sociology*, Free Press, New York

Merton, R.K. (1976) *Sociological Ambivalence and Other Essays*, The Free Press, New York

Merton, R.K. (1978, orig. 1938) *Science, Technology and Society in Seventeenth Century England*, Humanities Press, New Jersey

Merton, R.K. (1979) 'Remembering Paul Lazarsfeld', in Merton *et al.* (eds) *Qualitative and Quantitative Social Research:*
Papers in Honor of Paul F. Lazarsfeld, Free Press, New York

Merton, R.K. (1981) 'Our Sociological Vernacular', *Columbia,* November, pp. 42-4

Merton, R.K. (1982) 'Socially Expected Durations: A Temporal Component of Social Structure', The ASA Career of Distinguished Scholarship Award Lecture, 8 September, San Francisco

Merton, R.K. (1982a) *Social Research and the Practising Professions,* ABT Books, Cambridge, Mass.

Merton, R.K. (1982b) 'Alvin W. Gouldner: Genesis and Growth of a Friendship', *Theory and Society,* Vol. 11, pp. 915 -38

Merton, R.K. (1984) 'Socially Expected Durations: A Case Study of Concept Formation in Sociology', in Powell and Robbins (eds) *Conflict and Consensus: A Festschrift for Lewis A. Coser,* Free Press, New York, pp. 262-83

Merton, R.K. and Nisbet R. (eds) (1976) *Contemporary Social Problems,* 4th Edition, Harcourt, Brace Jovanovich, New York

Merton, R.K., Coleman, J.S., and Rossi, P.H. (eds) (1979) *Qualitative and Quantitative Social Research: Papers in Honor of Paul F. Lazarsfeld,* Free Press, New York

Miller, S.M. and Tomaskovic-Devey, D. (1981) 'Symposium on Poverty in the United Kingdom', *British Journal of Sociology,* Vol. 32, No. 2, pp. 266-78

Mills, C. Wright (1948) *The New Men of Power,* Kelley, New York

Mills, C. Wright (1951) *White Collar,* Oxford University Press, New York

Mills, C. Wright (1956) *The Power Elite,* Oxford University Press, New York

Mills, C. Wright (1958) *The Causes of World War Three,* Simon and Schuster, New York

Mills, C. Wright (1960) *Listen Yankee: The Revolution in Cuba,* Secker and Warburg, London

Mills, C. Wright (1963) 'The Bureaucratic Ethos', in Stein and Vidich (eds) *Sociology on Trial,* Prentice-Hall, Englewood Cliffs, New Jersey, pp. 12-25

Mills, C. Wright (1970, orig. 1959) *The Sociological Imagination,* Penguin, Harmondsworth

Mitchell, J. and Oakley, A. (eds) (1976) *The Rights and Wrongs of Women,* Penguin, Harmondsworth

Morris, T. and Morris, P. (1963) *Pentonville,* Routledge & Kegan Paul, London

Myrdal, G. (1944) *An American Dilemma,* Harper and Brothers, New York

Newby, H. (1977) *The Deferential Worker,* Allen Lane, London

Newby, H. (1982) *The State of Research into Social Stratification in Britain,* Social Science Research Council, 1982

Newby, H. and Bell, C. (1979) 'From Epistemology to Methods: Narcissism or Reflexivity in Recent Sociology',paper presented to the BSA/SSRC Conference on 'Methodology and Techniques of Sociology', Lancaster University, January 3-5

Nicolaus, M. (1972) 'The Professional Organisation of Sociology: A View from Below', in Blackburn (ed.) *Ideology in Social Science,* Fontana/Collins, London, pp. 45-60

Nisbet, R.A. (1969) 'Sociology as an Idea System', in Horowitz (ed.) *Sociological Self-Images: A Collective Portrait,* Sage, London, pp. 193-204

Nisbet, R.A. (1970) *The Sociological Tradition,* Heinemann Education Books, London

Oakley, A. (1974) *The Sociology of Housework,* Martin Robertson, Oxford

Oakley, A. (1974a) *Housewife,* Allen Lane, London

Oakley, A. (1976) 'Wisewoman and Medicine Man: Change in the Management of Childbirth', in Mitchell and Oakley (eds) *The Rights and Wrongs of Women,* Penguin, Harmondsworth, pp. 17-58

Oakley, A. (1980) *Women Confined: Towards a Sociology of Childbirth,* Martin Robertson, Oxford

Oakley, A. (1981) *Subject Women,* Martin Robertson, Oxford

Oakley, A. (1981a) 'Interviewing Women: A Contradiction in Terms', in Roberts (ed.) *Doing Feminist Research,* Routledge and Kegan Paul, London, pp. 30-60

Oakley, A. (1984) *Taking It Like A Woman,* Jonathan Cape,London

O'Neill, J. (1975) *Making Sense Together: An Introduction to Wild Sociology,* Heinemann Educational Books, London

Orwell, G. (1937) *The Road to Wigan Pier,* Gollancz, London

Packard, V. (1961) *The Status Seekers,* Penguin, Harmondsworth

Parker, H. (1974) *The View from the Boys,* David and Charles, London

Parkin, F. (1968) *Middle Class Radicalism,* Manchester University Press, Manchester

Parkin, F. (1971) *Class Inequality and Political Order,* MacGibbon and Kee, London

Parkin, F. (ed.) (1974) *The Social Analysis of Class Structure,* Tavistock, London

Parkin, F. (1980) 'Reply to Giddens' *Theory and Society,* Vol. 9, pp. 891-94

Parsons, T. (1968, orig. 1937) *The Structure of Social Action,* 2 volumes, Free Press, New York

Parsons, T. (1952) *The Social System,* Routledge and Kegan Paul, London

Parsons, T. (ed.) (1968) *American Sociology,* Basic Books, New York

Parsons, T. (1968a) 'An Overview', in Parsons (ed.) *American Sociology,* Basic Books, New York, pp. 319-35

Parsons, T. (1968b) 'Introduction', in Parsons (ed.) *American Sociology,* Basic Books, New York, pp. ix-xix

Parsons, T. (1975) 'The Present Status of "Structural-Functional" Theory in Sociology', in Coser (ed.) *The Idea of Social Structure: Papers in Honor of Robert K. Merton,* Harcourt Brace, Jovanovich, New York, pp. 67-83

Payne, G., Dingwall, R., Payne, J., and Carter, M. (1981)*Sociology and Social Research,* Routledge and Kegan Paul, London

Phillips, D.C. (1973) *Abandoning Method,* Jossey-Bass, San Francisco

Plummer, K. (1979) 'Misunderstanding Labelling Perspectives' in Downes and Rock (eds), *Deviant Interpretations,* Martin Robertson, Oxford, pp. 85-122

Plummer, K. (1983) *Documents of Life,* George Allen and Unwin, London

Poggi, G. (1983) *Calvinism and the Capitalist Spirit,* Macmillan, London

Popper, K.R. (1945) *The Open Society and its Enemies,* 2 Vols., Routledge and Kegan Paul, London

Popper, K.R. (1957) *The Poverty of Historicism,* Routledge and Kegan Paul, London

Popper, K.R. and Eccles, J.C. (1983) *The Self and Its Brain,* Routledge and Kegan Paul, London

Potter, D. *et al.* (1981) *Society and the Social Sciences,* Routledge and Kegan Paul, London

Powell, W.W. and Robbins, R. (eds) (1984) *Conflict and Consensus: A Festschrift for Lewis A. Coser,* The Free Press, New York

Prescod, C. (1979) 'Review of Colonial Immigrants in a British City', *Race and Class,* Autumn, Vol. XXI(2), 198-203

Purvis, Trevor and Hunt, Alan (1993) 'Discourse, ideology, discourse, ideology, discourse, ideology ...', *British Journal of Sociology,* Vol. 44(3), pp. 473-499

Radcliffe-Richards, Janet (1980) *The Sceptical Feminist,* Routledge and Kegan Paul, London

Rex, J. (1961) *Key Problems of Sociological Theory*, Routledge and Kegan Paul, London

Rex, J. (1973) *Discovering Sociology*, Routledge and Kegan Paul, London

Rex, J. (1974) *Sociology and the Demystification of the Modern World*, Routledge and Kegan Paul, London

Rex, J. (ed.) (1974a) *Approaches to Sociology*, Routledge and Kegan Paul, London

Rex, J. (1975) *The Present State of Sociology*, transcript of a seminar given to the University of Alberta at Edmonton, June 1975

Rex, J. (1981) *Social Conflict*, Longman, London

Rex, J. (1982) 'The Neo-Kantian Approach to Structure', paper presented to a symposium on *Varieties of Structural Analysis in Sociology*, Dubrovnik, Yugoslavia

Rex, J. (1983) 'British Sociology 1960-1980 - An Essay', *Social Forces*, Vol. 61, No. 4, June, 999-1009

Rex, J. (1983, 2nd edition) *Race Relations in Sociological Theory*, Routledge and Kegan Paul, London

Rex, J. and Moore, R. (1967) *Race, Community and Conflict*, OxfordUniversity Press, Oxford

Rex, J. and Tomlinson, Sally (1979) *Colonial Immigrants in a British City*, Routledge and Kegan Paul, London

Rhea, B. (ed.) (1981) *The Future of the Sociological Classics*, George Allen and Unwin, London

Richards, M.P.M. (ed.) (1974) *The Integration of a Child into a Social World*, Cambridge University Press, Cambridge

Riesman, D. (1950) *The Lonely Crowd*, Yale University Press,New York

Roberts, Helen (1981) 'Some of the Boys Won't Play Any More: The Impact of Feminism on Sociology' in D. Spender (ed.), *Men's Studies Modified*, Pergamon Press, Oxford, pp. 73-81

Roberts, Helen (ed.) (1981a) *Doing Feminist Research*, Routledge and Kegan Paul, London

Rock, P. and McIntosh, M. (eds) (1974) *Deviance and Social Control*, Tavistock, London

Rodger, J. (1979) 'Review of *Policing the Crisis*', *Sociological Review*, May, Vol. 27(2), 394-6

Rogers, Mary F. (1980) 'Goffman on Power, Hierarchy and Status' in J. Ditton (ed.), *The View from Goffman,* Macmillan, London, pp. 100-33

Rogers, Mary F. (1983) *Sociology, Ethnomethodology, and Experience*, Cambridge University Press, Cambridge

Rubel, M. and Manale, M. (1975) *Marx Without Myth,* Basil Blackwell, Oxford

Runciman, W.G. (1966) *Relative Deprivation and Social Justice,* Routledge and Kegan Paul, London

Runciman, W.G. (1978) *Weber: Selections in Translation,* Cambridge University Press, London

Runciman, W.G. (1983) *A Treatise on Social Theory,* Cambridge University Press, Cambridge

Runciman, W.G. (1983a) 'Capitalism Without Classes', *British Journal of Sociology,* Vol. xxxiv, No. 2, June, 157-82

Runciman, W.G. (1993) 'Has British capitalism changed since the First World War?', *British Journal of Sociology,* Vol. 44(1), pp. 53-67

Sahlins, M. (1972) *Stone Age Economics,* Aldine, Chicago

Saunders, P. (1980) *Urban Politics,* Penguin, Harmondsworth

Saunders, P. (1982) *Social Theory and the Urban Question,* Hutchinson, London

Schwendinger, H. and Sehwendinger, J.R. (1974) *The Sociologists of the Chair,* Basic Books, New York

Secombe, W. (1973) 'The Housewife and her Labour under Capitalism', *New Left Review,* No. 83, 3-24

Selltiz, C., Jahoda, M., Deutsch, M. and Cook, S.W. (1965) *Research Methods in Social Relations,* Methuen, London

Serge, V. (1963) *Memoirs of a Revolutionary,* Oxford University Press, London

Seve, L. (1975) *Marxism and the Theory of Human Personality,* Lawrence and Wishart, London

Shaw, C.R. (1966, 5th edition) *The Jack-Roller,* University of Chicago Press, Chicago

Shils, E. (1960) 'Imaginary Sociology', *Encounter,* Vol. 14, 78-82

Shils, E. and Young, M. (1953) 'The Meaning of the Coronation', *The Sociological Review,* December, Vol. 1(2) 63-81

Simey, T S. (1962) 'Review of J. Rex (1961) *Key Problems of Sociological Theory',* *Sociological Review,* Vol. 10, 117-18

Sorokin, P.A. (1964, orig. 1928) *Contemporary Sociological Theories,* Harper and Row, New York

Sorokin, P.A. (1964a) *Social and Cultural Mobility,* Free Press, Chicago

Spender, D. (ed.) (1981) *Men's Studies Modified,* Pergamon Press, Oxford

Spender, D. (1981a) 'Introduction' in D. Spender (ed.), *Men's Studies Modified,* Pergamon Press, Oxford, pp. 1-10

Stacey, Margaret (1982) 'Social Sciences and the State: Fighting Like a Woman', *Sociology*, Vol. 16(3), 406-21

Stein, M. and Vidieh, A. (eds) (1963) *Sociology on Trial*, Prentice-Hall, Englewood Cliffs, New Jersey

Stinchcombe, A.L. (1975) 'Merton's Theory of Social Structure' in L.A. Coser, *The Idea of Social Structure: Papers in Honor of Robert K. Merton*, Harcourt Brace, Jovanovich, New York, pp. 11-33

Stouffer, S. *et al.* (1949) *The American Soldier*, Princeton University Press, Princeton

Talmon, J.L. (1952) *The Origins of Totalitarian Democracy*, Seeker, London

Tawney, R.H. (1938) *Religion and the Rise of Capitalism*, Pelican, London

Taylor, I., Walton, P. and Young, J. (1973) *The New Criminology*, Routledge and Kegan Paul, London

Taylor, L. (1968) 'Erving Goffman', *New Society*, 5 December, pp. 835-37

Taylor, L. and Walton, P. (1971) 'Industrial Sabotage: Motives and Meanings' in S. Cohen (ed.), *Images of Deviance*, Penguin, Harmondsworth, pp. 219-45

Thomas, W.I. and Znaniecki, F. (1918) *The Polish Peasant in Europe and America*, 5 Vols., University of Chicago Press, Chicago

Thomas, W.I. and Thomas, D.S. (1928) *The Child in America*, University of Chicago Press, Chicago

Titmuss, R. (1970) *The Gift Relationship*, George Allen and Unwin, London

Townsend, P. (1957) *The Family Life of Old People*, Penguin, Harmondsworth

Townsend, P. (1962) *The Last Refuge*, Routledge and Kegan Paul, London

Townsend, P. (ed.) (1970) *The Concept of Poverty*, Heinemann Educational Books, London

Townsend, P. (1970a) 'Introduction' in P. Townsend (ed.), *The Concept of Poverty*, Heinemann Educational Books, London, pp. ix-xi

Townsend P. (1973) *The Social Minority*, Allen Lane, London

Townsend P. (1976) *Sociology and Social Policy*, Penguin, Harmondsworth

Townsend, P. (1979) *Poverty in the United Kingdom*, Penguin, Harmondsworth

Townsend, P. (1983) 'Peter Townsend's Rejoinder ...', Network, *British Sociological Assocation*, October, No. 27, 11-13

Townsend, P. and Davidson, N. (1982) *Inequalities in Health: The Black Report*, Penguin, Harmondsworth

Troeltsch, E. (orig. 1931, 1956) *The Social Teachings of the Christian Churches*, George Allen and Unwin, London

Trotsky, L. (1967 edition) *History of the Russian Revolution,* Sphere, London

Turner, B.S. (1981) *For Weber,* Routledge and Kegan Paul, London

Turner, S.P. and Factor, R.A. (1984) *Max Weber and the Dispute over Reason and Value: A Study in Philosophy,Ethics, and Politics,* Routledge and Kegan Paul, London

Urry, J. (1977) 'Review of A. Giddens *New Rules of Sociological Method',* *Sociological Review,* Vol. 25, 911-15

Urry, J. (1981) 'Sociology as a Parasite: Some Vices and Virtues' in P. Abrams *et al., Practice and Progress: British Sociology 1950-1980,* George Allen and Unwin, London, pp. 25-38

Vidich A.J., Lyman, S.M. and Goldfarb, J.C. (1981) 'Sociology and Society: Disciplinary Tensions and Professional Compromises', *Social Research,* Summer, Vol. 48, No. 2,322-61

Vidich, A.J. and Lyman, S.M. (1984) *American Sociology: Worldly Rejections of Religion and their Directions,* Yale University Press

Waton, A. (1980) 'United at Last', *Network,* No. 17, May, 1-2

Weber, M. (1930) *The Protestant Ethic and the Spirit of Capitalism,* Unwin University Books, London

Weber, M. (1948) 'Politics as a Vocation' (orig. 1918) in Gerth and Mills (eds), *From Max Weber,* Routledge and Kegan Paul, London, pp. 77-128

Weber, M. (1949) *The Methodology of the Social Sciences* trans. E.A. Shils and H.N. Finch, Free Press, New York

Wedderburn, D. (ed.) (1974) *Poverty, Inequality and Class Structure,* Cambridge University Press, Cambridge

Wedderburn, Dorothy (1981) in Miller *et al., British Journal of Sociology,* Vol. 32, No. 2, 274-78

Whyte, W.F. (1943) *Street Corner Society,* University of Chicago Press, Chicago

Wiatr, J.J. (ed.) (1971) *The State of Sociology in Eastern Europe Today,* Southern Illinois University Press, Carbondale and Edwardsville

Wiatr, J.J. (1971a) 'Status and Prospects of Sociology in Eastern Europe: A Trend Report' in J.J. Wiatr (ed.) *The State of Sociology in Eastern Europe Today,* Southern Illinois University Press, Carbondale and Edwardsville, pp. 1-21

Willer, D. (1967) *Scientific Sociology: Theory and Method* Prentice-Hall, Englewood Cliffs, New Jersey

Williams, R. (1958) *Culture and Society,* Chatto and Windus,London

Williams, R. (1976) *Keywords,* Fontana, Glasgow

Williams, R. (1983) *Towards 2000,* Chatto and Windus /The Hogarth Press, London

Willis, P. (1977) *Learning to Labour,* Saxon House, Farnborough

Winch, P. (1958) *The Idea of a Social Science,* Routledge and Kegan Paul, London

Wolf, E.R. (1982) *Europe and the People Without History,* University of California Press, Berkeley

Worsley, P, (1970, orig. 1957) *The Trumpet Shall Sound,* Granada, London

Worsley, P. (1970a) 'Groote Eylandt Totemism and *Le Totemisme Aujourd'hui'* in Emmet and MacIntyre (eds) *Sociological Theory and Philosophical Analysis,* Macmillan London, pp. 204-22

Worsley, P. (1974) 'The State of Theory and the Status of Theory', *Sociology,* Vol. 8(1), January, 1-17

Worsley, P. (1975, orig. 1964) *The Third World,* Weidenfeld and Nicolson, London

Worsley, P. (1975a) *Inside China,* Allen Lane, London

Worsley, P. (1982) *Marx and Marxism,* Ellis Horwood/ Tavistock, Chichester/London

Worsley, P. (1984) 'Multilateralism or Cant?', *Network,* No. 28, January 14-15

Worsley, P. (1984a) *The Three Worlds,* Weidenfeld and Nicolson, London

Wuthnow, R., Davison Hunter, J., Bergesen, A. and Kurzweil, E. (1984) *Cultural Analysis,* Routledge and Kegan Paul, London

Young, T.R. (1971) 'The Politics of Sociology: Gouldner, Goffman, and Garfinkel', *The American Sociologist,* Vol. 6, November, 276-81

Young, M. and Willmott, P. (1957) *Family and Kinship in East London,* Routledge and Kegan Paul, London

Zeitlin, M. (ed.) (1980) *Political Power and Social Theory,* JAI Press, Connecticut

Zorbaugh, H.W. (1929) *The Gold Coast and the Slum,* University of Chicago Press, Chicago